CONTACT LANGUAGES AND MUSIC

CONTACT LANGUAGES AND MUSIC

EDITED BY
Andrea Hollington
Joseph T. Farquharson
Byron M. Jones Jr.

The University of the West Indies Press
Jamaica • Barbados • Trinidad and Tobago

The University of the West Indies Press
7A Gibraltar Hall Road, Mona
Kingston 7, Jamaica
www.uwipress.com

© 2022 by Andrea Hollington, Joseph T. Farquharson and Byron M. Jones Jr.

All rights reserved. Published 2022

A catalogue record of this book is available from the National Library of Jamaica.

ISBN: 978-976-640-923-4 (print)
978-976-640-924-1 (ePub)

Cover design by Robert Harris

The University of the West Indies Press has no responsibility for the persistence or accuracy of URLs for external or third-party internet websites referred to in this publication and does not guarantee that any content on such websites is, or will remain, accurate or appropriate.

Printed in the United States of America

Contents

1. Introduction \ 1
   Joseph T. Farquharson, Andrea Hollington and Byron M. Jones Jr.

Part 1 Language, Music and Identity

2. Discoursing the State of a Caribbean Nation \ 17
   Hubert Devonish

3. "Dennery Segment ka mennen": Exploring the Dominance of Creole Languages in St Lucian Popular Music \ 37
   Ronald T. Francis and R. Sandra Evans

4. Singing in Creole or Portuguese?: Santomean Musical Manifestations \ 64
   Marie-Eve Bouchard

5. Wi Ful a Patan: A Quantitative Approach to Language Use in Jamaican Popular Music \ 89
   Byron M. Jones Jr.

6. Styling through Rhyming: Gender and Vowel Variation in Jamaican Dancehall Lyrics \ 103
   Nickesha Dawkins

7. Language Use in Peter Ram's Soca Performances \ 138
   Guyanne Wilson

8. Singing the King's Creole: The (Ethno)Linguistic Repertoire of Clifton Chenier \ 159
   Nathan A. Wendte

Part 2 Translocal Perspectives

9. Rap Kriolu Revisited: From the Transnational Diaspora to Cape Verde and Back \ 193
   Christina Märzhäuser

10. Authentic Crossing?: Jamaican Creole in African Dancehall \ 231
   Anika Gerfer

11. Jamaican in Transatlantic Contact Spaces:
   Linguistic Practices in African Reggae, Dancehall
   and Other Popular Musics \ 258
   Andrea Hollington

12. Jamaric Reggae: Jamaican Speech Forms in Contemporary
   Ethiopian Reggae Music \ 284
   Renato Tomei

13. Caribbean Identity in Pop Music: Rihanna's and Nicki
   Minaj's Multivocal Pop Personas \ 313
   Lisa Jansen and Michael Westphal

List of Contributors \ 337

Index \ 339

Chapter 1

Introduction

JOSEPH T. FARQUHARSON, ANDREA HOLLINGTON AND BYRON M. JONES JR.

Music and language have a manifold relationship: Language is a crucial part of many musical forms and practices, while musical features are seen in language as well. They share contexts, spaces and histories in many sociocultural expressive forms. Links between language and music have been explored by scholars in various contexts. For example, Jackendoff and Lehrdahl adapted Noam Chomsky's linguistic generative approach to music. While this aimed at finding a common theoretical approach, studying "universal musical grammar" and a formal description of musical understanding, the approach does not seem to be very influential today. In recent decades, and especially since the beginning of the twenty-first century, sociolinguistic accounts of popular music have become quite common, such as hip-hop (Alim 2006; Alim, Ibrahim and Pennycook 2009; Terkourafi 2010) or reggae and dancehall (Devonish 1996, 1998, 2006; Devonish and Jones 2017; Farquharson 2005; Hollington 2016, 2018; Jones 2019). Exploring various connections of language and music as social practices opens up a large field of possibilities and perspectives.

This is where the present volume comprises and ties in chapters that seek to look at various intersections and connections of language and music. Different accounts shed light on language variation, the use of Creole language in music, language ideologies, authenticity, language and identity, the ethnography of communication, multilingualism and language contact, language attitudes, linguistic creativity and transnational flows. Instead of concentrating on a specific music genre, this volume presents a colourful collection of different practices in various music genres and styles, as well as in different parts of the world. The shared focus of this book is that each contribution sheds light on one or more aspects of (a) contact language(s) and the ways linguistic practices feature in and impact on various music styles.

Numerous creolized cultures, as well as societies characterized by linguistic pluralism and contact, have yielded rich musical practices in which contact languages are used. In many cases, music, as a social and cultural form of expression, has constituted a domain in which contact languages have gained prestige, preserved historical linguistic forms and served as strong markers of identity. Especially in colonial and postcolonial contexts, contact languages referred to as Creole have usually been regarded as low prestige varieties with little power, especially in official and political domains. Here, music has offered spaces in which Creole languages could not only flourish but also be celebrated as cultural heritage. Despite these important aspects, no book-length volume on the interplay of contact languages and music exists to date. This volume presents a number of original case studies from mainly anglophone Caribbean and African contexts that have not been discussed in previous works. It also explores some other contact varieties in francophone and lusophone contexts. Additionally, this volume aims at filling the aforementioned research gap by providing insights into a number of Creole language and musical practices from Jamaica to São Tomé, and from Louisiana to Trinidad and Tobago. Apart from documenting and analysing the use of contact languages in music practices, the volume seeks to explore, in particular, questions of identity and authenticity, which are addressed by the various contributors in their respective chapters with regard to methodological, theoretical and ideological standpoints and perspectives:

1. How is the intersection between contact languages and music deployed by artistes to construct and negotiate various identities?
2. How do the intersectionalities between contact languages and notions of race, authenticity, class and nationality "play out" in music?
3. How are linguistic performances in music by second-language speakers of contact languages assessed and evaluated as authentic by first-language and second-language speakers?
4. What is the basis of the evaluations made by audiences at home and abroad about the authenticity of contact languages as second languages in music?

Contact Languages and/in Music

The preparation of this volume has been dogged by the constant presence of the intervening slash between the conjunction "and" and the preposition "in". At first, it was put in to leave the field as broad as possible as we worked out the exact scope of the volume. As the work progressed, it morphed into a marker of inclusiveness, signalling that we were interested in the confluence between contact languages and music as well as the ways in which the former are deployed in the latter. The coordinating conjunction does not preclude an interest in those communities where contact languages are present but in which they are excluded from one or more genres of local music (Farquharson 2017). While the majority of the chapters in the current volume deal with contact languages *in* music, we acknowledge that cases in which they are under-represented or absent from an entire song, genre or some sections of a song can be equally as informative. Although some work has been done over the years on contact languages and/in music, we believe that we have not even scratched the surface in exploiting the full potential of this academic pursuit.

The Subfields of Linguistics

For example, lyrics provide a ready source of raw data for linguistic analysis; however, the potential of lyrics as data has not been fully exploited by contemporary linguists. This is particularly telling for contact languages, many of which continue to be dominated by oral as opposed to scribal channels. In the areas of phonetics and phonology, of particular note are Devonish (2006), who looks at the manipulation of diphthongs in the service of rhyme schemes, and Dawkins (2016), who concentrates on the manipulation of vowels for stylistic purposes. The overwhelming majority of existing studies on contact languages and music belongs to the sub-discipline of sociolinguistics, and so it comes as no surprise that the variety of topics is quite large. For example, with regard to Jamaican music, there are works which apply Austin's (1955) speech act theory and Brown and Levinson's (1987) politeness framework in relation to Jamaican dancehall songs that address the topic of sexuality, while others look at the link between diglossia and language use patterns in Jamaican folk and popular music (Devonish 1996; Farquharson 2005, 2019; Jones 2019). The latter ties in with works that investigate the sociology of language, such as Winer's (1986) exploration of language use patterns in Trinbagonian calypso, Cooper and Devonish (1995) and Devonish and Jones (2017) on language in the popular music of post-Independence Jamaica, and Farquharson (2017) on the interaction between linguistic codes in both secular and religious music in Jamaica from the colonial period to the present. Other studies concentrate on meaning-making in songs by exploring the (non-)deployment of specific languages or language varieties by artistes in constructing/projecting a particular type of identity: the use of calypso in Costa Rica as a marker of Afro-Limonese identity (Herzfeld and Moskowitz 2004), or Haitian in the multilingual space of Montreal rap and its role in code-switching practices (Sarkar, Winer and Sarkar 2005). Moreover, especially in contexts characterized by migration and multilingualism, music practices involving contact varieties even become sites of language contact themselves, often illustrating complex language ideologies (Hollington 2016). In fact, language ideologies constitute an interesting domain for the study of the language and music intersection as both language and music are commonly employed by people to express, negotiate and promote language ideologies, attitudes and metalinguistic awareness (see, for instance, Sippola, Schneider and Levisen 2017).

Other studies focus on diachronic language use and change in contact situations, using music lyrics as data (Jones 2019). As the previous paragraph demonstrates, phonology, sociolinguistics and linguistic anthropology are the better-explored areas in the study of contact languages and music. This is curious for the linguistic study of contact languages given that scholars constantly complain about the lack of readily available data. Because music represents a specific genre in which sometimes special language is used, scholars rarely turn to song lyrics for data for morphosyntactic studies. Jakobson's (1960) poetic function of language focuses on *how* a code is used, and it also sheds light on the use of language. Rather than assuming that only the channel has changed, the role of the linguist would be to determine, for example, whether and to what extent morphosyntax, voice, ways of speaking and so on of the language(s) found in songs differ from that found in day-to-day speech and writing. In cases where there are several ways of phrasing a particular expression, is there a marked preference in singing for one way over another? Which roles are played by rhyme and style in this context? How do authenticity and aesthetics play into these practices? And how do individual practices by singers and musicians influence society at large?

Methods and Approaches

It has already been mentioned that what unifies this emerging field is the data that stands at the centre of analyses. It needs to be stressed, however, that "data" in this context is a very versatile phenomenon given the plurality of musical aspects, styles and practices that are investigated here. No method or approach has emerged as *the* way of studying contact languages and music, and rightly so! The heterogeneity that exists allows us to get a much broader view of both language and music. The field is dominated by qualitative approaches that focus on the pragmatic and discursive aspects of song lyrics, especially with regard to meaning-making and identity construction, but also include aspects of multilingualism, authenticity, style, language ideologies and attitudes. There is a real sense in which the works that apply quantitative methods to the study of contact languages in music are pioneering. In the quantitative paradigm, we are aware of the work of Dawkins (2016 and chapter 6, this volume), whose sociophonetic work unearths gendered patterns of language use that elude the naked ears but are clearly part of the competence of performers and audience members. Jones (chapter 5, this volume) explores the use of Jamaican and English in Jamaican popular music by making use of quantitative methods with a focus on variationist sociolinguistics. Gerfer (2018) explores nine phonetic variables, seven morphosyntactic variables and lexical features used by seven white non-Jamaican reggae artistes. Jones (2019) uses a corpus-based approach in examining the use of syntactic features in Jamaican and English in the lyrics of Jamaican popular music over a fifty-year period, using quantitative methods to map language change and mechanisms of such a change.

The Sociolinguistics of Globalization and Diaspora

Whether under forced or voluntary migration, people move across borders bringing their languages, songs, music practices and other intangible cultural artefacts. The high transglobal mobility of the past half millennium requires an approach that is sensitive to the sociolinguistic dynamics resulting from diasporic settings. This is starting to be addressed by an emerging eclectic approach being referred to as the sociolinguistics of diaspora. According to Hinrichs (2011, 1–2), the central questions of diasporic sociolinguistics are as follows:

- What happens to individual heritage languages as they are transplanted into new settings, creating new dialect contact situations?
- What happens to established models of sociolinguistic description?
- What role does language play in the representational politics of diaspora communities?

Music provides an arena for the sociolinguistics of globalization (Blommaert 2010) and the sociolinguistics of diaspora (Hinrichs 2011) to play out. This is evident in the global diffusion of African American English (also known as African American Vernacular English), not through migration but through old and new media. Music (e.g. rap and hip-hop) plays an important role in communities across the world, particularly in areas where young people feel marginalized and oppressed. Among migrants and their descendants, where the sociolinguistic dynamics of their host countries cause them to restrict use of their heritage language to private informal in-group interactions, music furnishes a public space for the use of the heritage language. This is true of Cape Verdean Creole by migrants in rap kriolu in diaspora communities in New England (United States), Lisbon and Rotterdam (Märzhäuser, chapter 9, this volume); Ghanaian Pidgin English and Nigerian Pidgin English (Naija) in the rap/reggae/dancehall of artists from those nationalities living abroad; Jamaican Creole as used in the reggae and dancehall music produced by Jamaican migrants in Canada, the United States and the United Kingdom; as well as Haitian in the rap music produced by Haitian migrants and their descendants in Quebec, Canada (Low, Sarkar and Winer 2009; Sarkar and Winer 2006). Where language is introduced to a new environment via migration, it is used in popular music in the host country, and music becomes one of the key sites of diffusion to other ethnolinguistic groups, both migrant and non-migrant.

Music bears testament to Blommaert's (2010, 106) characterization of linguistic repertoires as "truncated complexes of resources often derived from a variety of language, and with considerable differences in the level of development of particular resources". This is illustrated by the use of multiple codes in a single song, as described, for example, by Tomei (chapter 12, this volume) for reggae in Ethiopia; Sarkar, Winer and Sarkar (2005) for hip-hop in Montreal; and Hollington (chapter 11, this volume) for dancehall music in various African societies. Making full use of the sociolinguistic turntable that popular music provides, musical artistes produce highly interesting ways of linguistic interaction by drawing on and mixing resources from their linguistic repertoires.

Jansen and Westphal (2017) propose that singers become "transnational linguistic agents", exposing a global audience to a creative bricolage of linguistic resources. This transnationalization is of particular importance to under-resourced languages, a category to which the majority of Creole languages belongs. What Jansen and Westphal (2017) describe for Rihanna is also true of several other artistes with a similar social and linguistic background, for example, Michi Mee and Kardinall Offishall in Canada (Farquharson 2019).

An interesting aspect is provided by the observation of the roles that language and music play in diaspora communities in the transnational spread of contact languages in the absence of the vast economic and institutional resources for dissemination available to big or more established standard(ized) languages. This process may involve several phases. First, the contact language gains a limited foothold in the host country when it is mainly used in closed networks by native speakers and their descendants among themselves. If the community is marginalized, or physically or culturally isolated, this may lead to fossilization or death after the first couple of generations. If the migrant community shares living and working space with members of the host community and other migrant groups and uses its language in public settings, then the language may be picked up by out-group individuals as an additional language or register. Despite the imbalance in resources many contact languages have, music opens up spaces for the establishment of communities of practice centred on informal language teaching/learning.

Jamaican dancehall music created in countries such as Ghana, Guyana, Nigeria, and Trinidad and Tobago creates a complex (socio)linguistic space. It is interesting to observe contexts where a contact language exists in a society and is in regular use when at the same time artistes enregister the original language associated with the genre (e.g. Jamaican) to index both linguistic and professional authenticity, while also utilizing the local contact language to establish ethnic bonds with their home audience. The complexities in these contexts might be further complicated by historical ties and parallel developments in the contact varieties that come into contact with each other in the respective music practices. In this way artistes make conscious use of heteroglossic strategies, leveraging their linguistic resources to connect to people, express complex identities and to expand their audience/market.

The various contributions to this volume are arranged in two larger sections, namely *language, music and identity* and *translocal perspectives*. Though all contributions touch upon aspects of identity with regard to language use in music in the respective contexts, the chapters in the first part focus more on local, national or regional contexts, while the chapters in the second part address issues of translocality, global linguistic flows and diasporic identities.

Overview of the Contributions

Part 1: Language, Music and Identity

Music and nationality are the focus of the contribution by Hubert Devonish (chapter 2). By investigating four songs from Trinidad and Tobago, the author looks at discourses of national identity and ethnic relations.

Employing the notion of performative speech acts, he shows how artistes use different strategies of negotiating meaning and identity with their audiences. By switching between performer/narrator and performer/first-person participant, the artistes take on different personae and are thus able to engage in a multivocal discourse of negotiating (national) identity. The artistes use lyrics and music to affirm and deny performative speech acts, as the author illustrates.

Ronald T. Francis and R. Sandra Evans in chapter 3 explore Creole language use in St Lucia. By focusing on dennery segment, a recent musical genre developed on the island, the authors shed light on a new music phenomenon and investigate the roles language plays by employing Bourdieu's practice theory, in particular the concepts of linguistic habitus and linguistic market. The authors illustrate and discuss the use of Kwéyòl and Vernacular English of St Lucia in dennery segment, and analyse language use in different sociocultural domains commonly found in the lyrics. Furthermore, the chapter sheds light on the local, regional and international influences and resonances of the music genre.

Chapter 4 by Marie-Eve Bouchard investigates language ideologies in the music of São Tomé and Príncipe. By looking at language choices and the use of Creole varieties, the author discusses the role of music and musicians with regard to the valorization and maintenance of the Santomean Creole languages. The archipelago is in the process of language shift in favour of the dominant language, Portuguese, and the use of Creole varieties in music, in particular Forro and Angolar, serves as a marker of identity and authenticity as the author illustrates.

Byron M. Jones's chapter (chapter 5) provides an overview of the socially diagnostic factors that determine the use of Jamaican Creole and English in Jamaican popular music. The author does this by examining the frequency distributions of all eight factors that were identified in the onset of the study, after which the list was narrowed to include only the most salient factors, measured by their strength of association. The chapter links the saliency of these factors to changes in language attitudes in the wider Jamaican society.

Nickesha Dawkins in her sociophonetic study (chapter 6) introduces both a technical and a gender component. Through the measurement of acoustic features, focusing on vowel formants, she finds an unexpected pattern in the phonetic realization of vowels produced by dancehall artistes during performance. Both male and female artistes increase the pitch of vowels, raise the height of the tongue and produce the vowels as more front when addressing/targeting female audiences, but lower the pitch of vowels, lower the height of the tongue, and produce vowels as further back when addressing/targeting male audiences.

In chapter 7, Guyanne Wilson examines language use practices in Peter Ram's performance of soca music. The author analyses samples of Ram's studio recordings and live performances with the aim being to discover how Ram constructs identity through Creole use, what phonological patterns exist in his music and how these patterns change over time. The author concludes that performers have to navigate a linguistic space conditioned not only by stylistic preferences but also by issues of prestige, power and identity.

Nathan A. Wendte in chapter 8 presents a linguistic analysis of a corpus comprising fifty songs from the musical work of Clifton Chenier, the dubbed "King of Zydeco". The author aims to show the interaction of Characteristic Louisiana Creole and Characteristic Louisiana French in Chenier's work to better understand what language variety (or varieties) typify zydeco music (a Louisiana-based musical genre). The author concludes the chapter with a discussion stating that the linguistic description presented can expand our understanding of language's diverse forms in zydeco music, which may prove helpful in ongoing Louisiana Creole language revitalization efforts.

Part 2: Translocal Perspectives

Christina Märzhäuser's contribution (chapter 9) analyses the deployment of Capeverdean Creole in rap kriolu in the Cape Verdean homeland and its diasporas. The study takes a detailed ethnographic approach including song texts, interviews with MC's and other involved individuals, analysis of social media platforms, and documentary and fictional films. Marshalling all of this evidence, Märzhäuser conducts what she refers to as a linguistic market analysis looking at how artistes, singers and producers contribute to and influence access to Capeverdean and the functional expansion of the language to deal with topics and themes not normally treated in homeland varieties.

Anika Gerfer's chapter (chapter 10) takes up the sociolinguistic debates about crossing – the phenomenon of appropriating linguistic practices or emblematic language features of another cultural group – and the notion of authenticity. She explores African dancehall music and presents insights into song examples from Ghana, Nigeria and Kenya. Her analysis investigates which linguistic features of Jamaican Creole have been used by African dancehall artistes. She discusses the implications of these instances of crossing with regard to authenticity by looking at the multilingual practices and contexts of the respective artists.

Andrea Hollington, in chapter 11, casts a wider net by looking at the musical production of several African countries and the dominant status of Jamaican language, despite the absence of any significant population of native speakers of Jamaican in these countries. She attributes the dominance of Jamaican language practices to the high global visibility of Jamaican music, as well as the historical and ideological links between Africa and Jamaica, her diasporic daughter. Exploring songs from English-official African countries, such as Ethiopia, Kenya, Uganda, Zimbabwe, Ghana and Nigeria, Hollington frames music as a site of transatlantic contact of genres (reggae, dancehall, African pop) and linguistic varieties (e.g. Ghanaian/Nigerian Pidgin English, Jamaican Creole, African American Vernacular English and Swahili). Her analysis reveals the conscious use of Jamaican linguistic practices alongside expressions that are probably motivated by shared worldviews and experiences shaped by historical social practices such as colonialism and exploitation.

When elements of intangible culture get transplanted from one location to another they often outlive the generation that transported them and take on a life of their own. This is the focus of Renato Tomei's chapter (chapter 12), which looks at the musical and linguistic legacy of the Jamaican Rastafarian community in Ethiopia. Ethiopian youth take up not only the music of the community but also the accompanying language varieties (i.e. mainstream Jamaican Creole and Dread Talk). Tomei mines song lyrics, advertising and promotional material, social media posts, interviews, and audio/video recordings for Jamaican speech forms. His work uncovers a modern linguistic flow involving the incorporation of Jamaican words into music produced by Ethiopians corresponding to the decades-old ebb in which Jamaican singers (in Jamaica) incorporated Ethiopian words into their music.

In chapter 13, Lisa Jansen and Michael Westphal explore identity processes and the role of language in transnational and global music practices by Rihanna and Nicki Minaj. The authors shed light on the multilayered and diverse personas of these artistes and discuss their roles in promoting the spread of Caribbean English Creole. A qualitative multimodal analysis of the linguistic practices represented in the music and performances of these two artistes sheds light on the identity process expressed through creative performative means. Jansen and Westphal use the concepts of multivocality as well as multimodality in their analysis in order to present a nuanced picture of the translocal and global identities in pop music.

Conclusion

Although scholars have been studying contact languages and/in music for some time, the studies tend to be presented in disparate publications. This edited collection represents the start of a conversation that takes the topic to a new level by bringing together various case studies that together create a broad perspective on language and music in the contexts of migration, diaspora and language contact. It therefore adds to the body of knowledge on contact languages and music. There is scope for the application of various sociolinguistic models and theories that are suitable but have so far remained un(der)utilized. For example, Le Page and Tabouret-Keller's (1985) acts of identity model should prove useful in exploring the music produced in diaspora communities by second and subsequent generations. Moreover, concepts of language and migration as well as creative ways of handling large linguistic repertoires (Lüpke and Storch 2013) can be fruitfully examined in music practices in many societies. Additionally, the study of contact languages and music has largely involved linguists working in disciplinary silos. We are yet to exploit the enriching insights to be gained from collaborating with scholars from other disciplines such as psychology, sociology and ethnomusicology. For example, the latter could contribute significantly to a true ethnography of communication where we investigate music as its own system of communication, not merely as a scaffold for the lyrics. Such an interdisciplinary project would study how the instrumentals work in tandem with the lyrics to produce complete communicative acts.

A final point is that when we first started preparing the concept of this volume, we had anticipated a much broader spread in terms of regions and linguistic contexts. The reader will notice that there is a heavy focus on Caribbean contexts, especially on the Jamaican language in both local and diasporic spaces. This might be evidence of the state of academic work on contact languages and music, which apparently has a lopsided concentration on either North American (hip-hop) or English and English-related language communities. This is a signal that there are still many interesting and unresearched phenomena to uncover. Therefore, we hope that this volume will also inspire further research on the multifaceted connections between language and music.

References

Alim, Samy H. 2006. *Roc the Mic Right: The Language of Hip Hop Culture*. London and New York: Routledge.

Alim, Samy H., Awad Ibrahim, and Alastair Pennycook, eds. 2009. *Global Linguistic Flows: Hip Hop Culture, Youth Identities, and the Politics of Language*. London and New York: Routledge.

Austin, John L. 1955. *How to Do Things with Words*. Harvard: Harvard University Press.

Blommaert, Jan. 2010. *The Sociolinguistics of Globalization*. New York: Cambridge University Press.

Brown, Penelope, and Stephen C. Levinson. 1987. *Politeness: Some Universals in Language Use*. Cambridge: Cambridge University Press.

Cooper, Carolyn, and Hubert Devonish. 1995. "A Tale of Two States: Language, Literature and the Two Jamaicas". In *The Pressures of the Text: Orality, Texts and the Telling of Tales*, edited by Stewart Brown, 60–74. Birmingham: Centre of West African Studies.

Dawkins, Nickesha. 2016. "Gender as a Sociophonetic Issue in Jamaican Lyrics". PhD diss., University of the West Indies, Mona.

Devonish, Hubert. 1996. "Kom Groun Jamiekan Daans Haal Liricks: Memba se a Plie wi a Plie – Contextualizing Jamaican 'Dance Hall' Music: Jamaican Language at Play in a Speech Event". *English World Wide* 17 (2): 213–37.

———. 1998. "Electronic Orature: The Deejay's Discovery". *Social & Economic Studies* 47 (1): 33–53.

———. 2006. "On the Status of Diphthongs in Jamaican: Mr. Vegas Pronounces". In *Exploring the Boundaries of Caribbean Creole Languages*, edited by Hazel Simmons-McDonald and Ian Robertson, 72–95. Kingston: University of the West Indies Press.

Devonish, Hubert, and Byron Jones. 2017. "Jamaica: A State of Language, Music and Crisis of Nation". *La Revue des Musiques Populaires* 13 (2): 129–44.

Farquharson, Joseph T. 2005. "Faiya-bon: The Socio-pragmatics of Homophobia in Jamaican (Dancehall) Culture". In *Politeness and Face in Caribbean Creoles*, edited by Susanne Mühleisen and Bettina Migge, 101–18. Amsterdam: Benjamins.

———. 2017. "Linguistic Ideologies and the Historical Development of Language Use Patterns in Jamaican Music". *Language & Communication* 52: 7–18.

———. 2019. "Language Use in Jamaican Reggae Music and its Implication for the Concept of Diglossia". Paper presented at the 6th *Global Reggae Conference* held at the University of the West Indies, Mona, 13–16 February.

Gerfer, Anika. 2018. "Global Reggae and the Appropriation of Jamaican Creole". *World Englishes* 37: 668–83.

Herzfeld, Anita, and David Moskowitz. 2004. "The Limonese Calypso as an Identity Marker". In *Creoles, Contact, and Language Change: Linguistic and Social Implications*, edited by Geneviève Escure and Armin Schwegler, 259–84. Amsterdam: Benjamins.

Hinrichs, Lars. 2011. "The Sociolinguistics of Diaspora: Language in the Jamaican Canadian Community". *Texas Linguistics Forum* 54: 1–22.

Hollington, Andrea. 2016. "Movement of Jah People: Language Ideologies and Music in a Transnational Contact Scenario". *Critical Multilingualism Studies* 4 (2): 133–53.

———. 2018. "Transatlantic Translanguaging in Zimdancehall: Reassessing Linguistic Creativity in Youth Language Practices". *The Mouth* 3: 105–23.
Jakobson, Roman. 1960. "Closing Statement: Linguistics and Poetics". In *Style in Language*, edited by Thomas A. Seboek, 350–77. Cambridge, MA: MIT Press.
Jansen, Lisa, and Michael Westphal. 2017. "Rihanna Works Her Multivocal Pop Persona: A Morpho-syntactic and Accent Analysis of Rihanna's Singing Style. Pop Culture Provides Rich Data that Demonstrate the Rich Play of World Englishes". *English Today* 33 (2): 46–55.
Jones, Byron. 2019. "Beyond di Riddim: A Quantitative and Qualitative Approach to the Evolution of Language Use in Jamaican Popular Music, 1962-2012". PhD diss., University of the West Indies, St. Augustine.
Lehrdahl, Fred, and Ray Jackendoff. 1983. *A Generative Theory of Tonal Music*. Cambridge, MA: MIT Press.
Le Page, R.B., and Andrée Tabouret-Keller. 1985. *Acts of Identity: Creole-based Approaches to Language and Ethnicity*. Cambridge: Cambridge University Press.
Low, Bronwen, Mela Sarkar, and Lise Winer. 2008. "'Ch'us mon propre Bescherelle': Challenges from the Hip-Hop Nation to the Quebec Nation". *Journal of Sociolinguistics* 13 (1): 59–82.
Lüpke, Friederike, and Anne Storch. 2013. *Repertoires and Choices in African Languages*. Berlin: Mouton de Gruyter.
Sarkar, Mela, and Lise Winer. 2006. "Multilingual Codeswitching in Quebec Rap: Poetry, Pragmatics and Performativity". *International Journal of Multilingualism* 3 (3): 173–92.
Sarkar, Mela, Lise Winer, and Kobir Sarkar. 2005. "Multilingual Code-switching in Montreal Hip-hop: Mayhem Meets Method or, 'Tout Moune qui Talk Trash Kiss Mon Black Ass du Nord'". In *Proceedings of the 4th International Symposium on Bilingualism*, edited by James Cohen, Kara T. McAlister, Kellie Rolstad, and Jeff MacSwan, 2057–74. Somerville, MA: Cascadilla Press.
Sippola, Eeva, Britta Schneider, and Carsten Levisen, guest eds. 2017. "Language Ideologies in Music – Emergent Socialities in the Age of Transnationalism". Special issue, *Language & Communication* 52.
Terkourafi, Marina, ed. 2010. *The Languages of Global Hip Hop*. London and New York: Continuum.
Winer, Lise. 1986. "Socio-cultural Change and the Language of Calypso". *Nieuwe West-Indische Gids* 60 (3/4): 113–48.

Part 1

Language, Music and Identity

Chapter 2

Discours*ing* the State of a Caribbean Nation

HUBERT DEVONISH

Introduction

Invited to the University of Cape Town in December 2018 to do a series of presentations, on my first visit to the African continent as a descendant of enslaved Africans in the Americas, I find my mind split in two. I look at the black Africans in the audience, allow myself a mental jaw drop and think, "Aha! So this is Africa and these are Africans on their own continent." Then the other half kicked in. The black people in the audiences were a minority, very odd coming from the Caribbean where, depending on the country, audiences would either be made up predominantly of people of African descent or a mix of people of African and Indian descent. This wasn't quite the Africa I was expecting to be confronted with on my first working day on the mother continent. And then one sees that the black people present do not act as confidently as I expect of people at home on their own continent. And then it dawns on me. This atmosphere and behaviour is very old-style Caribbean. And then comes the epiphany. Black majority rule in South Africa dates back to just the 1990s. My own experience of black people at least symbolically being in charge of their own "postcolonial" space is easily thirty years longer than that of the black South Africans in the audience. Maybe, after all, there is actually something we can teach. We can talk of our more than fifty-five-year experience on this postcolonial or, more properly, neocolonial road.

The message is simple. The elites who inherit the state at the end of colonization do so as part of a nationalist and political discourse carried on in the language of the European colonizing group. The mass of the population living within the borders of this new "independent" state have their own discourses. These are conducted in the mass vernacular languages rather than a language such as English and take place in an oral rather than written medium. These discourses, in the case of the Caribbean, frequently take place in the milieu of speech events associated with musical performance.

The present work, developed from the workshop presentations in South Africa, is part of a larger study on popular discourse on race, language and national identity in the former British Caribbean. The intent is to understand the content of debates on identity, nation and state as they take place among the ordinary folk, the "masses", in their vernacular language varieties. Also under study are the discourse structures within which these debates take place. Of most important interest is how, if at all, the medium, in the form of language choice and discourse features, and the message interact with each other.

Discoursing Nation and the State

With countries of the Commonwealth Caribbean acceding to political independence beginning in the 1960s, there has been extensive discussion and debate around nation building. At core has been the relationship between the people and the new states which supposedly represent their national aspirations. Colonialism created arbitrary geographically based states. This it did either by forcing together people belonging to what were previously multiple nations or ethnicities, occupying that space, or importing people from other places and forcing them to work and exist in a new place which happens to be a European colony. On independence, the state and its supporting institutions are inherited by the elite to whom the departing colonizer hands over political control. The people, nations and ethnicities within the entity that is the postcolonial state are then forced to negotiate a relationship between each other and with the state. This is a study about the role of language in this negotiation, firstly in relation to the kinds of popular language discourse that take place and the issue of what role these play in the state that supposedly represents them and governs in their best interest.

The states which emerged in the postcolonial era are peculiar, best defined by what they were not. They did not naturally develop out of ethnic groups in a particular locality negotiating with each other, over time, albeit with the requisite use of force or threat of such use. They did not emerge as expressions of the history of the relationship between the peoples ruled by the state and the state itself. Rather, the Caribbean states which grew in the wake of European colonialism are constructed out of national and ethnic units forced together by the colonizer. Peoples find themselves together within the borders of a postcolonial state by virtue of having been forced together by colonialism. These were the classic plural societies produced by British colonialism as described by theorists at the time of independence, notably the Jamaican scholar M.G. Smith (1965).

The enforced coexistence within the newly independent formerly British Caribbean state, as just described, has to be rationalized and made acceptable to the citizens of the postcolonial state. This state responds to this challenge by developing an official discourse around the theme of unity, as seen in the national mottoes of Jamaica, "Out of Many, One People"; of Trinidad and Tobago, "Together we aspire, together we achieve"; and of Guyana, "One people, one nation, one destiny". These official discourses take place in the official language, English, and among the educated classes competent in this language, and in domains such as parliament and the mass media dominated by the state. An examination of the mottoes points to one conclusion. The ideal being aspired to is that of the nation state. Here, unlike in the multinational state, a single nation is governed by itself within the boundaries of a state-controlled geographical area. Within this model, the state is the highest expression of the nation, and, in the absence of a pre-existing nation, the first task of the independent Caribbean state is "nation-building".

Discourse on issues of nation formation and the relationship of ethnic groups and subordinate social classes to the state cannot be, by definition, the preserve of the state and its associated educated elite. These matters are the everyday reality of the mass of the population who have to coexist within the newly independent state. As might be expected, the general population develop their own discourse on these questions, within domains controlled by them, notably popular music. These discourses are, of course, conducted in the mass Creole vernacular within which they conduct their daily lives. One of the main forums for these mass-based discourses is musical performances involving lyrics performed to music live but more often recorded and replayed via amplification or broadcast on the radio and other electronic media. This body of discourse provides a very audible means of following the negotiating process taking place among the ethnic and social groups forced together inside these still relatively newly independent states.

The Songs

This is a study of four songs from Trinidad and Tobago. They are, in the order in which they will be discussed, "Trinbago Babu" by All Rounder (1996), "Come With It" by Black Stalin (1992), "Sundar" also by Black Stalin (1995) and "Ah Fraid Karl" by the Mighty Chalkdust (1972). They were selected because of the complexity of their discourse style and the nature of their subject matter.

One of the songs, "Ah Fraid Karl", is a traditional slow-tempo political commentary calypso or kaiso. The other three are of the genre classified as "soca". The name is a linguistic blend of the word *soul*, with reference to the soul music of 1960s African Americans, and the first syllable of *calypso*, the popular musical style associated with Trinidad and Tobago up to the late 1970s.

Most of the lyrics of these songs are in the English-lexicon Creole of Trinidad and Tobago. In the interest of avoiding extensive translation, we will transcribe the lyrics of the songs in the most anglicized transcription possible, providing bracketed explanations where these are required.

Embedded Performative Speech Acts

Defining Embedded Performatives

The notion of the performative speech act is well established in the literature on speech act theory. Non-performative language communication involves utterances which have a meaning and significance outside of the actual utterance itself. Thus, a statement such as "The cat is in the house" has a meaning which refers to some reality or suggested reality outside of the sentence itself.

In performative speech acts, the actual act of speaking fulfils the requirement for meaning. Utterances, including phrases such as "I pray", "I beg", "I ask", "I announce", "I pronounce" and "I report", typically signal performative speech acts. Thus, in a sentence in which a soldier says to his superior officer, "I am reporting that the weapons have been secured", the actual pronouncement is the meaning. The reporting is accomplished by the soldier uttering the sentence. As Searle (1989) suggests, with reference to performative speech acts, "the successful performance of the speech act is sufficient to bring about the fit between words and world, to make the propositional content true". Alternatively, the soldier could have said, "The weapons are secured, sir." Given the nature of the reporting relationship known to exist between the soldier and the officer, the absence of the introductory phrase, "I am reporting that . . .", including as it does the performative verb "report", does not change the intended or interpreted meaning of the utterance. Thus, we can modify our understanding of the quote from Searle (1989) by suggesting that "the successful performance of the speech act is sufficient to bring about a fit between words, *whether uttered or implied from the context*, and the world". We can treat the first example of the soldier's words as a case of an explicit performative speech act and the second as an implicit performative.

A particular manifestation of the performative speech act is of particular interest to us here. This occurs when a performative has embedded within it another speech act. In reporting speech acts, this takes the form of "X reporting that Y says Z". The Z is a separate speech act which has to be enacted within the larger speech act in order to establish what Y says. This enactment could be in the form of indirect speech, in which case only the content of what is said is preserved. Alternatively, Z could be re-enacted in the form of direct speech, in which case both the linguistic form and the message content of the original utterance are preserved.

In the songs to be analysed in this study, all involve the performer in the role of narrator, essentially reporting to an audience on a set of acts that are proposed to have taken place. Some of those reported acts are speech acts. At that point, the performer shifts from being a reporter or narrator to performing the embedded speech act as the "I" or "we" source of the utterance. The performer shifts from being performer/reporter to performer and first-person participant in the embedded speech act. The only way for the performer/participant not to perform the embedded speech act is for the performer/reporter not to initiate the reporting process. In two of the four songs to be discussed, the performer/reporter behaves lyrically, musically or both, in a way which denies that the embedded speech act is being performed by the singer in the role of performer/first-person participant. In the fourth song, the performer/reporter uses the musical performance to undermine the truth value of the embedded speech act being reported on.

Performative Affirmed by Lyrics and Music: "Trinbago Babu"

The narrative of the performer/reporter presents a speech event within which the song "Trinbago Babu" is supposed to be performed. This speech event is framed by a spoken word introduction which precedes the first verse. Indian-style tassa drums beat and we hear a speaking voice say, "Ah can't afford to loss this competition tonight. Ganraj ha(s) to sing plenty to beat me." We are about to hear a song, itself a speech act, which is supposed, as part of the narrative, to have taken place within a speech event, a singing competition.

The performer of the song, All Rounder, is about to sing against a competitor, Ganraj, and All Rounder is determined to win. A performative speech act is being carried out here. The performer, All Rounder, is telling us the story of the competition by way of him going through the speech act routines appropriate to a singing competition.

The music then comes in to accompany the drumming. It is a tune associated with a traditional song sung by Guyanese of Indian descent. The original song has the lines "Bengali babu, Bengali babu, I am the very best of Bengali babu." "Babu", a pejorative term used by outsiders to describe somebody of Indian descent and, as in this context, is used by the Indian community itself as a marker of internal group solidarity. In recent decades, the "Bengali Babu" song has been converted into "Guyana babu, Guyana babu, I am the very best of Guyana babu". The best known singer of this version of the traditional song is Terry Gajraj. Gajraj is probably the intended target of the All Rounder song, albeit with the slightly altered name of Terry Ganraj.

From the introduction which presents All Rounder as performing in a competition, we move to the first verse. Here, the perspective changes. In the verse, All Rounder gives a narrative of the competition between him and Terry Ganraj from Guyana. We presume, later to be confirmed by the chorus, that the teller of the story in the song is Trinidadian. We learn in the first verse that Terry Ganraj from Guyana claims he has the best chutney soca (an Indian-influenced style of soca). According to the narrative, a competition is set up between All Rounder, who will represent Trinidad and Tobago, and Terry Ganraj, representing Guyana. From Ganraj's name, we presume him to be Indian. The rules of the competition are that the lyrics can be changed, but the tune must remain the same when the two competitors take turns at singing. All Rounder accepts the challenge, saying:

> I say that is kicks
> So I started to croon (All Rounder 1996)

The preceding lines of the verse transition us from the narrative as presented by the performer/reporter in the verse to the singing performance in the competition presented to us by All Rounder, now in his role as performer/first-person participant. We have the embedded speech acts reported in the form of what he says. We also then have the introduction to another embedded speech act, one which he croons. This serves also as the intro to the chorus. Here, by performing in the role of a competitor in the song competition, All Rounder has shifted to being a performer/first-person participant.

> *Chorus*
> Guyana babu, Guyana babu
> Trinbago babu is the sweeter babu (All Rounder 1995)

This is the ultimate insult, from the perspective of the Guyanese competitor in the song, Terry Ganraj. The very music and lyrical structure used to extol the virtue of being the very best of Guyana babu is being hijacked by All Rounder to assert that Trinbago babu is the sweeter babu. This is a performative which relies for its effectiveness on the fact that a song normally used by Guyanese to extol their own virtues has been captured by the contestant from Trinidad and Tobago (aka Trinbago), All Rounder, to announce the virtues of Trinbago babu.

The second part of the chorus shifts the performer back to the role of performer/reporter and carries us back to the narrative describing what is taking place. The focus becomes the audience witnessing the competition, and that it is made up of babus all over – in the front, back, left and right – enjoying themselves.

> Look a babu on the left then a babu on the right
> Trinbago babu they wanted whole night
> A babu in the back then a babu all in front
> Trinbago babu whole night that they want
> A babu, a babu, a babu for so [many many *babus*]
> Look a babu babu babu, a babu for so
> A babu, a babu, for sweet Trinbago. (All Rounder 1995)

As the chorus ends, the audience have their voices represented in the form of encouragement to the Trinidad and Tobago contestant, All Rounder. We hear, in a speaking voice, "Hehoi, Sing bai [boy/brother]."

In the next verse, the stakes in the story are laid out. It's a big sell-out club at a venue called Himalaya; the prize is a house, some land and a car, in addition to a trip to India. The introduction of India into the narrative reminds us that the Trinidad and Tobago representative, All Rounder, is of African descent. He is, however, performing in a medium associated with people of Indian descent. The Guyanese contestant in the musical competition being reported on, Terry Ganraj, has a name which suggests that he is of Indian descent. His real-life avatar, Terry Gajraj, is certainly of Indian descent. This sets up, for the presumably Trinidad and Tobago Indian audience, a conflict between racial/ethnic allegiance, on one hand, and national identity on the other. This conflict is resolved by a member of the audience who announces his allegiance by indicating who he is betting on and why.

> A old Indian man say, "Mi na racial, [I am not racial]
> All mi [my] paisa [money] going on the kilwal [creole/black man]" (All Rounder 1995)

This verse ends with a clear message. National identity is supposed to reign supreme over racial or ethnic identity. The chorus then shifts us back into the mode of the actual musical competition between the representatives of the two countries, with All Rounder back to functioning as performer/first-person participant.

This victory of nationalism over race and ethnicity is consolidated in the third verse. We are told by All Rounder, as performer/reporter, that when Ganraj realized that he was losing, he packed up his things and said he was going. All Rounder coaxes Ganraj to stay and finish the competition. This is done by rubbing salt in the wound, since All Rounder assures Ganraj that even if the latter is losing, it is Ganraj's tune that is being sung by him, the winner.

In the fourth verse, we are told that the inevitable has happened. The judges have declared All Rounder the winner and he is called onto the stage to say something:

> So I tell Ganraj come, he started crying,
> I tell he "Man, No, is both of us win
> It is just a show, no fuss, no fight,
> Africans and Indians must always unite." (All Rounder 1995)

This is the second element in the identity message, that of unity between Africans and Indians. All Rounder, the African performer from Trinbago, has already been, within the story as narrated, accepted by Indians from Trinbago as their legitimate representative in a competition in a musical genre associated with their ethnic group. He goes on to win the competition against a Guyanese of Indian descent. By this manipulation of the storyline, the superiority of the nation state of Trinidad and Tobago over Guyana is established. However, what remains is a potential enmity between an African from Trinbago who has "appropriated" an Indian Guyanese song and won a competition with it. The last lines of the last verse quoted earlier, serve to defuse that conflict, and reaffirm the African–Indian unity message intended by All Rounder for his audience in Trinbago.

The song closes with an outro which emphasizes both All Rounder's superiority as singer and lyricist and his legitimacy with his Trinbago Indian audience. Having won the competition, we are told by All Rounder, in his role as performer/reporter, that his presumably Trinbago Indian audience wants him to continue singing.

> I tired and resting, they still want babu
> Ah had was to get up and give them babu.

Ahaha, ahaha
Hehoi
Nani want babu, daata want babu, papa want babu. (All Rounder 1995)

The song constantly slides between the perspective of the singer as performer/reporter narrating events and his perspective as performer/first-person participant producing an embedded performative. In this song, the two perspectives reinforce each other. Contrary to what one might expect, this is not a necessary relationship, as will be seen in the discussion of the remaining three songs.

Performative Denied by Lyrics/Affirmed by Music: "Come With It"

One aspect of discourse at the level of the emerging nation is the issue of the artistic forms which define it and the desire to keep them "pure", to preserve them for posterity. Part of the internal discourse has surrounded domains of popular music and their role in promoting the "highest" values appropriate to the emerging nation. There is a view that, given the influence which popular music has over the young, it should be reserved exclusively for exploring topics of high social, moral or political significance. Some performers have a reputation for covering such topics. They then are seen as sell-outs to commercialization when they "descend" into more prosaic topics such as that of dancing and partying.

Black Stalin, stereotyped as a "conscious" calypsonian, had sung in 1991 "Black Man Feeling to Party", an ode to his wife and the sacrifices she made in raising the family. The song, with appropriate swing and beat, summons her, now that the children are grown, to stop the housework she is doing, "put on something sexy", go out and have some fun, and "party the way we used to when we was young". The song was ambiguous, straddling social commentary in the form of recognition of the contribution made to the family by female labour and the partying celebration of that contribution. Stalin, with that as one of his songs, won the Calypso Monarch Competition in 1991. Not surprisingly, some of Stalin's fans would have viewed the very "partyness" of the song as signalling a sell-out to some kind of escapism.

It is to the implication that Black Stalin may have sold out that he responds the following year with "Come With It". He begins the song in his role as performer/reporter. He sets the context by referring to his hit of the previous year, "Black Man Feeling to Party". In the first lines, he suggests that people are "vexed like hell" that he is taking his wife to party. Before one knows it, journalists are criticizing him in the newspapers for singing lewd and suggestive songs. At this point, the denial of the performer/first-person participant kicks in:

> Before them reporters put my career in more jeopardy
> Not me, not me to sing again about party. (Black Stalin 1992)

He is promising that he will never again sing about party. However, the only way to not sing again about the topic of party is not to sing about it. To sing another song, claiming that one is not going to sing again about the topic is to, by a performative act, to deny the claim being made in the lyrics. He is, by claiming to yield to his critics, defying them by again singing about party. In addition, to do so in an uptempo "sweet soca" musical style similar to the song he is being criticized for doing, denies, by way of musical style, the truth value of what is being stated in the lyrics. This a performative speech act, denied by both the lyrics themselves and the music.

The performer/reporter ends the narrative in the first verse by stating that when his fans hear what he had to say, wherever he went, "They keep bawling out, 'No way!'" This ending sets up the chorus which continues to quote from the words of the fans. At this point, the performer/reporter shifts role. He becomes the performer/first-person participant, singing in the guise of the disgruntled fans.

> No, No, No! This party can't done, Blackman, jam another one,
> This party can't done, this party can't done.
> Come with it, with a party song
> Is you make we boogie-boogie
> All night long. (Black Stalin 1992)

The lyrics of the chorus in songs, as normally the only repeated set of lyrics, tend to identify the main theme or topic of the song. Often, listeners only remember the chorus. In this case, the chorus is made up of the words of the fans and is stereotypical of a party song genre. The lyrics call on the singer to sing another song, stating that the party must go on. And then there is the slogan, "Come with it!" All of this fits the style and content of the chorus of a party song intended for dancing and participatory singing. The chorus is a quotation from the fans who rebel against the performer's/reporter's narrative in the verse that has him resolving never to sing another party song. His audience, the fans, in the voice of Black Stalin as performer/first-person participant, defy the newspaper reporter critics. Singing the defiant words of his fans, he is enabled to sing a party song. All of this takes place against the background of seeming to concede to critics by promising not to sing another party song.

By the second verse, we realize that we are being treated to a dialogue between Black Stalin and his fans. This verse is their chance to reply to his propositions in the first verse. In his performer/first-person participant voice, he represents the fans as saying to him, with reference to his pledge not to sing another party song, "Is joke you making, Just jam, Just jam, Just keep on jamming." They tell him that they love his music and that he should not let any newspaper reporter put an end to it. At this point in the narrative, we get an insertion into the mouths of the fans of a direct counter to the claim that his music has lost its social and political focus. They say, "You sing and try to bring the whole Caribbean together", that he has tried to make a better life for the elders, so that now is good time for him to realize that "party people is people too". This becomes the pretext for the singing of the second chorus which begins with the lines, "No, no, no, this party can't done."

In the third verse, Black Stalin reintroduces himself as performer/reporter with the line, "Ah tell me fans, Ah tell me fans." What he tells them is that he is afraid of the reporters because they can put his career in danger. As a result, he will not again sing about party. Going forward, he would be restricting himself to politics and history. The fans, through a shift by Black Stalin to the role of performer/first-person participant, are reported as replying that he should forget the "foolish reporter". Since the press does not know the difference between social commentary and party, then he should just write music exclusively for party people. This transitions to the chorus where Black Stalin continues as performer/first-person participant representing the speech of the fans, and sings, "No, no, no, this party can't done."

Back in his role as performer/reporter in the fourth verse, he tells us that wherever he sang during the course of the year, people came to him and thanked him for singing the song he sang for them, with reference to the offending "Black Man Feeling to Party". Whatever their ages, they were made to feel like coming out to party. He then shifts, in reporting their exact words, to the performer/first-person participant mode, in which he, on their behalf, sings, with himself as addressee, "Keep on, man, keep on, man, Just keep on singing" and that the critics in the press should go to hell. He is congratulated for realizing that party people should get a break. This voice is maintained into the chorus of the fans, "No, no, no, this party can't done, Black Man, your fans having fun."

Black Stalin's thesis is that the song he sang the previous year, "Black Man Feeling to Party", was social commentary, albeit done in party-song style. He is attacked for singing a party song. "Come With It", in 1992, involves

Black Stalin in two guises. One is himself as performer/reporter narrating events, the criticisms levelled at him for singing a party song the previous year, and his resolve to not do it again. On the other hand, there is him as performer/first-person participant speaking in the voice of his fans, addressing himself. The fans, in the actual content of their argument as well as by employing stereotypical party lyrics such as "Come with it" and "This party can't done", aided and abetted by an uptempo musical accompaniment, produce a party song. All of these elements come together to subvert the storyline of Black Stalin as performer/reporter that he would not be singing another party song.

The main alternative guise adopted by the singer is that of the fans. Black Stalin produces this as a performative embedded within the reported narrative. This "party" guise is combined with musical arrangement. Together, these undermine the proposition made by the singer in the guise of performer/reporter producing the narrative. This pattern contradicts the straight alignment between the two guises adopted by All Rounder in "Trinbago Babu" as well as the alignment of these with the musical form.

Performative with Truth Value Affirmed and Denied by Lyrics/Denied by Music: "Tribute to Sundar Popo"

In the case of Black Stalin's 1995 song "Tribute to Sundar Popo", we have access to video footage of the live performance at the Dimanche Gras show on the stage of the Savannah in Port-of-Spain, Trinidad. He is performing as a contestant in the Calypso Monarch Competition of that year. He takes the microphone as he comes on stage. His costume is ethnically ambiguous. He wears saffron-coloured pants similar in style to a traditional Indian dhoti. Both colour and style signal "Indian". The shirt is made of madras cloth. Though associated with Indian female headwear in the Caribbean, it is strongly stereotyped as characteristic of traditional African Creole wear as well. Further playing with the ambiguity, his turban has the same ethnically ambiguous madras cloth design as the shirt, supplemented by a saffron-coloured addition hanging at the back, definitely signalling "Indian". In speaking voice, as competition contestant, Black Stalin announces, "Dedicated to one of our number one composer, dedicated to the man himself, Brother Sundar Popo." This speech act is a tribute. There is a break when he signals to the backing band to up the tempo. The musical style is chutney soca. In gesture and voice, Black Stalin assumes the guise of the performer/reporter and belts out the following lines:

Travelling on a plane to Toronto,

> With Roy Cape and me good friend, Sundar Popo
> I tell him that I want to sing a chutney
> And he is the right one to help me (Black Stalin 1995)

Black Stalin is being promised a chutney musical composition by Sundar Popo with which to perform. Chutney is a style of Caribbean music associated with the community descended from indentured servants from the Indian subcontinent. Sundar Popo is a foremost composer and performer of this style of music. On stage, at the musical level, there is a performative act taking place since the actual musical style in which the Black Stalin song is being performed is chutney soca, a musical fusion of chutney with those of the calypso subgenre, soca. Critical to understanding the contribution of the musical element is the realization that calypso and soca are associated with the community of African origin in Trinidad and Tobago.

Black Stalin, in his role as performer/reporter, narrates to us that Sundar Popo has promised that, once he gets back home, he would do for Black Stalin a very nice chutney composition. Black Stalin then complains that years have passed and he is yet to get the promised song. The listener, hearing the chutney soca music style of the song, however, wonders whether what is being performed and heard is not indeed, in at least some metaphorical sense, the promised song.

As the chorus begins, Black Stalin shifts from performer/reporter narrating a story to a third party, transforming himself into a performer/first-person participant addressing Sundar in the second person.

> Sundar, where me song
> Where me song
> Sundar where the song
> You promise me so long? (Black Stalin 1995)

Black Stalin, in the second verse, shifts back to the role of performer/reporter. He tells us that he has been friends with Sundar Popo from the time of his earliest chutney hit "Nani and Nana", and that he paved the way for the more modern chutney performers. Addressing his audience as "you" in the following lines, Black Stalin sings:

> Now that I going to do for you a chutney jam,
> I must go to the best composer in the land.
> And the best chutney composer everybody know
> Is nobody else but Sundar Popo. (Black Stalin 1995)

The pretext created in the narrative by Black Stalin of trying to get the best chutney song to perform is what turns the speech act into a tribute. He is able to praise Sundar Popo's composition abilities, not explicitly but indirectly, by way of the story he is telling. At this point, the chorus starts. Black Stalin shifts back to his role as performer/first-person participant, who is now addressing Sundar Popo and asking for the song that was promised so long ago.

In the third verse, again in Black Stalin's performer/reporter guise, we hear all the invitations Black Stalin has received to perform the song that he is awaiting from Sundar:

> Everybody waiting on this chutney jam
> Sundar leave me like Alice in Wonderland
> Ah find he carrying this thing too blinking far
> Like he don't want me be no superstar. (Black Stalin 1995)

After the third occurrence of the chorus, Black Stalin in a speaking voice says, "Nuff respect to the man." This is a kind of reality check, reminding us that all we are hearing is part of an artistic device to pay tribute to Sundar Popo.

There is, against this background, a wider intent. This is expressed in the lyrics of the final verse.

> Every day them politicians talking
> Every day is only race I hearing
> So I want him write a song about unity
> Between Africans and Indians in this country
> I want him write a song so that the world could know
> In we music ent have no race in Trinbago
> Is just some politicians looking for vote
> Want to push racialism down we throat. (Black Stalin 1995)

Promoting unity between ethnic Africans and Indians in the country is the ultimate purpose of the song. The backgrounds of the two protagonists in the song narrative play an important role in realizing the goals of the speech act. Black Stalin is a very accomplished African Trinidadian musical composer and performer in a genre associated with the African ethnic group in Trinidad and Tobago. He is paying musical tribute to Sundar Popo who is of Indian ethnicity and who is an accomplished composer and performer in a musical genre associated with the Indian community of Trinidad and Tobago. The music of the song, chutney soca, is a blend of the two ethnically associated genres. The theme of the song is African–Indian unity. Black Stalin as performer/reporter in the last verse states what the song that Sundar writes should say. By reporting the contents of the speech act he would want from Sundar, he is creating the very song he says he wants Sundar to write. However, by suggesting that Sundar should do it, Black Stalin is denying the fact that he is performing the speech act that he pretends to want Sundar to create. The chutney soca music, with its blend of African and Indian musical forms, affirms that the speech act, in the form of the song, which Black Stalin is asking for, is actually the one in progress. However, Black Stalin, in the chorus where he functions as performer/participant, is denying having received the song from Sundar.

What then is the truth that Black Stalin intends us to take away from the song performance? The storyline up to the beginning of the fourth verse suggests that Black Stalin has not received the song from Sundar Popo. However, the lyrics of the fourth verse, giving us all that the song from Sundar Popo should say, and the musical composition, which is chutney soca, all point in one direction. They all suggest that Black Stalin has received, at least in some metaphorical sense, the song he is claiming not to have yet been given. In the actual stage performance, determining the truth value of the proposition made by Black Stalin is further disrupted. Towards the end of the last chorus, the real Sundar Popo comes dancing on stage with sheets of paper in his hand, presumably the song, which are handed over in a bundle to Black Stalin. The two men embrace.

"Tribute to Sundar Popo" illustrates a point made in the discussion of embedded performatives. In the case of a reporting performative speech act, if it includes within it another performative speech act, that embedded speech act has to be performed. That performance has the potential to undermine the claim made in the reporting speech act that the embedded one did not take place. In the case of musical performances such as "Tribute to Sundar Popo", the music accompanying the performance can further undermine the perceived truth of such claims.

Performance of Performative Denied by Lyrics: "Ah Fraid Karl"

"Ah Fraid Karl" by the Mighty Chalkdust is a 1971 song challenging the then recently amended Sedition Act in Trinidad and Tobago. Draconian elements of the amended act, attributed to the then-attorney-general Karl Hudson-Phillips were introduced in the wake of the 1970 Black Power Revolution, which saw large-scale demonstrations and an army mutiny which threatened the foundations of the postcolonial state. A key element in it was the call for unity across the racial divide of oppressed Africans and Indians of the country, who together constituted the vast majority of the population. The song makes several allusions to the incidents which brought the Sedition Act into being.

In setting out to challenge the Sedition Act, the Mighty Chalkdust begins in the role of performer/reporter. He is recounting to the listener the fact that his friends do not have his best interests at heart. They want the police to hold him and put him in jail. Then he reports all the things that the friends want him to do that would put him in trouble:

> They want me to sing and say
> Who move the Labas [garbage dump] from the highway
> And have the whole stench install
> Right inside the heart of Whitehall [the government administrative centre]
> (Mighty Chalkdust 1971)

He pointedly does not say who is responsible. The Sedition Act is claimed to be the cause of his reticence. He uses this formula to establish that the reporting of an embedded speech act requires that one actually performs it. In this context, this could breach the amended Sedition Act. He then expresses two kinds of fear. The first is fear of Karl Hudson-Phillips, the perceived driver behind the Sedition Act.

> But Not me
> Ah fraid Karl
> Ah fraid Karl
> Ah fraid he jail me
> Like he jail Rex Lassalle (Mighty Chalkdust 1971)

The reference here is to Lt Rex Lassalle, one of the leaders of the army mutiny which took place in solidarity with the young Black Power demonstrators who had brought the state of Trinidad and Tobago to the point of collapse in the early part of 1970. We later get a juicy piece of gossip directed at the political elite and the second source of his fear.

> They say a minister was found
> In a hotel with a call girl in town
> But I ain't singing bout that
> Ah fraid the sedition act. (Mighty Chalkdust 1971)

The song is set up to protect against the risk of being jailed by Karl Hudson-Phillips under the Sedition Act. The performer/reporter, therefore, gives as a report things that his "friends and them" say and want him to repeat. For the duration of the report, introduced by "They say", he is functioning as performer/first-person participant, as required when one delivers an embedded performative speech act. He then quickly switches back, in the third line, to the "I" of the performer/reporter, who reports that he will not actually sing what has already been sung. We have a situation in which the performer/reporter is seeking to deny that that which is performed by the performer/first-person participant has actually ever been performed.

The formula just outlined is repeated over the course of the song. This can be seen in the following lines:

> Like me friends and them ain't consider
> What happen to Weekes and Granger
> Is when they jail my backside
> That they going be satisfied (Mighty Chalkdust 1971)

George Weekes, a prominent trade union leader, and Geddes Granger, a student leader, played prominent roles in the demonstrations that constituted the Black Power Revolution of 1970. They were subsequently detained under a state of emergency which was declared by the government. This is the jailing to which the song refers. All these ostensible fears frame the constant performance of speech acts involving the singing of utterances, the contents of which could trigger prosecution under the Sedition Act.

The song, using this device, travels to the heart of events associated with the introduction of the amendments to the Sedition Act. This it does by attacking two figures at the heart of the legal response to the army mutiny that took place in support of the Black Power demonstrations. With reference to Bruce Procope, the prosecutor in the mutiny trial of the soldiers who were brought before an international court martial, Chalkdust sings:

> In the trial Bruce Procope did so well
> That he leave he home and live in Hilton Hotel
> But ah fraid, ah fraid. (Mighty Chalkdust 1971)

And then, with reference to a member of that court martial, then Col Danjuma from Nigeria, Chalkdust sings, with reference to an outstanding bill at the Trinidad Hilton Hotel:

> They say Danjuma who tried our soldiers here
> Still owe Hilton two thousand dollars for beer
> But I keeping out a that
> Ah fraid the sedition act. (Mighty Chalkdust 1971)

The fact that the Mighty Chalkdust could get away with all of this without being charged under the Sedition Act says something about the relative freedom of speech given to calypsonians within the musical and political culture of Trinidad and Tobago. To an extent, however, the cleverness with which the song exploits the difference between the calypsonian as performer/reporter, who would be expected to be responsible for his words, and the calypsonian as performer/first-person participant, performing the words of a reported speech act, may have played a role. The distancing creates enough of what is now called "plausible deniability" that the state might not have felt sufficiently provoked to react in the form of prosecution.

Nation Discoursing Nation

One cannot pretend that a hand-picked sample of four songs from the tens of thousands that would have been produced in post-independence Trinidad and Tobago can be used to make any definitive statements about the nature of popular discourse on nation and state. However, we can say something about a tiny part of that discourse, as constituted by the four songs discussed. We see that popular discourse in songs examines exactly the same issues as discussed by academic and political elites. This is so even though the latter carry out their discourses in English and with a strong orientation towards written texts and ideas originating in Europe and North America.

The common feature across these songs has been the manipulation of discourse. This has involved the relationship between the role of performer as reporter/narrator and as mouthpiece of what others are saying. Shifting roles allow for ambiguity which can be exploited.

We see in the songs an effort at defining of the nation which is performance oriented. Who does or does not belong to the nation of Trinidad and Tobago, sometimes referred to as Trinbago in the songs, is determined by, as in "Trinbago Babu", victory in performance battle with a nearby "other", in this case, Guyana. The victory is achieved by the appropriation of a musical symbol, a tune, from Guyana and using it to win a competition with the best of Guyanese in that musical genre. That the Trinbago champion is not of the ethnic group associated with the musical genre, yet receives support on nationalist grounds from compatriots of the appropriate ethnic group, signals nation over ethnicity. There is then the theme of African–Indian unity across national boundaries, Trinbago and Guyana, which serves to reinforce the theme of unity across the ethnic groups within the boundaries of the state of Trinidad and Tobago.

That same theme is performed in Black Stalin's "Tribute to Sundar Popo". The symbolism of a syncretic musical form, chutney soca; ethnically ambiguous performance costume; and a cross-ethnic musical tribute combine in a sung musical performance. The ambiguity of whether the song being sung is the song being asked for across the ethnic divide is reinforced because the actually performed song is being done in a tribute across that divide.

What is the role of the artist within the nation? Should that role be to entertain, educate or a combination of the two? When does entertainment become escapism? And most importantly, when does the need to live and have fun override the requirement and expectation to transform society? And does that transformation include not just the political and economic structures but also those within the family, notably man and woman? The ambiguity of Black Stalin's "Come With It" leaves the listener very unclear as to where the artist stands or sits on these overlapping issues.

In Chalkdust's "Ah Fraid Karl", we see the people in the process of nation formation, in conflict with the postcolonial state. The state is, in the wake of a challenge to existence, seeking to control speech. The calypsonian exploits the difference between the role of performer/reporter, on the one hand, and performer/first-person participant in a reported speech act, on the other. When the performers take the latter role, they use the first-person perspective to speak in the voice of the people. They can, however, deny that which they perform on the grounds of "plausible deniability" since it is "they" who are saying it and "I" am only performing it on their behalf.

Performance brings the nation into being, as in its unified African–Indian form promoted by All Rounder and Black Stalin. Performance, as done by Black Stalin, presents the arguments surrounding the role of the performing artiste in relation to the morals and values of the nation. Finally, denying performing speech acts, which are performed as part of the denial, provides the means by which the nation can challenge state control over speech acts. The nation that is presented in these songs is not an abstract or intellectual one. The four songs examined in this study, by way of performative speech acts, are discoursing the nation into being.

References

All Rounder [Anthony Hendrickson]. 1996. "Trinbago Babu". Album *JW Productions: Various Artists*. Trinidad and Tobago. Accessed 15 October 2019. https://www.youtube.com/watch?v=iUNhs2_EsSA.

Black Stalin [Leroy Caliste]. 1992. "Come With It". Album *Cry of the Caribbean*. Trinidad and Tobago. Accessed 15 October 2019. https://www.youtube.com/watch?v=7J5KG3CfE6U.

Black Stalin. 1995. "Tribute to Sundar Popo. Soca Monarch Competition". Trinidad and Tobago. Live video performance. Accessed 15 October 2019. https://www.youtube.com/watch?v=r8mNGbE_MGw.

Mighty Chalkdust [Hollis Liverpool]. 1971. "Ah 'Fraid Karl". Album *Mighty Chalkdust: First Time Around.* Trinidad and Tobago. Accessed 15 October 2019. https://www.youtube.com/watch?v=z0z1DpCQuBo.

Searle, John R. 1989. "How Performatives Work". *Linguistics and Philosophy* 12 (12): 535–38.

Smith, M.G. 1965. *Plural Society in the British Caribbean.* Kingston: Sangster's.

Chapter 3

"Dennery Segment ka mennen"

Exploring the Dominance of Creole Languages in St Lucian Popular Music

RONALD T. FRANCIS AND R. SANDRA EVANS

The connection between language and music has been explored in several contexts. In the Caribbean, research has focused on larger territories, mainly on Jamaican dancehall (Devonish 1996, 1998; Devonish and Jones 2017; Farquharson 2005) and, to a lesser extent, soca in Trinidad and Tobago (Leu 2000). In St Lucia, "Dennery Segment", also referred to as "Lucian Kuduro", is an emerging genre of soca music that has gained momentum on the island, in the wider Caribbean and in the Caribbean diaspora in North America and Europe.[1] This chapter explores this genre, focusing specifically on language use and the sociolinguistic basis of its growing popularity. The first section lays the groundwork by exploring the linguistic situation of St Lucia, and the origin of the genre and its musical composition. It also provides brief notes on the data collection procedures used for this chapter and contextualizes the analysis by summarizing Bourdieu's theory of practice and its application in the subsequent sections. The second section dissects the lyrical composition and content of the genre, and forms connections between its content and the sociocultural context within which it emerges. Finally, the last section examines how the music is being received by various markets (in both the economic and Bourdieusian sense), the growing popularity and dominance of the genre, and the role of Creole languages in forging this dominance.

Language in St Lucian Society

St Lucia is one of few English-official territories in the Caribbean where a French-lexicon Creole (Kwéyòl) is widely spoken. This contemporary linguistic situation resulted from a turbulent colonial history in which the island was occupied for extended periods of time by both the British and the

French, ultimately remaining British until it gained independence in 1979. This frequent change in colonial power has had far-reaching ramifications for the island's cultural, social, religious and political development, and the historical reality of dual colonialism is perhaps most evident in the language situation extant in the island, which has been variously described in the relevant literature as bilingual, trilingual and multilingual (Alleyne 1961; Midgett 1970; Le Page 1977; Le Page and Tabouret-Keller 1985; Isaac 1986; Pollard 1990; Simmons-McDonald 1988, 1994, 1996, 2014; Garrett 1999, 2003). The trilingual and multilingual classifications distinguish a third language, in addition to Kwéyòl and Standard English, that is referred to in the literature by various terms: Vernacular English of St Lucia, St Lucian English-Lexicon Vernacular, St Lucian Creolized English and a Creole-Influenced Vernacular. While there is little consensus on nomenclature, there is much consensus on its nature. Scholars contend that this contact variety contains phonological, syntactical, lexical and semantic features influenced by Kwéyòl and is more structurally akin to Kwéyòl than Standard English (Garrett 2003, 157; St-Hilaire 2011, 2; Simmons-McDonald 2014, 121).

Isaac (1986, 32–33) delineates a continuum in St Lucia in which three main (four distinct) codes may be identified: St Lucian Standard English (SLSE); an acrolectal variety or what may be deemed Internationally Acceptable English; and St Lucian Creolized English (SLCE), an umbrella term for two varieties, one mesolectal and one basilectal, and Kwéyòl. Exploring bilingualism in St Lucia, Isaac treats SLCE as an interlanguage and distinct linguistic system from both Kwéyòl and SLSE, and contends that 20 per cent to 80 per cent of St Lucians use it as an L1 (35, 40–41). St-Hilaire supports this claim, arguing that "many, if not most, St Lucians who claim to speak English actually speak [SLCE]" (2011, 2–3). This chapter adopts Isaac's distinctions and the well-established notions that SLCE is composed mostly of Creole forms. Therefore, SLCE and Kwéyòl are the two codes referred to as Creole languages in this chapter.

It is noteworthy that SLCE has no local name in St Lucia. In fact, many St Lucians (the artists included) name English and Kwéyòl as the two languages that they speak, and they do not identify SLCE as a language that is distinct from any other type of English. For instance, Evans (2013) found that out of eighty-one St Lucian police officers who were asked to name the languages that they speak, none of them named SLCE by any of the aforementioned terms or by any other name.

In order to contextualize the changing dynamics of language use in St Lucia through music, which this chapter addresses, it should also be emphasized that Standard English has been institutionalized as not only the de facto official language but also the socially dominant language. Its functions are governed by a social code, which prescribes it as the appropriate variety for use in public formal domains such as schools, public administration and the courts (Brown-Blake 2014, 55). This socially distinguishes SLSE from the two Creole languages, which both have wider local currency. Kwéyòl, which has always been more widely spoken in rural districts, has historically been regarded as the national language of St Lucians and the most patent index of their national and cultural identity, but it is not regarded with the same social prestige as Standard English. Like Kwéyòl, SLCE is mainly used in informal spaces by St Lucians throughout the island, particularly by young people. It is the predominant language of the capital, Castries, and, increasingly, the rest of the island for daily, popular and informal communication, steadily replacing Kwéyòl for this function, particularly among the youth (Garrett 2003).

Dennery Segment

Dennery segment is currently the most popular genre of music in St Lucia. According to Inglis and Justin (2017), who have explored the origin of the genre, it began to take shape on the island in 2009 and gradually morphed into the more distinct and more prevalent musical genre that it is today. It owes its origin, popularity and prevalence to the persistence of young local artists, whose music was often disregarded by established musicians, musical engineers and producers. Propelled by a desire for acceptability and accessibility, they continued to produce music, which, over time, became readily consumed by young St Lucians at clubs as well as house and street parties. The majority of these young artists hail from rural villages in St Lucia, particularly the village of Dennery, after which the variety is named.

A key characteristic of these villages, from which dennery segment continues to emerge, is a strong presence of Creole languages and creole culture as symbols of St Lucian identity. Therefore, it is not surprising that the lyrics of the songs are couched in the local Creole languages rather than in Standard English. They also tap into many aspects and ideologies of rural creole culture that reflect, symbolize and legitimize the lived realities of the artists and resonate with the adherents of dennery segment, particularly young St Lucians from rural areas. Another feature that also seems to resonate with a young audience is the salaciousness of the lyrics. This was aptly captured by Preedy, a Trinidadian artist who collaborated with dennery segment producers on the 2019 song "Lost and Found", who was told by a dennery segment producer that "anything you could make sexual in a song, put it on a Dennery beat and you have a hit" (MussBuss T.V. 2018). Another notable element of the dennery segment is the track instrumentals or riddims that underlie the songs, which are mainly produced by blending dancehall, soca, zouk and African beats. They are also influenced by African solo and sewenal rhythms that are a longstanding part of rural creole culture. Although dennery segment has been likened to a type of music from Angola, so much so that it was initially dubbed "Lucian Kuduro", its origin cannot be narrowed to a single musical predecessor. In fact, the songs bear semblance to dancehall, soca and other traditional Caribbean genres due to the inclusion of some variation of the tresillo rhythm (see figure 3.1), which underlies a lot of Latin American and Caribbean music such as habanera, bèlè, buigine, zouk, Jamaican dancehall and soca (Kattari 2009, 113–14; Sublette 2007, 134; Vurkaç 2012, 51):

This rhythm is undoubtedly an important rhythmic component of dennery segment production. Lashley "Motto" Winter, arguably the top producer in the genre, demonstrating the basic rhythmic underlay of dennery segment on his YouTube channel (Team Foxx), forms a tresillo rhythm with two claps followed by a tom drum beat, which he explains "brings the beat together".[2] It would be somewhat premature to characterize the genre solely by this rhythmic pattern without comprehensive musical analyses yet available. However, based on analyses of the production videos by the artists, the tresillo appears to be the most distinctive rhythmic feature of the genre. However, producers tend to vary the instrumental composition of the riddims to suit the collaborators. When producing zouk and groovy riddims, for example, they feature a more sustained use of melodic instruments than in soca riddims. Therefore, dennery segment can perhaps primarily be distinguished from other genres of Caribbean music only by the prioritization of percussive instrumentation over melodic instrumentation and the pervasive use of the tresillo. Even when melodic instruments feature heavily on a riddim, they tend to be used very percussively without sustained notes. This does not mean that melodic instruments are seldom used, but they are never the focus. For instance, a rhythmic, strummed guitar line, which is a key feature of calypso, is rarely featured in Dennery

Figure 3.1 Tresillo rhythm.

Segment. The artists themselves characterize and distinguish the genre by the heavy use of percussion:

> Anything above 140 [bpm can be] Lucian Kuduro, anything below that [can] not. It's usually a straightforward bass line. Other soca is more melodic, there are more chords and arrangements. Lucian Kuduro only has one lead instrument, and that one instrument usually carries the entire beat or carries the entire drum on the rhythm. (Lashley "Motto" Winter quoted in Prosper 2018)

While a musical definition of the genre is beyond the scope of this chapter, it treats any song made by dennery segment artists, be it likened to dancehall, zouk or soca, as belonging to the genre once it has been named dennery segment or Lucian Kuduro, and produced by the artists or performed by them in part or whole.

Dennery segment has gained wide popularity in St Lucia and is growing rapidly in popularity in the wider Caribbean, as well as in St Lucian diaspora in North America and Europe. Lashley "Motto" Winter, for example, has collaborated with many major soca artists from around the region. His 2018 "Pim Pim" and "Gwada" riddims featured many prominent and well-established soca artists including Fay Ann Lyons, Lyrikal, Shal Marshall, Bunji Garlin and Machel Montano from Trinidad and Tobago; Skinny Fabulous and Hypa 4000 from St Vincent; and Fadda Fox from Barbados, just to name a few, who all seem to be drawn to what Motto describes as "the new Lucian sound" (Mottosoca 2019). Motto was also recognized by New York State Senator Jesse Hamilton for spreading Caribbean music and culture around the world (Mottosoca 2019). Motto's increasing regional and international popularity is just one example of the growing popularity of the genre.

Data Collection

The data for this chapter were collected entirely via social media using a purposive sampling method. They consist of filmed radio interviews on YouTube featuring dennery segment artists and producers, blogs and online newspaper interviews, YouTube production videos in which the artists explain their creative processes, as well as some of the most popular dennery segment songs posted to YouTube between 2016 and 2019, approximately 75.[3] The interviews and vlogs were transcribed partially, all the songs were transcribed completely, and two separate corpora were formed: (1) interviews and production, and (2) lyrics. The videos and articles that were selected for the interview corpus all feature the artists and producers describing the instrumental underlay of the genre and the use of language in their music. The sections of each video that outline their creative processes were transcribed orthographically, and information irrelevant to the study, such as elaborate introductions and party promotions, was omitted. The corpus of lyrics was divided into verses and tagged for the use of Kwéyòl, SLCE and Standard English. A thematic analysis and a textual description of the lyrics were conducted to identify the cultural tropes that are reflective of St Lucian society and the impact of the music in various markets.

Theoretical Framework

This chapter employs Bourdieu's theory of practice (in a broad sense) as a theoretical guide for exploring the dominance of Creole language usage in the lyrics of dennery segment as well as the growing linguistic currency of Creole languages engendered by the increasing popularity of the music. Bourdieu's exploration of practice[4] delves into the inherent social heterogeneity of linguistic competence and performance. He contests the Saussurean and Chomskyan notion that linguistic performance is the generation of grammatical structure by an ideal speaker-listener and contends instead that every expression or utterance is an insoluble product of a "linguistic habitus" produced within a "linguistic market" (Bourdieu 1991, 37, 43–45; Thompson 1991, 17). These two concepts as well as the concept of *capital*, elaborated next, are the three pillars of Bourdieu's practice. These interlocking concepts can be summarized by the following formula: [(Habitus)(Capital)] + Field = Practice, which states that one's practice results from relationships "between one's dispositions (habitus) and one's position in a field (capital), within the current state of play of that social arena (field)" or market (Maton 2014, 50). This formula serves as a guide for this sociolinguistic analysis. This theoretical approach is apt for this chapter, as it is an ideal discursive framework for going a step beyond linguistic structure and analysing the sociocultural context that leads to the dominance of Creole languages in this burgeoning genre.

Linguistic Habitus

According to Bourdieu, "linguistic habitus" is a set of socially constructed dispositions that involve both our linguistic capacity to generate language and the social capacity to use our linguistic competence adequately in a specific situation (1991, 37). These dispositions are inculcated, structured, durable, generative and transposable (Thompson 1991, 12–13). Inculcation refers to the gradual inscription of these dispositions into our bodies through training and learning that makes them second nature (Thompson 1991, 12). They are also structured in that they reflect the social condition under which they were inscribed (Thompson 1991). "Durable" refers to the lifelong nature of these inscriptions, which are pre-conscious in that they are not "readily amenable to conscious reflection and modification" (Thompson 1991, 13). These dispositions are also generative and transposable because they produce multiple linguistic outcomes in practice and can be used outside of the social fields in which they were inscribed (Thompson 1991). In sum, according to Bourdieu (1991, 37), every speech act is, in part, the product of these inscribed dispositions.

The authors contend that dennery segment artists produce a socially conditioned lyrical product that is essentially the practice of their linguistic habitus. Their social spaces and cultural realities have inscribed their linguistic performance and these inscriptions are transposed to their lyrical choices. Commenting on the most constructive way to analyse Jamaican dancehall lyrics, Devonish (1996) states that one "needs to be as concerned about the cultural context within which language communication takes place, as with the actual linguistic structures employed" (221). While Devonish does not coin his approach as linguistic habitus, his analysis of the lyrics is underpinned by the cultural context within which dancehall music is created and performed, and through this lens, he is able to show how other scholars who have negated this approach have misinterpreted the lyrical content of dancehall. This chapter undertakes a similar exploration of the lyrical content of dennery segment through the critical lens of linguistic habitus in order to account for the pervasive occurrence of Creole languages.

Linguistic Market

Bourdieu (1991) uses the terms *market*, *field* and *game* interchangeably to refer to a "system of sanctions and censorship" within which linguistic signification and symbolic value are given to speech and various forms of capital are exchanged (37). Bourdieu identifies several forms of capital, namely economic capital (material wealth), cultural capital (knowledge, skills, cultural acquisitions, educational or technical qualifications) and symbolic capital (prestige or honour) (43–65). Bourdieu also identified "linguistic capital", which is an individual's capacity to produce a legitimate competence within a market, producing a "profit of distinction" during social exchanges (55). In essence, markets bestow a certain symbolic value on every linguistic product produced within them and an individual's linguistic capital, therefore, is based on one's capacity to produce a product that is appropriate for a particular market (Thompson 1991, 18). Within these markets, one form of capital can be converted into another, for example education (cultural capital) in exchange for a lucrative job (economic capital) (Thompson 1991, 14). Linguistic exchanges are a symbolic relation of power in which the producer of an utterance is endowed with linguistic capital that is converted into economic and symbolic wealth based on the value ascribed to the utterance by the market upon which it is enacted. This symbolic power equates to the legitimacy or recognition of speech based on the socially or politically dominant language of the market which excludes speakers who lack the capacity to produce the legitimate language (Bourdieu 1991, 55).

This chapter treats various groups of consumers as the linguistic markets within which the music/riddims and the lyrics of the genre are all given a symbolic value. There are four main markets: local St Lucian consumers, the diasporic St Lucian community (in Europe and North America), the wider English-official Caribbean (particularly Trinidad) and the French-official Caribbean (namely Martinique and Guadeloupe). The dennery segment producers are skilled in creating riddims that are suited for each market. As each type of riddim/beat (be it dancehall, groovy or zouk) is valued differently in each market, each accrues different quantities of cultural capital depending on the market. Zouk riddims, for example, are highly valued in the French Antilles as zouk is a medium through which Martinique and Guadeloupe (which are still departments of France) assert their Antillean identity (Guilbault et al. 1993, 9). The lyrics and the music are inseparably intertwined. Consequently, when the riddims grow in cultural capital, the linguistic capital of lyrics attached to these riddims also grows in symbolic value. Also, the various linguistic codes used in the genre are valued differently on the various markets. This growth of the linguistic capital because of the highly valued (musical) cultural capital as well as the variance in symbolic capital ascribed to the different languages used is what has been termed "dominance" in this chapter.

Language Use in Dennery Segment

It is impossible to divorce the musicality of dennery segment from its lyrical context or the lyrics from their social context. This section briefly explores the lyrical composition of the songs in the corpus. It also identifies various cultural tropes that point to the social experiences of the artists that have formed their linguistic habitus. It shows how their varied and unique St Lucian cultural identity has equipped them with a mastery of various fields that has allowed them to convert their cultural and social capital to economic and symbolic capital.

Lyrical Composition and Language Use

As per the data used for this chapter, it appears that dennery segment lyrics are composed mainly of SLCE and Kwéyòl. It has already been established that most St Lucians do not identify SLCE as a language and may consider their use of what is, in fact, SLCE to be the use of SLSE. However, they recognize Kwéyòl as a marker of cultural identity. The artists themselves define the music that they produce as an indivisible admixture of the riddims and the Kwéyòl lyrics to which they credit the uniqueness and appeal of the genre. Subance, a prominent artist, stated in a blog interview, "We mix the Creole with the English . . . when the beat drops and you have the lyrics, you fall in love with the music" (Christie 2017). This same sentiment is even echoed in the lyrics of one of the songs, which states, "That's my lingua / Mix English with the Patois."[5]

The data show that the Creole languages are the dominant languages used in the genre as the sum of Kwéyòl lyrics, SLCE lyrics and lines composed of the two together account for 64 per cent of the data (see following list). The corpus of lyrics is composed of 380 unique lines (repeated lines were counted once). Rhymes were used to determine the end of each line. The language(s) used in each line was first identified and then a total number of lines for each language was calculated. From these totals, the percentage language distribution was derived as shown in the following list:

Language	%
Kwéyòl	27
SLCE	29
Kwéyòl and SLCE	8
SLSE	30
Other	6

Kwéyòl

Many artists are from rural communities where the use of Kwéyòl is more prevalent, and they craft entire songs in the language. Many of the riddims themselves, particularly the zouk ones, are given a Kwéyòl title, for example, the "Manicou Wousi" (Roasted Opossum) and "Gwen (Gwan) Bois" (Big

Wood) riddims. These songs are often entirely in Kwéyòl, although they sometimes feature English lexis to facilitate a rhyme, as in "vagrant" and "infant" in example 1, or to refer to things for which there is no Kwéyòl lexical equivalent, like "CD" or "vacuum", as in example 2:

(1) *Jus' ban nou dé bonm wonm*   (just give us two buckets of rum)
     *Nou pa vlé pyès **vagrant***   (we do not want any vagrants)
     Moun ka dansé moun anlè moun   (people are dancing close together)
     *La pa ni pyès **infant***   (there are no infants)

(2) *Na koupé **CD***   (I am cutting CDs)
     *Wèsté la pou mwen sa **vacuum** ou*   (stay there for me to vacuum you)

SLCE

It was shown earlier that SLCE should be treated as a separate language from SLSE due to its structural semblance to Kwéyòl forms and its English lexical base. However, some clarification is required on what is categorized as a "Kwéyòl form" in the context of analysis. A list of phonological, syntactic, semantic and lexical features of SLCE (discussed later) was created and each line/lyric with an English lexical base was examined according to these criteria. If an individual lyric was composed completely, or almost completely, of these grammatical forms, it was classified SLCE and counted as an SLCE lyric. These forms included:

1. The selection of tense vowels where SLSE required lax vowels. Consider example 3, an orthographic and phonemic transcription of a verse of "Bad in Bum Bum", which is one of the most popular dennery segment songs:

(3) *Your man say you not perfec'*   /jɔ mʌn seː juː nɔt pəˈfɛk/
     Frien' say makeup not good   /fɹɛn seː meːˈkʌp nɔt guːd/
     But when you get in the mood   /bʌt wɛn juː gɛt in diː muːd/
     Everyfing looking good   /ˈɛvɹiːfiŋ luːkin guːd/

Mighty's pronunciation in this verse features one of the key phonological traits of St Lucian speech, the selection of tense vowels where lax vowels would be used in most standard varieties of English. This is evident in words like "good" and "in", which are articulated here as /guːd/ and /in/ instead of Standard English /gʊd/ and

/ɪn/. While there is generally variation between these lax and tense counterparts in St Lucia, St Lucians who are more Kwéyòl-dominant tend to select the more tense counterparts, which are closer to the vowel system of Kwéyòl, instead of the Standard English variants. See Lieberman (1974, 128–90) for some discussion on undifferentiated vowels in SLCE due to Kwéyòl influence.
2. T/D deletion (deletion of alveolar stops in word final consonant clusters) as observed in the pronunciation of the words /pɜːˈfɛk/ and /fɹɛn/ in example 3.
3. The use of /f/ where SLSE uses /θ/ as seen in /ˈɛvɹiːfiŋ/ and /d/ as opposed to SLSE /ð/ in words like "them" /dɛm/. The phonemic substitution of Standard English dental fricatives with alveolar plosives and/or the voiceless labiodental fricative is common in St Lucia (Isaac 1986, 104–5; Lieberman 1974, 129) but is neither unique to St Lucia nor English-lexicon Creoles in general. However, when considered with other phonological patterns, it forms part of the phonological structure of SLCE.
4. The omission of a copula with locative, temporal or adjectival phrases, for example, *I behind da truck, it nice and round* and *it 6:30*, which mirrors the structure of declarative sentences of the same type in Kwéyòl (Carrington 1984, 115–16).
5. The marking of durative/continuous and iterative/habitual aspects with V + -ing and no auxiliary, for example, *Girl, I eh lying uh* (durative) and *when you wining* (iterative). This is a well-documented feature of St Lucian speech and has been found to be more common than the use of *does + V*, which is used, but to a lesser extent, to mark iterative aspect (Carrington 1969, 264, 278; Garrett 2003, 167; Isaac 1986, 135–37).
6. The well-established use of unmarked non-stative verbs with past tense, completive aspect reference, for example *I take lessons already* and *God give everybody a little something*. SLCE shares this feature with Kwéyòl (as well as other Creoles) in which the unmarked stative verb indicates completive aspect with a preceding subject or the imperative mood without a subject (Carrington 1984, 117; Holm 2000, 141).
7. The dearth of inflectional markers on plural nouns, for example *hot like pepper*. Kwéyòl, like other Creole languages, does not mark the noun morpheme for gender or number, and the unmarked noun designates either the totality or an unspecified part of the referent (Carrington 1984, 67–68; Holm 1988, 193). The literature on the

SLCE noun shows that, like Kwéyòl, it remains unmarked when plural or generic (Garrett 2003, 169; Isaac 1986, 110–12).
8. Negation marked with the particles *doh, eh, not* and *cya*, for example *we doh want that*. The auxiliary verb "to do" is not used in SLCE, neither in negation nor in the formation of interrogatives, and sentences are negated by using any of the aforementioned particles with the same syntactic function as the Kwéyòl negator "pa" (Carrington 1984, 154; Garrett 2003, 170; Isaac 1986, 167).
9. The semantic broadening of English words to match the breadth of meaning in Kwéyòl. Consider *all Cuba, all China* from example 10 where the word *all* is equivalent to the Kwéyòl "tout", which can mean both "all" and "all the way to". Isaac (1986), who examined students' writing, posited that this semantic broadening is due to the polysemy of Kwéyòl lexical items and students' inability to "discriminate between SE forms covering the same semantic field but belonging to specific contexts, determined by the particular nuance of meaning which is conveyed" (185). Garrett (2003) also noted this, commenting on the broadening of the English semantic fields of words like "scratch", "come" and "again" to match their broader Kwéyòl equivalents (171).

These examples, which highlight the grammatical relationship between SLCE and Kwéyòl, reify claims in the literature that SLCE is structurally similar to Kwéyòl and the authors' treatment of SLCE as a Creole language. The artists often code-switch between these two Creole languages in the same line. The lyrics in example 4 contain the grammatical features detailed in items 4 and 8 listed earlier and also a language switch to Kwéyòl:

(4) *Your bumpa not sézi*   (seized/frozen/stuck)
    My girl, you doh have fwédi   (cold/draft/arthritis)
    Your clothes not on **kwédi**   (credit/loan)

SLSE

There are many lyrics in the data that are grammatically acceptable Standard English phrases and sentences. A lot of these are instructions such as *Pop your tail*. In order to be very precise about what was considered SLCE in the data, these were not considered SLCE unless there were other forms that match the SLCE criteria within the same lyric. However, as there is lexical overlap between SLSE and SLCE, the presence of SLSE forms may not be a matter of preference for SLSE on the part of the artists and may have more to do with shared lexis and a few shared grammatical features. For example, a lot of the songs are instructive, and the imperative mood is formed in both SLSE and SLCE with the bare, uninflected verb. In the very same song that contains the lyric *Pop your tail*, most of the non-instructive lines with an English lexical base contain the features of SLCE explored earlier, for example *I in your back* (adjectival predicate – zero copula) and *what you say* (absence of auxiliary verb "to do" in interrogatives), among others.

Other

All forms that could not be classified as one of the three codes under study were labelled "other". These included mainly Jamaican Creole words such as *pon*, exclamations such as *whoy* and onomatopoeic lyrics like *Bidip-bang* and *tic tac*.

Performing Linguistic Habitus

As many of the artists were initially rejected by the mainstream music industry in St Lucia, they were left with no alternative but to create and produce their own music. As a result, they have inscribed their social realities and linguistic identities into the music. Further, they recognize that their creole identities are part of the authenticity of the music:

> You have to remain natural, you have to be yourself. You can't go around yourself and try to be something else, 'cause you go be without nothing. If you don't have yourself, you have nothing. So I always try to put local in everything I do, in everything I say, in my singing, even in my running, I run in creole. It is something that I always do, so big up to de people that staying true to themselves and that's just that. (Freezy quoted in Gooding 2017)

This infusion of self may be deliberate, as Freezy outlined, but also a subconscious enactment of inculcated dispositions. Either way, many aspects of St Lucia culture, particularly in rural communities, are evident in the lyrics of the genre. This section explores a few themes through the lens of Bourdieu's habitus. It demonstrates how some key features of their sociocultural context, which act as a structuring field, have shaped the lyrical choices of the artists.

Kwéyòl Music

Within rural communities in St Lucia, where the use of Kwéyòl is widespread, there is great appreciation for music composed in the language.

This appreciation has spurred the institutionalization of formal and public spaces for exploring the music. For years, the artists created the music but never formally promoted it. However, because music composed in Kwéyòl is highly valued within rural markets, the songs grew in popularity without any impetus from the creators of the music themselves. This momentum in the rural communities created a demand that incited the creation of more music and the eventual establishment of formal structures that facilitated the growth of the genre. For example, the rural community of Dennery has held its own soca monarch competition outside of the national competition since 2014. Through this district competition, songs that would ordinarily have not been included in national competition before the current burst of popularity were given a platform. For example, Mighty's "Gros[6] Lo (Big Portion)", composed entirely in Kwéyòl, placed second in the inaugural competition.

The demand for Kwéyòl music is longstanding, particularly in rural communities, as the language has always been the primary indicator of St Lucian cultural identity. As such, there have been formal cultural spaces like calypso competitions, for example, in which Kwéyòl is not just accepted but valued. Belle Vue Kwéyòl Song Competition is one such cultural space, which unlike other spaces, requires artists to perform songs composed entirely in Kwéyòl. St Lucia also has a very strong folk music culture and the language of folk music is Kwéyòl. The two flower festivals, La Marguerite and La Rose, are celebrated and performed mainly with folk music in Kwéyòl, and many of the participants who enact the various roles in these festivals, particularly those who are members of La Rose, are monolingual speakers of Kwéyòl (Guilbault 1987, 100). These rural communities and formal cultural spaces have acted as a field within which the linguistic habitus of the artists has been structured. As they continue to produce popular riddims, accompanied by Kwéyòl lyrics, within a market that values Kwéyòl lyrics, they convert their cultural and linguistic capitals to economic and symbolic capital, and structure the very field that in turn structures their habitus.

Local Food and Farming

The lyrics often feature references to local food like fruits and ground provisions, which are all staples of St Lucian cuisine. While these are not unique to St Lucia and can be found in most tropical areas, the lyrics, as in example 5, clearly position them within St Lucia and demonstrate the connection between the daily experience of the writers and their music:

(5) *I just love Saint Lucia*
 Sweet mango ripe banana
 Coconuts, jelly water
 Juicy yams and guavas
 That's our national dish
 Plantain and banja (yams)
 Local bread and cassava
 From country

This is comparable to other genres of music indigenous to the Caribbean. For example, the band Kassav, who popularized zouk music, chose that name with reference to cake made of cassava, an indigenous food item that represents the "Indigenous mixture of music", which is zouk's musical structure and the fact that it "indexes their French Antillean identity" (Zamor 2012, 144).

Most of the ground provisions in St Lucia are farmed in rural areas where agriculture is an important part of the communities and, as a result, references and allusions to farming are sometimes featured in the music as well. It is possible that many of the artists, who emerged from these rural agrarian communities, have had some personal connection to agriculture, and so this agrarian identity sometimes serves as inspiration for the lyrics. Consider example 6:

(6) *Manman-mwen ni bwapen* (My mother has breadfruit)
 Mé i pa sa tjouwi'y   (But she cannot pick it)

These lyrics do not always deal with food and farming in and of themselves but are sometimes transposed into the literary wordplay and craft of the lyrics. In examples 7 and 8, the artists use *balanmin*, "a digging tool made of iron flattened at one end", and cocoa to refer to male genitalia (Frank 2001, 17):

(7) *Turn around* (×6)
 On de balanmin

(8) *Mwen kay fouté'w tak kako* (I will give you some cocoa)
 Pa di mwen i yak, kako   (Don't tell me it's yuck, cocoa)
 Vini vin pwen tak kako   (Come, come and get some cocoa)
 Kako-a pa'n mak, kako   (The cocoa has no marks, cocoa)

Folklore and Religion

Another sociocultural feature of St Lucian society that emerges from the lyrics is religion and folklore. Commenting on folklore in St Lucia, Simmons (2017, 257) states, "The island is supposed to be inhabited by a host of [*jan gajé*], a generic term for a wide number of supernatural manifestations." In St Lucia, as in many postcolonial societies, there is rarely a clear distinction between Christian practices and remnant domestic rituals from African traditional religions. Elements of Christianity and African traditional religions are part of the everyday life of St Lucians, most of whom are of African descent (Anthony 1998, 558). This duality, which is commonplace in St Lucian society, is reflected in the lyrics of the genre:

(9) *Lanné sa la mwen vini*   (this year I come)
    pou bwilé tout gajé   (to burn all witches)
    Alkali, mwen ka fouté, Alkali (Alkali, I am giving/striking with Alkali)
    Ou pa ni pou pè gajé   (You must not be afraid of witches)
    Alkali épi Bondyé   (Alkali and God)

Migration

One of the most poignant and enduring structural characteristics of Caribbean society is the transnational and migratory nature of its people (Thomas-Hope 2002, 3). Women, in particular, often migrate "for securing employment and ultimately some measure of upward mobility", and they often spearhead the migration of other members of their families (Thomas-Hope 2002, 4). Baldwin and Mortley (2016) have shown how love and the power that love has to inspire certain tasks have also motivated Caribbean women, who are socialized to care for their loved ones, to migrate. The complex group of factors that motivate both intra-regional and extra-regional migration is beyond the scope of this chapter. However, this migratory reality is undeniably a common feature of St Lucian (and the wider Caribbean) society and, consequently, it forms part of the linguistic habitus of artists who acquire their dispositions within these transnational realities. This is evident in the following verse where one artist chastises women who seek economic and social mobility through extra-regional marriages:

(10) *La ni fanm ka mandé mayé* (There are women asking for marriage)
     Pou machin, loto èk papyé (for vehicles, lottery and papers/citizenship)
     Lè ou tann dènyé papyé   (When you hear of the last paper)

For England and the UK
St Lucia or USA
Florida and Aruba
All Cuba, all China   (All the way to Cuba, China)

Politics and Social Commentary

Caribbean music has always been an avenue for sociopolitical commentary. Often, ideas and events that are part of popular public discourse are satirized in Caribbean music. Dennery segment is no exception to this trend. For example, when a politician, while criticizing the work done on maintaining the roadside, allegedly "flubbed" during a news interview, an artist used his exact words (example 11) in the lyrics of a song. That same politician was quoted again verbatim after a heated exchange between this politician and the speaker of the house of assembly ensued and was broadcast live during a sitting of parliament (example 12). The satirizing of topical political issues is common in St Lucian music – more so in calypso than this genre – and while it is not as common in dennery segment, it is not surprising that political discourse sporadically features in these songs:

(11) *They cut de grass behind de grass and put it*
     On de side of de road
(12) *Since when that's your role*

Regional Influences

Finally, on the matter of content and habitus, there is evidence of foreign cultural influences that have been acculturated by St Lucians in the lyrics of the genre. In St Lucia, American hip-hop and Jamaican dancehall music are both very popular and have consequently formed part of the social field that has moulded the linguistic habitus of the artists. An example of this is the use of the phrase "one drop" in dennery segment, which is a dancehall song (and dance of the same name) by Jamaican dancehall artists QQ and Venomous. The term is featured in the title of a 2019 Umpa and Sully dennery segment song and is used in the song's instructive, dance lyrics:

(13) *Now make that bumpa bump and lock*
     Stick out your tongue and do ***one drop***
     Make that ting just tic toc

Conquering the Fields

This section explores the markets, which are, in effect, fields of power, and how the artists and the music are positioned within these fields. It maps out the structures of each market that promote the growth of the genre through the legitimization and sanctioning of the music. It focuses specifically on the cultural and linguistic capital endowed by the various fields that are exchanged for symbolic and economic capital, and shows how the characteristics of the genre, often its lyrical composition, give it a different type of currency within each market.

St Lucia

The island of St Lucia was the first market within which dennery segment was produced and ought, therefore, to be the first consideration in exploring the dominance of the genre. On a national level, the initial reception was not positive. Formal musical establishments, like radio stations and national soca competitions, rejected the genre, perceiving it as vulgar and lacking musical sophistication. Consequently, the initial rise in popularity of the genre originated in rural, informal spaces. Through social media, the songs gained traction among young people who embraced them as dance music, particularly because they are not seasonal nor linked exclusively to carnival. Most of the lyrics are raunchy and salacious, which is also part of their appeal to young people. The majority of the artists are young men who appeal to young women through this instructive dance music. The artists often address the young women with commonly used terms of endearment in St Lucia such as *my girl, jenn tifi* (young girl), *jenn fanm* (young woman) and *gyal*, some of which are shown in examples 14 to 16:

(14) *Jenn fanm* (Young girl)
    Akoupi (×3) (stoop)
    Stoop down
    Lemme see you akoupi on it (Let me see you stoop on it)

(15) *Girl come brace on de big poto* (pole)
    Make dem know you not papicho (nonsense)

(16) *My girl, just work de bumpa*
    My girl, just roll de bumpa

The heterosexual male gaze upon the female body is neither novel in St Lucian music nor unique to St Lucian soca. The female body has always been commodified and "instructed" by the lyrics of male artists in the male-dominated field of Caribbean soca music, and an overt, unapologetic female sexuality has even been embraced by some female calypso and soca artists themselves (Goddard-Scovel 2016, 152–53; Leu 2000, 55). Therefore, the highly sexual (often smutty) lyrics are arguably legitimized by the response of women who are fans of the genre and who welcome them, dance to them and follow the instructions. Their sanctioning acceptance has so structured the field that the vast majority of the lyrical content of the genre is a lascivious pursuit of these young women. Young men also identify with the artists who reflect their own intentions and consciousness in the Creole languages that they know and use. They participate in the gaze, in the dancing and in the same pursuit of women that the artists promote in their songs. These rural youth were the first (sub)field that sanctioned the genre, even as it was being initially censored by the wider national audience for this overt sexuality. Many artists are still banned from radio stations and are viewed as outsiders within the local soca industry (Inglis and Justin 2017).

Over time, the national market began to accept the genre as a unique St Lucian creation. The strong percussive riddims and the use of Creole languages, as well as the cultural content, began to be perceived not only as music but as a cultural movement and a product with export potential. Interest in the riddims from outside of the country, like collaborations with Trinidadian soca artists, influenced St Lucian public opinion and the local musical establishment. The genre grew in cultural capital because the dynamics of the field evolved. Once the potential to convert cultural capital into economic capital was recognized, the symbolic value of the music increased and it began to dominate the local music industry. Collaborations with established St Lucian soca artists increased and, in an effort to cash in on the economic capital of the genre, these collaborators embraced the blatant sexuality of the genre. One result of this embrace, a kind of linguistic convergence, was a renewed pride in Kwéyòl specifically and an increase in the prevalence of Creole lyrics in St Lucian soca in general.

English-Official Caribbean

Outside of St Lucia, dennery segment is most popular in Trinidad and Tobago, although it has been embraced by many English-official markets, particularly in the Lesser Antilles. Some songs like "Split in de Middle" (Freezy) and "Bad in Bum Bum" (Mighty and Subance), which feature only St Lucian artists, have gained a lot of traction. However, the rise in popularity of the genre in Trinidad and Tobago can be attributed mainly to collaborations with Trinidadian artists. The riddims are certainly the primary point of interest in the genre in these territories, not the lyrics. Songs sung entirely in Kwéyòl have not successfully broken into this field. In fact, the artists have made a conscious effort to sing in SLCE (which again they identify as English) when collaborating with regional artists:

> Changing the ratio of English to Kreyòl lyrics certainly played a role in raising Lucian soca's profile. Increasingly, artists from across the waters, including Machel Montano, Patrice Roberts and Problem Child, have looked to St Lucia and collaborated with artists and producers associated with the Dennery Segment. (Prosper 2018)

There is a great deal of mutual intelligibility and grammatical overlap between SLCE and other English-lexicon Creoles, which has aided in the legitimization of the genre in these English-official markets. For example, in his collaboration with Lyrikal, "Party Lit", Motto sings "sometimes they does ask us how we does do it", which contains "does" as a preverbal marker of iterative aspect, a common syntactic feature of Creole languages and a common lexical particle with this syntactic function in English-lexicon Creoles. This lyric is grammatical both in SLCE and in Trinidadian Creole. These shared features and the high degree of mutual intelligibility can help to explain why the use of SLCE is so prominent in these collaborations and the widespread acceptance of its use within this market. Arguably, most soca songs in the English-official Caribbean are written in the respective English-lexicon Creole, so it is not surprising that the use of SLCE is highly valued within this field.

While the use of Kwéyòl is minimal in each song, the language features frequently in collaborations. Tokens of Kwéyòl are generally limited to a few lexical items. For example, Machel Montano's 2018 collaboration with Motto, "Issa Vibe", features one repeated line in Kwéyòl, *annou alé* (let's go). As previously mentioned, the mixture of Kwéyòl with the riddims is often viewed by the artists as the defining composition of the genre. It is this precise concoction that imbues it with cultural capital. Therefore, the use of some Kwéyòl lyrics, even though not pervasive, maintains the St Lucian fingerprint of the collaboration and, consequently, increases the legitimacy of the music across markets for both collaborators. St Lucian collaborators capitalize on the opportunity to perform with established soca artists within the soca mecca, Trinidad, while Trinidadian artists who sing a few lyrics in Kwéyòl authenticate their music for Kwéyòl-speaking markets. Machel Montano, commenting on his collaborations with the artists and the reach and growth of soca in St Lucia, Dominica and the French Antilles, states, "we starting to reach into de other islands and we starting to talk their language" (OJO

TTRN – Trinidad & Tobago Radio Network Limited 2017). He underscores the power of language as a point of entry into various Caribbean markets. Both groups of collaborators are capitalizing on the cultural capital of the lyrics to better position themselves within foreign fields.

French-Official Caribbean

French Creole is one of the strongest links between Martinique and Guadeloupe and the English-official islands of Dominica and St Lucia, and zouk has hereto been the musical genre that, by virtue of the shared language, has kept the islands musically connected (Guilbault et al. 1993, 9, 16–17). The artists themselves are cognizant of this connection, with one song stating "Tun sa Matinik, Sent Lisi, Dominik, Gwadloup / An'n fè an bagay" (hear this Martinique, St Lucia, Dominica, Guadeloupe / Let's do something). They exploit the linguistic connection to appeal to this market. When analysed through a Bourdieusian lens, it can be asserted that the French Antilles are all fields of power within which zouk riddims, soca music and French Creole are all highly valued. Therefore, dennery segment artists, who produced zouk-like soca rhythms with French Creole lyrics, enter this field with a great degree of cultural and linguistic capital. According to Inglis and Justin (2017), the genre gained acceptance on the radio in Martinique even before it gained widespread acceptance in St Lucia, and it was a Martiniquan radio personality, Nigel Nicholas, who coined it "Lucian Kuduro".

Within a market, certain linguistic products are sanctioned while others are censored. While dennery segment generally features very vulgar and sexually charged lyrics, songs that are written on zouk riddims with predominantly Kwéyòl lyrics do not possess this blatant salaciousness. Instead, there is a great deal of craft in the lyrical structure in which the sexual content is often concealed with double entendre. Consider example 17:

(17) *Kòk la ka bat* (the rooster is beating)
I di mwen Slah, annou fè chimen (she told me, Slah, let's make way)
Koki-o-ko (sound of the rooster)
Kok sa la an chay lajan i kay fè (that rooster will make a lot of money)
Volé, mouté ho, gonflé an lézè (fly, go up high, swell in the air)
Fanm-lan di mwen kòk sa a benyen chalè (the woman said this rooster is full of heat)

The structure of the French-official market may account for this phenomenon. According to Guilbault et al. (1993, 155):

> Zouk singers have stayed away from so-called pornographic songs (with the exception of Frankie Vincent), which were popular during the preceding dancehall era. Instead they focus on actual stories that can be understood by a wide audience and on generic themes that evoke Antillean ways of life and social conditions.

This "censorship" (in both the denotative and Bourdieusian sense) can explain why songs that feature this lyrical structure are strongly positioned within this market. It also accounts for why many artists feature wordplay instead of overt sexuality on these zouk riddims. The nature of zouk as a genre, which breaks the physical boundary of the market, acts as a structuring field that has informed the habitus of the artists. Further, Kwéyòl lyrics in St Lucia, even within other genres of music, like calypso, follow the very same pattern of clever wordplay.

St Lucian Diaspora

There are two dimensions to be considered within this market: (1) St Lucian and other Caribbean nationals living abroad and people of Caribbean descent, and (2) the wider North American and European audience that encounters the music. For St Lucians in the diaspora, what draws them to the music is its authenticity, its connection to their national and Caribbean heritage and identity. Many artists have been invited to perform at events being thrown by Caribbean nationals in the United States and Canada as well as in parts of Europe, mainly the United Kingdom and France. However, the very same challenges that the artists face with breaking into the Trinidadian market plague them within this market as well. Some members of their audience do not speak or comprehend Kwéyòl. Therefore, for the wider North American and European field, their linguistic products are not highly valued. In order to combat this, they made a conscious effort, as was done with the wider English-official Caribbean, to include more English lyrics in the genre. "It just wasn't something people were used to hearing," commented Hyper of Blackwidow Sounds, a collective of St Lucian DJs currently based in Philadelphia, who goes on to state:

> We'd have to ease the sound in with other mixes when we played out in parties in the States. As the times change, so does the music. The easiest way to have the music appeal to mainstream is simple, just sing parts of it in English. And that's

what the artists began to do, and it worked. Small adjustments can go a long way. (Prosper 2018)

This change of musical structure and language was, in essence, an attempt to make the genre more valued within this field, but in so doing, the music may lose the characteristics of the field that structured it. The artists appear to be aware of this reality. Hyper is proposing that the genre be "eased" into other sounds for greater acceptance, not altered completely, and "parts" of the songs are to be sung in English but not the whole. It can be asserted that to change these characteristics would render the music unauthentic.

In 2018, several artists and their management teams, with the support of the St Lucian government, undertook a promotional tour of the United States (30 August to 10 October) with the intention of showcasing "high quality Saint Lucian culture and music to international audiences with the hope of attracting major investments" (St Lucia News Online 2018). Even with this undertaking, this field remains the one within which the artists are worst positioned to excel for multiple reasons. There is intense competition from other genres of music and more established varieties of soca. They also currently lack the financial capital to promote the product and, as has been explored, one of the things that authenticates the genre, the use of Creole languages, particularly Kwéyòl, disadvantages them within this field. It is possible that through collaborations, the dominance experienced within the English- and French-official Caribbean will diffuse into these diasporic markets. However, this is left to be seen.

Conclusion

This chapter has explored the origin and linguistic nature of dennery segment and has attempted to account for its growing popularity nationally, regionally and internationally. Through a thematic analysis of the lyrical content, rooted in Bourdieu's theory of practice, it has shown how the sociocultural context within which the producers and performers of the genre were groomed has influenced their linguistic habitus and the types of music and lyrics that they produce. It has also accounted for the popularity of the genre within various markets in the Caribbean and beyond. Whether a subconscious transposition of habitus, or a deliberate, conscious exchange of cultural capital for economic and symbolic capital, the artists remain keenly aware of the value of the Creole languages to their music. For Kwéyòl in particular, the growing popularity of the genre has engendered a renewed pride in the language, and it has gained wider currency among the youth. As it stands, the dominance of dennery segment is playing a critical role in the revitalization of Kwéyòl, and, if the genre continues to thrive, it will, no doubt, continue to contribute to the promotion and preservation of the language in St Lucian society.

Abbreviations

CIV	Creole-influenced vernacular
SLCE	St Lucian Creolized English
SLEV	St Lucian English-lexicon Vernacular
SLSE	St Lucian Standard English
VESL	Vernacular English of St Lucia

Notes

1. The chapter title translates to "Dennery Segment is dominating".
2. In his production videos on YouTube (https://www.youtube.com/user/09lashley), "Motto" Winter identifies several types of beats including hot soca, zouk, Jab soca and dennery segment. The rhythmic distinctions among these subgenres are not always clear, although he makes an effort to emulate other songs in the target market, for example, the Jab soca beat is similar to other Grenadian soca songs that fall within the Jab soca genre.
3. It is difficult to determine the exact number of songs or the artists who perform each of them in the corpus of lyrics because some of the videos used were DJ compilations and it is sometimes unclear where one song ends and another begins. Also, in the DJ compilations, the entire song is not used so only the first verse and chorus are available.
4. Bourdieu's theory of practice is an approach to the study of language, sociology and anthropology that spans decades of research and is only summarized in this chapter.
5. Lyrics in Kwéyòl were transcribed using the writing system in the *Mouvman Kwéyòl Sent Lisi* handbook (MOKWEYOL): Louisy, Pearlette, Paul Turmel-John, Jean Bernabé, and Lawrence D. Carrington. 1983. *A handbook for writing Creole*. Castries: Research St. Lucia Publications.
6. *Gwo* in MOKWEYOL.

References

Alleyne, Mervin C. 1961. "Language and Society in St. Lucia". *Caribbean Studies* 1 (1): 1–10. Accessed 20 May 2019. www.jstor.org/stable/25611645.

Anthony, Patrick A. 1998. "Popular Catholicism and Social Change in St Lucia". *Social Compass* 45 (4): 555–74. doi: 10.1177/003776898045004004.

Baldwin, Andrea Natasha, and Natasha K. Mortley. 2016. "Reassessing Caribbean Migration: Love, Power and (Re)Building in the Diaspora". *Journal of International Women's Studies* 17 (3): 164–76.

Bourdieu, Pierre. 1991. *Language and Symbolic Power.* Cambridge, MA: Harvard University Press.

Brown-Blake, Celia. 2014. "Expanding the Use of Non-dominant Caribbean Languages: Can the Law Help?" *International Journal of Speech Language and the Law* 21 (1): 51–82. doi: 10.1558/ijsll.v21i1.51.

Carrington, Lawrence D. 1969. "Deviations from Standard English in the Speech of Primary School Children in St. Lucia and Dominica: A Preliminary Survey (Part II)". *IRAL: International Review of Applied Linguistics in Language Teaching* 7 (4): 259–82.

———. 1984. *St. Lucian Creole: A Descriptive Analysis of Its Phonology and Morpho-Syntax.* Amsterdam: Benjamins.

Christie, A.C. 2017. "Subance; Artist Best Known for Dennery Segment; the New St Lucian Music Genre". *ilovecarnivall*, 25 June 2017. http://ilovecarnivall.co.uk/subance-artist-best-known-for-dennery-segment-the-new-st-lucian-music-genre/.

Devonish, Hubert. 1996. "Kom Groun Jamiekan Daans Haal Liricks: Memba Se A Plie Wi A Plie: Contextualizing Jamaican 'Dance Hall' Music: Jamaican Language at Play in a Speech Event". *English World-Wide* 17 (2): 213–37. doi: 10.1075/eww.17.2.05dev.

———. 1998. "Electronic Orature: The Deejay's Discovery". *Social and Economic Studies* 47 (1): 33–53. Accessed 20 May 2019. www.jstor.org/stable/27866164.

Devonish, Hubert, and Byron Jones. 2017. "Jamaica: A State of Language, Music and Crisis of Nation". *JME!* 13 (2). doi: 10.4000/volume.5321.

Evans, R. Sandra. 2013. "An Examination of the Language Use Patterns and Practices of the Legal System in St Lucia". PhD diss., The University of the West Indies.

Farquharson, Joseph T. 2005. "Faiya-bon: The Socio-pragmatics of Homophobia in Jamaican (dancehall) Culture". In *Politeness and Face in Caribbean Creoles*, edited by Susanne Muehleisen and Bettina Migge, 101–18. Amsterdam: Benjamins.

Frank, David. 2001. *Kwéyòl Dictionary.* Government of Saint Lucia, Ministry of Education.

Garrett, Paul B. 1999. "Language Socialization, Convergence, and Shift in St. Lucia, West Indies". PhD diss., New York University. https://search-proquest-com.ezproxy.sastudents.uwi.tt/docview/304515003?accountid=45039.

———. 2003. "An 'English Creole' that Isn't: On the Sociohistorical Origins and Linguistic Classification of the Vernacular English in St Lucia". In *Contact Englishes of the Eastern Caribbean*, edited by Michael Aceto and Jeffrey P. Williams, 155–210. Amsterdam: Benjamins.

Goddard-Scovel, Ekeama. 2016. "Functions of Gender in Soca: An Historical and Lyrical Analysis of St. Lucian Soca". PhD diss., Purdue University. https://search-proquest-com.ezproxy.sastudents.uwi.tt/docview/1973276611?accountid=45039.

Gooding, Kerri. "Split in de Middle's Freezy Not Giving Up His Creole Roots". *Loop*, 4 August 2017. http://www.loopslu.com/content/split-de-middles-freezy-not-giving-his-creole-roots-2.

Guilbault, Jocelyne. 1987. "Oral and Literate Strategies in Performances: The La Rose and La Marguerite Organizations in St. Lucia". *Yearbook for Traditional Music* 19: 97–115.

Guilbault, Jocelyne, Gage Averill, Edouard Benoit, and Gregory Rabess. 1993. *Zouk: World Music in the West Indies*. Chicago: University of Chicago Press.

Holm, John A. 1988. *Pidgins and Creoles: Volume 1, Theory and Structure*. Cambridge: Cambridge University Press.

———. 2000. "The Creole Verb". In *Language Change and Language Contact in Pidgins and Creoles*, edited by John H. McWhorter, 133–99. Amsterdam: Benjamins.

Inglis, Dylan Norbert, and Sant Justin. 2017. "Mini Documentary: What is Lucian Dennery Segment Music (Lucian Kuduro)". YouTube video, 15:03. Accessed 20 May 2019. https://www.youtube.com/watch?v=-1cwZ4RYbyM.

Isaac, Martha F. 1986. "French Creole Interference in the Written English of Secondary School Students". Master's thesis, The University of the West Indies, Cave Hill.

Kattari, Kim. 2009. "Building Pan-Latino Unity in the United States Through Music: An Exploration of Commonalities Between Salsa and Reggaeton". *Musicological Explorations* 10: 105–36.

Le Page, Robert B. 1977. "De-creolization and Re-creolization: A Preliminary Report on the Sociolinguistic Survey of Multilingual Communities Stage II: St Lucia". *York Papers in Linguistics* 7: 107–28.

Le Page, Robert B., and Andrée Tabouret-Keller. 1985. *Acts of Identity: Creole-Based Approaches to Language and Ethnicity*. Cambridge: Cambridge University Press.

Leu, Lorraine. 2000. "'Raise Yuh Hand, Jump up and Get on Bad!': New Developments in Soca Music in Trinidad". *Latin American Music Review / Revista De Música Latinoamericana* 21 (1): 45–58. doi: 10.2307/780413.

Lieberman, D. 1974. "Bilingual Behavior in a St. Lucian Community". Doctoral dissertation, University of Wisconsin.

Maton, Karl. 2014. "Habitus". In *Pierre Bourdieu: Key Concepts*, edited by Michael J. Grenfell, 60–76. London: Routledge.

Midgett, Douglas. 1970. "Bilingualism and Linguistic Change in St Lucia". *Anthropological Linguistics* 12: 158–70.

Mottosoca. "About". webpage, 2019. Accessed 20 July 2022. https://mottosoca.com/about/.

MussBuss T.V. 2018. "PREEDY Talks Dennery Segment, KROME Da Producer". YouTube video, 1:22. Accessed 20 May 2019. https://www.youtube.com/watch?v=vWMxBOgCElA.

OJO TTRN – Trinidad & Tobago Radio Network Limited. 2017. "Motto & Machel's 'Issa Vibe' Fuses Bouyon & Dennery Segment Music Together With WCK". YouTube video, 15: 25. Accessed 20 May 2019. https://www.youtube.com/watch?v=m5GdnsGkWM8&t=437s.

Pollard, Velma. 1990. "The Speech of the Rastafarians of Jamaica, in the Eastern Caribbean: The Case of St. Lucia". *International Journal of the Sociology of Language* 85: 81–90. doi: 10.1515/ijsl.1990.85.81.

Prosper, Meg. 2018. "Bad in Bum Bum: Charting the Rise of the Dennery Segment, St. Lucia's Scorching Soca Sound". *LargeUp*, 23 February 2018. https://www.largeup.com/2018/01/03/dennery-segment-st-lucia-soca/.

Simmons, Harold. 2017. "Notes on Folklore in Saint Lucia". In *The Road to Mount Pleasant*, edited by John R. Lee and Embert Charles, 246–59. Castries: The Msgr. Patrick Anthony Folk Research Centre.

Simmons-McDonald, Hazel. 1988. "The Learning of English Negatives by Speakers of St. Lucian French Creole". PhD diss., Stanford University. https://search-proquest-com.ezproxy.sastudents.uwi.tt/docview/303699153?accountid=45039.

———. 1994. "Comparative Patterns in the Acquisition of English Negation by Native Speakers of French Creole and Creole English". *Language Learning* 44 (1): 29–74. doi: 10.1111/j.1467-1770.1994.tb01448.x.

———. 1996. "Language Education Policy (2): The Case for Creole in Formal Education in St Lucia". In *Caribbean Language Issues, Old & New: Papers in Honour of Professor Mervyn Alleyne on the Occasion of His Sixtieth Birthday*, edited by Pauline Christie, 120–42. Saint Andrew Parish: University of West Indies Press.

———. 2014. "Instructional Models for a Creole-influenced Vernacular Context: The Case of St Lucia". In *Education Issues in Creole and Creole-influenced Vernacular Contexts*, edited by Ian Robertson and Hazel Simmons-McDonald, 119–50. Saint Andrew Parish: University of West Indies Press.

St-Hilaire, Aonghas. 2011. *Kwéyòl in Postcolonial Saint Lucia: Globalization, Language Planning, and National Development*. Amsterdam: John Benjamins Publishing.

St Lucia News Online. "Government of Saint Lucia Endorses and Sponsors Dennery Segment US Promotional Tour". 14 August 2018. https://www.stlucianewsonline.com/government-of-saint-lucia-endorses-and-sponsors-dennery-segment-us-promotional-tour/.

Sublette, Ned. 2007. *Cuba and Its Music: From the First Drums to the Mambo*. Chicago: Chicago Review Press.

Team Foxx. "St Lucia 'Dennery Segment' Music Explained (Lucian Kuduro) | Lashley 'Motto' Winter". YouTube video, 3:54. Accessed 20 May 2019. https://www.youtube.com/watch?v=3UMEGanU85k.

Thomas-Hope, Elizabeth M. 2002. *Caribbean Migration*. Saint Andrew Parish: University of West Indies Press.

Thompson, John, ed. 1991. Introduction to *Language and Symbolic Power*, by Pierre Bourdieu, 1–31. Cambridge, MA: Harvard University Press.

Vurkaç, Mehmet. 2012. "A Cross-Cultural Grammar for Temporal Harmony in Afro-Latin Musics: Clave, Partido-Alto and Other Timelines". *Current Musicology* 94: 37–65.

Zamor, Héléne. 2012. "Constructing French Creole Identity Through Language, Music and Dance". In *Language, Culture and Caribbean Identity*, edited by Jeannette Allsopp and John R. Rickford, 146–57. Saint Andrew Parish: University of West Indies Press.

Chapter 4

Singing in Creole or Portuguese?

Santomean Musical Manifestations

MARIE-EVE BOUCHARD

Introduction

São Tomé and Príncipe is a former Portuguese colony and has Portuguese as its only official language since its independence in 1975. Since the beginning of the twentieth century, a process of nativization of Portuguese related to the loss of proficiency in the three native Creole languages of the islands (Forro, Angolar and Lung'ie) and to a language shift from these Creoles to Portuguese has been under way in the country. The native Creoles are at different stages on the ethnolinguistic vitality scale: Forro is shifting, Angolar is threatened and Lung'ie is nearly extinct (Eberhard, Simons and Fennig 2022). In this Santomean context of language shift and (possible) loss, there are two opposite driving forces: on the one hand, language ideologies that belittle and denigrate the use of Creole languages in favour of Portuguese, and on the other hand, the association of the Creole languages to Santomean cultural and national identity. I suggest that the study of musical manifestations brings to the surface these contradictions, which may be less visible in other contexts. In this chapter, I discuss the ways in which these opposite forces are embedded in singing practices and how they emerge in the discourse around musical expression.

Music is one of the social forms in São Tomé and Príncipe where the use of Creole is still common, and sometimes even expected and valued. Traditional songs are in Creole, but contemporary singers (e.g. Kalú Mendes, Gapa and Nino Jaleco) and bands (e.g. Grupo Tempo and Sangazuza) also do sing in Creole (mainly Forro, but also Angolar). This suggests that singers and musicians might have an important role to play in the valorization of the creoles of the islands.

Following Schneider, Sippola and Levisen (2017, 2), I consider language choices in music to mirror social and linguistic realities; these choices are "indexically related to the social discourses in which they emerge". An ideological approach to Santomean musical expression gives access to beliefs that Santomeans hold about the languages of the islands and their speakers and to the symbolic meaning of the languages singers choose to sing in. Studying language in and around music sheds light on local expressions of identity and authenticity, and on the discourses that shape them.

To my knowledge, language ideologies in and around musical expression in São Tomé and Príncipe have not been explored. Actually, little work on language ideologies and music in São Tomé and Príncipe exists. Exceptions to this are Bouchard (2017, 2018, 2022) on language ideologies and Bialoborska (2016) on the classification of Santomean music. This study fills a gap in the literature on the languages of São Tomé and Príncipe, and it proposes to take a linguistic anthropological approach to language use and choice in music.

In this chapter, I aim to answer the following questions: (1) What language ideologies, explicit and implicit, are expressed in and around musical expression? (2) How are language ideologies interrelated with identity and authenticity, and how is this expressed through language choice in music? (3) What is the role of musicians in the valorization and maybe maintenance of the use of Creoles in the Santomean society? By asking these questions, I aim to identify the ideologies behind the discourses on language choice, identity and authenticity, and understand the ways in which they work.

The chapter is organized as follows. The second section is a brief historical and sociolinguistic overview of São Tomé and Príncipe. The third section introduces the different Santomean musical genres, and the fourth section presents the research setting, study material and analytical framework. The following two sections discuss the two main driving forces coexisting in the actual context of language shift: one gives an account of the ideologies that surround the Santomean creoles and European Portuguese in the musical world, showing how the negative stereotypes and beliefs associated with the use of Creoles in everyday life is also mirrored in language choice for musical expression, and the other section discusses how singing in Creole is associated with local identity and authenticity. In this section, I also discuss two linguistic practices that can be observed in musical manifestations (*tirar versos* [singing in metaphors], and mixing languages), as well as their meaning in the Santomean context. The last section is a wrap-up of this study, and it considers the role of musicians and singers in slowing the language loss process underway on the islands.

A Brief Sociohistorical Overview of São Tomé and Príncipe

The islands of São Tomé and Príncipe were taken into Portuguese colonial control in the 1470s. The first inhabitants of these islands were Portuguese, Africans and probably a few Spanish Jews (Seibert 2007). The African population, whose great majority was brought by force to work as enslaved people, came mainly from the Bight of Benin in the first years (approximately 1485–1520) and from the kingdoms of Kongo and Angola in the following years (Ferraz 1979; Rougé 2004; Hagemeijer 2011). Mixed unions between blacks and whites were encouraged to populate the island, as Portugal did not have enough people to settle in its colonies (Hagemeijer 2018). This contact between Europeans and Africans most probably favoured the linguistic contacts from which appeared the first forms of Creoles in the Gulf of Guinea. Three indigenous groups to the islands were formed during this first phase of colonization (1485–1600) related to slave trafficking and sugar cultivation: the Forros, the *filhos da terra* (children of the land); the Angolares, descendants of enslaved marrons who escaped from the plantations and formed their own community on the southern side of São Tomé Island; and the Principenses, the *minu ie* (child [of the] island), the natives of Príncipe Island.

From the beginning of the seventeenth century to mid-nineteenth century, the Portuguese lost interest in their islands of the Gulf of Guinea. According to Seibert (2006, 30), because of the decrease in the number of white settlers on the islands, the remaining inhabitants, whom he calls the creoles, "became steadily more African by blood". But around 1830, the Portuguese returned on the islands to cultivate coffee and cocoa. Coffee cultivation did not last very long, as it was labour-intensive and the price on the market was falling, but cocoa became important for Portugal's economic prosperity (Hodges and Newitt 1988). The cocoa production required a high number of workers. The native creoles and the newly freed refused wage labour on the plantations, which they considered degrading and beneath their free-man status (Seibert 2006). But the demand for a workforce was high, so the Portuguese decided to bring in labour from abroad. Those workers were called *serviçais* (servants) or *contratados* (contract labourers). Many of these indentured labourers came from Angola in the first few years, and then from Cape Verde. With those contracted labourers, São Tomé and Príncipe witnessed a population boom (Lorenzino 1998). Such a demographic event had an impact at the linguistic level, as these non-native speakers of Portuguese came with their respective languages. Among those languages, the main ones were

Cape Verdean Creole, and Kimbundu and Umbundu (from Angola) (Hagemeijer 2009a). On the one hand, Cape Verdeans were numerous and often arrived with their families, which facilitated the use and the preservation of their native Creole. As a consequence, Cape Verdean Creole is still spoken on both islands, especially in Príncipe, where about 31 per cent of the population speaks it (INE 2012a). On the other hand, as Hagemeijer (2009b, 17) wrote, "the predominance of the speakers of Kimbundu and Umbundu in certain plantations led to the appearance of a contact language called the Portuguese of the Tonga (Rougé 1992; Baxter 2002, 2004)".[1] The Tongas are the descendants of the *serviçais*; they are children who grew up on plantations and who learned the Portuguese L2 (second language) spoken by the people in their surroundings.

With the independence of São Tomé and Príncipe, all these ethnolinguistic groups were given equal social status (at least, in theory), and Portuguese was chosen as the official language of the new country. Portuguese would represent a homogeneous nation; it would play a role of national symbol to unite all Santomeans of different racial backgrounds under one nation. Today, Portuguese is the majority language, spoken by 98.4 per cent of the population according to the last census (INE 2012b) and the main language of social interaction among Santomeans. It is also the only language of education. Forro, Angolar and Lung'ie are national languages with no special status or recognition. Older Santomeans recall teachers complaining about children speaking Creole in school and being forbidden to speak Creole by their parents and teachers. One of the reasons parents and teachers started to forbid their children to speak Creole was to avoid mixing Creole and Portuguese (Afonso 2009). This was especially common in and around the capital among Forros. However, note that Forro (the most widely spoken Creole of the islands, still today) is sometimes perceived as a language of social cohesion among Santomeans in the diaspora. Many Santomeans start to give more value to the native Creoles of their country when abroad, and they speak it more frequently abroad then when on the islands. Creoles are then viewed as "the spoken embodiment of their Santomean identity" (Bouchard 2017, 195).

Musical Manifestations of São Tomé and Príncipe

There exists little documentation of musical manifestations in São Tomé and Príncipe; material to investigate music in all its forms before the twentieth century is practically non-existent, and historical sources scarcely discuss the matter.[2] Some of the Santomean musical genres are gradually disappearing, and knowledge of songs and music is not being transferred from one generation to another anymore (Bialoborska 2016). Traditional Santomean music is only listened to by Santomeans (on the islands and in the diaspora). It does not span across different cultures, not even in the Portuguese-speaking world, as does Angolan kizomba for example. Lyrics are in Creole or Portuguese (depending on the musical genres and the singers), and they are grounded in local history and reality. Bialoborska (2016, 2020), who conducted the most exhaustive study of Santomean music to date, proposes the classification of Santomean musical genres as shown in table 4.1.

Bialoborska (2016) divides the Santomean musical manifestations into two main groups: the ones that are not associated with other cultural practices or activities, and the ones that are. In the first group are the traditional musical genres created on the islands before the beginning of the twentieth century; the genres created by musical bands and influenced by African, South American and Antillean music from the beginning of the twentieth century to the 1980s; and the most recent genres created with computers. In the second group are the musical genres that accompany rituals such as djambi (a healing ritual brought from *serviçais* coming from Angola), theatrical manifestations,[3] folk tales, religious celebrations and everyday life activities.

Table 4.1 Classification of Santomean Musical Genres

Group	Subgroup	Musical Genre
Independent music manifestations	Traditional music	Irmandade, lumandádgi, lundum,ússua, puíta, quiná, dêxa, socopé, tafua, bulawê
	Band music	Rumba santomense, samba-socopé, puxa
	Mechanized musical creation	Rhythm similar to kizomba angolana, buladuro
Music that accompanies cultural manifestations	Rituals	Djambi
	Theatre	Tchiloli, Danço Congo, Auto de Floripes
	Folk tales	Soya cantada
	Religious celebrations	Tlundu, Estleva, Plo Mon Dessu, Vindes Meninos
	Everyday life activities	Work-related songs, nursery rhymes, lullabies

Some of these musical genres emerged among the different ethnolinguistic groups of the islands (e.g. irmandade and ússua come from Forros, quiná from Angolares, and dêxa from Principenses); others came with the Angolan *serviçais* and were adapted and assimilated later into Santomean culture (e.g. puíta and djambi); still others are emblems of creolization and represent a mixture of European and African artistic manifestations (e.g. Tchiloli on São Tomé Island, and Auto de Floripes on Príncipe Island – they are dramatic interpretations of texts written by Europeans). But today, with the globalization and transnational distribution of music, local and traditional Santomean music is being replaced by popular music styles from abroad, especially from the Portuguese-speaking world (e.g. kizomba from Angola and sertanejo from Southeast and Centre-West Brazil). Also, with the ongoing language shift from the Santomean Creole languages to Portuguese, the loss of these Creoles might entail losing part of the traditional musical manifestations if no effort of preservation and transmission is made. But for now, I believe that music offers a point of entry to investigating language ideologies, the performing of local identity and authenticity, and the symbolic meanings of the languages of São Tomé and Príncipe.

Research Setting, Study Material and Analytical Framework

I conducted fifteen months (between June 2015 and March 2017) of ethnographic fieldwork and semi-structured interviews in São Tomé and Príncipe (mainly on São Tomé Island). I continued to live in São Tomé after my fieldwork research was completed, for a total of two years and a half in the country. I have also spent six weeks (Winter 2018–19) in the Netherlands and Portugal to conduct interviews with Santomeans living in the diaspora. The purpose of these interviews was to investigate the speech of Santomean immigrants living in Europe. Interviews were carried out employing techniques from both sociolinguistic interviews (Labov 1984) and ethnographic interviews (Spradley 1979). I did a total of 120 interviews with Santomeans around the country, and 54 interviews in the Santomean diaspora. Informants were between twelve and seventy-three years old. During the interviews, I elicited comments on language, identity and localness to arrive at a clearer picture of the ideologies underlying linguistic choices and national identity within the speech community. Interviews were conducted in Portuguese. When I conducted these interviews with Santomeans, music was not central to my research, and musical manifestations of any sort were only discussed when informants would themselves bring up the topic. This means that I did not discuss music with all informants, but also that discussions about music were totally free, with no directed questions or topics. I was not looking for music-related information in particular; this study is built on material gathered for studying language use, generally speaking.

Observations made through participant observation were also integral to this study in order to understand community and local practices, and to examine language choice and use in action. I have participated (as an observer) in many musical performances, including a night of djambi and tchiloli performances, demonstrations of popular traditional music and dances (bulawê, socopé, etc.), and shows with young and older Santomean singers and bands.

The analytical framework of this study focuses on three key terms and their intersections: language ideology, identity and authenticity. Language ideology is the link between forms of talk and social structures; it is "the cultural system of ideas about social and linguistic relationships, together with their loading of moral and political interests" (Irvine 1989, 255). Language ideology comprises the social value of some languages as opposed to others; the symbolic quality of languages as emblems of nationhood; the sociopolitical meaning of the use of some languages over others; and values and ideals such as authenticity, modernity, progress and many more (Blommaert 1999). According to Hill (2008), linguistic ideologies persist because they support the interests of elites who share these ideologies. In fact, language ideology is a way of thinking loaded with political, social and economic interest (Irvine 1989). I believe that investigating ideologies in musical manifestations is relevant to the understanding of the loss of the Creole languages in São Tomé and Príncipe. The language ideologies discussed in this chapter come from beliefs clearly articulated during the interviews, and from more subtly expressed beliefs enacted through language use and practices.

Identity is central in language, and theorizations about the relationship between identity and language have been significant in the past thirty years or so (De Fina 2012). The constructionist approach to identity (cf. Berger and Luckmann 1967) views the relation between the individual and the social world as a reality that is continuously created and recreated. Social interaction is central to the processes of identity construction. In this chapter, I take interest in the local understanding of national identity.

Embedded in the concept of identity are ideas of authenticity. Authenticity is often rooted in local concepts of purity, and authenticating discourse is performed to "display, impugn, vie for, and enact forms of ethnic identity"

(Shenk 2007, 195). Here, I explore the concept of local authenticity as viewed by Santomean musicians and expressed thought in the use of language in songs.

Finally, I combine this analytical framework with discourse analysis. I analyse relevant samples of metalinguistic discourse held by Santomeans (mainly singers) to access ideologies, identity and authenticity as expressed in the Santomean musical world.

Language Ideologies and Purism as Inhibitors

In an effort to develop into a unified society, São Tomé and Príncipe is moving away from the plurilingual society that it might have been in the past, and is becoming more and more monolingual (Bouchard 2019). Portuguese is the only official language of the country, and European Portuguese is perceived by Santomeans as the "right" language and variety to speak (Bouchard 2017). Silverstein (1996) called this ideology "Monoglot Standard". This ideology of Monoglot Standard is based on the following ideas: only one variant of a form, variety, or language is "correct", thus depicting correctness as a grammatical fact instead of a social and political decision; ways of speaking can be ranked according to their correctness and prestige; the status of the standard language can be explained with a set of convincing arguments to justify its prestige and correctness, although these arguments usually differ from what scholars and linguists would say on the matter; and speaking the standard opens doors to social and economic possibilities and benefits, therefore learning to speak it is important (Silverstein 1996; Milroy and Milroy 1999; Hill 2008).

Since the eighteenth century, one of the key ideological ingredients in the construction of group and national identities is a perceived cultural and linguistic homogeneity; "modern nations require one unambiguous name, one homogeneous identity, one common history, one language" (Blommaert 2014, 1). These singular symbols are ideologically and socially constructed, and they render invisible the great diversity that exists within the numerous speech communities of this world (Silverstein 1998; Blommaert 2014). In São Tomé and Príncipe, the Forros in power at the time of the independence decided that Portuguese would represent a homogeneous nation; the Portuguese language then acquired the symbolic role of uniting and unifying Santomeans. On the islands since colonial times, languages are socially stratified, with Portuguese at the top of the pyramid, and the Creole languages and the restructured varieties of Portuguese (e.g. Portuguese of the Tonga) at the bottom of this pyramid (Afonso 2009, 91). This relates to Bourdieu (1991) who argued that competence in the legitimate language (Portuguese in the Santomean case) is the most valuable linguistic capital in what he calls the standard linguistic market. Linguistic capital refers to the different language resources available to an individual, and to the values attributed to these recourses. It functions in relation to a certain linguistic market (cf. Del Percio, Flubacher and Duchêne 2007; Heller 2003, 2010), meaning that the linguistic capital varies from one linguistic market to another. The linguistic market is a place where linguistic capital is exchanged, and the different languages and language varieties have different symbolic values. On the standard linguistic market, more value is attributed to standard varieties because of the overt prestige associated with them and, most importantly, because of the social power of its speakers. These ideologies are perceived through the linguistic choices of Santomean singers and songwriters.

Traditionally, during colonial times, songs were written and sung in Creole languages. But the ideologies that surround the languages of the islands and drive the languages shift also had an impact on the musical scene: singing in Creole started to be disvalued. In excerpt 1, Mateus (all names of participants are pseudonyms), lead singer of the band Anguené (which means "Angolar" in the Creole language of the same name), explains how Santomeans negatively received their musical performances in Creole.

Excerpt 1: The Spite of Creole Languages

> *Criamos uma banda em Angolares [ok] começamos a cantar em língua Angolar [sim] quando íamos pa cidade pa parque popular, cantavam "Foooraaa!" o forro dizia "Foooraaaa! Cantam bicho!" porque desprezava essa língua angolar, fomos desprezado muitas vezes.*

> We created a band in São João dos Angolares [ok] and we were singing in Angolar [yes] when we'd go to the city to the central park, they'd shout "Get out!" Forros would say "Get out! You sing in the animal's language!" because they despised Angolar, we were despised many times.

Mateus recalls these experiences with pride because his band resisted the social pressure and continued to sing in Angolar. Referring to Creole languages as *línguas de bicho* (animal's language), starting in the middle of the twentieth century, was frequent, according to my informants. It is at that point that the language shift (from the Creole languages to Portuguese) was intensified. The Creole languages of the islands were also considered to be primitive, inferior and backward (Bouchard 2017). Such pejorative beliefs regarding Creole languages are common in colonial and postcolonial settings (e.g. Rickford 1983; Wassink 1999; Winford 1976; among many others). The ideologies of the Portuguese language superiority are founded upon such beliefs. Some of the consequences of these language ideologies are the deprecation of the Creole languages, the growing loss of the Creoles and the prejudices attached to Creole speakers; although, this latter part seems to be slowly changing. Even so, with time, Anguené became a famous band in São Tomé and Príncipe; it participated in different national events on the islands and performed in Portugal, Gabon and France. This suggests that musicians and singers might somehow play a role in the valorization of the Creole languages in São Tomé and Príncipe. But this is a great challenge for the young songwriters, who do not speak Creole as a first language anymore, and when they do speak it, it is not considered to be the "real" Creole as spoken by their ancestors.

Language ideology encompasses issues of purity of languages (cf. Das 2008). Purism functions as an ideology; it is a mental construct that plays a role in the process of linguistic norm formation (Brunstad 2003). Preference for purism is often manifested as a dispreference for loanwords (Kroskrity 2017, 11). According to Kroskrity (2009, 75), elders often "display linguistic authority but discourage younger speakers from adapting their heritage languages to the contemporary world". In this sense, ideologies of purism may inhibit language valorization and revitalization instead of supporting it (Dorian 1994; Zuckermann and Walsh 2011). In fact, these ideologies can restrain the linguistic emancipation of individuals and, in the case of the Santomean songwriters, cause them to refrain from writing songs in Creole, as explained by the singer Ricardo in excerpt 2.

Excerpt 2: Consequences of Singing in Creole

Muitas pessoas perguntam porque que você não faz uma música em dialeto não sei que, digo ya, fazer uma música em dialeto não é fazer só, ou eu faço uma música em dialeto com cabeça tronco e membro, ou não faço, porque se for pa mim fazer aquele dialeto misturado com português mal falado e quê, corro o risco até de matar a língua, tá a perceber, assim que que vai acontecer? As pessoas quando vão me ouvir a cantar assim vão pensar que é assim que se fala quando não é assim, quando não estou a falar a língua correta, automaticamente sofro duas penalizações, sofro penalização da parte de quem vai ouvir a música, e sofro penalização próprio dos nossos antepassados nossos mais velhos que vão me dar na cabeça a dizer "não, você está a cantar uma coisa que você não sabe, quando é assim pergunta primeiro, pergunta aos mais velhos porque se não você vai matar a nossa língua, nossa cultura."

> Many people ask me why I haven't written a song in dialect or whatever, but I'm like making music in dialect[4] is not that simple, I do it with my head, my torso, and my limbs, or I don't do it at all, because if I make a song with that dialect mixed with broken Portuguese, I take the risk of killing the language, you understand, so what's gonna happen? People will hear me sing like this and they'll think that's how you're supposed to speak it, even if it's not the case, even if I'm not speaking it right, I automatically get two penalties, one from the people who are listening to my music, and one from our ancestors, our elders who will pull my ears and say, "No, you're singing something that you don't even know, when that's the case, ask first, ask the elders because if you don't, you'll kill our language, our culture."

Excerpt 2 suggests that linguistic purism is a preoccupation for Santomean singers. Ricardo stresses the pressure that songwriters feel, as they are expected to write using *a língua correta* (the correct language). Singers who do not use a variety of Creole that Santomeans consider to be "correct" take the risk of misguiding their fans and of being dismissed by elders. Another consequence of singing in a non-correct version of Creole is the "kill[ing of] our language, our culture". Ricardo's discourse suggests that not all spoken forms of Creole are legitimate, that code switching is bad (*dialeto misturado com português mal falado* "dialect mixed with broken Portuguese"), and that there is no space for a variety of Creole that would be influenced by Portuguese. Although the elders are not (yet) the last remaining proficient speakers of the Creole languages in São Tomé and Príncipe, they are still perceived as exemplary and authoritative speakers (cf. Kroskrity 2009 about indigenous communities in the United States). The idea that elders speak and represent the purest form of Creole is still a deeply rooted ideology. That being said, such ideologies of linguistic purism may create unrealistic expectations.

Creole as Marker of Identity, Authenticity and Nativeness

Language is a semiotic resource for identity marking, and music can be a space for performing this identity (cf. Alim 2006; Alim, Ibrahim and Pennycook 2009; Hollington 2016, 2018; Sippola, Schneider and Levisen 2017; among many others). For Santomeans, the Creole languages of the islands are a central marker of their Santomeanness (even when they do not speak it), and singing in Creole is a way to perform this local understanding of national identity. In this manner, the use of Creole in songs conveys a sense of locality and Santomean identity. Of locality, because Creoles are perceived as rooted in the islands. According to Woolard (2005, 2), "within the logic of authenticity, a speech variety must be perceived as deeply rooted in social and geographic territory in order to have value". And of Santomean identity because the Creoles of the islands are indexed to display authenticity and nativeness. Still today, these Creoles are iconic representations of being Santomean, of *Santomensidade* (Santomeanness). Santomeans often make the distinction between the native Creole languages of São Tomé and Príncipe as being *ours*, and Portuguese as being *theirs*, or *of others*, even if Portuguese is the first (and often only) language of the vast majority of the population. In excerpt 3, Mateus justifies his band's choice to sing in Creole by contrasting these possessive markers (*our* and *of others*).

Excerpt 3: Our Own Language and Other People's Language

> *Decidimos cantar em angolar porque somos de angolar, nunca ninguém tinha cantado em angolar, será que nossa própria língua íamos desprezar a nossa língua e valorizar língua dos outros? Não, valorizamos a nossa língua angolar.*

> We decided to sing in Angolar because we are from São João dos Angolares, nobody had sung in Angolar before,[5] you think that our own language we were going to despise our own language and value other people's language? No, we value our language Angolar.

Mateus refers to Angolar as *nossa própria língua* (our own language), and Portuguese as *a língua dos outros* (other people's language). I have heard such statements on many occasions among Santomeans (descendants of both Forros and Angolares). For many, especially among older generations, Portuguese is still viewed as the language of the colonizers. This distinction between Creoles and Portuguese made by Mateus in excerpt 3 brings me to discuss the concept of authenticity.

Authenticity and anonymity are ideologies of linguistic authority that exist simultaneously (Woolard 2005). On the one hand, ideologies of authenticity locate "the value of a language in its relationship to a particular community", and they refer to what is perceived as a "genuine expression of such a community" (Woolard 2005, 2). When a language is the legitimating ideology of a national identity, one must speak this language to be perceived as authentic. In this sense, ideologies of authenticity in São Tomé and Príncipe point out the knowledge of a native Creole of the islands to be recognized as and considered to be *filho da terra* (child of the land). On the other hand, ideologies of anonymity hold a language to be public, accessible and neutral. It is nonethnic in character (cf. Woolard 2005, 6; Fishman 1965, 149). While authenticity is understood as "being from somewhere", anonymity refers to "being from nowhere" (Woolard

2005). In this sense, Portuguese would be the language of anonymity in São Tomé and Príncipe. It is the language of authority, the dominant language and the language of power. In this section, I will focus mainly on authenticity. Following Shenk (2007), I view authenticity as a social construct, a negotiated accomplishment and an outcome of interactional processes, loaded with the speakers' ideologies.

In excerpt 4, language is used by the Santomean singer Nino Jaleco to authenticate Elguy, a young Santomean singer who now lives in Europe. The underlying belief held by Jaleco is probably that an authentic Santomean speaks Creole. Elguy recalls the meeting between the two at the *Rádio Nacional* in São Tomé City in December 2018.

Excerpt 4: To be a *Filho da Terra* (Child of the Land)

[Nino Jaleco] começou a falar o dialeto de São Tomé comigo, pa tentar perceber se eu era mesmo original mesmo santomense, se percebia dialeto, quando o senhor começou a falar, eu respondí, foi um bocadinho um momento difícil mas eu conseguí responder, a pergunta eu ainda lembro que a pergunta que o senhor me fez era "Kê aglasa sun?" isso é em português é como...como é teu nome, e depois eu respondí meu nome é Fábio e tal, disse ah ok, depois começou a falar mais coisas e só falava em dialeto porque é uma pessoa antiga. [. . .] Senhor falou assim "Bô sa ngê téla vede", depois em português eu posso dizer que você é mesmo gente da terra, filho dos pais santomenses, realmente você viveu aqui, percebe crioulo perfeitamente, então você é da terra.

[Nino Jaleco] started to speak Forro with me, to see if I was really genuinely Santomean, if I understood Forro, when he started to talk, I answered, it was a bit of a tough time but I was able to answer his question, I still remember the question he asked, it was "Kê aglasa sun?" in Portuguese that is what . . . what is your name, and then I answered my name is Fábio and all, he said ah ok, then he said some things in Forro because he's an elder. [. . .] Then the man said like this "Bô sa ngê téla vede", then in Portuguese I can say that you are really from our land, son of Santomean parents, you really lived here, you understand Creole perfectly, so you are from the land.

Excerpt 4 is an example of authenticating practices among Santomeans. Jaleco, who is older than Fábio and known for his songs in Forro, is testing the authenticity of the young singer. In this authenticating discourse, Fábio displayed his Santomeanness by answering Jaleco's question (*Kê aglasa sun?* "What is your name?") in Forro. As a recognition of Fábio's authenticity, Jaleco tells him that he is really Santomean (*Bô sa ngê téla vede* "You are really from our land"). In Jaleco's view (as for many others), speaking Forro is like a badge (cf. Woolard 2005) for identifying real Santomeans, the ones who are *da terra* (from the land). Although the question he asked appears (to me, at least) as a basic and easy question that many "non-real" Santomeans could answer, no mention regarding this was made during my interview with Fábio. This interaction between Jaleco and Fábio stresses the importance of speaking Creole for being considered authentically Santomean.

In the following paragraphs, I discuss two linguistic practices used by Santomean singers to perform and display their identity and express their stance regarding the languages of the islands. The first one, which Santomeans refer to as *tirar versos* (singing in metaphors), is mainly used by older singers who possess great knowledge of the Creoles, and the second one, the mixing of languages, is used by young singers, probably to show that they are part of the local and the global musical scene at the same time.

Tirar Versos, or Singing in Metaphors

I name "singing in metaphors" what Santomeans refer to as *tirar versos* (*vesu* in Forro and *semplu* in Angolar). According to the Portuguese dictionary Infopedia, *versos* (written *vesso*) is "an oral literary form composed mainly of proverbs and based on traditional tales, facts, or imagination".[6] I add to this definition that *vesu*[7] also has a moral or pedagogical meaning. For a long period of time in São Tomé and Príncipe, songs were performed in Creole languages. This is not surprising as most Santomeans probably had one of the Creole languages as their first language. Because the Portuguese had lost interest in the islands for a period of two centuries (from the beginning of the seventeenth century to the mid-nineteenth century) and few Portuguese nationals were then living on the islands, we cannot assume that Santomeans were bilingual in Portuguese. Santomeans who have told me about *vesu* considered them to be *outro tipo de forro* (another kind of Forro), *um tipo de vocabulário que a gente invente* (a kind of vocabulary that we invent) or *uma forma de comunicação que nós usávamos entre os escravos naquela época colonial* (a form of communication used by slaves in colonial time). In other words, *tirar versos* can be seen as a secret code, only available to insiders. This performing peculiarity is explained by Ricardo in excerpt 5.

Excerpt 5: The Stone for Mashing Chili Should Mind Its Own Business

> *Uma música do meu pai que diz assim "Budu ê, bô sa budu mola magita, ken tê bô de dumu angu ê", quer dizer, "budu" é pedra, chama-se de pedra, "mola" é pisar, "magita" é malagueta, né? Então, "budu, bô sa budu mola magita, ken tê bô de dumu angu",*

> você é pedra de pisar malagueta, o que que você tem de vir pisar angu, [. . .] se você é pedra de pisar malagueta, você não pode pisar angu, porque você . . . uma pedra que pisa malagueta é uma pedra que arde né, então diz, você é pedra de pisar malagueta, que que tem você ir pisar o angu, quel é a ousadia que você tem de ir pisar o angu, mas, pra quem percebe, pensa que está a falar mesmo da pedra mas a mensagem não é essa, isso é um provébio, uma metáfora, que ele tá a passar pra outra pessoa, tá a perceber, é mesma coisa que estar a dizer assim, você tá a meter, não sabe nada da minha vida, o qué que tem você vir meter comigo?

> There is a song from my father that goes like this "Budu ê, bô sa budu mola magita, ken tê bô de dumu angu ê", that means, *budu* is stone, it's called a stone, *mola* means to mash, *maguita* is chili, right? So, "budu, bô sa budu mola magita, ken tê bô de dumu angu", you are a stone for mashing chili, why would you mash *angu*,[8] [. . .] if you are a stone for mashing chili, you cannot mash *angu*, because you . . . a stone that mashes chili is a stone that burns, right, so it says, you are a stone for mashing chili, why would you mash *angu*, why would you dare mash *angu*, but for those who don't understand, they'd think that the song is really about a stone but that's not the message, it's a proverb, a metaphor, that the singer is passing along to another person, you understand, it's the same thing as saying you're not minding your own business, you don't know anything about me, why do you put your nose in my business?

In the song written by Ricardo's father, the nosy person is being compared to a stone used for mashing chili. This stone used to mash chili should not be used to mash things that are not spicy because it will make these things spicy as well. Doing so is wrong, this is not what the chili stone is made for. Santo means use one stone for the chili and a different one for the *angu*; they should not be interchanged.

As explained in the interview with Ricardo, songs with metaphors were written to send a message to someone, *de uma forma que a mensagem não seja direta* (in a way that the message would not be too direct). Telling someone to mind their own business would be considered rude, but writing a song about it appears more socially acceptable. The complete meaning of the songs written in metaphors is for insiders, the ones who know the full story behind the song. These stories and meanings were transferred, together with the songs, from older to younger generations. This is how Ricardo learned Forro and came to understand the hidden meanings of his father's songs.

Singing in metaphors is an instrument for showing local and authentic Santomean identity. For the Santomeans I interviewed, it is associated with Santomeanness, with great knowledge of Creole, and it may only be performed in Creole. When I asked Ricardo about singing in metaphors in Portuguese, he said it was too "difficult" (*difícil*), and that the songs in Portuguese "lose that thing" (*perde aquele coiso*), "thing" being that essence that makes *tirar versos* what it is. In other words, it needs to be in Creole to be authentic.

Mixing Creole and Portuguese

As mentioned earlier, singing in Creole conveys a sense of locality and identity. But singing in Portuguese, as most of today's young Santomean singers do, probably conveys a sense of modernity and globality. This brings me to question the symbolic meanings conveyed by mixing languages. What stance does mixing languages express? I suggest that mixing languages is a meaning-making resource and an instrument for making an identity that is local *and* transnational. By using a Creole language and Portuguese, Santomean singers show that they are part of both the local and global musical cultures. A good example for this is the *song Bomu kêlê* ("Vamos acreditar" in Portuguese; "Let's Believe It"), sung in Forro[9] and Portuguese by Calema. This song was very popular in 2015 when I first arrived in São Tomé and Príncipe – popular enough for me to have accidently learned this song by heart. Calema is a musical band formed by two brothers (Fradique and António Mendes Ferreira) from the region of São João dos Angolares. They now live in Europe, and they are among the very few Santomean musicians who have a career abroad. During the STP Music Award 2015, the brothers won prizes for best album, best song ("Bomu kêlê"), most popular artists on the Internet and best band. In excerpt 6 are the lyrics of the song "Bomu kêlê".

Excerpt 6: "Bomu kêlê", by Calema

Original Version[10]	Translation
Encontramo-nos no meio do mar	We are in the middle of the sea
Duas ilhas que formam um país	Two islands that form a country
Tudo o que precisamos está lá	All we need is there
É só acreditarmos e seguir	We only need to believe and move forward
Vamos dar as mãos num só coração	Let's shake hands with one heart
Bomu kêlê ni scola, ni tlaba	Let's believe in schools and work
E ni tudu kuá cu nom ca pô fé	And in everything we can do
Vamos conseguir pois vamos ver	We'll do it, we'll see

São Tomé e Príncipe a desenvolver	São Tomé and Príncipe is developing
Cu tudu fôça nom cu cloçon nom	With all our strength and our heart
Bomu kêlê ni scola, ni tlaba	Let's believe in schools and work
E ni tudu kuá cu nom ca pô fé	And in everything we can do
Iné manu nom cu iné mana nom	Our brothers with our sisters
Bomu kêlê ni kuá cu nom tê	Let's believe in what we have
Nom tê cacau, nom tê baná	We have cocoa, we have bananas
Nom tê côcô, nom tê vadô-panha	We have cocoyam, we have flyingfish[11]
Nom tê téla, nom tê awá êêê	We have the land, and we have water
Côcôndja fluta e café	Coconut, breadfruit, and coffee
Piá kwá cu nom ka pô fé	See everything we can do
Cu tudo kuá cé ni téla nom	With everything from our land
Vamos conseguir pois vamos ver	We'll do it, we'll see
São Tomé e Príncipe a desenvolver	São Tomé and Príncipe is developing
Cu tudu fôça nom cu cloçon nom	With all our strength and our heart
Bomu kêlê ni scola, ni tlaba	Let's believe in schools and work
E ni tudu kuá cu nom ca pô fé	And in everything we can do

Language mixing within popular songs is not uncommon around the world. Code-mixing and code-switching usually involve the languages in contact in the singers' linguistic communities, or a language of power such as English. In fact, singing in English appears as a means to penetrate the anglophone musical market and to internationalize one's work (Bentahila and Davies 2002). This is, of course, part of a broader movement of globalization of popular music. For Santomeans, it is the Portuguese language that gives them access to a larger market and that contributes to the internationalization of their music. But why choose to mix Creole and Portuguese instead of singing only in Portuguese? Singing in Creole (even if only in part, as in "Bomu kêlê") could be perceived as excluding of non-Santomeans or of non-speakers of Creole. But the Western market nowadays is open to music from different cultures and different languages. I believe that mixing languages in their songs symbolizes the identity of a very specific group among the Portuguese-speaking world: Santomeans. Singing in Creole roots them in their native land, and singing in Portuguese opens them to the world. This symbolizes the reconciliation of conflicting trends of globalization and localization (Bentahila and Davies 2002).

It is important to mention that code-mixing in "Bomu kêlê" is not representative of language mixing in the everyday conversations of Santomeans. Further studies on code-switching based on conversational data between Santomeans are necessary.

Discussion and Conclusion

Language choice in Santomean music is meaningful, and the symbolic meanings conveyed by the different languages are shaped by language ideologies that have been circulating in São Tomé and Príncipe since the colonial times. The process of meaning-making in music is context-bound (cf. Aleshinskaya and Gritsenko 2017, 58). Research findings indicate that in São Tomé and Príncipe, singing in a Creole language indexes melodic and rhythmic structure, authenticity and locality, and it is ideal for *tirar versos* (which itself also marks Santomeanness); singing in Portuguese indexes modernity, expansion, professionalism; and mixing these languages indexes a transnational identity. Some musicians see their mission as preserving Creoles through their musical performance (e.g. Mateus and Calema), but others view singing in Creole as a barrier to their expansion in the musical world. This belief is explained by Ricardo in excerpt 7.

Excerpt 7: Creole as Not Good Enough for the International Market

> Nossas músicas, feitas em São Tomé, principalmente aquelas músicas nas nossas línguas, ela só funciona no mercado ali, ela não escoa o produto, então qué que acontece, as novas gerações, mesmo aquelas gerações antigas, também quando vêm pa fora, querendo já internacionalizar os seus trabalhos, tentam ir já mais pra outras línguas, como calão angolano, brasileiro, como crioulo caboverdiano, que são os países onde que a música tá tendo mais saída então eles já entram alí, alguns tentam misturar, pôr alguma coisa . . . alguma coisa da nossa língua, alguma coisa da nossa língua mas, não chega a ser . . . não chega a ser suficiente, o que nos obriga então a cantar em português, cantar em brasileiro, cantar no calão angolano, cantar no crioulo de Cabo Verde.
>
> Our songs, made in São Tomé, specially these songs in our languages, they only work in the market there, they don't sell the product, so what happens, the new generations, or even the older generations, when they move abroad and want to internationalize their work, they turn toward other languages, like Angolan slang, Brazilian, like Cape Verdean Creole, because they're countries where people listen to music, so they do that, some try to mix languages . . . put

something from our language, something from our language but it is not ... it is not enough, and that compels us to sing in Portuguese, in Brazilian, in Angolan slang, in Cape Verdean Creole.

In this view, singing in Portuguese is a marketing strategy. Songs in Creole "only work in the market there", which is not enough for singers who aim for an international career. As a commercial product, songs "are likely to be adapted to the requirements of the public(s) they target" (Davis and Bentahila 2008, 247). Interestingly, even singing in Cape Verdean Creole seems to be more appealing than singing in a Santomean Creole. This is probably due to the fact that the vast majority of Cape Verdeans proudly speak Creole as a first language and because their native Creole is tightly attached to their national identity. Although São Tomé and Príncipe and Cape Verde are both former Portuguese colonies, the musical and linguistic practices and language ideologies in these countries are very different (see Martin's, 2012, work about music and ideologies in Cape Verde; and Märzhäuser's, 2011a and 2011b, about language choice among bilingual Cape Verdean singers in Portugal).

The Santomean singers I interviewed exhibit awareness of the authenticating discourse around language and identity in the music world, and they know that their language choice expresses a stance, a position regarding their identity. They feel the tension of the contradictory forces, of the competing ideologies, driving the language shift from Creoles to Portuguese in São Tomé and Príncipe, and at the same time, maintaining the Creoles as a marker of Santomean identity. I believe that there is a need for reformulation in terms of the Creoles' role as a marker of social identity in this still multilingual but shifting nation. The purist ideologies held by elders limit the contexts for expressing the Creole languages. By mixing Forro and Portuguese in its songs, Calema challenges these purist ideologies and the beliefs that Creoles are incompatible with a globalized musical career. In this view, music can be seen as a space that promotes a redefinition of Santomean identity. It is also a space where ideologies are expressed, transmitted and reproduced, and where musicians and singers may be authenticated (or not).

Santomeans are struggling to maintain their languages. There are no official language policies and no real public discussions on the matter. Most efforts to preserve the Creole languages are observed on local radio and television, which have a few programs that promote the maintenance and practice of the Creoles, and through the work of musicians and singers. As the Creole languages are pushed to extinction by educational, administrative, technological and the global marketplace forces, Santomean artists and their songs written in their native Creoles appear as a tool to slow down the language loss process. From this point of view, songs and song texts play an important role in language valorization (and revitalization) and, to a broader extent, in cultural valorization. But that being said, songs alone cannot lead to the restoration of everyday use of the Creoles in conversational speech (cf. Crum and Crum 2002; Pietikäinen 2010).

Acknowledgements

This research was supported by the Swedish Wenner-Gren Foundation and the Department of Romance Studies and Classics at Stockholm University. I am grateful to musicians, singers and music lovers in São Tomé, Portugal and the Netherlands.

Notes

1. My translation of *a predominância de falantes do Kimbundu e do Umbundu em algumas roças levou ao surgimento de uma língua de contacto chamada Português dos Tongas*.

2. Exceptions to this are, for example, Almada (1884) and Negreiros (1895) in the nineteenth century, and Amado (2010), Bragança (2005), Reis (1969, 1973) and Santo (1998) in the twentieth century. But as noted by Bialoborska (2016), these documents do not offer in-depth and exhaustive analyses of Santomean cultural manifestations.

3. Tchiloli is the most studied Santomean cultural activity; for more on the topic, refer to Gründ (2006), Neves (1995), Reis (1969), Ribas (1965), Seibert (2009) and Valverde (1998), among others.

4. The term *dialeto* (dialect) is often used to refer to Forro (Bouchard 2017).

5. He is probably referring here to popular contemporary bands, as traditional songs were sung in Angolar.

6. My translation of *Forma de literatura oral constituída sobretudo por provérbios e que se baseia em contos tradicionais ou em factos verdadeiros ou imaginados*.

7. Plural marking in Forro is not formed by adding the morpheme -*s* at the end of a noun (as it is the case in Portuguese, its lexifier), but rather by adding the pluralizing markers *iden* or *den* (see Hagemeijer, 2011, for more on the topic). I decide to write *vesu* for both the singular and plural forms in this text.

8. Typical Santomean dish made with mashed bananas.

9. The members of Calema grew up in the region of the Angolares, but they sing in Forro. This points out the higher prestige of Forro among the Creole languages of São Tomé and Príncipe (Bouchard 2017).

10. Note that the Creoles of the Gulf of Guinea have no official orthography. But a proposition was made in 2010, called the Unified Alphabet for the Writing of the Native of São Tomé and Príncipe (Alfabeto Unificado para a Escrita das Línguas Nativas de São Tomé e Príncipe, ALUSTP). Refer to Araujo and Agostinho (2010) for more information on the topic. I found the lyrics of "Bomu kêlê" on Calema's web page and video clip. They are not written according to the ALUSTP. The spelling of the words is quite different than what is suggested in Araujo and Hagemeijer (2013).

11. Vadô-panha is a very common type of fish in São Tomé and Príncipe called voador in Portuguese or Atlantic flyingfish in English.

References

Afonso, Helena Lima. 2009. "Interferências Linguísticas: Um Contributo Para o Ensino da Língua Portuguesa em São Tomé e Príncipe". Master's thesis, Universidade de Lisboa.

Aleshinskaya, Evgeniya, and Elena Gritsenko. 2017. "Language Practices and Language Ideologies in the Popular Music Show *The Voice Russia*". *Language & Communication* 52: 45–59.

Alim, Samy H. 2006. *Roc the Mic Right: The Language of Hip Hop Culture*. London and New York: Routledge.

Alim, Samy H., Awad Ibrahim, and Alastair Pennycook, eds. 2009. *Global Linguistic Flows. Hip Hop Culture, Youth Identities, and the Politics of Language*. London and New York: Routledge.

Almada, Vicente Pinheiro Lobo Machado de Mello. 1884. *As Ilhas de S. Thomé e Principe (Notas de Uma Administração Colonial)*. Lisbon: Typographia da Academia Real das Sciencias.

Amado, Lúcio Neto. 2010. *Manifestações Culturais São-tomenses. Apontamentos, Comentários, Reflexões*. São Tomé: UNEAS.

Araujo, Gabriel Antunes de, and Ana Lívia dos Santos Agostinho. 2010. "Padronização das Línguas Nacionais de São Tomé e Príncipe". *Língua e Instrumentos Linguísticos* 26: 49–810.

Araujo, Gabriel Antunes de, and Tjerk Hagemeijer. 2013. *Dicionário livre do santome-português*. São Paulo: Hedra.

Baxter, Alan Norman. 2002. "Semicreolization? The Restructured Portuguese of the Tongas of São Tomé, a Consequence of L1 Acquisition in a Special Contact Situation". *Journal of Portuguese Linguistics* 1: 7–39.

———. 2004. "The Development of Variable NP Plural Agreement in a Restructured African Variety of Portuguese". In *Creoles, Contact and Language Change: Linguistics and Social Implications*, edited by Geneviève Escure and Armin Schwegler, 97–126. Amsterdam: John Benjamins.

Bentahila, Abdelâli, and Eirlys E. Davies. 2002. "Language Mixing in Rai Music: Localisation or Globalisation". *Language & Communication* 22: 187–207.

Berger, Peter, and Thomas Luckmann. 1967. *The Social Construction of Reality*. Harmondsworth: Penguin.

Bialoborska, Magdalena. 2016. "Vungu Téla, Estudo da Música Santomense: Uma Proposta de Métodos, Técnicas e Objetivos". *Cadernos de Estudos Africanos* 32. https://journals.openedition.org/cea/2121.

Bialoborska, Magdalena. 2020. "Dexâ puíta sócó(m)pé. Música em São Tomé e Príncipe do colonialismo para independência". PhD diss., Instituto Universitário de Lisboa.

Blommaert, Jan. 1999. *Language Ideological Debates*. Berlin and New York: Mouton de Gruyter.

———. 2014. *State Ideology and Language in Tanzania*. Edinburgh: Edinburgh University Press.

Bouchard, Marie-Eve. 2017. "Linguistic Variation and Change in the Portuguese of São Tomé". PhD diss., New York University.

———. 2018. "A Distinctive Use of R as a Marker of Santomean Identity". *Journal of Belonging, Identity, Language, and Diversity*, 2 (1). http://bild-lida.ca/journal/volume_2_1_2018/bouchard/.

———. 2019. "Becoming Monolingual: The Impact of Language Ideologies on the Loss of Bilingualism in São Tomé and Príncipe". *Languages* 4 (50): 1–15.

———. 2022. "Redefining Forro as a marker of identity: Language contact as a driving force for language maintenance among Santomeans in Portugal". *Multilingua: Journal of Cross-Cultural and Interlanguage Communication*, 41 (1): 85–104. https://doi.org/10.1515/multi-2020-0082.

Bourdieu, Pierre. 1991. *Language and Symbolic Power*. Translated by Gino Raymond and Matthew Adamson. Cambridge, MA: Harvard University Press.

Bragança, Albertino. 2005. *A Música Popular Santomense*. São Tomé e Príncipe: UNEAS.

Brunstad, Endre. 2003. "Standard Language and Linguistic Purism". *Sociolinguistica* 17: 52–70.

Crum, Beverly, and Earl Crum. 2002. *Newe Hupia. Shoshoni Poetry Songs*. Logan: Utah State University Press.

Das, Sonia. 2008. "Between Convergence and Divergence: 'Reformatting Language Purism in the Montreal Tamil Diasporas'". *Journal of Linguistic Anthropology* 18 (1): 1–23.

Davis, Eirlys, and Abdelâli Bentahila. 2008. "Translation and Code Switching in the Lyrics of Bilingual Popular Songs". *The Translator* 14 (2): 247–72.

Del Percio, Alfonso, Mi-Cha Flubacher, and Alexandre Duchêne. 2017. "Language and Political Economy". In *The Oxford Handbook of Language and Society*, edited by Ofelia Garcia, Nelson Flores and Massimiliano Spotti, 55–76. Oxford: Oxford University Press.

Dorian, Nancy. 1994. "Purism vs. Compromise in Language Revitalization and Language Revival". *Language in Society* 23 (4): 479–94.

Eberhard, David, Gary Simons, and Charles Fennig, eds. 2022. *Ethnologue: Languages of the World, 25th edition*. Dallas: SIL International. Accessed 13 August 2022. http://www.ethnologue.com

Ferraz, Luiz Ivens. 1979. *The Creole of São Tomé*. Johannesburg: Witwatersrand University Press.
Fina, Anna de. 2012. "Discourse and Identity". In *The Encyclopedia of Applied Linguistics*, edited by Carol A. Chapelle. Oxford: John Wiley and Sons. https://onlinelibrary.wiley.com/doi/full/10.1002/9781405198431.wbeal0326.
Fishman, Joshua. 1965. "The Status and Prospects of Bilingualism in the United States". *Modern Language Journal* 49: 143–55.
Gründ, Françoise. 2006. *Tchiloli: Charlemagne à São Tomé sur l'île du Milieu du Monde*. Paris: Magellan & Cie.
Hagemeijer, Tjerk. 2009a. "Aspects of a Discontinuous Negation in Santome". In *Negation Patterns in West African Languages and Beyond*, edited by Norbert Cyffer, Erwin Ebermann and Georg Ziegelmeyer, 139–65. Amsterdam/Philadelphia: Benjamins.
———. 2009b. "As Línguas de São Tomé e Príncipe". *Revista de Crioulos de Base Lexical Portuguesa e Espanhola* 1: 1–27.
———. 2011. "The Gulf of Guinea Creoles: Genetic and Typological Relations". *Journal of Pidgin and Creole Languages* 26: 111–54.
———. 2018. "From Creoles to Portuguese: Language Shift in São Tomé and Príncipe". In *The Portuguese Language Continuum in Africa and Brazil*, edited by Laura Álvarez López, Perpétua Gonçalves and Juanito Ornelas de Avela, 169–84. Amsterdam/Philadelphia: Benjamins.
Heller, Monica. 2003. "Globalization, the New Economy, and the Commodification of Language and Identity". *Journal of Sociolinguistics* 7 (4): 473–92.
———. 2010. "The Commodification of Language". *Annual Review of Anthropology* 39: 101–14.
Hill, Jane. 2008. *The Everyday Language of White Racism*. Oxford: Wiley-Blackwell.
Hodges, Tony, and Malyn Newitt. 1988. *São Tomé and Príncipe: From Plantation Colony to Microstate*. Boulder and London: Westview Press.
Hollington, Andrea. 2016. "Movement of Jah People: Language Ideologies and Music in a Transnational Contact Scenario". *Critical Multilingualism Studies* 4 (2): 133–53.
———. 2018. "Transatlantic Translanguaging in Zimdancehall: Reassessing Linguistic Creativity in Youth Language Practices". *The Mouth* 3: 105–23.
Infopédia. 2019. "Vesso". Accessed 1 July 2019. https://www.infopedia.pt/dicionarios/lingua-portuguesa/vesso.
Instituto Nacional de Estatística (INE). 2012a. "Características Educacionais da População". *IV Recenseamento Geral da População e Habitação*. Accessed 1 July 2019. http://www.ine.st/Documentacao/Recenseamentos/2012/TemasRGPH2012/11CARACTERISTICAS%20EDUCACIONAIS%20%20DA%20POPULACAO%20Recenseamento%202012.pdf.
———. 2012b. "Estado e Estrutura da População. *IV Recenseamento Geral da População e Habitação*". Accessed 1 July 2019. http://www.ine.st/Documentacao/Recenseamentos/2012/TemasRGPH2012/2_ESTRUTURA%20DA%20POPULACAO%20Recenseamento%202012.pdf.
Irvine, Judith. 1989. "When Talk isn't Cheap: Language and Political Economy". *American Ethnologist* 16 (2): 248–67.

Kroskrity, Paul. 2009. "Language Renewal as Sites of Language Ideological Struggle: The Need for 'Ideological Clarification'". In *Indigenous Language Revitalization: Encouragement, Guidance and Lessons Learned*, edited by Jon Reyhner and Louise Lockard, 71–83. Flagstaff: Northern Arizona University Press.

———. 2017. "Indigenous Tewa Language Regimes across Time: Persistence and Transformation". *International Journal of the Sociology of Language* 246: 7–300.

Labov, William. 1984. "Field Methods of the Project on Linguistic Change and Variation". In *Language in Use: Readings in Sociolinguistics*, edited by John Baugh and Joel Sherzer, 28–53. Englewood Cliffs: Prentice-Hall.

Lorenzino, Gerardo. 1998. "The Angolar Creole Portuguese of São Tomé: Its Grammar and Sociolinguistic History". PhD diss., City University of New York.

Martin, Carla. 2012. "Sounding Creole: The Politics of Cape Verdean Language, Music, and Diaspora". PhD diss., Harvard University.

Märzhäuser, Christina. 2011a. "Creatividade Bilingue em Letras de Rap de Lisboa". In *Múltiplos Olhares Sobre o Bilinguismo*, edited by Christina Flores, 145–82. Colecção Hespérides, Braga: Universidade do Minho.

———. 2011b. "Motivações na Escolha de Língua em Letras de Rap. Um Estudo com Falantes Bilingues (Português – Caboverdiano) en Lisboa". In *Linguística do Português. Rumos e Pontes*, edited by Mathias Arden, Christina Märzhäuser and Benjamin Meisnitzer, 429–52. München: Meidenbauer.

Milroy, James, and Leslie Milroy. 1999. *Authority in Language: Investigating Standard English*. New York and London: Routledge.

Negreiros, Almada. 1895. *Historia Etnographica da Ilha de S. Thomé*. Lisbon: Antiga Casa Bertrand–José Bastos.

Neves, Rosa Clara. 1995. "Tchiloli de São Tomé. Identidade Cultural Numa Nova Nação Africana". *CIOE. Multicultural*, 4.

Pietikäinen, Sari. 2010. "Sámi Language Mobility: Scales and Discourses of Multilingualism in a Polycentric Environment". *International Journal of the Sociology of Language* 202: 79–102.

Reis, Fernando. 1969. *Povô Loga, o Povo Brinca. Folclore de São Tomé e Príncipe*. São Tomé: Câmara Municipal de São Tomé.

———. 1973. "Folclore de São Tomé e Príncipe". Separata do *Boletim Cultural da Guiné Portuguesa* 28 (109).

Ribas, Tomás. 1965. "O Tchiloli ou as Tragédias de S. Tomé e Príncipe". *Espiral* 1 (2): 70–71.

Rickford, John. 1983. "Standard and Non-standard Language Attitudes in a Creole Continuum". (Society for Caribbean Linguistics, Occasional papers, 16). St. Augustine, Trinidad, 1983. [Reprinted in *Language of Inequality*, edited by Nessa Wolfson and Joan Manes, 145–60. The Hague: Mouton, 1985.]

Rougé, Jean-Louis. 1992. "Les Langues des Tonga". In *Actas do Colóquio Sobre Crioulos de Base Lexical Portuguesa*, edited by Ernesto de Andrade, Maria Antónia Mota and Dulce Pereira, 171–76. Lisbon: Colibri.

———. 2004. *Dictionnaire Étymologique des Créoles Portugais d'Afrique*. Paris: Karthala.

Santo, Carlos Espírito. *A Coroa do Mar*. Lisbon: Caminho, 1998.

Schneider, Britta, Eeva Sippola, and Carsten Levisen. 2017. "Introduction: Languages Ideologies and Music". *Language & Communication* 52: 1–6.

Seibert, Gerhard. 2006. *Comrades, Clients and Cousins: Colonialism, Socialism and Democratization in São Tomé and Príncipe*. Leiden, Netherlands: Brill.

———. 2007. "500 Years of the Manuscript of Valentim Fernandes, a Moravian Book Printer in Lisbon". In *Iberian and Slavonic Cultures: Contact and Comparison*, edited by Beata Elbieta Cieszynska, 79–88. Lisbon: CompaRes.

———. 2009. "Carlos Magno no Equador: A Introdução do Tchiloli em São Tomé". *Latitudes* 36: 16–20.

Shenk, Petra Scott. 2007. "'I'm Mexican, Remember?' Constructing Ethnic Identities Via Authenticating Discourse". *Journal of Sociolinguistics* 11 (2): 194–220.

Silverstein, Michael. 1996. "Monoglot Standard in America". In *The Matrix of Language*, edited by Donald Brenneis and Ronald Macaulay, 284–306. Boulder: Westview Press.

———. 1998. "The Uses and Utility of Ideology: A Commentary". In *Language Ideologies: Practice and Theory*, edited by Bambi Schieffelin, Kathryn Woolard and Paul Kroskrity, 123–45. Oxford: Oxford University Press.

Sippola, Eeva, Britta Schneider, and Carsten Levisen, eds. 2017. "Language Ideologies in Music – Emergent Socialities in the Age of Transnationalism". *Language & Communication* 52: 1–116.

Spradley, James. 1979. *The Ethnographic Interview*. New York: Holt, Rinehart, and Winston.

Valverde, Paulo. 1998. "Carlos Magno e as Artes da Morte: Estudo Sobre o Tchiloli da Ilha de São Tomé". *Etnográfica* II (2): 221–28.

Wassink, Alicia Beckford. 1999. "Historic Low Prestige and Seeds of Change: Attitudes Toward Jamaican Creole". *Language in Society* 28 (1): 57–92.

Winford, Donald. 1976. "Teacher Attitudes toward Language Varieties in a Creole Community". *Linguistics* 175: 45–75.

Woolard, Kathryn. 2005. "Language and Identity Choice in Catalonia: The Interplay of Contrasting Ideologies of Linguistic Authority". *UC San Diego: Institute for International, Comparative, and Area Studies*. Accessed 2 July 2019. https://escholarship.org/uc/item/47n938cp.

Zuckermann, Ghil'ad, and Michael Walsh. 2011. "Stop, Revive, Survive: Lessons From the Hebrew Revival Applicable to the Reclamation, Maintenance and Empowerment of Aboriginal Languages and Cultures". *Australian Journal of Linguistics* 31 (1): 111–27.

Chapter 5

Wi Ful a Patan

A Quantitative Approach to Language Use in Jamaican Popular Music

BYRON M. JONES JR.

Introduction

In societies where more than one language coexist, language use and language attitudes are a frequent topic of discussion. Most people see language as a mere means of communication, hardly ever stopping to note the intricacies of the language they speak. For some, it is an element of status and prestige, giving power and authority to the "ordinary" people who speak it. In Jamaica, many individuals are conscious of the stereotypical views attached to respective language forms in existence in society. This awareness is often manifested in instances where predominantly Jamaican Creole (hereafter JC) speakers, appearing in English domains (especially the media), try to produce their "best" (closest to the standard) variety of English (cf. Kouwenberg et al. 2011). However, awareness of language stereotypes does not always result in individuals gravitating towards using the language that is aligned to prestige. Some individuals, for various reasons, eschew the prestigious language and use more of the language that is considered low in status. The reasons surrounding such an occurrence are not always obvious, but commonly, it is done to mark solidarity as well as to create or maintain an identity (cf. Ryan 1979, 149).

It has been stated that "music ... has always provided a more liberal space giving access to a variety of languages, styles, and voices" (Farquharson 2017, 8). Though more linguistic freedom exists in the music domain, there have been very specific times in the history of Jamaican music where language use was an issue. The first of such instances occurred during the early post-emancipation period when ska was emerging as the first popular indigenous genre of Jamaican music, and the art form was garnering recognition from international music investors. Some artistes who were scouted by international producers received language tutelage, because it was seen as the key ingredient for overall musical success. The most notable case was that of Millie Small, who had experienced early local success with her ska music. Due to this local dominance, international success was expected. She was scouted and taken to England by Jamaican-born producer Chris Blackwell, who ensured that she was enrolled in speech classes very early (Spectropop 2016).

The second key moment was aligned with Chris Blackwell too, this time with Bob Marley. Blackwell had a deliberate policy that ensured that Marley sang mostly in English in an effort to be understood by his audience. According to Winer (1990), "full appreciation of the message of [R]eggae songs, considered important by its singers, depends on comprehension of the lyrics, sing in Jamaican English Creole (JamC), standard Jamaican English (JamE), or both". This desire of Blackwell for artistes under his management to be understood was thought to be the key ingredient of their success.

The most recent conversations similarly seek to warn Jamaican music industry players of the many barriers that the use of JC in their music entails. The school of thought is that the songs which are done in the Jamaican vernacular appeal to a limited market – only the people who understand it. This, the patois (JC) critics say, restricts the mass appeal of the music, because a very large percentage of the foreigners who make up the overseas markets do not understand the language (Reid 2002).

These debates about language use introduce elements of language control and language choice and the possible implications of these choices. Two questions arise from these issues: How exactly is language used in Jamaican music? How does language use correlate with success? The present chapter aims to answer the first question[1] by providing a descriptive quantitative examination of language use in Jamaican popular music to determine its patterns, if they exist, and to identify the factors that determine these patterns. The first section provides a summary of the data used, focusing specifically on corpus design and construction. The second section provides a description of the preliminary output of the statistical analysis of the study. The third section provides a summary discussion of the statistical output.

Understanding the Data

Within the design of the data for the study, it was decided that if popular music was the element of examination, popularity needed to be defined within the scope of the study. Though defining popular music is a complex undertaking, "popularity" within this research as applied to music is seen as quantitative popularity. In this sense, popular music is "the music [that] is widely liked by relevant evaluators . . . [that] has a high degree of consumption and approval . . . [and hence] a relation to an audience" (Fisher 2011, 409). I decided that the most suitable way to maintain the idea of popularity in this study is to use music charts as the main guideline for data selection.

The Charts

Music charts were an appropriate selection frame, since they had a measure for popularity index (sales, radio request and party selection), and they removed any subjectivity and researcher bias. Therefore, the data for the study comprise transcriptions of lyrics of songs chosen from music charts. These music charts were originally taken from two different sources: the Jamaica Broadcasting Corporation (hereafter JBC) Top 100 music charts and the X-News top music charts. JBC produced annual charts, whereas X-News directed most of its attention to weekly top twenty charts. Since JBC chart production ended in 1996, I used its charts for the period 1962–96 and X-News for the rest of the period (1997–2012). To create annual charts from X-News' weekly charts, I created a system where a point inverse formula was used to rank songs by awarding points to an entry for each week it stayed on the chart. From position one to twenty, points were awarded inversely, hence, number one had a twenty-point allotment and number twenty a one-point allotment. The ranking of entries was thereafter derived by their aggregate score. From these two charts, I created annual charts of the top twenty songs of each year.

Since the final charts were drawn from two different sources, I had to ensure that these two sources were comparable. In ensuring the comparability of these two sources and the data they suggested, the switch between sources was done from the Jamaica Broadcasting Corporation – a media house with radio and television divisions – to the Community Television Systems, Videomax and Mediamax Limited (CVM), another media house with television, radio and newspaper (X-News). Comparability checks the extent to which the two sources produce similar results ensuring that neither source was inferior to the other. From these two sources, the JBC and X-News charts, the Jones Annual Music charts (JAM) were created. These comprise an annual chart for each of the fifty years covered by this research. These charts formed the main pool of data analysed in this study. The pool consisted of 1,050 songs from 1962 to 2012.

Triangulation

In this triangulation process, annual charts were compared and matched against several notable compilations to check the similarity of the pool of charts and the ranking of each entry within the pool. In this process, Edward Seaga's *Reggae Golden Jubilee: Origins of Jamaican Music* and the Fab Five's *50 Years of Jamaican Music* compilations were the bases against which the JAM charts were matched. The composers of these compilations did a screening for each year since independence and selected their top song for each year. I checked if all the songs on these compilations were present on my charts. Not only were the songs from the compilations required to be on my charts, they were required to be the number one song for the respective year or they had to be highly ranked.

Quality Control and Verification

Throughout the period of the study where charts were being compiled, I received constant feedback and warning against the use of charts as my source of data, as the issue of payola (paying for airplay) would render them inaccurate. To counter this possible issue, I added a measure of quality control by assembling a team of seven experts who vetted the JAM charts. The team, who I classified as the Knowledgeable Others, comprised radio and party disc jockeys, radio broadcasters, artiste managers and music analysts. These committee members were selected based on several criteria. They should have been in the music industry for more than fifteen years, they must be popular and credible individuals among the Jamaican music and entertainment industry, and their knowledge of music should span all the genres of Jamaican music. Upon their selection, they were presented with the JAM charts which they independently vetted and provided feedback on. They were asked to check the songs in the pool to see if they should be present and that their rankings were accurate. They provided feedback on the removal, addition and re-ranking of songs, which was used to corroborate the decisions on the entries that made the final JAM charts.

Transcription and Tagging

The transcription of the songs on the JAM charts had two stages. The first stage was a "search and convert" process, where lyrics for songs on the JAM charts were retrieved from different websites, and CD sleeves and booklets. At this stage, I screened lyrics by listening to each song while following the lyrics to confirm accuracy; if lyrics were incorrect, they were amended. The second stage of transcription was a more typical process. Here, a "listen and transcribe" approach was taken to provide song lyrics which were not obtained in the first stage. I listened to the remaining songs and transcribed their lyrics. Once all songs were transcribed, they were then tagged using special codes. These tags were markers for all the variables that could impact language use in the music. These variables were both social variables, such as *gender*, and music specific variables, such as a song's *position on the charts* or the *delivery style* an artiste used in his song. The variants of these variables were identified based on observed patterns in the data rather that predetermined options. In this regard, for example, *gender* – a category that typically has dichotomous options – had a third option (both) present. In this study, gender was used in reference to the artiste delivering the song. However, in an effort to capture simultaneous delivery by a male and female, the *both* category was introduced. The independent variables identified and coded in this study were *gender, theme of song, audience, speaker within the song, period/year, song position on chart/popularity, delivery style, song stanza* and *genre*. Special codes were also created to identify each language being studied – one for English and one for JC.

Impact and Hierarchy of Factors

Within the study, a three-tier[2] analysis was done; however, the scope of this chapter warrants only the first two levels to meet the aims outlined. The first level presents a univariate analysis, which details the frequency distribution of all the variables (factors) coded in the study. Such a distribution outlines the frequency (absolute frequency), relative frequency and percentage frequency for each variable. Chiefly, this univariate analysis provides the relative frequencies of the use of JC and English in the lyrics of Jamaican popular music. The second level provides a bivariate analysis which explores the relationship between each variable and language use. This bivariate analysis allowed me to examine each factor and its influence on how language is used in Jamaican popular music.

Frequency of Use of JC and English

Absolute frequency (hereafter *f*) in this analysis refers to the total number of occurrences for a particular variant, while relative frequency (hereafter *f/n*) refers to the comparative measure of a proportion or number of actual values to the total number of occurrences of a variable. On this basis, in this database of Jamaican popular music, *f* of English versus JC variants is 14,754 and 12,520, respectively. Expressed as *f/n*, it can be said that in this study, there is a .541 and .459 *f/n* of use for English and JC in the lyrics of Jamaican popular music, highlighting a chief finding of the study. Put differently, it can be said that over the fifty-year period covered by this research, English and JC have a 54 per cent and 46 per cent frequency of use, respectively, in the lyrics of Jamaican popular music.

Exploring the Factors

There were nine variables that were examined in the study as possible factors to influence language use over the fifty-year period. As previously stated, gender had an atypical categorical breakdown: the typically dichotomous variable (male and female) had a third category classified as *both*. This category was used to mark instances where there was simultaneous singing or deejaying. Under gender, it was realized that *males* had the highest *f* of all the gender values at 25,502 (*f/n* .935, 93.5%*f*) followed by *females* at 1708 *f* (*f/n* .062, 6.3%*f*). These figures are a direct result of more songs in the data set being done by males. Noticeable observations were made for decade[3] where it was realized that there was a steady increase for each of the five decades. There was an increase from an absolute frequency of 2,987 (*f/n* .110, 11.0%*f*) in the first decade to 7,388 (*f/n* .271, 27.1%*f*) in the fifth and final decade. This increase can be explained when the statistics for *genre* are examined. The greater frequency is found between *dancehall* and *reggae* with absolute frequencies of 13,977 (*f/n* .512, 51.2%*f*) and 10,281 (*f/n* .377, 37.7%*f*), respectively. These two genres dominated the mid to final decades, and as such, the increase in the frequency seen in the last decade is expected. The remaining occurrences are distributed across five genres with the highest being that of *rocksteady* with an absolute frequency of 1,275 (*f/n* 0.47, 4.7%*f*) and the lowest being *gospel* with 76 occurrences (*f/n* .003, .3%*f*). *Soca* and *ska* occupy the mid-range of the lower spectrum with 366 (*f/n* .012, 1.2%*f*) and 784 (*f/n* .029, 2.9%*f*) instances, respectively.

There were four delivery styles identified and coded in the data. Of the four, *toasting*, with the lowest frequency of 255 (*f/n* .009, 0.9%*f*), was marginally smaller than the category with the closest frequency, *talking* 1001 (*f/n* .037, 3.7%*f*), but considerably lower than the two categories with the highest frequencies. *Singing* has a high of 56.8%*f* (*f/n* .568, 15,499 *f*), which is 18.2% higher than *deejaying* with a percentage frequency of 38.6%*f* (*f/n* .386, 10519 *f*). For the *position on chart* variable, there is an almost equal frequency distribution. *Position 1–5*, which has the highest absolute frequency at 7,187 instances (*f/n* .264, 26.4%*f*), has a mere 433 instances more than *position 6–10*, which has an absolute frequency of 6,754 (*f/n* .248, 24.8%*f*). *Position 11–15*, which is 78 occurrences less than *position 6–10* at 6676 (*f/n* .245, 24.5%*f*), is only marginally larger than *position 16–20* at 6657 (*f/n* .244, 24.4%*f*). The *stanza* variable marks the location in the song where the linguistic variable is identified. For this variable, the most noticeable point of reference is the exponentially higher absolute frequency for *verse*, at 21012 or 77% (*f/n* .770), than *chorus*, which has the second highest frequency but only at 4,278 or 15.7% (*f/n* .157). None of the other values surpassed the five percentage frequency. *Intro* was the closest at 4.7%*f* (*f/n* .047, 1276 *f*), which was more than twice that of *bridge*, which had a mere 2.2%*f* (*f/n* .022, 591 *f*). *Outro* had the lowest percentage frequency at .4%*f*, which marked a significant gap between the highest and lowest frequencies for *stanza*.

Within the *theme* variable, *warning/reprimand* has the highest frequency at 4308 (*f/n* .158, 15.8%*f*). However, this frequency is marginally higher than *love and romance* and *lifestyle*, whose frequencies are 4,290 (*f/n* .157, 15.7%*f*) and 4129 (*f/n* .151, 15.1%*f*), respectively. *Dispute*, *entertainment* and *social commentary* also have similar figures with differences of 1% and .3%, respectively. The frequencies for this set of values are only marginally lower than that of the high-frequency categories. Jamaican musicians often assume different personalities within their songs to the extent where songs have an entire discourse in which a single artiste will have dialogues undertaking various roles which see different speakers being introduced and audiences addressed. As a result, there were variables identified and coded to represent speaker and audience. Among the *speaker* variable, the most frequent category, *protagonist*, is approximately four times more frequent than the second most frequent category, *zero*.[4] *Protagonist* has a 74.3% frequency (*f/n* .743, 20,268 *f*) and *zero* 13.9%*f* (*f/n* .139, 3785 *f*). These were the only categories with a double-figure frequency percentage. Other notable categories were *narrator* with 5.94%, *male* 2.86% and *female* 2.08%. Among the *audience* variable, there were three prominent categories. *General* had the highest percentage frequency at 66%*f* (*f/n* .660, 17999 *f*) followed by *female* and *male* at 22.7%*f* (*f/n* .227, 6,178 *f*) and 7.9%*f* (*f/n* .0079, 2,148 *f*), respectively.

All the variables introduced earlier were coded and the frequency distribution examined to provide a clear understanding of the factors that may contribute to language use in Jamaican popular music. Later we will see the relationship between these factors[5] and language use. From this bivariate analysis, we will be able to determine if the effect of these variables on language use is statistically significant and, if so, what the effect size is.

Extra-Linguistic Factors Impacting Language Use in Jamaican Popular Music

In this section, the effect of each independent variable on language use will be assessed by its chi-square and Cramer's V values. Pearson's chi-square (X^2) test is used when we want to see whether there is a relationship between two categorical variables (Field 2013, 688). When we conduct this test, a significance value will be given. It has an allowance of .05 for a researcher to reject the null hypothesis (the default statement that says that there is no relationship between the dependent and the independent variables). Therefore, if the significance value is greater than .05 then the null hypothesis is true and there is no statistical significance and no relationship between the two variables being examined. Cramer's V is a measure of the strength of association between two categorical variables (Field 2013, 695). "Cramer's V provide[s] a test of statistical significance and also provides information about the strength of the association . . . a strong association is closer to 1" (Morgan et al. 2012, 136). Therefore, for all statistically significant variables, their effect size will be examined to create a hierarchy of their impact.

Table 5.1 provides a summary of the impact each variable has on the use of language in Jamaican popular music. We can see that, based on the chi-square and significance values, all nine coded variables are statistically

Table 5.1 Significant Value and Effect Size of Extra-Linguistic Variables

Variable	Chi-Square	Cramer's V
Delivery style	7076.82; $p < .05$	.51
Genre	7184.70; $p < .05$	.51
Theme	4166.60; $p < .05$	.40
Decade	4378.25; $p < .05$	.40
Audience	1440.713; $p < .05$	.23
Speaker	493.04; $p < .05$	.13
Stanza	480.00; $p < .05$	.13
Gender	103.67; $p < .05$	.06
Position on chart	16.11; $p < .05$	.02

significant. This allows us to reject the null hypothesis and conclude that there is a noteworthy relationship (instead of one of chance) existing between each variable and language use. The key question that remains is, to what extent does these factors determine what language is used? In answering this question, we turn our attention to the Cramer's V value of each variable, which indicates that, with an equally large effect size of .51, *style* and *genre* are the two variables with the strongest impact on language use. A further analysis of the data reveals that, with *style*, *deejaying* has the highest percentage frequency for JC use at 77.4% (f/n .774) and therefore the lowest for English use with 22.6% (f/n .226). The ranking was reversed for *toasting*, which had the highest percentage frequency for English use at 89.4% (f/n .894) and the lowest JC use at 10.6% (f/n .106). *Singing*, which had the highest absolute frequency of all delivery styles, had the second highest and second lowest relative frequencies for English and JC use with 75.1% (f/n .751) and 24.9% (f/n .249), respectively. *Talking* had almost equal use of English and JC use with 51.0% (f/n .510) and 49.0% (f/n .490), respectively.

With *genre*, the percentage frequencies for *reggae* and *dancehall* were ranked among the lowest for the use of English.[6] *Dancehall* had the lowest with 29.9% (f/n .299) but had the highest percentage frequency for JC of all genres with 70.1% (f/n .701). After *dancehall*, only *soca*, at 62.5% (f/n .625), had a lower percentage frequency of use for English than *reggae* at 75.8% (f/n .758). The other genres all had percentage frequencies of use for English over 90%. *Rhythm and Blues* had 99.8% (f/n .998) followed by *rocksteady*, *ska* and *gospel* with 96.3% (f/n .963), 93.8% (f/n .938) and 93.4% (f/n .934), respectively. Noteworthy is the fact that *soca*, a non-indigenous genre to Jamaica, has the highest relative frequency of JC occurrences after *dancehall*. Additionally, the relative frequencies for *reggae* and *dancehall* are reversed, as the former has 76% and 24% English to JC use, while the latter has 30% and 70% English to JC use.

Theme and *decade* had an identical medium effect size, demonstrated by their Cramer's V value of .40. When we look at *decade* diachronically, there were sharp decreases in the percentage frequency of English with a simultaneously sharp increase for JC. There was a 96.3% (f/n .963) and 3.7% (f/n .037) use for English and JC in the 1st *decade*, which moved to 80.2% (f/n .802) and 19.8% (f/n.198) and then to 52.9% (f/n .529) and 47.9% (f/n .479). For the remaining two decades, the decrease and increase were steadied with 43.1% (f/n .431) and 56.9% (f/n .569) moving to 36.6% (f/n.366) and 63.4% (f/n.634) in the last decade. Under *theme*, there were sixteen categories. *Love and romance* had the second highest percentage frequency at 85.6% (f/n .856), ranked only behind *equal rights and justice* at 95.5% (f/n .955). *Dispute* and *spirituality* had almost identical frequencies at 72.0% (f/n .720) and 71.2% (f/n .712), respectively. *Unity* at 62.9% (f/n .629) and *social commentary* at 54.0% (f/n .540) were the only other categories with percentage frequencies over 50%. The list is completed by *marijuana* (42.3%f, f/n .423), *entertainment* (40.8%f, f/n .408), *lifestyle* (38.2%f, f/n .382), *sex* (32.0%f, f/n .320), *gyallis*[7] (29.5%f, f/n .295), *badman* (22.4%f, f/n .224) and *politics* (13.0%f, f/n .130). With mirrored images of English use expected for JC use, *politics* and *equal rights and justice* had the highest (87.0%f, f/n .870) and the lowest (4.5%f, f/n .045) percentage frequencies, respectively. Apart from *equal rights and justice*, only *dispute* (28.0%f, f/n .280), *love and romance* (14.4%f, f/n .144), *social commentary* (46.0%f, f/n .460), *spirituality* (28.8%f, f/n.288) and *unity* (37.1%f, f/n .371) had percentage frequencies lower than 50%.

The remaining five variables, though statistically significant, had a small effect size. *Audience* had the best effect size of these variables with .23. This may be as a result of the fact that the absolute frequency of the variable was dominated by three categories. *General* audience had the highest absolute frequency for both English and JC with 8,579 (47.7%f) and 9,420 (52.3%f) followed by *female* and *male* with 4,458 (72.2%f) and 1,720 (27.8%f) and 1,170 (54.5%f) and 978 (45.5%f) instances, respectively. The remaining ten categories had absolute frequencies ranging from 5 to 88 for English use and 0 to 174 for JC, many of which had 100% frequency for English use.

Speaker and *stanza* had an identical effect size of .13. Like *audience*, many of the categories of the *speaker* variable had low absolute frequencies for both English and JC use. For the use of both languages, *protagonist* with 10,380 and 9,888 had the highest absolute frequency followed by *zero* with 2532 and 1253 and *narrator* with 958 and 662. In exploring the percentage frequency of the variable, I noticed that it is an English-dominant variable, as eleven of its twelve variants have a higher frequency for English use. *Male* is the only category, at 53%, that had a higher percentage frequency for JC.

For *stanza*, *verse* and *chorus* had the highest absolute frequencies totalling 21,012 and 4,278, respectively, of a total of 27,274. *Outro* had the second highest percentage frequency for the use of English variants with 71.8% (f/n .718) behind *bridge* with 97.3% (f/n .973). *Verse, intro* and *chorus* had similar frequencies with 52.4% (f/n .524), 54.8% (f/n .548) and 55.9% (f/n .559), respectively. The relative frequencies for JC use for *chorus, intro* and *verse* remain close with 44.1% (f/n .441), 45.2% (f/n .452) and 47.6% (f/n .476). *Bridge*, which had the highest frequency for English, had the lowest for JC use at 2.7% (*f/n* .027), directly preceded by the *outro* at 28.2% (*f/n* .282).

As mentioned earlier, there were a great deal more songs in the data that were done by males than females, contributing to the small effect size of .06. This imbalance further contributed to the absolute frequency for *males* being over ten times that of *females* for both languages. All three categories of *gender* had a greater percentage frequency for English use. *Both* had the highest frequency at 100% followed by *females* at 62%, while *males* had the lowest frequency with 52%.

In the Introduction, one of the claims that was made is that the use of JC in music has dire consequences that will inevitably affect the success of a song. However, if we look at the effect size of *position* of the song (marking how popular a song was), we can see that it had the smallest effect size of .02. A breakdown of the variable indicates that all categories had a higher percentage frequency for English use than JC. *Position 16–20* had the highest frequency percentage for English use at 55.4% (*f/n* .554, 3,687 *f*). However, this figure was only marginally larger than *position 6–10* and *position 11–15*, which were equal at 54.5% (*f/n* .545, 3679 and 3639 *f*). The top five positions have the lowest per cent frequency for English use at 52.2% (*f/n* .522, 3749 *f*), which tells us that, though the songs in the top-five position had a higher use of English than JC, the songs occupying these positions had a higher percentage frequency use of JC than any other position on the chart. Therefore, the language used in the songs did not impact their popularity greatly, since the higher up on the charts the songs were found, the use of JC increased.

Discussion

Within the music domain, as the statistics indicate, there is a pattern at work, which dictates the course of action to be taken when a song is being penned. There are several factors, some more influential than others, which seemingly determine the language to be used in a particular song. When we examined *decade*, we saw that there was a move from a predominance of English use to one of JC. On the charts that furnished the data, it was observed that in the early part of the first decade, many songs fell within the genre of *rhythm and blues*. However, most of these songs were covers of American songs that were placed on riddims with a Jamaican finish. As such, the language used in these songs was English, the language of the originals. When ska became the dominant genre later in the decade, the influence of the American music industry was still present, specifically in the language used. "While numerous commentators pointed out the musicological influence of rhythm and blues on the development of Jamaican popular music of the 1960s (i.e., ska, rocksteady, *reggae*), nobody has noted the strong linguistic impact of the former on the latter" (Farquharson 2017, 10). A shift in language was observed when ska and other original genres of Jamaican music became dominant and popular. By the mid-decade, the use of JC was almost equal to that of English. This was attributed to the introduction of dancehall, a JC genre, along with an increase in the themes and delivery style which accompanied the genre.

As the data in the previous section indicate, the factors with the largest effect size were *decade, genre, theme* and *delivery style*. This observation is one of significance within this research. Though all factors were statistically significant, these four factors had the greatest impact on the patterns of language use observed. We noted that over the decades, language use changed, which is in line with a prediction of the *Language Attitude Survey* conducted by the Jamaican Language Unit in 2005. The results from the survey identified that there was a change in attitude towards JC, as more individuals were identifying with the language. However, the survey did not indicate or hint at the structure of the change. In the music, the shift in language over the decades was driven by, as stated earlier, the introduction and popularity of dancehall. Though the genre coexisted in the same space with reggae, there were elements that separated them. As the frequency distribution from the bivariate analysis indicates, similar to the fact that dancehall seems to be the genre of JC, reggae seems to be the genre of English. To say definitively that they are JC and English genres, respectively, a multivariate analysis is required, which was not examined in this chapter. This analysis would examine the frequency distribution for both *dancehall* and *reggae* over the final two decades when dancehall was popular to see the rate of increase of JC in both genres.

As these genres had their language of association, so did they have *themes* and *delivery styles* that were linked to them. *Deejaying* was aligned to *dancehall* and *singing* to *reggae*. Similarly, *love and romance* was a reggae theme, while *sex* and *badman* themes were more common with dancehall. Therefore, the fact that these themes and delivery styles are associated with a particular genre that has a preference for a particular language means that they will also have a preference for the language of the genre they are linked to.

The prediction of a change in attitude towards JC brought with it an acceptance and popularizing of the genre, and by extension, the themes and delivery style of the language. Therefore, the combination of genre, delivery style, decade and theme presents the best model to dictate and predict the language that is used within Jamaican music, while the desire for success seems secondary. JC has a special place in the global space, which is supplied by the music being exported from Jamaica. This should come as no surprise because JC is more popular internationally than Jamaican English (Mair 2013, 263). Jamaican music and its patterns of language use have forged a special marker, or brand, of (national) identity, and audiences' desire to be associated with this brand and to experience the identity that comes with it appears to be the decisive element of success.

Notes

1. Greater research beyond the scope of this chapter is required to address the second question.
2. The third was a multivariate analysis by way of logistic regression.
3. Years were recoded as decades to make the variable easier to analyse.
4. No addressee was present, so the artist was performing the song as himself/herself.
5. Independent variables.
6. This is attributed to the fact that these two genres had a high absolute frequency split across both languages, while the other genres had smaller absolute figures.
7. The *gyallis* category referenced all statements by male artistes about their, or other males', abilities of having multiple women with whom they are romantically involved.

References

Farquharson, Joseph. 2017. "Linguistic Ideologies and the Historical Development of Language Use Patterns in Jamaican Music". *Language and Communication* 52: 1–12.

Field, Andy P. 2013. *Discovering Statistics Using IBM SPSS Statistics: And Sex and Drugs and Rock 'n' Roll*. Los Angeles: Sage Publications.

Fisher, John Andrew. 2011. "Popular Music". In *The Routledge Companion to Philosophy and Music*, edited by Theodore Gracyk and Andrew Kania, 405–15. London: Routledge.

Jamaican Language Unit. 2005. *The Language Attitude Survey of Jamaica. Technical Report*. Kingston: The Jamaican Language Unit.

Kouwenberg, Silvia, Winnie Anderson-Brown, Terri-Ann Barrett, Shyrel-Ann Dean, Tamirand De Lisser, Havenol Douglas, Marsha Forbes, et al. 2011. "Linguistics in the Caribbean. Empowerment Through Creole Language Awareness". *Journal of Pidgin and Creole Languages* 26: 387–403.

Mair, Christian. 2013. "The World System of Englishes". *English World-Wide* 34 (3): 253–78.
Morgan, A. George, Nancy L. Leech, Gene W. Gloeckner, and Karen C. Barrett. 2012. *IBM SPSS for Introductory Statistics: Use and Interpretation*. New York: Routledge.
Reid, Tyrone. 2002. "Dancehall – No Problem Mon!". *Jamaica Gleaner*, 28 April 2002. Accessed 9 March 2013. http://old.jamaica-gleaner.com/gleaner/20020428/ent/ent1.html
Ryan, Ellen Bouchard. 1979. "Why do Low-Prestige Language Varieties Persist?" In *Language and Social Psychology*, edited by Howard Giles and Robert St Clair, 145–57. Oxford: Blackwell.
Spectropop. 2016. *Spectropop Welcomes Millie Small*. Spectropop Express, n.d. Web. 24 November 2016. http://www.spectropop.com/MillieSmall/index.htm.
Winer, Lise. 1990. "Dread Ina Babylon: The Intelligibility of Reggae Lyrics in North America". *English World-Wide* 11 (1): 35–58.

Chapter 6

Styling through Rhyming

Gender and Vowel Variation in Jamaican Dancehall Lyrics

NICKESHA DAWKINS

Introduction

This work is derived from a subsection of my 2016 dissertation that examines the acoustic variation of vowels in Jamaican dancehall music lyrics, and how this variation is impacted by the social phenomenon of gender. The major task of the research is to conduct a sociophonetic exploration of acoustic phonetic features as a significant characteristic of gender identity and style in Jamaican dancehall music lyrics. This study combines two traditional areas in linguistics, phonetics and sociolinguistics, which produce a relatively new area under the aforementioned discipline known as sociophonetics. These combined areas provide the opportunity for further insights into the culture of Jamaican dancehall music.

Background of the Jamaican Language Situation

The Statistical Institute of Jamaica reports that Jamaica currently has a population of approximately three million people, and according to Meade (2001), the majority of this population are speakers of Jamaican Creole (JC), or Patois as we call it. English is the official language of Jamaica, while Jamaican Creole is the national language. English is the assigned medium of instruction in education; it is also the main language of the media and business. Although the government has formally recognized JC to some extent, there is still some stigma attached to the language and its speakers. Jamaican Creole is associated with the lower socioeconomic strata of the Jamaican society, and as the language of focus for this study, it is important to note that it is also the language of the Jamaican dancehall.

Table 6.1 JC Vowel Phoneme Inventory

Front Vowels (Both High and Low)	Back Vowels (Both High and Low)
/ɪ/: [ɪ], /i/: [i]	/ʊ/: [ʊ] /u/: [u]
/ɛ/: [ɛ]	/ʌ/: [ʌ]
/a/: [a], [ɐ], [ɑ]	/ʊʌ/: [uo], [ʊʌ], [ua]
/a:/: [a:], [ɐ:], [ɑ:]	/ʌʊ/: [ɐu], [ʌu], ʌʊ], [au],
/ɪɛ/: [ɪɛ], [ɪɐ]	
/aɪ/: [aɪ], [ɐɪ], [ɐɛ]	

Jamaican Creole Vowels

For this study, the vowels are the most important linguistic variables under investigation. Therefore, significant attention will be paid to these phonemes and not consonants. Moreover, the vowel system proposed by Meade (2001) will be adopted (see table 6.1).

Dancehall Music

Dancehall music is one of the most popular musical genres in Jamaica today; "its songs are 'climbing charts' and 'making waves' in other parts of the world such as Europe, Asia and the Americas" (Dawkins 2009, 2013). Cultural studies expert Hope (2006) captures the genesis of this music and culture, stating that the intense social pressures operating in Jamaica during the early 1980s demanded a catharsis – the opening of a safety valve to release the pent-up frustrations of many dislodged Jamaicans. Popular culture responded to "the vacuum that had developed in the society. It projected a cultural music product that was indelibly marked by the political, economic and social tensions at work in the society. This was the evolution of dancehall music and culture" (Hope 2006, 9). Hope explains that the term *dancehall* is also defined as a place for the staging of dances.

This type of music is performed by artists known as deejays (DJs) (Devonish 2006; Hope 2010). These artists are usually black, inner-city (ghetto) youth. Stanley Niaah states that "dancehall is synonymous with Jamaica. Its very identity is reflective of Jamaica's motto, 'Out of many, one people,' unifying yet divisive and exclusionary" (2010, 1). She goes on to say that dancehall is created by the people, the disenfranchised youth, many of whom are from African descent who "continually seek tomorrow's dinner from a 'noisy' space that has been snubbed by the upper classes" (1).

Dancehall: A Culture of Masculinity

Dancehall is a male-dominated arena. Not only are men dominant in terms of their performance as artists of the genre, they are also the main supporters of dancehall events. In other words, they are the main attendees/audience at dancehall shows and festivals. In addition, approximately 98 per cent of producers, disc jockeys, studio engineers and show promoters of this musical genre are men. Hope (2010, 13) argues that

> while the dancehall exists within a space that encourages the widening or loosening of the traditional socio-patriarchal boundaries and facilitates male/female re-negotiation of traditional socio-political and socio-economic roles as desired by traditional Jamaican society, nevertheless, the dancehall is rigidly patriarchal and heavily male-dominated.

Very few women have made a substantial name for themselves within the genre, some of whom are Patra, Lady G, Lady Saw and Tanya Stephens. Lady Saw is the only female in the genre who maintained her presence at a superior level (a constant female hitmaker) prior to following her strict Christian teachings four years ago (2016). She is also dubbed the "Queen of Dancehall"; some of her titles have been "Muma Saw" or just "Muma" (meaning the "mother" of dancehall). Although Tanya Stephens has also maintained a significant presence in dancehall to date, the fame of Lady Saw surpasses this significant presence. However, as popular as any of these women may be, men are the "rulers" of the dancehall "kingdom". In support of this view, Hope (2010, 13) posits that "although popular female artists such as Lady Saw gained prominence and economic and social power within its boundaries, the dancehall evolved and still remains predominantly a masculine space under masculine power and control". Beenie Man is dubbed the "King of the Dancehall"; his popularity and successful reign in the genre almost seem unending. He is among many males (Bounty Killer, Sizzla, Buju Banton, Capleton, etc.) who have sustained tremendous success in the genre.

Stepping Out of Bounds: Crossing the Masculine Borderline

Although men's dominating presence in dancehall has always been noticeable, what is even more noticeable is that they are now crossing over into the limited space that was allotted to the females of the genre. This space being the role of dancing. Stanley Niaah (2010) states that "anxiety about male dancing surfaced in dancehall around 2003, when male dancers and dancing crews began to proliferate and to upstage female dancers in visible competitions for the stage, the street and video spotlight" (141). I have witnessed female dancers literally being pushed out of the view of the video camera by male dancers who wanted to be in the spotlight in 2009 at a famous dancehall event known as Hot Mondays. Fire Links, who served as both promoter and sound selector[1] at the event, was quite upset by the behaviour of these men and spoke out openly against the behaviour at the event.

Theoretical Framework: The Theory of Style

The theory of style is indispensable to this research because style is the ethos of the Jamaican dancehall musical culture. Within this culture, style is manifested in the art of dress, dance, rhythmic rhyming patterns, the syntax of the lyrics (the ordering of a number of words per line, per chorus bar) and, most importantly, there could be what I term a phonetic style.

Bell (1984) argues that "style is essentially speakers' response to their audience" (145). He postulates that speakers will style shift to sound like other speakers. The more attention that an audience pays to the speaker, the more likely it is that the speaker will be influenced to style shift. Thus, speakers design their style of talk for their audience. Bell further proposes that style refers to ways of speaking – how speakers use the resource of language variation to make meaning in social encounters. Like Bell (1984, 2001), Coupland (2007) is of a similar opinion; he asserts that speech style and social context interrelate. Style, according to Coupland, "refers to the wide range of strategic actions and performances that speakers engage in, to construct themselves and their social lives" (1).

Style and Its Application to Music Lyrics

The notion that musical artists style shift to sound like other artists with a different accent from their own is not unheard of either. Trudgill (1983) found that British punk music singers changed their pronunciation of particular phonemes to sound more American because the American style was seen as more prestigious by British audiences/fans. According to Bell (1984), "persons respond mainly to other persons, and speakers take most account of hearers in designing their talk" (159).

Bell (2001) revisits the whole concept of style that he had proposed in his 1984 work. He proposes that the sociolinguistic core question about language style is, "why did this speaker say it this way on this occasion". He outlines that the most crucial point to be made about such a catch line is the why factor. This involves the search for an explanation and presupposes a search for and the existence of patterns. Second, the question implies an alternative choice: a "that", which could have been chosen instead of a "this way".

A Theory of Identity

In examining the social aspects of language and gender, one cannot avoid the issue of identity, as this is directly related to theories of gender. Joseph (2004) posits that social identity is that part of an individual's self-concept which derives from his/her knowledge of his/her membership in a social group (or groups) together with the value and emotional significance attached to that membership. Baldwin and Hetch (1995) identify two types of identities: one of which is personal identity, which indicates "who I am", and the other is enacted identity, which indicates "who I am for others" (quoted in Joseph 2004, 81). He puts forward that one's deep personal identity is made up in part of the various group identities to which one stakes a claim by arguing that group identity finds its most "concrete" manifestation in a single symbolic person/individual.

Men and women can and do construct voices of the opposite sex to identify with particular groups of speakers. According to Gordon and Heath (1998), men and women may modify their articulatory lowering or raising of their formant frequencies to produce voices that aim towards archetypes of the opposite gender. This, they say, is motivated by social dynamics, such as those associated with the construction and performance of identity. Le Page and Tabouret-Keller (1985) state that acts of identity entail identities which people make within themselves as well as those that are shared with others. They further postulate that "the individual creates his systems of verbal behaviour so as to resemble those common to the group with which he wishes from time to time to be identified" (115). However, the process of choosing is neither necessarily conscious nor is it always unidimensional (Le Page and Tabouret-Keller 1985).

Linguistic Identity and Phonological Variation

Holmes (1997) shows how one woman constructs a stereotypical gender identity through her use of phonological variants which are more frequent in New Zealand women's speech than men's. For example, she uses the standard realization of the (ING) variable and the conservative aspirated variant of intervocalic /t/. Thus the speaker constructs a conservative feminine gender identity in this instance through a combination of phonological choices.

A study conducted by Torgersen (2002) on the phonological distribution of the "FOOT" vowel, /ʊ/, found that girls used the fronted variants more often than boys. In addition to Torgersen's work, Fought (1999) documents Chicano English speakers' participation in a majority sound change which involved the fronting of /u/. Patterns of fronting relative to gender and social class were not as salient, although "Female" and "Working Class" speakers generally showed a greater degree of fronting compared to "Male" and "Middle Class" speakers (Ward 2003). In similar case studies carried out by Eckert (2004) and Boberg (2005), it was revealed that the backing of /æ/ and the backing and lowering of /ɛ/ and /ɪ/ are features of Canadian English associated with what is called the Canadian Shift, and similar developments have recently been found in sociophonetic studies of California by Eckert (2005). Chambers and Hardwick (1986) argue that women in Toronto have the tendency to front and raise the diphthong /aw/ to produce [ew], while men lead in the backing and rounding of the diphthong [ow]. Also, Milroy and Milroy's (1985) observation of the Belfast speech community indicates that women lead linguistic change in the raising and fronting of [æ] to [ɛ], while the backing and occasional rounding of [a] are led by men.

Building on these works, this study considers how male and female artists of Jamaican dancehall music vary their vowel articulatory features by performing what appears to be a gendered linguistic identity via style associated with this musical genre.

Methodology

This is a quantitative study in which the researcher investigates the acoustic variation on vowels used in the song choruses of dancehall music and their correlation with gender, the contexts in which these gender-correlated features occur, and the likely social factors of the gender-based variation of the phonetic features (vowels).

Sample Size

Ten male artists and five female artists were selected for the study. They were selected based on their tenure (ten years and more) in the dancehall music industry. For this study, a total of 120 songs were examined. Eighty of these songs are sung by the ten males (eight songs per male), while the other forty are sung by the five female artists (eight songs per female). Forty of the eighty songs by men target men and the other forty target women. For the women in the study, twenty of the forty songs target men and the other twenty target women. The sample size is as such because men outnumber women in dancehall, having a 1:2 (5:10) ratio in their presence in this industry for more than ten years, and having a ratio advantage of 1:10:5 (90:444) in their numbers of songs on the overall charts (recorded in the overall database of my dissertation). The songs were obtained initially from VP Records' Simply the Best and Reggae Gold album charts, and were recorded by the artists between 1990 and 2014.

Data Synthesis

Mathematical measurements which involve the implementation of Praat analyses via tables, charts and graphs were incorporated. Praat is a computer programme used mainly to examine the physical properties of sound; the use of this programme is required for the measurement of F_0, F_1 and F_2 vowel formant measurements. F_1 is related to vowel height, F_2 to vowel frontness and F_0 to fundamental frequency,[2] which is related to vowel pitch. It is important to note that pitch is correlated with the physical feature of fundamental frequency; therefore, when considering speech at the prosodic level, it is preferable to use the concept of fundamental frequency rather than pitch.

Vowels were selected because they are more sonorous than consonants. That is, they are rich/full in vibratory quality and sound. They are also more distinguishable (visible) in the spectrogram than consonants. By way of illustration, figure 6.1 shows the word *man* in Praat in line final position in the chorus of the song "No Argument" by dancehall artist Bounty Killer.

The vowel is the darker shaded area in the timeline selection. The selection of the vowel is captured in the light gray selection of 0.246366 on the spectrogram, a pink hue in the backdrop, and the vowel formants are seen below it indetifiable by their very dark gray hue. The formants have the dotted lines (called formant trackers) running horizontally across them. On each side are the nasals [m] and [n]. You can see by this picture that the vowel is clearer than the nasal consonants which are also sonorous, but less so than the vowel; in this case, the low front unrounded lax vowel [a].

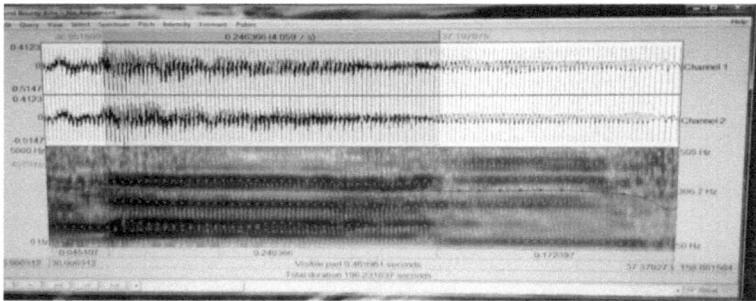

Figure 6.1 Spectrogram of Bounty Killer's [man] "man" in the chorus of "No Argument".

Making Vowel Selections in Words

Baranowski (2013) recommends that vowels in fully stressed syllables in mono- or disyllabic words should be selected for analysis. They should not be preceded by obstruent-liquid clusters, as those have a lowering and backing effect on the position of vowel nuclei. The vowels that form part of the rhyming pattern in the words of each song's chorus were selected for analysis; that is, vowels located in the same phonetic environments.

The vowels incorporated in the study are [i ɪ a ʊ], in the words [mi] "me", [mɪ] "me", [man] "man" and [jʊ] "you". These vowels were selected because the preliminary study (Dawkins 2016) found that these vowels form part of the most frequently used rhyme scheme in the choruses and extended choruses (chorus verses) of the songs being investigated. That is, words such as [man] "man", [mi] "me", [mɪ] "me" and [jʊ] "you" are commonly used by the artists to form rhymes in dancehall choruses. Although these vowels are contained in syllables that have other sonorous phonemes [m n j], these other segments are not as sonorous as the vowels which can be easily heard in the audio or distinguished by sight on the spectrogram. The Praat analysis was used to determine whether variation exists in the production of vowels for men versus women in dancehall music. If these phonological variations do exist, the researcher seeks to find out what social factors are correlated with these variations.

Vowel Measurement

The midsection (midpoint) of the vowels is measured because that is the most stable point in the production of vowels, and it also eliminates or lessens the interference of a preceding or following consonant. Labov (2001) recommends that a single point in the vowel be the ideal point of measurement because this point will be the central tendency of the nucleus, as it is the target the speaker is aiming at and the central acoustic impression that the listener obtains. This approach adopted here has been used in numerous sociophonetic studies of vowels (Baranowski 2007; Boberg 2008; Dinkin 2009). A single point of measurement in the vowel nucleus has proved to be effective at distinguishing social groups.

After the vowels were measured using the standard spectrogram settings,[3] the results were recorded in detailed tables (see Dawkins 2016), and summarized in the relevant tables and charts located in the Findings section of the chapter. Additionally, the statistical significance of the findings is determined by the use of chi-square tests.

Praat and Music

Praat was specifically selected as the main instrument for the acoustic analysis of the vowels because of its prevalent use by researchers conducting linguistic studies that concentrate on acoustic phonetics. Van der Meer (2015) outlines that Praat is the best programme for music analysis. He notes, "to have a microscopic insight into melodic contours, to see the precise pitch of a given note, to have precise measurements of the duration of beats – they are all impossible without such a program" (1).

Praat and Filters

Filters[4] were not used to separate the vocals (high or low frequencies involving F_0, F_1 and F_2) from the accompanying instrumental music because filtering is considered irrelevant. According to the Van der Meer (2015), there are many reasons why this technique is now considered obsolete. Instead of using filters, modern pitch extraction looks at the partials, sees their relative distances and then applies an algorithm for calculating the position of the fundamental frequency. If there is a main voice with some accompaniment, PRAAT is usually able to isolate the main partials, disregard the confusion of the partials of the accompaniment and come to a good estimate of the fundamental frequency of the main voice (Van der Meer 2015).

Determining the Target Audience

The artists in dancehall music usually perform songs with lyrics geared towards a specific audience. Information about the target audience was obtained directly from artists where possible during the primary interviews.

I also got target audience identification information from expert authors/ researchers of the dancehall music genre: Donna Hope who is a Full Professor of Culture, Gender and Society at the University of the West Indies and Sonjah Stanley Niaah, senior lecturer in cultural studies at the same university during the data collection period. This was done via interviews in both their offices, located at the University of the West Indies, Mona campus. Each expert was interviewed individually. Only the choruses of the songs were played and the respondent was asked, in both cases, to tell who the target audience of a specific song might be. In other cases, the target audience was determined through textual analysis.

Types of Audiences

According to Bell (1984), speakers accommodate their addressee primarily. Other types of audiences, such as overhearers and referees, affect style to a lesser but regular degree. The two types of audiences focused on in this research are the addressees and referees. The addressees are those audience members for which a song was specifically composed or those members who can benefit from or identify with the song lyrics. For example, these members include artists that are engaged in lyrical feuding. In Jamaican dancehall, we refer to these addressees as clash artists. They write what is known as a counteraction (a specific song that serves as a reply/response to a song by another artist that targets them). In American rap culture, they refer to this scenario as "beef" or "beefing". Additionally, this audience type (addressee) can be persons who may or may not personally know the artist, but can identify or relate in some way or another to the message in the song in a more specific way. The other audience type is the referee; these audience members are indirectly addressed or referred to. Bell (1984) notes that referee design is typical of mass media communication. For the songs under study, the referees include members of the general public that can benefit from or identify with the DJ's lyrics and concepts being portrayed. The artists may also refer to themselves or herself in a particular song to establish identification with a specific topic to which others can relate. Both addressees and referees have the potential to influence the utterer's language style.

It is important to note that an artist can have a song addressing more than one audience type. A song can target a particular audience and also refer to another group of listeners (that is, addressees versus referees). For example, Buju Banton's song "Boom Bye Bye" addresses the issue of homosexuality/gay men, but is addressed to heterosexual men, telling them to "shoot these men". This same situation is seen in Spragga Benz's song "Funny Guy Thing", where he addresses the same issue of homosexuality/gay men and reasserts his masculinity by stating that [wɪ nʌ ɪna nʌ fʌnɪ ɡaɪ tɪŋ; bad man nʌ wieɹ dʒi sʧɹɪŋ], which translates to "we do not partake in 'funny guy thing' [homosexual activities]; bad men [gangsters] don't wear G-strings [thongs]". Here, he uses both exclusive and inclusive language, where gay men are being referred to as "funny guys" and heterosexual men are being referred to as "bad man". There are also cases where the referees are females and the addressees are males, and vice versa. Example 1 shows a song by Beenie Man which was determined by the panel of experts to target women, as it tells women of his sexual prowess. In this song, females are the addressees.

Example 1: [nju sʊzikɪ] "New Suziki" by Beenie Man

IPA	English Gloss
[dɪ ada naɪt mɪ bʌk a gjal ina miɪ nju sʊzukɪ	The other night I ran into a girl while I was in my new Suzuki
ʃi nɛva ɛkspɛk nʌtn bɪg an spukɪ	She never expected anything big and spooky (reference to male genitalia)
naʊ dɪ gjal kjɑn lʊk ina mi fes	Now the girl cannot look me in the face
gjal nʊo sɛ ʃi luz dɪ ɹes	She knows she has lost the race
gjal kʌm dʒɹap ina mi nju sʊzukɪ	This girl throws herself (sits) in my new Suzuki
ʃi nɛva ɛkspɛk nʌtn bɪg an spukɪ	She never expected anything big and spooky
naʊ dɪ gjal kjɑn lʊk ina mi fes	Now the girl cannot look me in the face
gjal nʊo sɛ ʃi luz dɪ ɹes]	She knows she has lost the race

As evidenced in example 2, the panel of experts determined that this song by Lady Saw targets a male audience, as she challenges men by asking if their sexual prowess is adequate for her. This is seen in the lyrics where she states, "Can you manage what you have been after for so long" (in reference to a man being able to handle her in bed) and "make sure you have more than one combination to ease all of my frustrations" (in reference to different sexual positions). In this song, males are the addressees.

Example 2: [alıgeʃanz] "Allegations" by Lady Saw

IPA	English Gloss
[aım ieɹın diz siɹʌs alıgeʃanz	I am hearing these serious allegations
sɛ dı man dɛm waːn kʌm dʒɹap ina mı bɛd	that men want to throw themselves in my bed
a tjun dɛm waːn kʌm tjun in pan wı steʃan	They want to tune in unto our station (reference to sexual intercourse)
a ɹʌn dɛm waːn kʌm ɹʌn wı badı ɹɛd	they want to run our bodies red (to put one's body under pressure, excessive work: referring to sex)
kjan jʊ manidʒ we jʊ afta fı so laŋ	Can you manage what you have been after for so long (in reference to a man being able to handle her in bed)
an ıf a aːl naıt wɝk kjan jʊ stie sʈʃɹaŋ	and if it is an all night's work, can you stay strong
mɛk ʃʊoɹ jʊ av mʊoɹ dan wan kʌmbınieʃan	Make sure you have more than one combination (referring to different sexual positions)
fı ız aːl a mı fɹʌsʈʃɹieʃan]	to ease all of my frustrations

The next section presents the findings of the quantitative data collected. These are shown in the form of tables, charts and figures which display the number of artists, song titles, target audience and the vowels of interest.

Findings

Praat Data Presentation and Findings of F0, F1 and F2

The Praat data looks at vowels used in the same phonological environments, that is between or after the same consonant sounds in the syllables of the same rhyming words sung in lyrics by both male and female artists. These words occur in line final position for each of the song's chorus/chorus-verse in which they appear. A sample of the formant measurements of the male artists' vowels for F0, F1 and F2 values from the rhyming words of each song's chorus and target audience are shown in table 6.2. After which, the calculations of the findings are presented in table extracts, charts and diagrams. See Dawkins (2016) for the complete table.

Table 6.3 shows the mean of the formant frequency values relating to F0, F1 and F2 of the vowels produced by male artists when targeting both male and female audience members.

Table 6.2 Samples for the F0, F1, F2 and Vowel Duration Calculations for Male Dancehall Artists

Syllable Final Rhyming Vowel Word	Vowel	Male Artist Name and Song	Target Audience	F0 Value/Pitch Mean (Hz)	Vowel Duration from the Midpoint	F1 Value (Hz)	F2 Value (Hz)
Me [mi]	[i]	Buju Banton, "Too Bad"	Males	173.59	"	689.76	1701.40
Me [mi]	[i]	Buju Banton, "Wanna Be Loved"	Females	223.61	"	316.81	1966.37
Me [mi]	[i]	General Degree, "Mr. Riggi Up"	Males	87.01	0.032 s	1340.84	2579.55
Me [mi]	[i]	General Degree, "When I Hold You"	Females	332.17	0.032 s	686.57	1710.48
Man [man]	[a]	Beenie Man, "Boss Man"	Males	175.76	0.032 s	848.56	1497.64
Man [man]	[a]	Beenie Man, "Slam"	Females	226.68	0.032 s	758.51	1322.99
You [ʊ]	[o]	Shabba, "Whiney"	Males	76.08	0.032 s	746.49	2134.00
You [jʊ]	[o]	Shabba, "Pullu pum"	Females	376.80	"	818.69	1105.53

Variation on Vowel Pitch (F0): What Men Do When Targeting Men or Male-Like Issues, and Women or Female-Like Issues

The data in table 6.3 reveal that male artists produce a lower F0 value on all their vowels /i ɪ a ʊ/ in the rhyming syllables of their choruses that target men, and a higher F0 value on the same vowels in the same phonetic environment when targeting women. Figure 6.2 shows the mean formant frequency specifically for the mean F0 for male artists when targeting male and female audiences.

The data shows that the average pitch on the vowels /i ɪ a ʊ/ articulated in song choruses by male artists targeting men is lower than the average for the same vowels used to target females (150 Hz and 216 Hz, respectively). Thus, when compared to each male's average production on each selected vowel in the study, the findings reveal that men are more likely to have a lower pitch

Table 6.3 Mean F0, F1 and F2 Frequencies Produced on Selected Vowels by Male Dancehall Artists When Targeting Male and Female Audience Members

Formant	Target Audience	Vowels			
		/i/	/ɪ/	/a/	/ʊ/
F0	Males	155.86 Hz	152.52 Hz	160.81 Hz	133.20 Hz
	Females	231.01 Hz	228.57 Hz	193.70 Hz	211.54 Hz
F1	Males	621.22 Hz	788.61 Hz	813.57 Hz	847.53 Hz
	Females	464.27 Hz	670.62 Hz	773.38 Hz	767.68 Hz
F2	Males	1896.82 Hz	1927.53 Hz	1522.30 Hz	1729.04 Hz
	Females	1979.09 Hz	1801.307 Hz	1538.34 Hz	1721.25 Hz

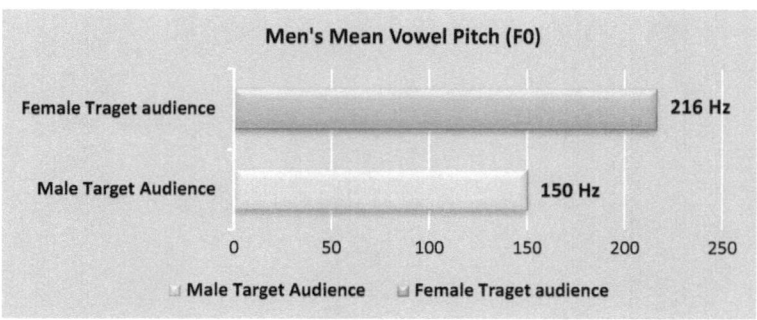

Figure 6.2 F0 mean values of vowels produced by male artists targeting men and women.

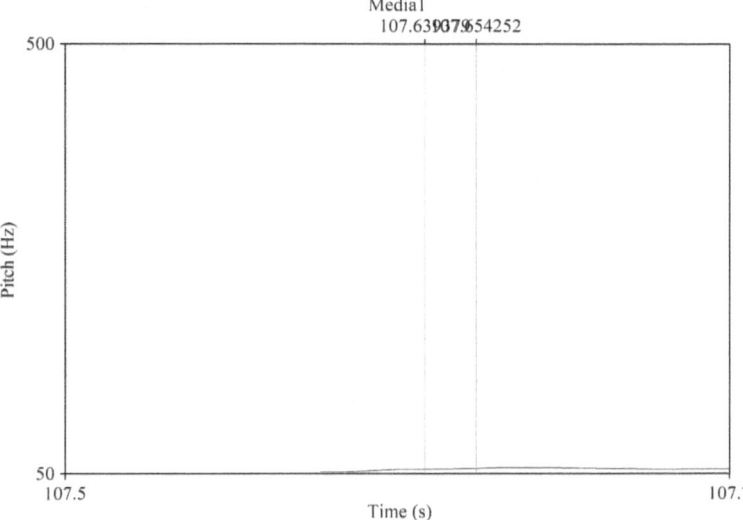

Figure 6.3 Capleton's [ɪ] vowel in [mɪ] "me" in the song "The More Dem Try" targeting men.

than their mean on their vowels when targeting men or male-like issues, and a higher pitch than their mean on their vowels in songs that target women or female-like issues. In addition, figures 6.3 and 6.4 (Praat pictures) show Fo variations based on gender of the target audience for male artist Capleton.

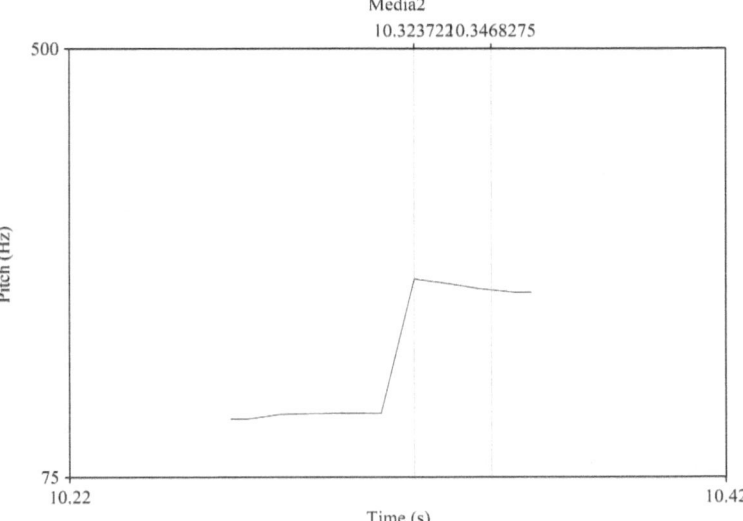

Figure 6.4 Capleton's [ɪ] vowel in [mɪ] "me" in the song "More Hot Girls" targeting females.

Figure 6.3 shows that Capleton's pitch (F0 value) of the high front unrounded lax vowel [ɪ] is 55.874 Hz. The vertical grid lines represent the midsection of the vowel that was measured; the penultimate horizontal line at the bottom between the grid vertical lines indicates the vowel pitch. This is very low compared to the vowel pitch demonstrated by him in figure 6.4, which shows that his pitch on the same vowel [ɪ] targeting females in the same phonetic environment has an F0 value of 270.99 Hz.

Variation of Vowel Height (F_1): What Men Do When Targeting Men or Male-Like Issues, and Women or Female-Like Issues

As seen in table 6.4, the male artists in the study produce higher F_1 values than their mean on their vowels /i ɪ a ʊ/ when targeting men or male-like issues, and produce these same vowels with lower F_1 values when targeting women and female-like issues. This therefore means these male artists lowered their vowels instead of raising them for men, and raised them instead of lowering the same vowels for women. This is indicated by the high F_1 values on the vowels produced in the songs that target men and the low F_1 values on the vowels in the songs that target women. A low F_1 value is indicative of a high vowel or vowels being produced higher in the oral cavity, while a high F_1 value is indicative of a low vowel, or vowels being produced lower in the oral cavity. Figure 6.5 shows the mean format values for the male artists for their songs targeting both male and female audiences.

The chart shows that male artists have an average F_1 value of 767 Hz when targeting a male audience, and a value of 668 Hz when targeting a female audience. Thus, men are more likely to produce their vowels lower in the oral cavity than higher when targeting men or male-like issues in their songs. Moreover, the chi-square test result for the F_1 data for the men proves to be statistically significant (see table 6.5).

Table 6.4 Average F_1 Frequencies Produced on Selected Vowels by Male Dancehall Artists When Targeting Male and Female Audience Members

Formant	Target Audience	Vowels			
		/i/	/ɪ/	/a/	/ʊ/
F_1	Males	621.22 Hz	788.61 Hz	813.57 Hz	847.53 Hz
	Females	464.27 Hz	670.62 Hz	773.38 Hz	767.68 Hz

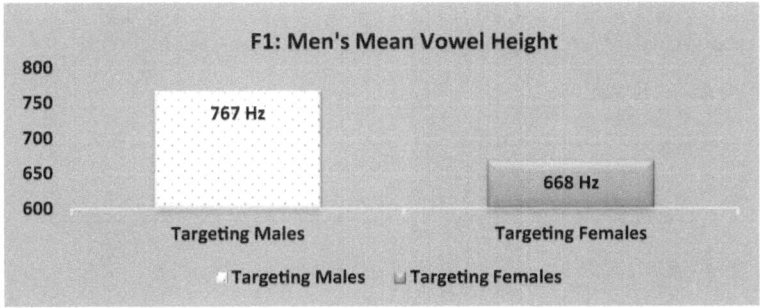

Figure 6.5 F1 mean values of vowels produced by male artists targeting men and women.

Table 6.5 Chi-Square Test for F1 Frequencies Produced on Selected Vowels by Male Dancehall Artists When Targeting Male and Female Audience Members

			Results			
	I	ɪ		A	ʊ	Row Total
Targeting men	621 (589.31) [1.70]	789 (792.98) [0.02]		814 (861.96) [2.67]	848 (827.75) [0.50]	3072
Targeting women	464 (495.69) [2.03]	671 (667.02) [0.02]		773 (725.04) [3.17]	676 (696.25) [0.59]	2584
Column total	1085	1460		1587	1524	5656 (grand total)

Note: The table provides the following information: the observed cell totals, the expected cell totals (in parentheses) and the chi-square statistic for each cell (in square brackets). The chi-square statistic is 10.7013. The p-value is .013456. The result is significant at $p<.05$.

Variation of Vowel Formants F2: What Men Do When Targeting Men or Male-Like Issues, and Women or Female-Like Issues

Men produced a lower F2 value on two out of four of their rhyming vowels; this indicates that these songs are produced more front, since F2 correlates with vowel frontness (see table 6.6). Half the songs produced by males are produced with these vowels being more front and half more back, irrespective of the target audience. This pattern is quite different from what was shown for both F0 and F1, and seems to depict that there is less variation with men's F2 when targeting either men or women. Men are more likely to vary their pitch and vowel height rather than front their vowels when targeting a specific audience. Figure 6.6 shows the mean F2

Table 6.6 Average F2 Frequencies Produced on Selected Vowels by Male Dancehall Artists When Targeting Male and Female Audience Members

Formant	Target Audience	Vowels			
		/i/	/ɪ/	/a/	/ʊ/
F2	Males	1896.82 Hz	1927.53 Hz	1522.30 Hz	1729.04 Hz
	Females	1979.09 Hz	1801.307 Hz	1538.339 Hz	1721.25 Hz

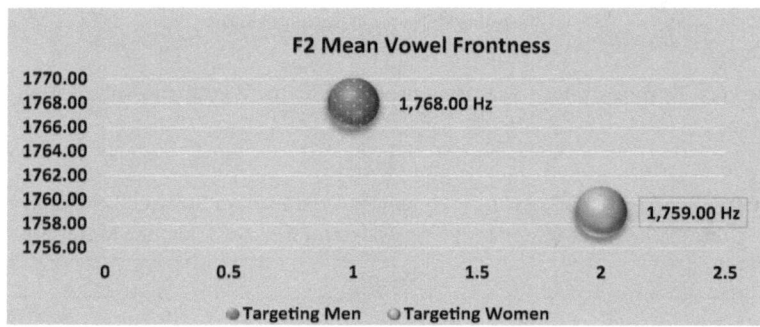

Figure 6.6 F2 mean values of vowels produced by male artists targeting men and women.

value for the male dancehall artists when targeting men and women, and the difference in the F2 values is only 9 Hz.

Milroy and Milroy (1985) state that women in their Belfast study tended to lead in the fronting of vowels, while men lead in the lowering and

Table 6.7 Chi-Square Test for F2 Frequencies Produced on Selected Vowels by Male Dancehall Artists When Targeting Male and Female Audience Members

	Results				
	I	ɪ	a	ʊ	Row Total
Targeting men	1897 (1943.08) [1.09]	1928 (1869.39) [1.84]	1522 (1534.01) [0.09]	1729 (1729.52) [0.00]	7076
Targeting women	1979 (1932.92) [1.10]	1801 (1859.61) [1.85]	1538 (1525.99) [0.09]	1721 (1720.48) [0.00]	7039
Column total	3876	3729	3060	3450	14115 (grand total)

Note: The chi-square statistic is 6.0653. The p-value is .108475. The result is not significant at $p < .05$.

backing of vowels. It can be deduced based on the data presented in this study that the men in dancehall lead in the backing of vowel production in the choruses of their songs irrespective of the gender of the target audience. The chi-square test result shows that the F2 data for the men is statistically insignificant (see table 6.7).

Although the chi-square test in this instance is insignificant, there is evidence of vowel variation among the men as it relates to their F2 values and specific target audience.

Praat Analysis for the Female Dancehall Artists

This section examines the Praat data for the female dancehall artists in the study. A sample of the calculations for these artists' vowels for F0, F1 and F2 are provided in table 6.8. In addition, the table displays the target audience and the words in which the vowels appear. See Dawkins (2016) for the complete table.

Table 6.9 shows the mean of the formant frequency values relating to F0, F1 and F2 of the vowels produced by female artists when targeting both male and female audience members.

Variation on Vowel Pitch (F0): What Women Do When Targeting Men or Male-Like Issues, and Women and Female-Like Issues

The data in table 6.9 reveal that female artists produced a higher pitch average on all their vowels /i ɪ a ʊ/ in the rhyming syllables of their songs' choruses that target women, and a lower pitch on the same vowels in the same phonetic environment when targeting men (241Hz and 179 Hz, respectively). Figure 6.8 shows the mean values of vowels produced by female artists targeting men and women.

Figures 6.8 and 6.9 show a Praat picture of Lady Saw's articulation of the vowel [ɪ] used in the rhyming words in a chorus that targets a male audience.

Figure 6.8 shows that Lady Saw's pitch (F0 value) of the high front unrounded lax vowel [ɪ] is 95.31 Hz. This is lower than her pitch for the same vowel used in the same phonological environment in her song "Dem No Like Me" targeted at women, which is seen in figure 6.9. This shows that Lady Saw's pitch (F0 value) of the vowel [ɪ] is 433.14 Hz.

Table 6.8 Samples of F0, F1, F2 and Vowel Duration Calculations for Female Dancehall Artists

Syllable Final Rhyming Vowel Word	Vowel	Female Artist Name and Song	Target Audience[a]	F0 Value/Pitch Mean (Hz)	Vowel Duration Midpoint (Hz)	F1 Value (Hz)	F2 Value (Hz)
Me [mi]	[i]	Lady Saw, "It's Raining"	Males	99.87	0.032 s	479.10	2134.92
Me [mi]	[i]	Lady Saw, "I Don't Care (IDC)"	Females	236.71	"	415.57	2300.57
Me [mi]	[i]	Macka Diamond, "Gwaan Bad"	Males	65.04	0.032 s	588.30	1711.68
Me [mi]	[i]	Macka Diamond, "Don't Talk to Mi"	Females	215.00	"	438.60	2353.011
Man [man]	[a]	Macka Diamond, "Ugly Man"	Males	310.28	0.032 s	966.26	
Man [man]	[a]	Macka Diamond, "Want a Man"	Females	412.63	"	821.62	1464.66
You [ju]	[o]	Ce'cile, "If Yu"	Males	63.13	0.032s	279.15	
You [ju]	[o]	Ce'cile, "Love Him Fi Yu"	Females	179.72	"	622.68	2005.46

[a] "Males" is the dependent variable, and "Females" the independent variable.

Table 6.9 Average F0, F1 and F2 Frequencies Produced by Female Dancehall Artists When Targeting Male and Female Audiences

Formants	Gender	Vowels			
		/i/	/ɪ/	/a/	/ʊ/
F0	Males	164.74 Hz	135.48 Hz	237.78 Hz	210.36 Hz
	Females	206.09 Hz	216.59 Hz	251.92 Hz	294.46 Hz
F1	Males	461.21 Hz	773.35 Hz	965.25 Hz	605.91 Hz
	Females	449.17 Hz	542.59 Hz	1063.84 Hz	579.64 Hz
F2	Males	2168.39 Hz	2145.93 Hz	1519.01 Hz	1531.64 Hz
	Females	2277.87 Hz	2098.48 Hz	1597.12 Hz	1903.03 Hz

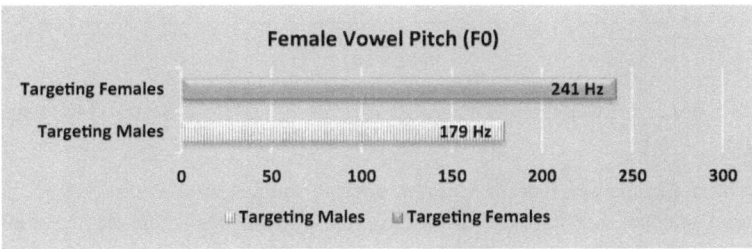

Figure 6.7 F0 mean values of vowels produced by female artists targeting men and women.

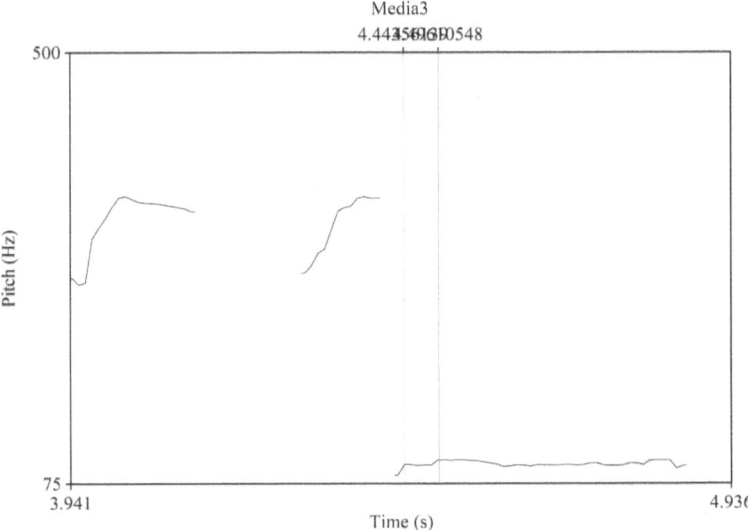

Figure 6.8 Lady Saw's [ɪ] vowel in [mɪ] "me" in the song "Ninja Bike" targeting males.

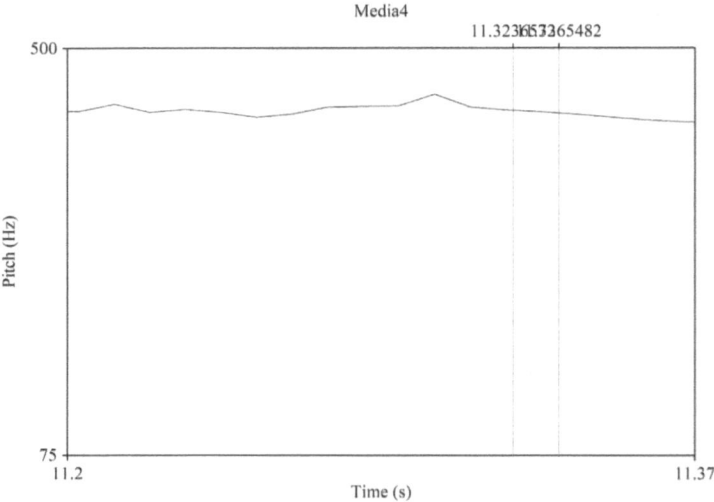

Figure 6.9 Lady Saw's [ɪ] vowel in [mɪ] "me" in the song "Dem No Like Mi" targeting females.

Table 6.10 Chi-Square Test for F0 Frequencies Produced on Selected Vowels by Female Dancehall Artists When Targeting Male and Female Audience Members

	Results				
	I	ɪ	A	ʊ	Row Total
Targeting men	165 (161.62) [0.07]	135 (153.35) [2.19]	238 (213.47) [2.82]	210 (219.56) [0.42]	748
Targeting Women	206 (209.38) [0.05]	217 (198.65) [1.69]	252 (276.53) [2.18]	294 (284.44) [0.32]	969
Column total	371	352	490	504	1717 (grand total)

Note: The table provides the following information: the observed cell totals, the expected cell totals (in parentheses) and the chi-square statistic for each cell (in brackets). The chi-square statistic is 9.7492. The p-value is .020822. The result is significant at $p<.05$.

The chi-square test conducted on the F0 data for the female artists when targeting male and female audience members proves to be statistically significant (see table 6.10).

Variation of Vowel Formants F1: What Women Do When Targeting Men or Male-Like Issues, and Women and Female-Like Issues

The data analysis in table 6.11 reveals that women tend to raise their vowels when targeting women or female-like issues, and tend to lower their vowels when targeting men and male-like issues. What is interesting to note is that this was the case for 3/4 /i ɪ ʊ/ of the selected vowels /i ɪ a ʊ/. The

Table 6.11 Average F1 Frequencies Produced by Female Dancehall Artists When Targeting Male and Female Audiences

Formant	Gender	Vowels			
		/i/	/ɪ/	/a/	/ʊ/
F1	Males	461.21 Hz	773.35 Hz	965.25 Hz	605.91 Hz
	Females	449.17 Hz	542.59 Hz	1063.84 Hz	579.64 Hz

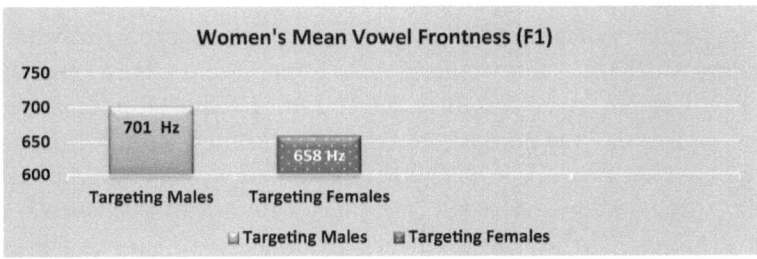

Figure 6.10 F1 mean values of vowels produced by female artists targeting men and women.

average F1 value for [a] was actually lower in production when targeted at women compared to its use in songs targeted at men. The vowel carried an average value of 9652.25 Hz when targeting males and an average value of 1063.84 Hz when targeting females. The higher the F1 value, the lower the vowel in the oral cavity, and the lower the F1 value, the higher the vowel. Figure 6.10 shows the mean for the female F1 values for all their vowels targeting men and women.

The chi-square test shows that the F1 findings for the female artists in the study are statistically significant (see table 6.12).

Table 6.12 Chi-Square Test for F1 Frequencies Produced on Selected Vowels by Female Dancehall Artists When Targeting Male and Female Audience Members

	Results				
	I	I	A	ʊ	Row Total
Targeting men	461 (469.22) [0.14]	773 (678.56) [13.14]	965 (1045.69) [6.23]	606 (611.53) [0.05]	2805
Targeting women	449 (440.78) [0.15]	543 (637.44) [13.99]	1063 (982.31) [6.63]	580 (574.47) [0.05]	2635
Column total	910	1316	2028	1186	5440 (grand total)

Note: The chi-square statistic is 40.3884. The *p*-value is <00.00001. The result is significant at *p*<.05.

Variation of Vowel Formants F2: What Women Do When Targeting Men or Male-Like Issues, and Women and Female-Like Issues

The data reveal that female dancehall artists tend to have higher F2 values on their vowels when targeting women, and lower F2 values on the same when targeting men (see table 6.13). Therefore, women tend to produce these vowels more front when targeting women and more back when targeting men. Figure 6.11 presents the mean F2 values for female artists' songs that target male and females audiences.

The data pattern displayed in figure 6.11 goes hand in hand with the literature which states that women tend to front their vowels, whether these vowels are back or not (Chambers and Hardwick 1986; Milroy and Milroy 1985). Unlike the literature which states that women tend to front their vowels more than men do (Chambers and Hardwick 1986; Milroy and Milroy 1985; Gordon and Heath 1998), this data reveals that women also back their vowels when targeting men and male-like issues in Jamaican dancehall music.

The chi-square test for F2 data for the female artists shows that the findings are statistically significant (see table 6.14).

Table 6.13 Average F2 Frequencies Produced by Female Dancehall Artists When Targeting Male and Female Audiences

Formant	Gender	Vowels			
		/i/	/ɪ/	/a/	/ʊ/
F2	Males	2168.39 Hz	2145.93 Hz	1519.01 Hz	1531.64 Hz
	Females	2277.87 Hz	2098.48 Hz	1597.12 Hz	1903.03 Hz

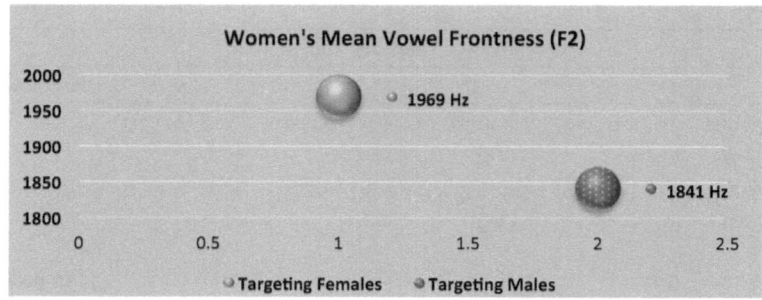

Figure 6.11 F2 mean values of vowels produced by female artists targeting men and women.

Table 6.14 Chi-Square Test for F2 Frequencies Produced on Selected Vowels by Female Dancehall Artists When Targeting Male and Female Audience Members

	Results				
	I	ɪ	A	ʊ	Row Total
Targeting men	2168 (2148.47) [0.18]	2146 (2050.85) [4.41]	1519 (1505.76) [0.12]	1532 (1659.92) [9.86]	7365
Targeting women	2278 (2297.53) [0.17]	2098 (2193.15) [4.13]	1597 (1610.24) [0.11]	1903 (1775.08) [9.22]	7876
Column total	4446	4244	3116	3435	15241 (grand total)

Note: The chi-square statistic is 28.186. The *p*-value is < 0.00001. The result is significant at *p* < .05.

Presentation of the Same Song Sung by Both a Male and Female Artist

Following are the lyrics and Praat values for a song performed by a male artist (Gyptian) and sung over (covered) by a female artist (Lady Saw) on the same rhythm, using similar lyrics and the same vocal styles in terms of the delivery of the melody.

Example 3: [ʊol jʊ] "Hold You" by Gyptian

Chorus 1

[gjæl mɪ waːn fi ʊol jʌ   Girl I just want to hold you
pʌt mɪ aɹmz ɹait aɹoun jʌ   Put my arms all around you
gjal jʌ gɪv mɪ dɪ taɪtɛs ʊol mɪ ɛva gɛt ɪn a maɪ laɪf   Girl you give me the tightest hole (literally means "hole" referring to vaginal entrance) I have ever gotten in my life

gjal mɪ dʒʌs waːn fɪ skwiz jʌ   Girl I want to squeeze you
pʊt mɪ tɪŋ aːl aɹoun jʌ   Put my thing right around you
gjal jʌ gɪv mi dɪ taɪtɛs ʊol mɪ ɛva gɛt ɪnæ maɪ laɪf]   Girl you give me the tightest hold I have ever gotten in my life

Example 4: Lady Saw's Cover of Gyptian's Song

Chorus 1

[bwaɪ mɪ glad sɛ mɪ ʊol jʌ   Boy I'm glad that I hold you
juz dɪ pʊsi kantʃɹʊol jʌ   Use my pussy to control you
bwaɪ jʌ gɪv mi dɪ bɪgɛs wʊd mɪ ɛva gɛt ɪn a maɪ laɪf   Boy you give me the biggest wood (literally penis) I have ever gotten in my life

Table 6.15 Praat Values for the /ʊ/ Vowel

Gyptian				Lady Saw			
Chorus Line	Vowel	F1 Value	F2 Value	Chorus Line	Vowel	F1 Value	F2 Value
Line 1	/ʊ/	666.528 Hz	1478.456 Hz	Line 1	/ʊ/	494.730 Hz	1183.642 Hz
Line 2	/ʊ/	784.194 Hz	1759.485 Hz	Line 2	/ʊ/	662.234 Hz	2396.693 Hz
Line 4	/ʊ/	833.100 Hz	1678.221 Hz	Line 4	/ʊ/	571.687 Hz	1636.244 Hz
Line 5	/ʊ/	771.764 Hz	1783.366 Hz	Line 5	/ʊ/	407.302 Hz	1676.083 Hz
Mean	/ʊ/	763.893 Hz	1674.882 Hz	**Mean**	/ʊ/	533.9875 Hz	1723.1655 Hz

Table 6.16 Praat Values for the /aɪ/ Vowel

	Gyptian				Lady Saw		
Chorus Line	Vowel	F1 Value	F2 Value	Chorus Line	Vowel	F1 Value	F2 Value
Line 3	/aɪ/	856.872 Hz	1798.621 Hz	Line 3	/aɪ/	600.202 Hz	2182.810 Hz
Line 6	/aɪ/	506.505 Hz	1628.27 Hz	Line 6	/aɪ/	1039.934 Hz	2043.558 Hz
Mean	/aɪ/	681.885 Hz	1713.445 Hz	**Mean**	/aɪ/	820.068 Hz	2113.184 Hz

bwaɪ mɪ nɛva bɪliv jʌ	Boy I never believed you
wɛn jʌ tɛl mɪ sɛ mɪ wʊda nid jʌ	When you told me that I would have needed you
bwaɪ jʌ gɪv mɪ dɪ bɪgɛs wʊd mɪ ɛva gɛt ina maɪ laɪf]	Boy you give me the biggest wood I have ever gotten in my life

Praat Values and Analysis

Table 6.15 contains the formant (F1 and F2) values for Gyptian's and Lady Saw's high back vowels taken from the chorus of "Hold You".

The back vowels for Gyptian's F1 value have a mean of 763.893 Hz compared to Lady Saw's high back vowels whose mean value is 533.987 Hz. This shows that her production of [ʊ] is higher than his. As it relates to their F2 values of the same vowel, Gyptian's has a lower mean of 1674.882 Hz compared to Lady Saw's 1723.1655. This indicates that his production is more back and retracted than hers which is more front.

Table 6.16 contains the formant (F1 and F2) values for Gyptian's and Lady Saw's high front vowels taken from the chorus of "Hold You".

When examining their production of the front diphthong [aɪ], Gyptian's F1 mean value is 681.885 Hz compared to Lady Saw's 820.068 Hz. The F2 values show that Gyptian produces the front diphthong more back and retracted than Lady Saw, showing values of 17143.445 Hz and 2113.184 Hz, respectively. The data reveals that the female artist (Lady Saw) is more likely to front her vowels, while Gyptian is more likely to produce his vowels more back and retracted in the same song, using the same or similar lyrics. This once again shows consistency with previous works carried out in the literature by various linguists such as Gordon and Heath (1998): women in the study tend to lead in the fronting of vowels, unlike men, who are more inclined to lead in the backing of vowels.

Summary

The findings consistently show that men and women demonstrate a phonetic style as it relates to the variation of vowels in the choruses of their songs. The data also portrays that the audience of the artists acts as a catalyst that sways these vowel variations produced by the artists. Both men and women demonstrate and manipulate different acoustic styles when addressing a specific target audience.

Most importantly, both male and female artists use a higher pitch when targeting female audiences or topics, and a lower pitch when addressing male audiences or topics. It was also observed that they both tend to raise their vowels when targeting a female audience and lower their vowels when targeting male audience members. Female artists tended to show more variations on their vowels than the men as it relates to their F2 (vowel frontness) productions. The findings revealed that women fronted their vowels more than men, and they did so more specifically when targeting female audience members.

Discussion

Style as a Phonetic Component of Jamaican Dancehall Music

After careful examination of the data, a clear pattern emerges that indicates that Jamaican dancehall music has a unique phonetic pattern, which I refer to as a phonetic style. This can be determined based on the results of the data findings, which consistently reveal that male and female dancehall artists demonstrate a specific linguistic style in the delivery of their songs' choruses. Earlier I mentioned that style is defined as speakers' responses to their audience; speakers design their talk for their audience (Bell 1984, 2001). In the findings, it was observed that artists will vary the formant frequencies (F_0, F_1 and F_2) of their vowels when targeting a specific type of audience. This, therefore, reveals that the artists' linguistic style is used in response to an intended audience, whether it be an addressee or referee. Thus, the artists' acoustic styles are audience driven. That is, they take into account the hearers in the design of their lyrics. This corresponds with Bell's (1984, 2001) argument which states that persons respond mainly to other persons, and speakers take most account of hearers in designing their talk. This brings me to the conclusion that although the gender of the artists is of importance, the gender of their intended target audience is even more significant. This revelation shows that the phonetic feature which is the variation of the vowels is influenced by the gender of the audience being targeted.

As it pertains to contexts in which these gender-influenced features occur – in other words, why did the artists say it this way on this occasion? – based on the findings, the artists will use a particular linguistic feature (a phonetic style which involves the variation of formant frequencies) when addressing or referring to a particular gender or a topic related to a particular gender.

Stylistic Variations on Pitch (F0), Height (F1) and Frontness (F2) Are Audience Driven

Moreover, what is significant in the findings is the phonetic style (vowel variation) that was observed in the artists' production of F0, F1 and F2. Both male and female artists used a higher pitch than their average on vowels that were in rhyming syllables targeted at women and a lower pitch on those that targeted men. It was also revealed that both men and women tended to raise their vowels (produced them higher in the oral cavity) when targeting women and lowered their vowels (produced them lower in the oral cavity) when targeting men. In addition, the findings show that female artists are more likely to front their vowels when targeting women and to back their vowels when targeting men; in other words, the women in the study fronted their vowels more than the men, and women fronted 70 per cent of their vowels, while the men fronted 53 per cent of their vowels. Devonish (2006) postulates that the vowels located in rhyming syllables in dancehall songs receive more stress (heavily emphasized). Other research, such as Fry's (1958), has found that in English languages, pitch is said to be the strongest cue in determining whether a syllable is stressed. I argue that these rhyming vowels in dancehall lyrics are phonetically important because they carry specific cues related to a specific social identity, in this case, gender.

It appears that there are certain social aspects that are associated with particular linguistic norms. Holmes (1997) states that sounds are inherently meaningless but can derive social significance from their distributional patterns, becoming associated with the culturally recognized attributes of the social groups who use them most frequently. This then leads me to the examination of the likely social factors of the gender-based variation of the phonetic features. Style appears to be to be a significant factor; the artists are establishing gendered identity through style, the phonetic style of dancehall.

Although the data revealed that the variation of vowel pitch and vowel frontness in the case of the men in the study are not as statistically significant as that of the women, it may be significant in the sense that because men are more linguistically secure as it relates to their voice pitch and F2 vowel productions in dancehall music, they are less likely to show much variation from their average formant frequencies. This may be due to the fact that men's social position in dancehall is more secure than that of women, whose position in that musical arena is less secure. Therefore, linguistic variation of the vowels for the women is more prevalent. According to

Trudgill (1974), "the social position of women in our society is less secure than that of men and subordinate to that of men. It is therefore more necessary for women to secure and signal their social status linguistically and in other ways" (183). Trudgill goes on to say that women are more aware of this type of signal. Therefore, women in dancehall may be more likely to show linguistic variation because they are aware of their social positions within this genre of music.

Establishing Identity through Style

Men to Men and Men to Women

The men and women of dancehall project different identities (in keeping with audience accommodation and identity projection) through their manipulation of acoustic and prosodic features on the vowels [i ɪ a ʊ] used in their rhyming syllables. They do this by modifying their voice quality. Based on the data, it appears that a low pitch is affiliated with maleness or male linguistic identity, and/or issues of masculinity, associated with sex and gun violence, which, according to the experts of the genre (Hope 2010; Stanley Niaah 2010), are things on which dancehall music lyrics focus. Pitch as a linguistic resource, carries meaning such as gender identity, and a low pitch is identifiable with men (Yuasa 2008). In songs where men target women, men use a higher pitch on the vowels of those rhyming syllables; it appears that a high pitch is associated with the feminine gender, or signals female identity.

Women to Women and Women to Men

The women also depict these behaviours. The female dancehall artists use a higher pitch on 75 per cent of their vowels in songs in which the rhyming syllables target women and female-like issues. Female artists raised their vowels in 65 per cent of these syllables, and fronted their vowels in these same syllables in 70 per cent of the songs. As it relates to women targeting men, the opposite occurs. The female artists used a lower pitch, lowered their vowels more and produced these vowels more back than their average production in the rhyming syllables of their songs' choruses. Again, there is a unique linguistic pattern as it relates to the manipulation of the acoustic and prosodic phonetic features. Women demonstrate a specific style on their rhyming syllable, depending on the gender of their target audience.

Personal versus Enacted Identity

Earlier in the chapter, we looked at two types of identities. These are personal and enacted identity. Personal identity is "who I am" and enacted is "who I am for others". Women in dancehall, like the men in this musical genre, are performers of the linguistic style(s) that are associated with this genre of music. Female artists in the study lower their pitch, and produce their vowels lower and more back in their rhyming scheme to identify with this culture, which is traditionally linked to masculinity. Although women are outnumbered by the men in dancehall, and are less secure, they are also able to be performers of masculinity within this musical genre. Connell (1995) warns that masculinity is not just a property of men. Therefore, women are also performers and consumers of masculinity. I argue that the women are establishing an enacted identity, that is, performing a role that is identified as not their own, but using a style that will associate/identify them with the genre of music in which they are a part, a musical genre which is male dominated and is associated with power and prestige.

Conclusion

Jamaican dancehall music has unique linguistic styles that are associated with the genre. These linguistic styles are audience driven and are correlated with acoustic phonetic variations (variation of vowel formant frequencies). These styles are demonstrated by both male and female artists of the genre. These linguistic styles also form the unique rhyming patterns/schemes in each song's chorus. As it relates to the variation of vowels, the pitch (F_0) of the vowels, the raising and lowering of the vowels (F_1), and the fronting and backing of the vowels (F_2) are all influenced by the gender of the target audience. Low pitch is identified with masculinity or male audiences, and high pitch is associated with femaleness/femininity or topics related to both concepts. The variation of the vowels is quite significant, and although the gender of the artists is of importance, the gender of the target audience is even more significant. This genre of music encapsulates the sociolinguistic theory of style to establish gendered identities within the genre.

Notes

1. A sound selector is an individual who "selects" the music records to play at a dance, party or any event being celebrated with recorded music. In other cultures such as America, the sound selector may be referred to as the MC or disc jockey (DJ). These individuals keep the crowd engaged by being very

vocal about their specific musical selections. In dancehall music, selectors are well-known figures and are instrumental in aiding new artists in finding their audience by playing their music at dances and hyping them up to the crowd.

2. Fundamental frequency is the lowest frequency of a periodic wave.

3. The standard settings for the spectrogram analysis window used for the measurements in Praat for calculating F0, F1 and F2 are set at 50 Hz–500 Hz, with a window length of 54.005, a dynamic range of 70.0 decibels (db) and a spectrum view range of 5000.0 Hz. All the audio versions of the songs collected for the study were converted to WAVE files because this quality is easier to read in the Praat programme.

4. Filters are used to define the highest and lowest frequencies of interest in the signal by letting audio above a certain frequency pass (high-pass filter) or audio below a certain frequency pass (low-pass filter). Anything outside those limits is attenuated. They are also called low-cut or high-cut filters, but the function is the same (Sound on Sound 2009).

References

Baldwin, John R., and Michael L. Hetch. 1995. "The Layered Perspective on Cultural (In) tolerance(s): the Roots of a Multi-disciplinary Approach to (In) tolerance". In *Intercultural Communication Theory*, edited by R.L. Wiseman, 59–91. California: Sage.

Baranowski, Maciej. 2013. "Sociophonetics". In *The Oxford Handbook of Sociolinguistics*, edited by R. Bayley, R. Cameron and C. Lucas, 403–24.Oxford: Oxford University Press.

———. 2007. *Phonological Variation and Change in the Dialect of Charleston, South Carolina*. Durham: Duke University Press.

Bell, Alan. 1984. "Language Style as Audience Design". *Language in Society* 13: 145–204.

———. 2001. "Back in Style: Reworking Audience Design". In *Style and Sociolinguistic Variation*, edited by Penelope Eckert and John R. Rickford, 139–69. Cambridge and New York: Cambridge University Press.

Boberg, Charles. 2005. "The Canadian Shift in Montreal". *Language Variation and Change* 17: 133–54.

———. 2008. "Regional Phonetic Differentiation in Standard Canadian English". *Journal of English Linguistics* 36: 129–54.

Chambers, Jack K., and Margaret F. Hardwick. 1986. "Comparative Sociolinguistics of Sound Change in Canadian English". *English World-Wide* 7: 23–44.

Connell, Raewyn W. 1995. *Masculinities*. Berkeley and Los Angeles: University of California Press.

Coupland, Nikolas. 2007. *Style: Language Variation and Identity*. New York: Cambridge University Press.

Dawkins, Nickesha. 2016. "Gender as a Sociophonetic Issue in Jamaican Dancehall Lyrics". PhD diss., University of the West Indies, Mona.

———. 2009. "Gender-based Vowel Use in Jamaican Dancehall Lyrics". *Sargasso* I: 95–114.

———. 2013. "She Se Dis, Him Se Dat: Examining Gender-based Vowel Use in Jamaican Dancehall". In *International Reggae: Current and Future Trends in Jamaican Popular Music*, edited by Donna P. Hope, 124–66. Kingston: Pelican.

Devonish, Hubert. 2006. "On the Status of Diphthongs in Jamaican: Mr. Vegas Pronounces". In *Caribbean Creole Languages*, edited by Hazel Simmons McDonald and Ian Robertson, 72–95. Kingston: The University of the West Indies Press.

Dinkin, Aaron. 2009. "Dialect Boundaries and Phonological Change in Upstate New York". PhD diss., University of Pennsylvania.

Eckert, Penelope. 2004. "California Vowels". Accessed 15 April 2014. http://www.stanford.edu/~eckert/vowels.html.

———. 2005. "Variation, Convention, and Social Meaning". Paper presented at the Annual Meeting of the Linguistic Society of America, Oakland, California.

Fought, Carmen. 1999. "A Majority Sound Change in a Minority Community: /u/-Fronting in Chicano English". *Journal of Sociolinguistics* 3: 5–23.

Fry, Dennis. 1958. "Experiments in the Perception of Stress". *Language and Speech* 1: 126–52.

Gordon, Matthew, and Jeffery Heath. 1998. "Sex, Sound, Symbolism, and Sociolinguistics". *Current Anthropology* 39 (4): 421–49.

Holmes, Janet. 1997. "Setting New Standards: Sound Changes and Gender in New Zealand English". *English World-Wide* 18 (1): 107–42.

Hope, Donna. 2006. *Inna Di Dancehall: Popular Culture and the Politics of Identity in Jamaica*. Kingston: University of the West Indies Press.

———. 2010. *Man Vybes: Masculinities in the Jamaican Dancehall*. Kingston: Ian Randle Publisher.

Joseph, John. 2004. *Language and Identity: National, Ethnic and Religious*. New York: Palgrave McMillan.

Labov, William. 2001. *Principles of Linguistic Change. Volume 2: Social Factors*. London: Blackwell.

Le Page, Robert, and Andree Tabouret-Keller. 1985. *Acts of Identity: Creole-based Approaches to Language and Ethnicity*. New York: Cambridge University Press.

Meade, Rocky. 2001. *Acquisition of Jamaican Phonology*. Netherlands: Foris.

Milroy, James, and Lesley Milroy. 1985. "Linguistic Change, Social Network, and Speaker Innovation". *Journal of Linguistics* 21 (2): 339–84.

Sound On Sound. 2009. "What Are Filters and What Do They Do?" Accessed 31 October 2012. https://www.soundonsound.com/sos/jul09/articles/qa0709_2.htm.

Stanley Niaah, Sonjah. 2010. *Dancehall: From Slave Ship to Ghetto*. Ottawa: University of Ottawa Press.

Torgersen, Eivind. 2002. "Phonological Distribution of the FOOT vowel, /ʊ/, in Young People's Speech in South-Eastern British English". *Reading Working Papers in Linguistics* 6: 25–38.

Trudgill, Peter. 1974. *The Social Differentiation of English in Norwich*. Cambridge: Cambridge University Press.
———. 1983. "Acts of Conflicting Identity: The Sociolinguistics of British Pop-song Pronunciation". In *On Dialect: Social and Geographical Perspectives*, edited by P. Trudgill, 141–60. Oxford: Blackwell.
Van der Meer, Wim. 2015. "PRAAT Manual for Musicologist". Accessed 22 October 2015. https://wimvandermeer.wordpress.com/praat-manual-for-musicologists/.
Ward, Michael. 2003. "Portland Dialect Study: The Fronting of /ow, u, uw/ in Portland, Oregon". PhD diss., Portland State University.
Yuasa, Ikuko Patricia. 2008. *Culture and Gender of Voice and Pitch: A Sociophonetic Comparison of the Japanese and Americans*. Oakville, CT: Equinox.

Chapter 7

Language Use in Peter Ram's Soca Performances

GUYANNE WILSON

Introduction

Although the Caribbean region is musically rich, to date, few studies have been undertaken which examine the musics of the Caribbean from a linguistic standpoint. The exception to this has been reggae, and to some extent dancehall, though the latter still receives a mostly sociological treatment. Yet the musics of the Caribbean offer rich fodder for linguistic study: they are performed in the full range of Caribbean languages (zouk, for example, is sung in various French Creoles, while chutney is performed in a mix of Trinidad English Creole and Bhojpuri); they show evidence of extensive code-mixing and code-switching; they are a repository of dying languages and other historical language sources (consider, for example, retentions of Trinidad French Creole in the island folk songs); and they capture changes in language ideologies over time (see Farquharson 2017). Music, especially singing, in the Caribbean has been and continues to be used as a means of rebellion and resistance (Lengemann 2012) and of shaping individual, national and regional identity. In this study, I look at language use in one of the relatively new, rapidly spreading and exceedingly popular Caribbean musical genres, soca, a musical genre which originated in Trinidad. Specifically, I look at language use by Barbadian soca star Peter Ram and explore how his language use reflects his identity both as a Barbadian and as a performer of soca music.

In the next section, I introduce soca music, its origins and its functions in contemporary Caribbean society. This is followed by an overview of the language situation in Barbados and in Trinidad, along with major features of the English-derived Creoles spoken on each island. From here, there will be a discussion of the key literature on language use in music. The third section presents the data used and the methods applied in the analysis of the data. The results of this analysis, starting with an analysis of Peter Ram's speech, are then presented in the following section. In the final section, conclusions are drawn and suggestions for future work are given. The results show that Peter Ram's language use over time mirrors his identity as a soca artiste from Barbados.

Background

Soca Music

Soca is a Trinidadian and Tobagonian musical form most often associated with the islands' pre-Lenten Carnival celebrations. It is also featured in carnivals on other islands and those hosted by Trinidadians and other Caribbean people living in the diaspora. Soca singers release new songs each year, hoping to win over listeners and to attain either the Road March title, for the song played most frequently during the parade of the bands on Carnival Monday and Tuesday, or the title of Soca Monarch champion.

The term *soca* was first introduced in the 1970s. According to some accounts, the word was first coined by Trinidadian singer Ras Shorty I (Garfield Blackman) as a blend of the word *calypso* and *kah*, the first letter of the Indian alphabet (Guilbault 2007). Other accounts say that the word arose as a blend between *soul* and *calypso*. Whichever account is true, soca distinguishes itself from calypso lyrically and musically. Whereas calypso is social commentary addressing a range of social issues, soca has become more synonymous with party music, and its lyrics focus mostly on the listener's enjoyment. In terms of tempo, soca is faster paced than its forerunner. Over time, soca has emerged as the more popular of the two genres, enjoying far more media coverage and greater government and private investment. This is perhaps best evidenced by the fact that the 2019 Calypso Monarch was awarded TT$700,000, but the winner of the 2019 Soca Monarch received TT$1,000,000.

Peter Ram

This chapter focuses on language use in the music of widely acclaimed Barbadian singer and songwriter Peter Ram (born Peter Wiggins). Caribbean music blogger Stefan Walcott (2013) notes that Peter Ram's musical career took off in the 1980s as a dancehall/dub artiste. However, Peter Ram soon crossed over into ragga soca and is more widely known for his performances in this genre. In 2015, "his song 'All Ah' We' took Crop Over's 'triple crown,' winning the titles of Stag Jam, Party Monarch and Tune of De Crop, the latter for having his song played throughout the entire parade route on Kadooment Day, Crop Over's climactic grand parade" (Serwer 2016). His 2016 hit "Good Morning" was lauded for addressing Barbados and Crop Over directly (Serwer 2016). In addition to his success in Barbados, Peter Ram is a regular fixture at other regional carnivals, notably Trinidad Carnival.

Language in Barbados and Trinidad

In Barbados and in Trinidad, as in the majority of the English-speaking Caribbean, standardized varieties of English are spoken alongside an English-lexifier Creole. This Creole is the first language of the majority of people on the island (Devonish and Thomas 2012). Caribbean Creoles exhibit a high degree of variability, often described on a spectrum referred to as the (post-)Creole continuum with its three main reference points: the basilect; the mesolect, an intermediate Creole; and the acrolect, often equated with the local standardized English variety. Both Barbadian English Creole (BEC) and Trinidadian English Creole (TEC), however, have been identified as intermediate Creoles (Winford 2000), that is, having no basilectal variety. For BEC, this intermediary status is accounted for by a number of demographic factors which led either to the high retention of superstrate features in the Creole or the eventual decreolization of a basilect which may have emerged around the eighteenth century (Winford 2000). The reasons for this are not the focus of the present chapter, but whatever they may be they have nonetheless resulted in BEC displaying a number of distinctive features at all linguistic levels.

With regard to phonology, BEC is unique among Caribbean Creoles as being a fully rhotic variety, so that words in the NORTH vowel set, for example, are realized variably with [aːɹ] or [ɒːɹ] (Blake 2008, 316). The only exception to this seems to be words in the NURSE vowel set, which are realized with [ʏ]. Other phonological features of BEC include the realization of voiceless stops in syllable final position as glottal stops, and the quality of the first element of the PRICE diphthong, which is often realized as [ʌɪ], resulting in a merger with the CHOICE lexical set for some speakers, since CHOICE can be realized either as [oɪ] or [ʌɪ] (Blake 2008, 316). BEC also shows variation in the realization of the FACE and GOAT vowels, which can either be monophthongs, [e], or [ɛ] and [o], respectively, or diphthongs, [eɪ] or [ɪɛ] and [oə], respectively. Finally, variation is also seen in the realizations of the CLOTH and THOUGHT vowels. CLOTH is generally realized as [ɒː] and THOUGHT may be merged with this or else realized as [aː].

On the basis of historical evidence, Barbadian English has been established as the model for other Englishes and English Creoles in the Caribbean (Devonish and Thomas 2012; Holm 1994, 345). All the same, there are a number of key differences which exist between BEC and TEC.

The latter, for starters, is non-rhotic, although there is increasing evidence for the use of a rhotic pronunciation in NURSE contexts by some speakers (Wilson 2014), and the use of glottal stops for syllable-final [p,t,k] is unique to BEC. Differences between the vowel systems of the two varieties are reported in table 7.1.

Table 7.1 shows that there are a number of phonological features which distinguish BEC and TEC from each other. But there are also features which the two share, along with other Caribbean Creoles. These include the fact that unstressed syllables are often realized with full vowels, the stopping of dental fricatives and the reduction of consonant clusters, though, of course, these latter two features are not peculiar to Creoles and are also attested in many non-standardized varieties of English.

Language in Music

The issue of language use in music, particularly popular music, has held linguists' attention for several decades. Trudgill's (1983) early work on the subject establishes quite clearly the centrality of American English accents in the genre. Trudgill identifies a core of five American English features, which Simpson (1999) later dubs the USA-5, which are used by the British pop and rock groups, notably The Beatles. The earlier findings are corroborated by a number of subsequent studies which routinely find that American features are used in pop, rock and country music singing (Duncan 2017; Gibson and Bell 2012; Simpson 1999). The overwhelming

Table 7.1 Phonological Differences between BEC and TEC

Lexical Set	BEC	TEC
LOT	[ɑ], [ɒ]	[ɔ],[ʌ], [ɒ]
CLOTH	[ɒː]	[ɔ], [ɒ]
NURSE	[ɤ]	[ɜː], [ɔ]
NORTH	[ɑːr], [ɒːr]	[ɔː]
FORCE	[oːr]	[ɔː]
PRICE	[ʌɪ]	[aɪ]
FACE	[eː], [eɪ], [ɛː], [ɪɛ]	[eː]
THOUGHT	[ɑː]	[ɔː],[ɒː]
GOAT	[o], [oə]	[oː]
MOUTH	[ʌu], [ʌʊ]	[ɔʊ]

Sources: Adapted from Blake (2008) and Youssef and James (2008).

preference for American-accented English in pop music is often attributed to the economic and cultural power of the United States in the music industry, and its use is taken by some to show alignment with the capitalist mainstream (Beal 2009).

This, however, is not the whole picture. In terms of pop music, singers often choose to reject the USA-5 and thus forge their identity as pop singers functioning outside of the mainstream; Beal's (2009) exploration of the retention of Sheffield dialect features by the British band the Arctic Monkeys has become an iconic example of this. Similarly, while African American Vernacular English remains the main reference language for performance, hip-hop's emphasis on authenticity and "keepin' it real" means that hip-hop artistes outside the United States also draw on their own language varieties, and especially on minority/low prestige varieties in their speech communities, with considerable code-switching across varieties not uncommon (cf. Pennycook 2007; Androutsopoulos 2010).

Choice of language use in singing, then, reflects both the identity the singer wishes to portray and the specifications required to produce an authentic performance in the genre. Generally, soca is performed in TEC (Leung 2017), though this was not always the case with its predecessor, calypso. Winer (1986) shows the progression of calypso as a genre that was performed first in Trinidad French Creole, then in standardized English, and then finally in TEC. Soca's offshoots, rapso/ragga soca and chutney soca, furthermore reflect the island's sociolinguistic complex. Lengemann (2012), in her study of rapso music, shows that while early rapso artists use TEC to assert their Trinidadian identity, more recent performers of the genre mix TEC with standardized Trinidad English. Similarly, chutney soca is sung either in TEC or a "mixed English and Hindi" (Mohammed 2007, 6). Moreover, the popularity of Jamaican dancehall music across the region, particularly among young people, has seen the introduction of Jamaican Creole English (JamC) elements into soca (Cf. Leung 2009; Guibaullt 2007, 176).

Research on language and music focusing on Caribbean languages and music has been largely concerned with reggae and its spread beyond its Jamaican roots. On the one hand, some scholars (Westphal 2017; Gerfer 2018) note the predominance of JamC as the language of reggae performance by non-Jamaican reggae artists performing outside of Jamaica. For these singers and their audiences, JamC, or at least some features of that variety, have become enregistered as the dialect most appropriate for reggae music performance. This use of JamC is not restricted to sung performances; Gerfer (2018) further notes how artistes also make use of an albeit limited repertoire of JamC features in interviews as a means of constructing and maintaining their identity as reggae singers. This is particularly noteworthy since it potentially sets non-Jamaican reggae artistes apart from their Jamaican counterparts, the latter group more often performing reggae in English (cf. Farquharson 2017). On the other hand, there is increasing evidence that, like hip-hop and pop, reggae music artistes increasingly draw on their own local languages. Westphal (2017) reports singing in German by one of the reggae musicians in his study and, perhaps more interestingly, Mazzoli (2017) and Levisen (2017) both report the use of extended pidgins or Creoles by reggae artistes in Nigeria and Vanuatu respectively.

The influence of JamC on non-Jamaican musical forms has also received some attention. Within the Caribbean, Leung (2009) looks at the use of JamC and features perceived to belong to JamC in Trinidadian ragga soca music. Critically, she notes that mixing of JamC and TEC are the linguistic requirements for successful performance of ragga soca (519) but that, at the same time, use of JamC and JamC-like features, what she calls Perceived Jamaican Creole English (PJCE), has decreased as the genre becomes more established and singers are found to use TEC features far more frequently. Beyond the Caribbean, Jansen and Westphal (2017) examine Barbadian-born pop star Rihanna's language use in her linguistically controversial song "Work", and find that she uses an assortment of her native BEC features, but also features associated with JamC or else shared by several Caribbean English Creoles. Thus these studies show that the influence of JamC is not limited to reggae but can also extend to other varieties of music.

With the possible exception of Rihanna, who is of course a native speaker of a Caribbean Creole and whose megastar status gives her immeasurable reach, the artistes drawing on JamC are involved in extensive referee design, where language use is modelled on a variety which the speaker (or singer) does not have immediately available to them in their speech community (Bell 1992). Referee design has previously been used to account for style shifting in the sung performances of New Zealand pop singers (Gibson and Bell 2012). By and large, the music of non-Caribbean reggae artistes is produced for audiences within their locale or region. As such, there is no native speaker censure with regard to the authenticity of their accents, a fact that is even acknowledged by some of the singers in Leung's (2009) study, who note that their pronunciations would not count as authentic to Jamaican audiences, even if Trinidadian audiences judge them thus. Indeed, it is the fact that some of the realizations are not legitimate JamC forms that leads Leung to use the term Perceived Jamaican Creole English (514) to describe them. The selection of JamC features singers use, their "truncated repertoire" (Westphal 2017 quoting Blommaert 2012), is both sufficient and appropriate for their audiences. Very few of them enjoy truly international reach, though it should be noted that those who do, such as Bermuda's Collie Budz and Germany's Gentleman, employ far more JamC features and do so far more consistently than others (Gerfer 2018).

The more recent literature on language and music with regard to the Caribbean, therefore, is largely biased towards JamC and reggae; even the two studies on soca and related genres consider the effect of JamC on the art form. However, where considerable attention has been given to non-Jamaican performers of reggae, the same has not been done for soca, even though soca artistes from Caribbean countries enjoy considerable success. As in Trinidad, soca has become a mainstay of Carnival celebrations on other islands, such as Spice Mas in Grenada and Crop Over in Barbados. Moreover, soca artistes from other islands are also increasingly popular among Trinidadian audiences. In 2019, for example, Grenadian soca star Mr Killa (Hollis Jonah Mapp) copped the coveted International Soca Monarch title, and Vincentian soca star Skinny Fabulous (Gamal Doyle) shared the Road March title with Trinidadians Machel Montano and Bunji Garlin (Ian Alvarez) singing a song composed by Doyle. Among Barbadian performers, Alison Hinds, Rupee (Rupert Clarke) and of course Peter Ram have distinguished themselves. Despite all of this, no research has been done on the language use of non-Trinidadian soca performers in the same way as that of non-Jamaican reggae singers.

Soca artistes are in general a highly mobile group, and often visit other islands and perform at their Carnivals throughout the year. This is particularly true of performances at Trinidad Carnival and competing for the coveted ISM title. Peter Ram in particular has competed in the competition several times, often as a finalist. His music is generally quite well received in Trinidad, with the popular steel band Desperados even opting to play an arrangement of his "Good Morning" in the 2017 Panorama competition. What this means, therefore, is that Peter Ram's music is not limited to Barbadian listeners, but also includes, in no small way, Trinidadian listeners. This makes his language use a particularly fitting starting point for research into language use by non-Trinidadian *soca* singers, especially given the differences between BEC and TEC.

This chapter answers the following questions:

1. How does Peter Ram use Creole to construct an identity as
    a. an authentic performer of *soca* music?
    b. an authentic performer from Barbados?

2. What features of Barbadian Creole are present in Peter Ram's speech and singing?
3. How does Peter Ram's language use, particularly with regard to phonology, differ in speech and singing?
4. What differences can be observed in Peter Ram's phonology over time?
5. What differences, particularly with regard to phonology, exist in language use in Peter Ram's performances geared to Barbadian and Trinidadian audiences?

Data and Method

In order to answer the preceding questions, recordings of Peter Ram's performances in both Trinidad and Barbados were obtained. Schneider (2016, 277) notes that YouTube provides a "treasure trove" of data for linguistic study and so all videos and recordings used in this study were accessed via YouTube. Where possible, studio versions of his songs prepared for Barbadian and Trinidadian audiences were also used. Finally, recordings of televised interviews that Peter Ram carried out in Barbados and Trinidad were obtained via YouTube.

The songs included in the analysis are "Good Morning" (2016), "All Ah We" (2015) and "I Need a Woman" (2008). The songs were selected based on their popularity in both Barbados and Trinidad. For the first two songs, both studio recordings and live performances were used, but for "I Need a Woman", only the studio recording was used. The spoken data for Barbados is taken from a clip from the YouTube channel LargeUp, in which Peter Ram holds a monologue about music in Barbados and his career. The interview data for Trinidad was obtained from Peter Ram's pre-Soca Monarch (2017) performance interview.

Variables under Investigation

As seen in table 7.1, BEC and TEC are phonologically distinct from each other in a number of ways. In this first exploratory study, the focus will be on a small selection of stereotypical features. In terms of consonants, rhotic pronunciation and glottal replacement for syllable-final unvoiced stops are examined. For vowels, the realization of vowels in the NORTH/THOUGHT and PRICE lexical sets are investigated. Although the main focus of this chapter is the phonological features, Jansen and Westphal (2017) argue the benefits of looking at different linguistic levels in the analysis of singing. Consequently, brief attention will be given to Peter

Ram's song lyrics and to aspects of language use such as the roll call in the live performances.

Method

The lyrics of each song were studied, and phono-opportunities (Coupland 1985), that is, instances in which Peter Ram could perform either TEC or BEC features, were isolated. A phono-opportunity approach is preferable since it allows the researcher to examine every realization of a variable. Soca lyrics are notoriously repetitive, which for these purposes is especially useful, since it allows us to have several tokens of the same word. Before the song lyrics in performance could be studied, an analysis of Peter Ram's speech was carried out. This was done in order to establish a baseline for comparison. It is well known that speakers of Caribbean Creoles often exhibit high levels of variation in terms of their overall use of individual features. Therefore, it was critical that the presence or absence of the features were examined both in speech and singing. For this, orthographic transcripts of Peter Ram's Trinidad and Barbados interviews were first produced and phono-opportunities identified. Then, for each phono-opportunity, the pronunciation Peter Ram used was noted phonetically.

Once this was done, an auditory analysis of Peter Ram's studio recordings of "I Need a Woman", "All Ah We" and "Good Morning" was done. In a first step, the lyrics of each song were obtained and phono-opportunities marked. Then, the recordings were listened to and a phonetic transcription of each of the phono-opportunities was made. The phono-opportunities in the recordings were then quantified and expressed as percentages in order to allow comparison of overall frequencies over time.

In a final phase, an analysis of live performances of "Good Morning" and "All Ah We" was carried out. For each phono-opportunity, the actual pronunciation Peter Ram used during Soca Monarch performances in Trinidad and Barbados was recorded. These were compared to his pronunciation of the same variants in speech and in the sung recordings. Although the initial aim was to quantify the features used in performance as had been done for the recordings, this was judged to be unwise. In the live performances, Peter Ram often appears out of breath and although he exerts considerable energy into his performance, he actually sings very little. Instead, a great deal of singing is done by backup singers or by the audience members themselves. Instead, Peter Ram interacts with the audience a great deal, particularly in the roll call segments. Furthermore, changes to lyrics for the live performances mean that some of the words containing phono-opportunities are not sung. Therefore, the comparison with the live performances will be qualitative.

Excluded from the phonetic analysis were

- Words ending [t] where [t] is part of a consonant cluster, such as <post>, since both varieties are susceptible to reduction/do not have a cluster as the underlying form.
- Instances where words ending in [t] were followed by another alveolar stop, since realization of the first alveolar may not be clear due to assimilation. Thus, in *start de drinking*, *start* is not analysed for the stop. The item could, and did, still serve as a token to test for rhotic pronunciation.
- Instances when the backup singers sang at the same time, since it was then difficult to determine who produced what sound.

For the lexical analysis, the song lyrics were closely studied. Lexical items associated with BEC or with Barbadian cultural events were highlighted. In addition to this, lexical items common in Caribbean Creoles, such as *liming* and *fete*, were noted. To be sure of their etymology, Allsopp and Allsopp's (2003) *Dictionary of Caribbean English Usage* as well as Winer's (2009) *Dictionary of the English/Creole of Trinidad and Tobago* were consulted. Additionally, "Good Morning", which had separate Trinidad and Barbados radio versions and which was performed on both islands, was analysed with reference to the differences in vocabulary that exist in the two versions of the song.

Results

Peter Ram's Speech

In the Barbados interview with LargeUp, Peter Ram makes consistent use of all of the BEC variants under consideration. This is hardly surprising since the programme is produced for Barbadian audiences and the topic is Barbadian music. Thus it is fitting that Peter Ram makes use of BEC features in order to signal his membership of and identification with the intended audience. However, comparison of Peter Ram's speech in interviews done in Trinidad and in Barbados shows that there is very little difference in Peter Ram's speech when addressing the two audiences. In both interviews, Peter Ram makes use of rhotic pronunciations in words such as *first*, *more*, *artists* and *Barbados*. Furthermore, there is evidence of glottal stopping in words like *do it*, *not only*, *but* and *like*. With regard to vowels, the PRICE vowel is realized mostly as [ʌɪ] as in *twice* and *style*, but occasionally, in the Barbados interview, also as [aɪ]. Finally, Peter Ram realizes the vowel in the NORTH/FORCE as [oɹ] as in *St George*. There were, however, no tokens of NORTH/FORCE in the Trinidadian interview with which this can be compared.

The Studio Recordings

The pronunciations used in the studio recordings differ both from those Peter Ram uses in the interviews as well as from one another.

Figure 7.1 shows that BEC features are always present in Peter Ram's sung recordings. In the earliest recording, "I Need a Woman", BEC features can be observed in pronunciations of phrases such as *by my side*, pronounced [bʌɪ mʌɪ sʌɪd], and *never*, pronounced [nɛvəɹ]. At the same time, there are instances in which PRICE vowels are realized as [aɪ] when rhotic pronunciations are not used. Only one token in which an unvoiced stop was replaced with a glottal stop was found in 2005, in the word *Cohoblapot*. In 2015, BEC features are limited to rhotic pronunciations of *nor* and glottal stopping in the word *bit*. In "Good Morning" (2016), even fewer BEC features appear.

As figure 7.1 illustrates, Peter Ram's overall use of BEC features in his studio recordings decreases over time. This is accompanied by an increase in TEC features, which generally, though not always, replace the BEC features. One major difference over the twelve-year period appears to be with the realization of words in the PRICE lexical set. In 2005, 50 of the

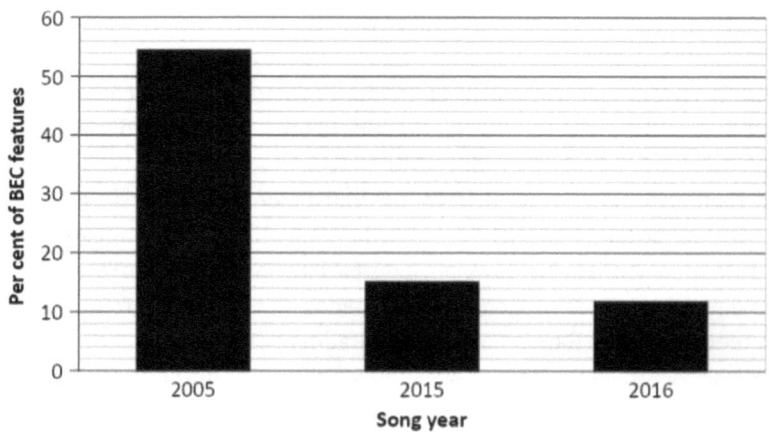

Figure 7.1 Per cent of BEC phonological features in Peter Ram's studio recordings.

130 phono-opportunities are for the words in the PRICE lexical set. Of these, thirty-two (64 per cent) are pronounced with [ʌɪ]. The only exception to this pronunciation seems to be with the pronoun *I*, which is alternately pronounced as [a] or [aɪ] and only on one occasion as [ʌɪ]. In comparison, in 2015, 22 per cent of PRICE tokens are pronounced with [ʌɪ], although it should be noted that it is based on a smaller number of tokens. By 2017, this percentage falls even further to 19.3 per cent, or six out of thirty-one possible tokens.

Rhotic pronunciations also display variability. In 2005, some 60 per cent of all possible rhotic pronunciations are realized with the [r], but in "All Ah We", only three of the thirty-five tokens, 8.5 per cent, are realized with [r] and in "Good Morning" (2016), only four out of seventy-six possible rhotic pronunciations, 5.3 per cent, are realized thus. Interestingly, two of these tokens occur in the phrase *foreday morning*. Foreday morning is a late night/early morning street party that takes place during the Barbadian Crop Over festivities, in which revellers are covered in paint and mud. The Trinidadian equivalent would be J'ouvert. It is noteworthy that Peter Ram uses the BEC pronunciation for the uniquely Barbadian event. This suggests that rhotic pronunciations may serve as an important index of Barbadian identity. Following the Labovian indicator–marker–stereotype trichotomy (Labov 1972 in Johnstone and Kiesling 2008), it is possible to argue that the use of rhotic pronunciations serves as a linguistic marker or, in Johnstone and Kiesling's (2008) terms, a second-order indexicality of Barbadianness, since second-order indexicalities can be linked to local and regional belonging. The use of the glottal stop in place of voiceless stops occurs rarely in all three years. Otherwise, not only is his pronunciation of *morning* consistently non-rhotic, he also does not appear to use the Barbadian THOUGHT vowel variants [ɑː] and [ɒː]. Instead, he uses the TEC variant [ɔː].

In addition to these features, "All Ah We" contains some phonetic features which more rightly could be described as belonging to JamC than to either TEC or BEC. These include the pronunciation of *little* as [lɪkl] and *whole* as [huol]. These, however, are used very rarely in the recordings.

The Live Performances

In general, the pronunciations employed during the live performances are consistent with those used in the studio recordings. With regard to "Good Morning", the main difference concerns the realization of the NORTH vowel in the word *morning*. While in the studio recordings, this is mostly produced with the TEC pronunciation [ɔː], in live performances, both in

Barbados and in Trinidad, Peter Ram consistently sings [aː]. This, however, is neither the BEC nor the TEC pronunciation, but rather the JamC realization of word in the NORTH set (Devonish and Harry 2008, 260). There are two possible explanations for the presence of the JamC feature in Peter Ram's performances. The first has to do with his biography. Before embarking on a career as a soca singer, Peter Ram sang dancehall, a Jamaican genre, and it is likely that features from the one genre are adopted by the other. Second, this could also be due to an observation which Martin Raymond, record producer and mastering sound engineer, unprompted, offers when he is consulted with regard to the recorded data. He writes, "One thing that has annoyed me is the attempt by singers to sound Jamaican. *All* has now became *arl*, bawl has become *barl* as in '*Mek arl de gyal dem barl out*' Don't get me started on '*Flag haffi wave*'" (Raymond, personal communication). Although Raymond does not accurately identify and describe the JamC features, his comments give insight into which forms are potentially perceived to be Jamaican by producers and performers, harking back to Leung's previous observation of the use of PJCE in ragga soca. Thus Peter Ram could be following this trend, applying JamC or PJCE features in soca music. The use of [aː] in NORTH means that the NORTH and START lexical sets become merged, since Peter Ram also uses this pronunciation for words in the START lexical set such as *start* and *party*.

When live performances in Trinidad and Barbados of "Good Morning" are further compared, few differences can be found on the level of phonology. In the live performances, the word *right* is replaced with *come*, which means there are fewer opportunities to observe the PRICE vowel, since this word occurs twenty-two times in the song and accounts for most of the PRICE tokens. Otherwise, a great deal of the actual singing of the song is left to the backup singers, and so many tokens are simply never produced. This is particularly true in Trinidad, where *morning* is also very rarely produced by the out of breath Peter Ram, despite *good morning* being the main hook in the song. At one point during the Trinidad performance, Peter Ram produces [ɑː] in the word *start*, and at another point, he produces [ɪt] where in the Barbadian performance [ɪʔ] is used.

In live performances of "All Ah We", few differences from the radio version can be noted on both islands. In the Barbadian performance, a previously non-rhotic realization of *here* is rhoticized, and in another, a previously raised and backed version of PRICE is lowered and fronted to [aɪ]. Given that these features are in the normal range of variation, these are hardly worth further consideration. The same is true of live performances of "All Ah We" in Trinidad. What does emerge in performances of "All Ah

We", however, both in Trinidad and Barbados, is an increase in JamC forms. Whereas in the recording *little* is pronounced as [lɪkl] only once, in the live performances the JamC pronunciation is used in all tokens. Furthermore, *all*, which in the radio version is pronounced as [ɔːl] or [ɒːl], varying between the BEC and TEC pronunciations, is alternately pronounced as [aːl] in the live performances.

Lexical Choices

Beyond phonology, there are a number of lexical choices worth examining in Peter Ram's soca songs. His early work locates him lexically in Barbados and particularly within the Barbados Crop Over festivities, since he makes overt reference to Cohobblopot, Calvacade and Power by Four, which are all events during Crop Over. At the same time, the song contains several references to girls and women in other locations such as *This one is for Canadian girls, New York/This one is for St. Lucia girls*. In the later songs, this heavy referencing to Barbados is not evident, except when singing about Crop Over or Foreday morning. However, as we have already seen, these references are removed from recordings for Trinidad in particular. Moreover, when performing "Good Morning" live in Trinidad, Peter Ram replaces *Crop Over* alternately with *Trinidad* or *Tobago*, as he does in the recordings. Furthermore, he inserts recognition markers like *Barbados* and at another point *Trinidad and Tobago* and then *Trinis and Bajans*.

The lyrics also include a number of shared Caribbean vocabulary items usually associated with Carnival such as *fete* (party), and *wine* (a type of dance), as well as the popular Carnival-bacchanal rhyming scheme. Finally, another lexical item which occurs both in "I Need a Woman" and in "Good Morning" is *liming*. Allsopp and Allsopp (1996, 349) establish this word as part of the Trinidadian lexicon, but the extent to which it might have been borrowed into other island Creoles is unknown. Although, on the boundary between morphology and syntax, a further point to be made regarding the use of Jamaican lexical items involves the item *pon*. In the radio version of "All Ah We", the lyrics are *stranger on your left*. However, in performances in both Trinidad and Barbados, *on* is changed to *pon*, which is a feature not typically associated with either island variety, but with JamC, although the spelling does not faithfully represent the word's phonology.

The analysis of phonological and lexical features in Peter Ram's speech and soca music illustrates how the different varieties of Caribbean Creoles are interwoven in the production of this genre. While TEC is clearly the dominant variety and seems to replace BEC in Peter Ram's more recent work, we see that the genre is also under the influence of JamC.

Language in the Roll Call

A prominent feature of live soca performances is the roll call segment. At this point, the artistes, using the formulation *Anybody from X*, attempt to excite the crowd by calling on groups from different towns or countries to identify themselves when called upon. In his performance of "Good Morning" in Trinidad, Peter Ram starts his roll call with Jamaica, then moves on, practically travelling southwards, to Antigua, St Lucia and St Vincent. When he arrives to Barbados, Peter Ram is audibly louder, and when the members of the crowd scream in response to his question, he replies, "I love you". Similarly, in live performances of "All Ah We", when he arrives to Barbados, there is additional commentary not given to the other islands. In the ISM semifinals performance, for example, Peter Ram asks, "Anybody from Barbados my island" and at the finals, "Anybody in here from my sweet likkle island Barbados". In so doing, Peter Ram affectionately asserts his identity as a Barbadian. On those occasions, he also takes on the role of host and tour guide, saying, "Welcome to the land of soca", simultaneously presenting himself as someone in the know about Trinidad, and especially about soca. Barbados is always the penultimate stop on the verbal cruise. The final port of call is always Port of Spain, and Trinidad and Tobago is always the last and most prominent member of the roll call. Indeed, Trinidad and Tobago receives considerable build up when it is announced, either by saying "somebody missing" or else by instructing the audience further to "make some noise". In the "Good Morning" performance at the ISM, Peter Ram goes so far as to pay special tribute to another aspect of Trinidad Carnival culture, first asking the audience if they "love pan" and then playing a track of the Desperados Steelband performing "Good Morning".

With regard to the phonetic features of Peter Ram's speech in the roll call segment, he sometimes appears to align himself not with TEC but with BEC and JamC. This is particularly evident in his pronunciation of certain vowel tokens. For words in the FACE lexical set, Peter Ram uses the onglide [ɪɛ], which is almost always used in FACE contexts by speakers of JamC and which he does not use when he is singing, opting instead for the [e:] shared by TEC and BEC. For words in the GOAT lexical set, Peter Ram uses JamC [uo] (Devonish and Harry 2008, 260), so that in the performance of "All Ah We" in Trinidad he instructs the whole [huol] audience to jump and wave [wɪɛv] to the soca [suokɐ], before advising them to stay [stɪɛ] alive by not drinking and driving. There are two particularly intriguing facts about Peter Ram's language behaviour at this point. Even though Peter Ram has the opportunity to produce typically Barbadian vowels in words such as *drive*, he does not do so. Furthermore, even though he is in Trinidad, performing for a largely Trinidadian audience, he defers to JamC vowels when referring to Trinidad's indigenous musical form, *soca*, and when giving the soca artiste's standard instruction to *jump and wave*.

Discussion

This analysis has highlighted several aspects of Peter Ram's language use in speech and singing. With regard to his speech, the fact that Ram does not appear to adopt TEC features in interviews geared towards Trinidadian audiences seems to underscore the importance of his Barbadian identity. Indeed, in both interviews, he states that he is Peter Ram from Barbados, thus clearly establishing his origin. In live performances, he makes continuous reference to the island, particularly in the roll call segments. In this way, Peter Ram's language use differs qualitatively from the language use of performers reported by Westphal (2017) and Gerfer (2018). Both previous studies find that performers of reggae music attempt to include JamC features even in speech as a way of claiming affiliation with JamC and reggae. But on the level of spoken language, Peter Ram reasserts his Barbadian identity, even and especially in performances in Trinidad. This Barbadian identity is seemingly at odds with another important aspect of Peter Ram's identity: his identity as a soca performer. In his speech, Peter Ram reinforces this side of himself by paying continuous homage to Trinidad and Tobago, soca's place of origin, both in interviews and in his live performances, thus situating himself as a performer of soca within this larger ecology.

Since his identity as a Barbadian is clearly so important to him, I would hesitate to argue, as Gerfer (2018) does, that what Peter Ram does when he adopts TEC features for singing is an example of crossing (Rampton 1995), since crossing involves important claims with regard to identity and group membership, which Peter Ram does not make. Instead, I would argue that Peter Ram is involved in style shifting, that is, changing his language use to match his stylistic needs, and not that he is trying to sound particularly Trinidadian. Since few differences exist in the language use either in the different recordings or live performances of his music in Barbados and Trinidad, it is equally unlikely that variation between speech and singing is the result of accommodation to different island audiences. It seems rather to be the case that TEC has become enregistered (Agha 2005) as the language of soca music performances, very much like the USA-5 features became enregistered in pop music performances or JamC features in reggae performance. Peter Ram wishes to establish himself as an authentic and successful performer of soca music and, consequently, makes use of TEC features in his recordings and performances. Peter Ram uses fewer stereotypical BEC features, particularly later in his career, highlighting his development as a soca artiste. In his Barbadian interview, he points out that he is a three-time Barbadian *soca* king, and in his Trinidadian interview, he asserts that he has given soca pride of place in his life, since it quenches his thirst. He acknowledges that Trinidad is the "land of soca", giving further credence to the argument that his aim is not necessarily to sound like a Trinidadian, but rather to sound like a soca artiste, which entails the use of TEC features. Here, again, Peter Ram is different from performers of other genres. Previous work on pop and hip-hop has found that singers move away from features associated with the genre's enregistered varieties as they establish themselves and become more successful as performers. This, however, is not what Peter Ram does.

At the same time, Peter Ram's use of JamC features was somewhat surprising, given the genre. In light of Peter Ram's musical biography, use of JamC features might be an important act of identity, revealing his allegiance to his earlier forays into dancehall. Musical and linguistic resources are mobile, and speakers and singers can draw on any combination of features in the projection of their identity. Furthermore, Peter Ram's use of JamC lends some insight into the relationship between the Englishes and Creoles in different Caribbean territories. In his World System of Standard and Non-Standard Englishes Model, Mair (2013) proposes that Jamaican English is a central variety in the Caribbean region, serving as a model to other Englishes. Moreover, and more importantly for current purposes, Mair argues that, due to the far-reaching popularity of the Jamaican musical genres reggae and dancehall, JamC could be regarded a supercentral variety, particularly in the entertainment sphere. This proposition is supported by the findings of this study on two levels. I have illustrated how Peter Ram makes use of JamC features both in singing and in speech during his performances. Furthermore, in the interview with Martin Raymond, the sound engineer also commented on the use of JamC pronunciations by soca performers, thus reinforcing Mair's observations with regard to the status of JamC in popular culture in the region. Raymond's firm stand against the use of JamC in *soca* complicates this, suggesting that JamC's dominance is not to be equated with omnipotence and that the relationships between Creoles are complicated.

Conclusion

As the number of soca singers of non-Trinidadian origin and their success with audiences both in their countries of birth and on other Caribbean islands increases, their language use in performance provides a rich source of linguistic data. Specifically, their language use permits us to examine not only language use in music but also the relationships between the different island Creoles, at least in one particular context. The presence of JamC features alongside TEC and BEC features in Peter Ram's performances suggests that language use and decisions about language use in performance are far more multifaceted than initially thought. Performers have to consider not only issues of stylistic variation in terms of choosing language that is appropriate to their genre but also issues of prestige, power and identity. Peter Ram's language use provides us with a first glimpse into this area, but future work on the language of other soca performers from other islands may well help enrich our understanding of the use of language in soca performance and the relationship between different Creoles.

References

Agha, Asif. 2005. "Voice, Footing, Enregisterment". *Journal of Linguistic Anthropology* 15 (1): 38–59.

Allsopp, Richard, and Jeannette Allsopp, eds. 2003. *Dictionary of Caribbean English Usage*. Mona: University of West Indies Press.

Androutsopoulos, Jannis. 2010. "Multilingualism, Ethnicity and Genre in Germany's Migrant Hip Hop". In *Languages of Global Hip Hop*, edited by Terkourafi Marina, (2010): 19–43.

Beal, Joan C. 2009. "'You're Not from New York City, You're from Rotherham' Dialect and Identity in British Indie Music". *Journal of English Linguistics* 37 (3): 223–40.

Bell, Allan. 1992. "Hit and Miss: Referee Design in the Dialects of New Zealand Television Advertisements". *Language and Communication* 12: 327–40.

Blake, Renée. 2008. "Bajan: Phonology". In *Varieties of English: The Americas and the Caribbean*, edited by Edgar Schneider, 312–19. Berlin and Boston: De Gruyter Mouton.

Coupland, Nikolas. 1985. "'Hark, Hark, the Lark': Social Motivations for Phonological Style-Shifting". *Language and Communication* 5 (3): 151–71.

Devonish, Hubert, and Otelemate G. Harry. 2008. "Jamaican Creole and Jamaican English: Phonology". In *Varieties of English: The Americas and the Caribbean*, edited by Edgar Schneider, 256–89. Berlin and Boston: De Gruyter Mouton.

Devonish, Hubert, and Ewart A.C. Thomas. 2012. "Standards of English in the Caribbean". In *Standards of English: Codified Varieties around the World*, edited by Raymond Hickey, 179–97. Cambridge: Cambridge University Press.

Duncan, Daniel. 2017. "Australian Singer, American Features: Performing Authenticity in Country Music". *Language & Communication* 52: 31–44.

Farquharson, Joseph T. 2017. "Linguistic Ideologies and the Historical Development of Language Use Patterns in Jamaican Music". *Language & Communication* 52: 7–18.

Gerfer, Anika. 2018. "Global Reggae and the Appropriation of Jamaican Creole". *World Englishes* 37 (4): 668–83.

Gibson, Andy, and Allan Bell. 2012. "Popular Music Singing as Referee Design". In *Style-Shifting in Public: New Perspectives on Stylistic Variation*, edited by Juan Manuel Hernández-Campoy and Juan Antonio Cutillas-Espinosa, 139–64. Amsterdam: John Benjamins Publishing.

Guilbault, Jocelyne. 2007. *Governing Sound: The Cultural Politics of Trinidad's Carnival Musics*. Chicago: University of Chicago Press.

Holm, John A. 1994. "English in the Caribbean". In *The Cambridge History of the English Language* 5, edited by Robert Burchfield, 328–81. Cambridge: Cambridge University Press.

Jansen, Lisa, and Michael Westphal. 2017. "Rihanna Works Her Multivocal Pop Persona: A Morpho-syntactic and Accent Analysis of Rihanna's Singing Style: Pop Culture Provides Rich Data that Demonstrate the Complex Interplay of World Englishes". *English Today* 33 (2): 46–55.

Johnstone, Barbara, and Scott F. Kiesling. 2008. "Indexicality and Experience: Exploring the Meanings of /aw/ -monophthongization in Pittsburgh 1". *Journal of Sociolinguistics* 12 (1): 5–33.

Lengemann, Maike. 2012. "'Did you know? Did you know? Dis Trini Could Flow': Mobilizing Sociolinguistic Resources in Trinidadian Rapso Music". *Zeitschrift für Anglistik und Amerikanistik* 60 (2): 217–35.

Leung, Glenda Alicia. 2017. "YouTube Comments as Metalanguage Data on Non-standardized Languages: The Case of Trinidadian Creole English in Soca Music". In *Data Analytics in Digital Humanities*, edited by Hai-Jew Shalin, 231–50. Cham: Springer.

Leung, Glenda Alicia E. 2009. "Negotiation of Trinidadian Identity in Ragga Soca Music". *World Englishes* 28 (4): 509–31.

Levisen, Carsten. 2017. "The Social and Sonic Semantics of Reggae: Language Ideology and Emergent Socialities in Postcolonial Vanuatu". *Language & Communication* 52: 102–16.

Mair, Christian. 2013. "The World System of Englishes: Accounting for the Transnational Importance of Mobile and Mediated Vernaculars". *English World-Wide* 34 (3): 253–78.

Mazzoli, Maria. 2017. "Language Nativisation and Ideologies in Ajégúnlè (Lagos)". *Language & Communication* 52: 88–101.

Mohammed, Aisha. 2007. "Love and Anxiety: Gender Negotiations in Chutney-Soca Lyrics". *Caribbean Review of Gender Studies* 1: 1–42.

Pennycook, Alastair. 2007. "Language, Localization, and the Real: Hip-Hop and the Global Spread of Authenticity". *Journal of Language, Identity, and Education* 6 (2): 101–15.

Rampton, Ben. 1995. *Crossing: Language and Ethnicity among Adolescents*. London: Routledge.
Schneider, Edgar W. "World Englishes on YouTube". In *World Englishes: New Theoretical and Methodological Considerations*, edited by Elena Seonane and Cristina Suarez-Gomez, 253–81. Amsterdam: John Benjamins Publishing.
Serwer, Jesse. 2016. "LargeUp TV: The Music of Barbados with Peter Ram". Accessed 9 April 2019. http://www.largeup.com/2016/07/29/largeup-tv-the-music-of-barbados-with-peter-ram/.
Simpson, Paul. 1999. "Language, Culture and Identity: With (another) Look at Accents in Pop and Rock Singing". *Multilingua – Journal of Cross-Cultural and Interlanguage Communication* 18 (4): 343–68.
Trudgill, Peter. 1983. "Acts of Conflicting Identity: The Sociolinguistics of British Popsong Pronunciation". In *On Dialect: Social and Geographical Perspectives*, edited by Peter Trudgill, 141–60. Oxford and New York: Basil Blackwell and New York University Press.
Walcott, Stefan. 2013. "Top 10 Bajan Dub (Dancehall) Records for Beginners". Accessed 9 April 2019. https://stefanwalcott.com/tag/peter-ram/.
Wilson, Guyanne. 2014. *The Sociolinguistics of Singing: Dialect and Style in Classical Choral Singing in Trinidad*. Muenster: Verlag-Haus Monsenstein und Vannerdat.
Winer, Lise. 1986. "Socio-cultural Change and the Language of Calypso". *Nieuwe West-Indische Gids/New West Indian Guide* 60 (3/4): 113–48.
———. 2009. *Dictionary of the English/creole of Trinidad & Tobago: On Historical Principles*. Canada: Queen's Press-Mc Gill-Queen's University Press.
Winford, Donald. 2000. "'Intermediate' Creoles and Degrees of Change in Creole Formation: The Case of Bajan". In *Degrees of Restructuring in Creole Languages*, edited by Ingrid Neumann-Holzschuh and Edgar Schneider, 215–46. Amsterdam: John Benjamins Publishing.
Youssef, Valerie, and Winford James. 2008. "The Creoles of Trinidad and Tobago: Phonology". In *Varieties of English: The Americas and the Caribbean*, edited by Edgar Schneider, 320–38. Berlin and Boston: De Gruyter Mouton.

Videography

"International Soca Monarch Finals – Peter Ram". YouTube video, 6:10, posted by Alban Edwards Ultra Stream Media, 26 December 2016. https://www.YouTube.com/watch?v=Q64WKpfdFTY.
"Peter Ram – All Ah We '2016 Soca' (Red Boyz Music)". YouTube video, 3:11, posted by JulianspromosTV, 5 June 2015. https://www.YouTube.com/watch?v=BiVQJ2xMbxo&list=RDwSrRWpGGoM4&index=2.
"Peter Ram All Ah We Performance at Party Monarc 2015 Kensington Oval". YouTube video, 4:15, posted by King Pin, 5 July 2015. https://www.YouTube.com/watch?v=y8kaq399Edg.
"Peter Ram All Ah We Soca Monarch Semi Final 2016". YouTube video, 3:28, posted by BajanSoundboy246, 25 January 2016. https://www.YouTube.com/watch?v=5HCPVck4aw0&t=114s.

"Peter Ram – Good Morning (Dj David Wolf Roadmix) Trinidad". YouTube video, 4:21, posted by DJ David Wolf, 17 January 2017. https://www.YouTube.com/watch?v=WlxZDmnD7SQ.

"Peter Ram Good Morning Official Video". YouTube video, 4:26, posted by JulianspromosTV, 30 November 2016. https://www.YouTube.com/watch?v=wSrRWpGGoM4&list=RDwSrRWpGGoM4&start_radio=1.

"Peter Ram Good Morning – Soca Monarch Finals 2017 (International Soca Monarch - ISM 2017)". YouTube video, 4:26, posted by Soca Hub, 25 February 2017. https://www.YouTube.com/watch?v=MJh33Wy75IY.

"Peter Ram – Woman By My Side | Official Music Video". YouTube video, 5:07, posted by VP Records, 5 June 2007. https://www.YouTube.com/watch?v=lRSI6jthKNE.

"The Music of Barbados with Peter Ram | LargeUp TV". YouTube video, 3:40, posted by LargeUp, 28 July 2016. https://www.YouTube.com/watch?v=WOA5FSb35e0.

Chapter 8

Singing the King's Creole

The (Ethno)Linguistic Repertoire of Clifton Chenier

NATHAN A. WENDTE

Introduction

Louisiana is home to a number of threatened French-lexified speech varieties, but the most endangered of these is Louisiana Creole (or Kouri-Vini). Intergenerational transmission has all but ceased, and it is virtually absent from school curricula. There are ongoing efforts to revitalize the language, but it is too soon to predict their long-term impact. Although Louisiana Creole's speakers historically come from a variety of backgrounds, the language is most closely associated with a subset of the black and mixed-race population known as Creoles (Dubois and Melançon 2000). Albert Valdman (1997, 12) speculates that one of the best vectors for the revitalization of the Louisiana Creole language is zydeco music, a popular genre that blends Louisiana's francophone folk music and African American rhythm and blues. If Valdman is correct, then it makes sense to look to zydeco for an idea of which language practices to target for transmission. Although the genre has produced an impressive number of distinguished artists, there is none who inspires so great a following as Clifton Chenier, the "King of Zydeco". Chenier made use of a diverse linguistic repertoire in his performances, employing features of both Louisiana Creole and Louisiana Regional French – often within the same song. This amalgam of forms may lead one to believe that his speech was somehow degraded or imprecise. Sara Le Menestrel (2015, 167) quotes a Louisiana musician who had this to say about Clifton Chenier: "I mean, hey, what's the big deal! He didn't create anything! . . . [H]e was a typical example of a blues band that used an accordion and sang in broken French." But Barry Ancelet (1996, 132) reminds us, "[N]either the late Clifton Chenier nor his Creole compatriots were in the habit of speaking nonsense in their own language." And as Chenier himself sings, "Jé konné kwa j'apé fé" (I know what I'm doing).[1]

This chapter provides a description of Chenier's linguistic repertoire through the lens of his non-English lyrics to better understand what language variety (or varieties) typify his zydeco music. I examine a lyrical corpus of fifty songs and analyse their linguistic traits. Ultimately, the results of this study expand our understanding of language's diverse forms in zydeco music, which may prove helpful in ongoing Louisiana Creole language revitalization efforts. Furthermore, these observations contribute to a richer picture of language's interaction with other aspects of Louisiana Creole ethnocultural identity.

Theory

At its broadest level, sociolinguistics seeks to explain the relationship between language variation and social meaning. Recent work in the field has shifted focus away from static notions of language varieties and social categories in favour of examining the dynamic means by which individuals and communities use linguistic resources to navigate social space (Eckert 2012). According to Augustin Ebongue and Ellen Hurst (2017, 1), "This reframing of sociolinguistics has led to an increasing number of studies looking at style, linguistic repertoire, communities of practice and so on." The notion of "repertoire" deserves further exposition. While formerly it might be assumed that a native speaker's language use would unambiguously reflect that same language's structure, linguistic repertoires capture the reality that individuals often possess knowledge of multiple language varieties, styles and registers. Knowledge of all these systems may or may not be complete within the repertoire, but the pieces from these systems are actively employed in order to reflect and create social meaning. One of the chief kinds of social meaning negotiated in such interactions is identity.

Sarah Benor (2010) deconstructs the idea of an ethnolect (that is, an ethnically determined way of speaking) and replaces it with the concept of an ethnolinguistic repertoire. The key difference is that, unlike an ethnolect, an ethnolinguistic repertoire is capable of being variably employed to meet the identity needs of its users. That is to say, in a given context, one may use linguistic features that are associated with a specific ethnic group in order to signal belonging with that ethnic group. On the other hand, that same individual may eschew these features in a different context in order to downplay belonging with that ethnic group. Such linguistic resources are said to belong to an ethnolinguistic repertoire because, in addition to fulfilling the functions of language, they also serve as signals of ethnic group membership. I have proposed a broadening of Benor's original concept to also include semiotic resources (that is, tools for making meaning) that are not explicitly linguistic, and I call this an ethnolinguistic identity repertoire (Wendte 2020a). The key theoretical addition here is that individuals often use an identity toolkit that includes both linguistic and non-linguistic indicators of ethnic group membership.

An example of a non-linguistic resource used to indicate ethnolinguistic group membership is music. Participation in certain genres of music can lead to associations with specific ethnolinguistic groups (reggae and Jamaicans, or konpa and Haitians, for example). Clifton Chenier, the focus of this chapter, undoubtedly drew from linguistic resources in his musical performances as a Louisiana Creole. However, he also used those linguistic resources in the context of zydeco music, a genre which has become a defining cultural characteristic of Louisiana Creoles today. Situating Chenier's lyrical material within the genre he helped create thus renders it a doubly potent piece of his ethnolinguistic identity repertoire.

Background

This section introduces the specific context of the word *creole* in the Gulf South, focusing on the history of its use as an ethnic and linguistic label. Next, we turn to the origins of zydeco and introduce one of its most influential artists, Clifton Chenier. The section concludes with a discussion of the contemporary zydeco music scene and the current state of the Louisiana Creole language.

Creole in the Gulf South

Although used in numerous locations at different points throughout history, the word *Creole* has developed local significations that can vary between and among communities. The Gulf South – a region that today encompasses portions of the states of Florida, Alabama, Mississippi, Louisiana and Texas – is no exception. Contemporary use of *Creole* as a label is primarily concentrated in Louisiana, and the precedents for its semantic evolution can usually be traced there as well.

Creole People

Creole (by most accounts, from Spanish *criollo*) was first applied to anything and anyone born in the New World; later, it both broadened and narrowed in meaning. Its first use in reference to a resident of what was then the colony of Louisiana occurred in the mid-eighteenth century. Robert Talon's death certificate designated him as "the first creole of the colony" (Gould

1996, 36). *Creole* would soon be extended to describe anything with Louisiana origins, including tomatoes, horses and even language (Hearn [1877] 1967). In its first uses, *Creole* made no further distinction than the origins of the thing being described. The word took on a more specific meaning with the Louisiana Purchase (or *La Vente de la Louisiane*) in 1803. Shortly thereafter, *Creole* was used to distinguish between the inhabitants of the former colony of Louisiana with their French language, Catholicism and *joie de vivre*, and the Anglo-American immigrants from the United States who flocked to Louisiana – particularly New Orleans – with their English language, Protestantism and more conservative social norms (Tregle 1992). This cultural divide was felt in both black and white society, highlighting the lack of racial connotations entailed by *Creole* at that time (Logsdon and Bell 1992). In the aftermath of the Civil War, however, the racial ambiguity of *Creole* was a major stumbling block. Louisiana's white elites rushed to defend the term as incontestably denoting "pure white blood" (Gayarré 1885, 3), denying that the word could ever properly apply to people of colour. But the colour-blind use of *Creole* in the colonial era was too pervasive to deny, and most whites eventually abandoned the term (Brasseaux et al. 1994, xii). This helped reinforce the false notion in the rest of the nation that a Creole was by definition someone of black or mixed ancestry. Among the non-white population, there was also friction over Creole identity. Prior to the Civil War, Louisiana society consisted of three tiers: free whites, the *gens de couleur libres* (free people of colour) and enslaved persons. While the system was clearly correlated with "race" and skin colour, it was not explicitly founded on these. Once Louisiana's slaves were emancipated, however, the free people of colour found themselves grouped socioeconomically with the formerly enslaved (freedmen). Some allege that, in order to preserve a modicum of separation from the freedmen, the former *gens de couleur libres* began calling themselves *Créoles de couleur* (creoles of colour) (Istre 2018, 16, 22). Formerly enslaved blacks charged these "Creoles" with artificially dividing non-whites when they ought to be uniting to demand greater rights (Logsdon and Bell 1992). In spite of these battles, the word *Creole* has remained in use among different sectors of the population up to the present.

In the 1960s, francophone whites would eventually find a new term on which to hang their hats: *Cajun*. Although the word had formerly been used derisively to refer to poor descendants of Acadian refugees, it had one advantage – it was only used for whites. Thus the French ethnic revival was kindled, and everything non-white about Louisiana's francophone heritage was subsumed and relabelled under "Cajunization" (Trépanier 1991). The

Anglo-American racial binary that had been imposed on Louisiana came to be reflected in the popular ethnolinguistic consciousness by the truism: Cajun=white; Creole=black. Consequently, corroborating the results of Sylvie Dubois and Megan Melançon, today's most widely accepted definition of a Louisiana Creole is a person of mixed or black ancestry who speaks – or whose ancestors spoke – some form of French, "preferably Creole French" (2000, 255). But just as *Creole* has been shown to be somewhat confusing as a label for groups and individuals, so, too, the term is polyvalent in reference to language varieties.

Creole Language

There are a number of factors that contribute to a remarkable amount of linguistic diversity in Louisiana. First, the origins of French in Louisiana were far from homogeneous (Picone 2015). In addition to the many regional languages of France spoken by the earliest colonists, there were also significant dialectal differences within French itself (including those varieties brought by Acadian and Québécois arrivals). Second, there were – and are – other languages besides French spoken in Louisiana. Indigenous languages were very important in the early administration of the colony, enslaved Africans carried their languages with them into bondage, non-French European immigrant groups brought their languages and a French-based creole had developed in Louisiana before the end of the eighteenth century. All of these speech varieties came into contact and changed as a result. The linguistic situation of Louisiana today owes its unique character to all of these influences. Third, the naming of languages is not a precise science – especially in Louisiana. This is particularly true when it comes to Creole and French. Thomas Klingler (2003b) demonstrates that the choice of glossonym (that is, language label) is highly correlated with ethnonym (that is, ethnic label). This means that the glossonym *Creole* has more to do with the ethnic identity of a speaker than any linguistic features of a given speech variety.

And yet there is also a long tradition of labelling speech as *Creole* in Louisiana. The first documented use of *Creole* as a glossonym is from a trial following a failed slave revolt in Pointe Coupée Parish in the late eighteenth century (Klingler 2003a, 44). This language was distinct enough from French and Spanish that it necessitated a translator for the court, although it was clearly known to the creoles (that is, Louisiana-born) of the era. But as described earlier, in the wake of the Civil War, the word *Creole* became problematic due to its imprecise racial quality. As people battled over who should count as Creole, they also sparred over what language should count as Creole. For those who saw *Creole* as only appropriate in designating whites, describing the language of non-whites with the same term was anathema. But setting aside the controversy of the glossonym itself, we now turn to some of the linguistic features of the speech variety popularly known as Louisiana Creole. The earliest linguistic descriptions of Louisiana Creole come from the last decades of the nineteenth century (Mercier 1880; Fortier 1884), and they list several traits that distinguish Creole from Louisiana Regional French. These traits include a distinctive set of pronouns, tense marking with pre-posed particles (as opposed to verbal conjugation), and phonological processes of shortening and agglutination. Later descriptions of Louisiana Creole indicate that the language may be adopting certain Louisiana Regional French traits (such as front-rounded vowels) and specific lexemes, but the two varieties have not demonstrably merged (cf. Lane 1935; Broussard 1942; Neumann 1985; Klingler 2003a). Perhaps the most perplexing phenomenon for language researchers is the tendency of speakers to mix characteristics from Louisiana Creole and Louisiana Regional French in their speech (Lane 1935, 8; Tentchoff 1975; Klingler 2005). This can make it very difficult to figure out where one ends and the other begins. Nevertheless, scholars seem to agree that – along with certain emblematic lexemes (cf. Neumann 1985, 52) – the best way to distinguish them is morphosyntactically (Valdman and Klingler 1997). In the sections that follow, and in an attempt to avoid accusations of superimposing glossonyms, I refer to the language variety described by the aforementioned "Creole" traits as Characteristic Louisiana Creole (CLC). This contrasts, then, with descriptions of "French" in Louisiana, which I refer to as Characteristic Louisiana French (CLF). Please note that these labels may or may not agree with local conventions of use.

Zydeco

The music known today as zydeco takes its name from a saying in Southwest Louisiana, "Les haricots est pas salés" (The green beans aren't salty), which refers to hard times economically (Spitzer 1986, 327; Ancelet 1996, 127). "Zydeco" is an approximate English pronunciation of the French *haricots*.[2] This expression can be heard as early as Alan Lomax's recordings of Louisiana musicians in the 1930s (Le Menestrel 2015, 14), and it eventually became the title of Clifton Chenier's genre-defining hit of the same name. Musically, the style derived from a number of earlier precedents: Louisiana French folk music known as *la-la*, religious *juré* chants, Afro-Caribbean polyrhythms and more. Creoles and Cajuns were very much united by the "French" music that they played, but race remained a significant boundary between the two groups. This boundary was sharply visible during the popularization of Cajun music, while Creole music was largely sidelined. In fact, under the influence of Cajunization (Trépanier 1991), zydeco was sometimes simply called "black Cajun music" (Spitzer 1986, 9). The history of mutual influence and performance among Creole and Cajun musicians is often glossed over in favour of a dichotomy borrowed from the Anglo-American socio-racial order. This was the context in which Clifton Chenier was raised. And as Ancelet advises, "To understand zydeco today, one must understand Clifton Chenier" (1996, 140).

Chenier was born in 1925 in a rural setting outside of Opelousas, Louisiana. In the 1940s, Clifton and his brother Cleveland joined a stream of migrants bound for Texas to take advantage of the economic opportunities created by the oil boom (see also Chambers 2014; Wendte 2020a, b). It was here that zydeco took its distinctive shape. Chenier managed to take the African-influenced French folk music of Southwest Louisiana and blend it with African American influences he encountered in Southeast Texas, namely blues and R&B. The results were at the same time old and new. This frustrated some musicians who claimed that Chenier's music was nothing special or original (Le Menestrel 2015, 97). Le Menestrel (2015) suggests that some of this animosity towards Chenier's style within the Creole community may be tied to old rivalries between creoles of colour and darker-skinned creoles. In particular, Le Menestrel highlights Chenier's musical use of a "Louisiana Creole speech variety", which she argues is associated with slavery (Ibid., 167). But innovative or not, Chenier's brand of zydeco is what was exported to far-flung corners of the globe, and it is the sound that most people today associate with the genre. His influence has been so great, in fact, that many young players today can see back no further than Clifton Chenier when they consider the roots of zydeco (Ancelet 1996, 142). Chenier's facility with multiple musical genres greatly expanded zydeco's audience, and it was likely his role in bringing zydeco to these new audiences that earned Chenier the title "King of Zydeco".

Contemporary Situation

As mentioned earlier, *Creole* today is a racialized label for many. The black–white dichotomy of contemporary Anglo-American society finds parallel expression in the differential uses of *Creole* and *Cajun* in Louisiana as both ethnic labels and linguistic labels. Labelling practices display ethnoglossic isomorphism, where ethnonyms come to stand in for glossonyms (Wendte 2020a, b). For example, black or mixed-race speakers of any French-lexified variety (whether CLC or CLF) dub the language *Creole* by virtue of their self-identification as creoles, whereas white speakers of the same variety will call it *Cajun* due to their self-identification as Cajuns. Thus, language labels are only reliable indicators of a speaker's identity, not the linguistic features of the language variety in question (Klingler 2003b; Dajko 2012; Spitzer 1986). There is, of course, no a priori link between a given ethnic identity and a language variety. However, ethnic groups often come to be associated ideologically with specific forms of language (Eastman and Reese 1981). Formerly, Creole identity was associated with a cultivated variety of French shared with other elites of francophone Louisiana (Domínguez 1986, 211; Cable 1884, 41). Today, Creole identity is more frequently associated with what was described earlier as CLC (Istre 2018, 109–53). Another aspect of this may be the contemporary revitalization efforts for "Louisiana Creole", which uniquely target CLC.

Of all the French-lexified speech varieties of the Gulf South, Louisiana Creole is by far the most threatened. Ingrid Neumann-Holzschuh and Thomas Klingler (2013) estimated a population of native speakers "well under 10,000", and Oliver Mayeux (2019, 59) estimates the current number to be just over 6,000. But even as intergenerational transmission tapers off and the number of native speakers dwindles, a limited revitalization movement has sprung up online. These efforts are thanks largely to the involvement of Dr. Christophe Landry, a Louisiana Creole who has put considerable time and energy into developing media, learning materials and awareness for the language. One important aspect of Landry's revitalization push is his decision to adopt and rehabilitate the glossonym *Kouri-Vini* to distinguish CLC from the CLF that occasionally gets labelled *Creole*. Kouri-Vini has historically been used as a somewhat derogatory way to refer to CLC (formed by combining the Louisiana Creole verbs "to go" and "to come"), but by reappropriating the term, it gives self-identified creoles an explicit language variety with which to associate (though not all self-identified creoles care to be associated with this speech variety). To further aid creoles in claiming a distinct ethnolinguistic identity, Landry and a team of community members developed a unique orthography for Kouri-Vini that distinguishes it from French on the one hand and from other French-based Creoles (like Haitian) on the other (Landry et al. 2016). The social weight of orthographic choices (Sebba 2007) ensures that this new orthographic system provides Louisiana Creoles (who choose to associate with Kouri-Vini) a visible index of identity apart from that of white-identified Cajuns. Such efforts constitute a kind of "strategic essentialism" (McElhinny 1996; Bucholtz 2003; Jaffe 2007; Barrett 2008) to validate a language variety and its associated identity. Mayeux (2014, 2015, 2019) compares the variety of Louisiana Creole used in the online revitalization community with the speech of the language's last native speakers. Although the differences between the two appear rather slight, if Louisiana Creole is to endure in the twenty-first century, it will likely be the variety championed by the revitalization movement.

Just as French influence – along with the word *Creole* – was once widespread throughout the Gulf South, so zydeco today transgresses neat boundaries and state lines. The contemporary spelling of *zydeco*, in fact, actually originated in Texas. According to Michael Tisserand (1998, 17–20) the term *zydeco* was specifically meant to refer to the blend of African American and Franco-Louisianan music that took root in Houston neighbourhoods settled by Louisiana migrants. This highlights the translocal character of zydeco, which has prompted Charles Wood and James Fraher (2006) to dub the combined regions of Southeast Texas and Southwest Louisiana the "zydeco corridor". As zydeco continues to evolve, Clifton Chenier is still widely regarded as the founding father of the genre. Chenier performed older waltzes and two-steps along with blues, instrumentals and even translations of popular songs. His eclectic musical repertoire was matched by his lyrical repertoire. Chenier would sing in English, CLC and CLF. In fact, he often mixed features of these last two speech varieties in innovative ways that often confound simple classification. His lasting influence on zydeco has ensured that his music and lyrics remain iconic within the genre. Given zydeco's continued importance to the Creole community as a badge of identity, Chenier's lyrics represent a great opportunity to learn about the linguistic features that make up a Louisiana Creole's ethnolinguistic repertoire (cf. Benor 2010; Wendte 2020a, b). These, in turn, may help provide future learning targets for the ongoing revitalization and reclamation of Louisiana Creole language and identity.

Methodology

In order to determine the language variety or varieties that Clifton Chenier used in his music, I transcribed fifty songs that included non-English lyrics, which are assumed to be either CLC, CLF or some mixture of the two. Taken together, these transcriptions form the Clifton Chenier Lyrical Corpus (CCLC). It should be noted that a lyrical corpus is bound to differ from natural speech in at least some aspects, but I believe the inherently performative nature of music makes such a corpus uniquely valuable in a study of ethnolinguistic repertoire. As seen in the earlier discussion, CLC distinguishes itself from CLF in a number of ways: phonologically, morphosyntactically and lexically. In this study, I examine five variables to determine whether a given lyric belongs to CLC or CLF: (1) first-person singular subject pronoun, (2) form of the perfect tense for dynamic verbs,[3] (3) form of "to have", (4) gender in possessive adjectives, and (5) syntactic position of direct object pronouns. Variables 1, 2, 4 and 5 are morphosyntactic, and variable 3 is lexical. The first three variables are taken from Klingler (2003b), and the last two variables proceed from the descriptive literature on Louisiana Creole referenced earlier (Lane 1935; Broussard 1942; Neumann 1985; Klingler 2003a). For each of the selected variables, there exist marked variants that belong either to CLC or CLF. The five variables and their variants are listed in table 8.1.

Within the CCLC, each song presents an environment for at least one of these linguistic variables to surface. For each environment present in a given song, I noted whether the lyrics contained the CLC variant, the CLF variant or some mixture of the two (either by alternating between forms or by using some kind of intermediate form). It is important to note that the songs in the CCLC are not assumed to be written exclusively in either CLC or CLF; rather, the purpose of analysing each song's lyrics is to note the presence or absence of variants associated with each linguistic variety in those environments where they would be expected to appear (that is, in those environments indicated by the five variables chosen for analysis). The results were compiled and relative frequencies tabulated. After presenting a cumulative summary of these results, I discuss each variable and provide transcriptions of lyrical segments from the CCLC that show a representative sample of the variants for each given variable.

I fully acknowledge that orthographic choices – while theoretically arbitrary – are never neutral (cf. Sebba 2007). Within this chapter, I have chosen to represent all non-English lyrical segments that demonstrate a CLC variant using the Kouri-Vini orthography (Landry et al. 2016). Alternatively, when the segment is used to demonstrate a CLF variant, I use a modified French orthography. These conventions are not meant to imply that an entire song or even utterance is exclusively in CLC or CLF; rather,

Table 8.1 Linguistic Variables for Determining CLC or CLF

Variable	CLC Variant(s)	CLF Variant(s)
1. 1S-pro	*mo* [mo]	*je* [ʒə]
2. perfect	bare verb	aux + verb (p.p.)
3. "to have"	*gin* [gẽ]	forms of *avoir* [a(v)waɾ]
4. poss. adj. gender	*mô* [mo] (m./f.)	*mon* [mɔ̃] (m.); *ma* [ma] (f.)
5. DO-pro syntax	SVO	SOV

I employ differential orthography to call attention to the language varieties with which the variant under consideration is most closely associated. In cases where a segment's linguistic features are of mixed or indeterminate provenance, Kouri-Vini orthography is the default. When phonological issues are being discussed, I also use the International Phonetic Alphabet (IPA). Following a discussion of the lyrics, I incorporate a brief analysis of the non-lyrical commentary audible on certain recordings. These comments provide some interesting perspectives on how Chenier saw his own ethnolinguistic identity and its relation to other ethnic and linguistic categories.

Results and Discussion

Table 8.2 gives the cumulative percentages of those songs that use CLC, CLF and both/other variants of the five linguistic variables discussed in the previous section.

Overall, the songs in the CCLC demonstrate a high degree of variability. No attempt is made here to discover which linguistic variants might implicate others, though this is a potential avenue for future research. One superficial observation: whenever a song in the CCLC contained environments for both the perfect tense and a direct object pronoun, both variants belonged to either CLC or CLF. Said differently, for the aforementioned two variables, there is no mixing of variants from different language varieties – if a song's lyrics express the perfect tense according to CLC/CLF conventions, then the syntax of direct object pronouns will also

Table 8.2 Frequency of Linguistic Features within the CCLC ($n=50$)

	1s-pro	perfect	"to have"	gender	DO-pro
CLC	10%	18%	70%	0%	14%
	$n=4$	$n=6$	$n=15$	$n=0$	$n=5$
CLF	14%	68%	25%	100%	72%
	$n=6$	$n=23$	$n=4$	$n=18$	$n=26$
Both/other[a]	76%	15%	5%	0%	14%
	$n=32$	$n=5$	$n=1$	$n=0$	$n=5$
Total[b]	$n=42$	$n=34$	$n=20$	$n=18$	$n=36$

[a] If, for a given variable, variants from both CLC and CLF appear within the same song, it is counted in the category "both/other".
[b] Totals reflect those songs within the CCLC in which an environment for a given variable was present.

adhere to that variety's norms. This suggests that there is at least some predictable patterning of the linguistic variables in certain configurations. In the following sections, I examine each of the five linguistic variables in detail and present a lyrical segment from the CCLC to demonstrate each variant of the linguistic variable under discussion. Then, I present the full lyrics of one song to illustrate the mixed characteristics that occur throughout the CCLC. Finally, I look at a number of non-lyrical segments of Clifton Chenier's speech to give an idea of Chenier's own metalinguistic awareness and attitudes.

Variable 1: First-Person Singular Subject Pronoun

Chenier shows a tendency to mix CLC and CLF variants of the first-person singular subject pronoun or use ambiguous forms like *mòj* that one could argue to be shared by both varieties. He does this in 76 per cent of the songs where an environment for this variable presents itself. He uses exclusively CLC variants in 10 per cent of the songs and exclusively CLF variants in 14 per cent of the songs. This seems to be the only variable for which innovative forms exist as opposed simply to a mixture of CLC and CLF variants within a song.

(1)
Mo   linm   la   kanmpony,   mo   Ø   in   ti   boug   la   kanmpony
1S.SBJ   love   DEF   country   1S.SBJ   COP   INDEF   little   boy   DEF   country
I love the country, I'm a little country boy (C5, 2:04)

(2)
J'ai   parti   dans   Lafayette   pour   faire   changer   mon   nom
1S-AUX   leave.PST.PRTCP   to   Lafayette   for   do   change   1S.POSS   name
I went to Lafayette to get my name changed (C33, 2:19)

(3)
Toukèkènn   ve   konné   kòfær   mòj   apé   kité
everyone   want   know   why   1S.SBJ   PROG   leave
Everyone want to know why I'm leaving (C32, 1:28)

(4)
Mòjé   Ø   las,   las,   las   isit
1S.SBJ   COP   tired   tired   tired   here
I'm tired, tired, tired here (C32, 1:46)

Example 1 demonstrates two clear instances of the most frequent CLC variant, *mo*. Example 2 demonstrates a somewhat less clear but still discernible CLF variant, *je* (in CLF, this form contracts with *ai* to produce *j'ai*). For examples 3 and 4, one could argue the *mòj* and *mòjé* are really just CLF variants with a preceding tonic pronoun [either *moi* (CLF) or *mò* (CLC)]. In International Standard French, this would have an emphatic effect, but in Louisiana French, subject doubling is a common pattern that does not necessarily carry the same pragmatic weight (Rottet 1996). Given the long history of contact between CLC and CLF, it seems possible that the tendency for subject doubling – along with CLF variants of those subjects – could have been borrowed into CLC. The differences in form between examples 3 and 4 seem to be due to phonotactic constraints. In example 3, the presence of an initial vowel in the progressive marker *apé* permits the apocope of [e] in the subject pronoun. In example 4, however, the [e] is retained because the next word (*las*) begins with a consonant.

One difficulty in determining the precise form of the first-person singular subject pronoun – especially when some form of *je* [ʒə] is involved – is that the final vowel often changes due either to contextual factors or phonological incorporation into CLC. According to George Lane (1935, 9), French [ə] frequently becomes [e] in Louisiana Creole. This means that if *je* were phonologically integrated into Louisiana Creole, the result would be pronounced [ʒe], which is homophonous with CLF *j'ai* (I have). I argue that this is precisely what one can observe in the CCLC. If this seems improbable, consider these two lines from the same Clifton Chenier song:

(5)
| Tu | me | linm | pi, | jé | Ø | mizérab | tou | lajounné |
2S.SBJ IS.OBJ love no.more IS.SBJ COP miserable all day
You don't love me anymore, I'm miserable all day long (C24, 1:13)

(6)
| Tu | me | linm | pi, | mo | Ø | mizérab | tou | lajounné |
2S.SBJ IS.OBJ love no.more IS.SBJ COP miserable all day
You don't love me anymore, I'm miserable all day long (C24, 2:27)

Examples 5 and 6 are identical except for the first-person subject pronoun, which makes it clear that *jé* [ʒe] is being used as an alternative to the more common CLC variant, *mo*.

Such an analysis of *jé* makes it easier to account for one of the more perplexing variants (a hapax) revealed in the data: *mé*.

(7)
| Mé | Ø | in | koshon | pou | twa, | Ø | vadé | fouyé |
IS.SBJ COP INDEF pig for 2S.OBJ IS.SBJ go.FUT root
I'm a hog for you, gonna root (C25, 2:15)

If we consider the "maximal" variant of the first-person subject pronoun to be *mòjé* (as in example 4), then *mé* (example 7) can be taken as an optionally contracted form that syncopates the medial segments [ɔ] and [ʒ]. Later in the same song, another variant appears in the same position: *jé*.

(8)
Jé	Ø	in	koshon	pou	twa
1S.SBJ	COP	INDEF	pig	for	2S.OBJ

I'm a hog for you (C25, 3:03)

In this case (example 8), one could argue that there is an aphesis of the initial segments [m] and [ɔ]. But ultimately, whether or not *jé* represents a contraction of the longer word *mòjé*, the preceding morphosyntactic data do not permit [mɔ.ʒe] to properly be classified as either CLC or CLF.

Variable 2: The Perfect Tense

Chenier favours forming the perfect tense with an auxiliary, which is the CLF variant of this variable. This occurs in 68 per cent of the songs where an environment for this variable presents itself. The bare verb is used for the perfect tense (the CLC variant) in 18 per cent of songs, and in 15 per cent of songs both ways of forming the perfect tense are attested.

(9)
Mo	ve	twa	tèl	kòm	to	vini-Ø	dan	péyi
1S.SBJ	want	2S.OBJ	such	as	2S.SBJ	come-PST	in	country

I want you like you came into the world (C45, 4:25)

(10)
C'est	là	t'as	'chappé	hier	au	soir
PRST[4]-PRS	there	2S.SBJ-AUX	escape.PST.PTCP	yesterday	at	night

That's where you got away to last night (C4, 0:32)

In example 9, the verb *vini* (to come) appears as a bare verb, indicating the CLC variant of the perfect tense. Example 10 illustrates the CLF variant of the perfect tense, which includes the auxiliary verb *as* (a form of *avoir* conjugated for the second-person singular) followed by the past participle *'chappé* (to escape, run away).

Examples 9 and 10 were chosen to demonstrate the two variants of the perfect tense with a second-person singular subject. The reason for this is to avoid the inherent ambiguity of the first-person singular subject pronoun in this context. Consider the following:

(11a)
Jé	arivé-Ø	asmatin,	é	çété	gran	jour
1S.SBJ	arrive-PST	this.morning	and	PRST.PST	full	day

I arrived this morning, and it was broad daylight (C36, 1:37)

(11b)
J'ai	arrivé	à	ce	matin,	et	c'était	grand	jour
1S.SBJ-AUX	arrive.PST.PTCP	at	this	morning	and	PRST-PST	full	day

I arrived this morning, and it was broad daylight (C36, 1:37)

In examples 11a and 11b, the sentence would be translated to "I arrived this morning, and it was broad daylight." The morphological breakdown, however, is not so clear. As mentioned earlier, one CLC reflex of the French pronoun *je* [ʒə] is *jé* [ʒe], which is phonologically identical to the CLF translation of the English phrase "I have" (that is *j'ai* [ʒe]). Additionally, Louisiana French routinely forms the perfect tense with a form of *avoir* plus the past participle of the verb. In the case of the first-person singular, that means that the perfect tense necessarily begins with *j'ai* [ʒe] (followed by the past participle of the verb). Based solely on the utterance [ʒe a.ri.ve], it is impossible to tell if Chenier is using a CLC reflex of *je* and a bare form of the verb (as shown in example 11a) or a compound form beginning with the CLF elements *j'ai* (as shown in example 11b). Within the CCLC, sometimes context gives clues as to the proper interpretation, but a certain mystery remains. At least for the first-person singular, then, this could also be a case of multiple causation (cf. Thomason and Kaufman 1988).

Compounding the ambiguity surrounding the canonical nature of this variable within the CCLC, there are also examples of song-internal variation:

(12)
Èl	kité-Ø	mò	tou	sèl
3SF.SBJ	leave-PST	1S.OBJ	all	alone

She left me all alone (C28, 0:55)

(13)
Elle	m'a	quitté	moi	tout	seul
3SF.SBJ	1S.OBJ-AUX	leave.PST.PTCP	1S.OBJ	all	alone

She left me all alone (C28, 2:28)

Examples 12 and 13, taken from the same song, display two different variants for expressing the perfect tense. Example 12 shows a bare verb in accordance with CLC norms, and example 13 shows a pattern in line with CLF norms. The fact that these two sentences are otherwise almost identical makes this variation all the more remarkable. Clearly an additional factor in analysing these sentences is the presence of a pre-verbal object pronoun in example 13, but that will be discussed in greater detail later.

Variable 3: "To Have"

Chenier displays a preference for the CLC lexeme *gin* whenever a form of "to have" is expected to surface. This is evident in 70 per cent of the songs where an environment for this variable occurs. In 25 per cent of songs Chenier uses the CLF variant *avoir* (or a form thereof), and in 5 per cent of songs both *gin* and forms of *avoir* occur.

(14)
Tu	*gin*	*dê*	*joli*	*ti*	*zyè-Ø*
2S.SBJ	have	INDEF.PL	pretty	little	eye-PL

You have pretty little eyes (C42, 2:23)

(15)
Tu	*devra*	*avoir*	*honte*
2S.SBJ	ought.FUT	have	shame

You ought to be ashamed (C11, 0:14)

Example 14, which translates as "You have pretty little eyes", illustrates a straightforward instance of the CLC variant *gin* being used to show possession. There is not a direct parallel for the CLF variant *avoir*, but example 15 does illustrate the use of *avoir* to idiomatically express the notion of being ashamed. In CLC, this notion could be expected to appear simply as *hont* or with the addition of "to have" as *gin hont*.

Chenier uses *gin* and *avoir* in a variety of ways within the CCLC:

(16)
Si	*tu*	*ve*	*amizé*	*tu*	*gin*	*pou*	*dépensé*	*tô*	*larjen*
If	2S.SBJ	want	amuse	2S.SBJ	have	for	spend	2S.POSS	money

If you want to have a good time you have to spend your money (C6, 1:06)

(17)
Mo	*ve*	*konné*	*kwa*	*gin*	*arivé*
1S.SBJ	want	know	what	have	happen

I want to know what's going to happen (C14, 2:24)

(18)
Mòj	*konné,*	*mòj*	*konné,*	*je*	*konné*	*pa*	*kwa*	*ina*	*avèk*	*twa*
1S.SBJ	know	1S.SBJ	know	1S.SBJ	know	neg	what	EX[5]	with	2S.OBJ

I know, I know, I don't know what's wrong with you (C35, 1:56)

(19)
Mé   ina   kishòj   disu   mô   nidé
But   EX   something   on   1S.POSS mind
But there's something on my mind (C43, 0:33)

(20)
Yé   pa   gin   pærsonn,   wèl,   pou   me   linmé
EX   NEG   EX   nobody   INTJ[6] for   1S.OBJ love
There's nobody, well, to love me (C28, 0:31)

(21)
Mo   jamé   i   de   lamour   dépi   twa   ê   gonn
1S.SBJ   never   have.PST   of   love   since   2S.SBJ COP   gone
I haven't had any love since you've been gone (C28, 2:34)

(22)
Mòj   té   gin   nidé   pou   te   kouri   wa
1S.SBJ   PST   have   mind   for   2S.OBJ   go   see
I had a mind to go see you (C8, 0:59)

In example 16, *gin* is used as part of the modal phrase *gin pou* (to have to), denoting obligation or necessity. According to the *Dictionary of Louisiana French*, a parallel construction exists that uses *avoir* (Valdman and Rottet 2010, 51). Example 17 features another auxiliary use of *gin*, this time to express the future (probably with an elided *pou*, cf. Neumann 1985, 227).

When Chenier does employ a form of the CLF verb *avoir*, it is possible to analyse these as fixed expressions or phrases borrowed from Louisiana Regional French into Louisiana Creole. In example 18, for instance, *kwa ina* represents an idiomatic way of saying "what's wrong", borrowed from an expanded CLF form *quoi il y en a*[7]. A very similar use of *ina* is in presentative constructions such as example 19. In this instance, *ina* can be translated as "there is". In both examples 18 and 19, however, the reflex of a form of *avoir* cannot be meaningfully isolated from the larger unit, *ina*. This calls into question whether such uses should truly be considered as uses of *avoir*. A contrastive form of the presentative construction can be seen in example 20, which uses the CLC variant *gin*. Another environment where forms of *avoir* occur in the CCLC is in the formation of CLF variants of the perfect tense (that is, aux + verb). In CLF (though not in International Standard French), the auxiliary used in forming the perfect tense is almost always a form of *avoir*. As has been mentioned before, this can cause ambiguity when the subject is first-person singular (see the earlier discussion and examples 11a and 11b). The one context in which Chenier does occasionally appear to use an unambiguous form of *avoir* is in the perfect tense. Example 21 would be translated as "I haven't had any love since you've been gone." Chenier uses the irregular form *i* (borrowed from CLF *eu*, the past participle of *avoir*) instead of the expected CLC variant *té gin*[8] (seen in example 22).

The preference for *gin* within the CCLC is significant for two reasons. First, it is the only CLC variant among the five variables analysed that Chenier clearly favours. Second, *gin* is a highly salient lexical marker of CLC (as opposed to CLF). Chenier's use of *gin* therefore indexes an identification with Louisiana Creole, despite the fact that for the other four linguistic variables he favours CLF (or ambiguous) variants. The association of *gin* with CLC is so strong, however, that this may outweigh his other linguistic choices that align more closely with CLF. The unexpected co-occurrence of *gin* with more CLF variants could also suggest that Chenier was deliberately transgressing linguistic norms.

Variable 4: Grammatical Gender in Possessive Adjectives

Of the five variables selected for analysis, grammatical gender in possessive adjectives is the only one that shows a completely uniform tendency: Chenier marks feminine gender in 100 per cent of songs where an environment for this variable occurs. This is the only variable for which Chenier shows no variability.

(23)

Moi	je	peux	dire	par	la	manière	tu	tiens	ma	main
1S.TON[9]	1S.SBJ	can	say	by	DEF	manner	2S.SBJ	hold	1S.POSS.F	hand

I can tell by the way you hold my hand (C27, 1:09)

In example 23, the noun *main* (hand) is marked as grammatically feminine by the presence of the possessive adjective *ma*. This form is a CLF variant, whereas a CLC variant in the same case would be *mô* (grammatically unmarked for the feminine). The present analysis may actually under-report the occurrence of this particular variable because it is only visible when there is a grammatically feminine noun being possessed. The gender system in Louisiana Creole is an emergent category that demonstrates variability across regions, speakers and time. Furthermore, as Mayeux (2019, 129) discusses, it is unclear whether this category is best seen as a strict two-gender system of masculine and feminine or a canonical one-gender system where masculine is the default but feminine is optional in some cases. Within the CCLC, there is no evidence that would point definitively to one system or the other. Chenier's use of gendered possessive adjectives makes it clear, however, that if feminine gender is only an optional feature for certain Louisiana Creole nouns, he elects to express it wherever possible.

There are two implications that arise from this observed behaviour. First, Chenier's sung speech variety can be assumed to have a fully developed system of number agreement. This follows from Mayeux's (2019, 130–31) finding that, in accordance with proposed language universals (cf. Greenberg 1980, 95), CLC speakers must first demonstrate the category of number before they demonstrate the category of gender. The second implication is that the variety of Creole employed by Chenier within the CCLC is closer to the regional dialect of Bayou Teche Creole than the regional dialect found along the Mississippi River. This proceeds from the observation that Teche Creole displays higher rates of gender agreement than Mississippi Creole (Mayeux 2019, 121).

Variable 5: Syntax of Direct Object Pronouns

The best descriptions of CLC indicate that the language is entirely subject–verb–object (SVO) (see variable 2). Nevertheless, when a personal object pronoun is present, Chenier favours a subject–object–verb (SOV) syntactic order that matches CLF. This occurs in 72 per cent of the songs containing an environment for this variable. Additionally, he uses an SVO ordering (associated with CLC) in 14 per cent of the songs, and in 14 per cent of the songs both syntactic orders are attested.

(24)
Mo   ve   twa   tèl   kòm   to   vini-Ø   dan   péyi
1S.SBJ want   2S.OBJ   such   as   2S.SBJ come-PST   in   country
I want you like you came into the world (C45, 1:34)

(25)
Moi   je   te   l'aime   avec   tout   mon   cœur
1S.TON   1S.SBJ   2S.OBJ   love   with   all   1S.POSS   heart
I love you with all my heart (C49, 1:01)

Example 24 illustrates the CLC variant (SVO): *mo* (1ps) *ve* (want) *twa* (2ps). This contrasts with example 25, which illustrates the CLF variant (SOV): *moi je* (1ps) *te* (2ps) *l'aime* (love). Examples 24 and 25 are both in the indicative mood, but there are at least two other environments where this variable can surface: the perfect and the infinitive. First, let us consider the perfect tense:

(26)

Yé	pélé-Ø	mò	fou, fou, fou,	mé	jé	konné	kwa	j'apé	fé
3PL.SBJ	call-PST	1S.OBJ	crazy	but	1S.SBJ	know	what	1S.SBJ-PROG	do

They call me crazy, but I know what I'm doing (C16, 0:38)

(27)

Tu	m'as	quitté	pour	t'en	aller
2S.SBJ	1S.OBJ-AUX	leave.PST.PTCP	for	2S.REFL	go

You left me to go away (C31, 0:38)

In example 26, the CLC variant syntactic order is exactly the same (SVO), the only difference being that the verb in its bare form here represents the perfect instead of the indicative (compare with example 20). In example 27, the CLF variant ordering is also retained, though now there is an intervening auxiliary between the verb's complement and the verb itself. Now let us turn to the infinitive:

(28)

Mo	vé	mariyé,	mo	vé	a	mariyé	twa
1S.SBJ	want	marry	1S.SBJ	want	to	marry	2S.OBJ

I want to marry, I want to marry you (C18, 1:34)

(29)

Yé	pas	gain	personne	pour	me	l'aimer
EX	NEG	EX	nobody	for	1S.OBJ	love

There's nobody to love me (C28, 1:40)

(30)

Mòj	ve	te	mariyé,	mòj	ve	mariyé	twa
1S.SBJ	want	2S.OBJ	marry	1S.SBJ	want	marry	2S.OBJ

'I want to marry you, I want to marry you' (C28, 1:12)

It is first important to note that in infinitive constructions, there is no explicit subject. What interests us, then, is the ordering of the infinitive verb and its object (which is expected to reflect the same syntactic order as in indicative or perfect clauses). And indeed, examples 28 and 29 correspond with the other examples for each respective variety. It is interesting to note, though, that there are instances like example 30 where both the CLC and CLF variants co-occur in close proximity to one another.

This variability of the syntactic order of direct object pronouns is somewhat unexpected (especially within the same song). This could be a consequence of phrasal borrowing where all elements – including "divergent" syntactical order – are transferred. For less extreme examples of co-occurrence, it is possible that certain verbs prefer certain syntactical ordering. For instance, the verb *linmé* (to love) appears rather frequently in the CCLC, and in all but one case it takes SOV ordering. Another interesting feature of this linguistic variable is that it is the only one that readily patterns with another variable. For all songs within the CCLC that contain possible environments for variables 2 and 5 (that is, the perfect tense and the syntax of direct object pronouns), the variables agree on either the CLC or the CLF variants.

(31)
Mo   ve   twa   tèl   kòm   to   vini-Ø   dan   péyi
1S.SBJ want 2S.OBJ such as 2S.SBJ come-PST in country
I want you like you came into the world (C45, 1:42)

(32)
Tu   m'as   fait   pleurer, tu   m'as   fait   brailler
2S.SBJ 1S.OBJ-AUX do.PST.PTCP weep 2S.SBJ 1S.OBJ-AUX do.PST.PTCP cry
You made me weep, you made me cry (C40, 0:22)

Example 31 demonstrates both a bare verb for the perfect tense and an SVO word order (both CLC variants), and example 32 demonstrates two instances of a composed perfect tense that uses an auxiliary as well as SOV word order (both CLF variants).

Analysis of "You Promised Me Love" (C48 in the CCLC)

To see how these variants all come together, I present the transcribed lyrics for one song in the CCLC:[10]

> Tu m'a promèt de lamour,   1
> Lamour va jamé mouri,   2
> Tu m'a promèt de lamour,   3
> Tu va dèt dan mô koté.   4
> Tu m'a promèt de lamour,   5
> Lamour va jamé mouri,   6
> Tu m'a kité,   7
> Avèk in nidé trakasé.   8
> *Bridge [spoken]:*
>
>> Tu konné? Lamour, lamour je mòj gin, va jamé mouri, shær. Tou lamour jé gin pou twa, lamour endan mô kœr, mo gonn mèt tou mâ amour dan tâ min.
>
> Tu m'a promèt de lamour,   9
> Lamour va jamé mouri,   10
> Mé tu m'a kité,   11
> Avèk in nidé trakasé.   12

In terms of the five linguistic variables under consideration, note the diversity of variants for the first-person singular subject pronouns occurring in the bridge. One can hear at least three: *mòj, jé* and *mo*. There are CLC, CLF and mixed variants. For the perfect tense, we see a CLF variant predominates in lines 1, 3 and so on. The form of the verb "to have" is unambiguously CLC *gin*, occurring in the bridge. Possessive adjectives display grammatical gender – the CLF variant – at the end of the bridge. Finally, we see that direct object pronouns display SOV syntax (occurring in the same lines as the perfect tense, namely line 1, line 3 and so on). Because the CLC variants only occur within the spoken bridge, one could argue that the song itself is in CLF. However, the featural mixture demonstrated elsewhere within the CCLC renders such an explanation a bit overly simplified.

Language Attitudes of Clifton Chenier

The final piece of data in this chapter concerns the non-lyrical content audible in certain Clifton Chenier recordings. Although the body of Chenier's songs varies somewhat from performance to performance, his interluding banter is unique for each given audience. These snippets provide some insight into the way that Chenier saw himself as a performer and a language user. These perspectives, then, help inform our understanding of the tools Chenier deployed to index his own ethnolinguistic identity.

(33) Clifton Chenier (CC):

I'm a Frenchman, see? Yeah, I talk that French. I didn't know how important it was to me until when, when I went to Paris last year. Yeah. When I got to Paris, boy, we start talkin' that French and that was it. I got right there, I laid right there with 'em, boy. They ain't had nothin' on me, Jack. I ain't lyin' either. (C15, 4:22–4:41)

(34) CC:

When I got in Paris, boy, talk that French, that was it ... I had the audience fooled in French. (C51*, 4:10–4:18)

(35) CC:

Komen ça va, misyè? Toukishòj ê mannifik? Toukishòj ê kòrèk?[11] Well, you know, I ... I speak French too, see, but it's different language, so ... (C52*, 0:03–0:18)

(36) CC:

They call me the Black Cajun ... Frenchman. (C52*, 0:58)

(37) Band member:

We gonna lay a little touch of Louisiana on you today – *parlez-vous français* and all that other stuff, you know. (C53*, 3:28)

In example 33, Chenier takes the opportunity to brag a little bit about his familiarity with the French language and its associated identity (Frenchman). This quote occurs at the end of C15, a traditional waltz with a feature mix somewhere in between CLC and CLF (not unlike the rest of the CCLC). This recording was made in 1971, which was still early in the days of "Cajunization" (Trépanier 1991). Rather than identify with today's common labels of *Creole* or *Cajun*, Chenier chooses the label *Frenchman*. This word is significant for a number of reasons. First, it is a word that does not have strict racial associations in the Gulf South. Second, it is a word that is common to an area larger than Southwest Louisiana, extending into Southeast Texas as well (Louder and Leblanc 1979, 326). Third, it makes an explicit connection between a label and language use. Chenier calls himself a Frenchman and his language, *French*. We cannot forget that this recording occurred in front of an audience. With Chris Strachwitz in the crowd – one of the most influential people in convincing Chenier to record "real" zydeco in French – it is probable that Chenier was flaunting what he realized made him unique (Ancelet 1996, 139). Chenier also seems to have been aware of the tinge of artifice surrounding the image he crafted for himself. In example 34, he jokes with the crowd that he could "fool" an audience in French.

Examples 33 and 34 were recorded in front of a largely anglophone audience (presumably). At the very least, they were recorded in the United States. In examples 35 and 36, however, Chenier and his band were in Montreux, Switzerland, among francophones. In example 35, Clifton opens with a fairly unmarked greeting (for Louisiana), but he is quick to make the audience aware of two things: he is a francophone, but his language is different than what they speak. In this way Chenier both ingratiates himself to the audience as being someone who can communicate with them in their own language, but he also creates distance from the audience by asserting a distinctiveness for his variety in particular. Later in the same track (example 36), Chenier seems to read off a list of buzzwords: *black*, *Cajun* and *Frenchman*. Rather than assume that Chenier thought of himself in terms of these labels, I believe he was speaking to whatever motivation may have brought his audience members there to see him perform. Chenier demonstrates his shrewdness by making himself relatable yet unique whether in front of an anglophone or a francophone audience.

A final example testifies to the flexibility of Chenier's image. In example 37, prior to taking the stage, one of Chenier's bandmembers tells the audience that they are going to present something uniquely Louisianan. And in order to make the audience understand what he means, he uses the phrase *parlez-vous français* (do you speak French). What is interesting about this phrase is how marked it would have been historically among native Creole and French speakers in the Gulf South. Such a "book French"[12] form is potentially a result of the efforts of the Council for the Development of French in Louisiana (CODOFIL) to revalorize French in Louisiana, which were well under way in 1983 when example 37 was recorded. But despite the phrase's unnaturalness to Chenier's linguistic origins, it serves to index the ethnolinguistic image of himself that Chenier was selling. Once he took the stage, his lyrics did justice to his linguistic heritage – however misleading his introduction might have been.

Conclusions

This chapter examined a corpus of Clifton Chenier's non-English lyrics to better determine the linguistic nature of the variety or varieties he used in his music. And while artistic uses of language are likely to be subject to different constraints than discursive uses, the results show that Chenier routinely mixed variants from CLC and CLF. Of the five linguistic variables analysed, the only CLC variant for which Chenier displayed a strong preference was the form of the verb "to have" (*gin*). For the remaining four variables – form of the first-person singular subject pronoun, form of the perfect tense for dynamic verbs, gender of possessive adjectives and the syntactic order of direct object pronouns – Chenier tends to choose CLF variants the majority of the time. Chenier alternatively positioned himself at the centre or at the periphery of the French language depending on his audience. His creativity and flexibility could be argued to be component behaviours of his ethnolinguistic identity repertoire, which allowed him to perform a multifaceted Creole identity.

The lyrical performance of Clifton Chenier is foundational to the contemporary understanding of zydeco music. This genre, in turn, is widely perceived to be one of the most highly salient markers of Creole identity in Louisiana and the broader Gulf South. As the number of native speakers of Louisiana Creole continues to decline, the time is ripe for a language revitalization movement – which thankfully has already begun. This chapter, through an analysis of Chenier's creative use of linguistic resources, has aimed to support these burgeoning efforts to revalorize Creole ethnic identity and the language varieties associated with it.

Directions for Future Research

An important next step for this research would be to compare the results drawn from the CCLC with a corpus of spoken Louisiana Creole (preferably from the Opelousas area). This would permit us to understand the ways in which performed or sung Louisiana Creole may differ from the spoken language. Additionally, though Clifton Chenier was arguably the most influential zydeco performer, he is far from the only one. It would be beneficial to add transcriptions of other zydeco artists who have recorded in Louisiana Creole and Louisiana Regional French to compare and contrast Chenier's linguistic behaviour with theirs.

Acknowledgements

I would like to thank the two anonymous reviewers whose comments and critiques greatly improved the final version of this chapter. All faults that remain are my own.

Notes

1. Clifton Chenier, 1975, "Sa M'Appel Fou (They Call Me Crazy)", track 2 on *Bogalusa Boogie*, Arhoolie Records CD 347, 1990, compact disc.
2. The source of the [z] sound is the liaison of the definite article *les* with the noun *haricots*.
3. "Dynamic" or "action" verbs are morphologically distinguished from stative verbs (Valdman et al. 1998, 9).
4. Presentative.
5. Existential.
6. Interjection.
7. See also Tentchoff (1975, 101).
8. In contrast to dynamic verbs, *té* is used to form the perfect tense with stative verbs like *gin*.
9. Tonic.
10. Clifton Chenier, 1966, "You Promised Me Love", track 1 on *Get It*, Demon S&C, 2012, digital release.
11. "How's it going, guys? Is everything great? Is everything alright?" (my translation).
12. This is a colloquial way that franco-creolophones of the Gulf South refer to International Standard French.

References

Ancelet, Barry Jean. 1996. "Zydeco/Zarico: The Term and the Tradition". In *Creoles of Color of the Gulf South*, edited by James H. Dormon, 126–43. Knoxville: University of Tennessee Press.

Barrett, Rusty. 2008. "Linguistic Differentiation and Mayan Language Revitalization in Guatemala". *Journal of Sociolinguistics* 12 (3): 275–305.

Benor, Sarah Bunin. 2010. "Ethnolinguistic Repertoire: Shifting the Analytic Focus in Language and Ethnicity". *Journal of Sociolinguistics* 14 (2): 159–83.

Brasseaux, Carl A., Keith P. Fontenot, and Claude F. Oubre. 1994. *Creoles of Color in the Bayou Country*. Jackson: University Press of Mississippi.

Broussard, James Francis. 1972 [1942]. *Louisiana Creole Dialect*. Port Washington: Kennikat Press.

Bucholtz, Mary. 2003. "Sociolinguistic Nostalgia and the Authentication of Identity". *Journal of Sociolinguistics* 7 (3): 398–416.

Cable, George W. 1884. *The Creoles of Louisiana*. New York: Charles Scribner's Sons.

Chambers, Glenn. 2014. "'Goodbye God, I'm Going to Texas': The Migration of Louisiana Creoles of Colour and the Preservation of Black Catholic and Creole Traditions in Southeast Texas". *Journal of Religion and Popular Culture* 26 (1): 124–43.

Dajko, Nathalie. 2012. "Sociolinguistics of Ethnicity in Francophone Louisiana: Language and Ethnicity in French Louisiana". *Language and Linguistics Compass* 6 (5): 279–95.

Domínguez, Virginia R. 1986. *White by Definition: Social Classification in Creole Louisiana*. New Brunswick: Rutgers University Press.

Dubois, Sylvie, and Megan Melançon. 2000. "Creole Is, Creole Ain't: Diachronic and Synchronic Attitudes toward Creole Identity in Southern Louisiana". *Language in Society* 29 (02): 237–58.

Eastman, Carol M., and Thomas C. Reese. 1981. "Associated Language: How Language and Ethnic Identity Are Related". *General Linguistics* 21 (2): 109–16.

Ebongue, Augustin Emmanuel, and Ellen Hurst, eds. 2017. *Sociolinguistics in African Contexts: Perspectives and Challenges*. Multilingual Education, Volume 20. Dordrecht Heidelberg: Springer.

Eckert, Penelope. 2012. "Three Waves of Variation Study: The Emergence of Meaning in the Study of Sociolinguistic Variation". *Annual Review of Anthropology* 41 (1): 87–100.

Fortier, Alcée. 1884. "The French Language in Louisiana and the Negro-French Dialect". *Transactions of the Modern Language Association of America* 1 (May): 96–111.

Gayarré, Charles. 1885. *The Creoles of History and the Creoles of Romance*. New Orleans: Crescent Steam Print.

Gould, Virginia Meacham. 1996. "Free Creoles of Color in Mobile and Pensacola". In *Creoles of Color of the Gulf South*, edited by James H. Dormon, 28–50. Knoxville: University of Tennessee Press.

Hearn, Lafcadio. 1967 [1877]. "Los Criollos". In *Occidental Gleanings*, vol. 1, 195–207. Freeport: Books for Libraries Press.

Istre, Elista. 2018. *Creoles of South Louisiana: Three Centuries Strong*. Lafayette: University of Louisiana at Lafayette Press.

Jaffe, Alexandra. 2007. "Contexts and Consequences of Essentializing Discourses". In *Discourses of Endangerment*, edited by Alexandre Duchene and Monica Heller, 57–75. 1st ed. New York: Bloomsbury.

Klingler, Thomas A. 2003a. *If I Could Turn My Tongue like That: The Creole Language of Pointe Coupee Parish, Louisiana*. Baton Rouge: Louisiana State University Press.

———. 2003b. "Language Labels and Language Use among Cajuns and Creoles in Louisiana". *University of Pennsylvania Working Papers in Linguistics* 9 (2): 77–90.

———. 2005. "Le problème de la démarcation des variétés de langues en Louisiane". In *Le français en Amérique du Nord: Etat présent*, edited by Albert Valdman, Julie Auger, and Deborah Piston-Hatlen, 349–67. Sainte-Foy, Québec: Les Presses de l'Université Laval.

Landry, Christophe, Cliford St. Laurent, and Michael Gisclair. 2016. "Kouri-Vini: A Guide to Louisiana Creole Orthography". Louisiana and Historic Cultural Vistas. www.mylhcv.com.

Lane, George S. 1935. "Notes on Louisiana-French II: The Negro French Dialect". *Language* 11 (1): 5–16.

Le Menestrel, Sara. 2015. *Negotiating Difference in French Louisiana Music: Categories, Stereotypes, and Identifications*. Jackson: University Press of Mississippi.

Logsdon, Joseph, and Caryn Cossé Bell. 1992. "The Americanization of Black New Orleans 1850-1900". In *Creoles of New Orleans: Race and Americanization*, edited by Arnold R. Hirsch and Joseph Logsdon, 201–61. Baton Rouge: Louisiana State University Press.

Louder, Dean R., and Michael Leblanc. 1979. "The Cajuns of East Texas". *Cahiers de géographie du Québec* 23 (59): 317–29.

Mayeux, Oliver. 2014. "Writing Louisiana Creole". BA thesis, SOAS, University of London.

———. 2015. "New Speaker Language: The Morphosyntax of New Speakers of Endangered Languages". MPhil diss., University of Cambridge.

———. 2019. "Rethinking Decreolization: Language Contact and Change in Louisiana Creole". PhD diss., University of Cambridge.

McElhinny, Bonnie. 1996. "Strategic Essentialism in Sociolinguistic Studies of Gender". In *Gender and Belief Systems: Proceedings of the Fourth Berkeley Women and Language Conference*, edited by Natasha Warner et al., 469–80. Berkeley: Berkeley Women and Language Group.

Mercier, Alfred. 1880. *Étude sur la Langue Créole en Louisiane*. New Orleans.

Neumann, Ingrid. 1985. *Le Créole de Breaux Bridge, Louisiane: Étude Morphosyntaxique, Textes, Vocabulaire*. Kreolische Bibliothek, vol. 7. Hamburg: H. Buske.

Neumann-Holzschuh, Ingrid, and Thomas A. Klingler. 2013. "Louisiana Creole Structure Dataset". In *Atlas of Pidgin and Creole Language Structures Online*, edited by Susanne Maria Michaelis, Philippe Maurer, Martin Haspelmath and Magnus Huber. Leipzig: Max Planck Institute for Evolutionary Anthropology. Available online at http://apics-online.info/contributions/53, Accessed 14 August 2022.

Picone, Michael D. 2015. "French Dialects of Louisiana: A Revised Typology". In *New Perspectives on Language Variety in the South: Historical and Contemporary Approaches*, edited by Michael D. Picone and Catherine Evans Davies, 267–87. Tuscaloosa: University of Alabama Press.

Rottet, Kevin J. 1996. "Language Change and Language Death: Some Changes in the Pronominal System of Declining Cajun French". *Plurilinguismes* 11: 117–52.

Sebba, Mark. 2007. *Spelling and Society: The Culture and Politics of Orthography around the World*. Cambridge and New York: Cambridge University Press.

Spitzer, Nicholas R. 1986. "Zydeco and Mardi Gras: Creole Identity and Performance Genres in Rural French Louisiana". PhD diss., University of Texas at Austin.

Tentchoff, Dorice. 1975. "Cajun French and French Creole: Their Speakers and the Questions of Identities". In *The Culture of Acadiana: Tradition and Change in South Louisiana*, edited by Steven L. Del Sesto and Jon L. Gibson, 87–109. Lafayette: The University of Southwestern Louisiana.

Thomason, Sarah G., and Terrence Kaufman. 1988. *Language Contact, Creolization, and Genetic Linguistics*. Anthropology Linguistics. Berkeley: University of California Press.

Tisserand, Michael. 1998. *The Kingdom of Zydeco*. 1st ed. New York: Arcade Publication, Distributed by Little, Brown and Co.

Tregle, Joseph G. 1992. "Creoles and Americans". In *Creoles of New Orleans: Race and Americanization*, edited by Arnold R. Hirsch and Joseph Logsdon, 131–88. Baton Rouge: Louisiana State University Press.

Trépanier, Cecyle. 1991. "The Cajunization of French Louisiana: Forging a Regional Identity". *The Geographical Journal* 157 (2): 161–71.

Valdman, Albert, ed. 1997. *French and Creole in Louisiana*. Topics in Language and Linguistics. New York: Plenum Press.

Valdman, Albert, and Thomas A. Klingler. 1997. "The Structure of Louisiana Creole". In *French and Creole in Louisiana*, edited by Albert Valdman, 109–44. Topics in Language and Linguistics. New York: Plenum Press.

Valdman, Albert, Thomas A. Klingler, Margaret M. Marshall, and Kevin J. Rottet, eds. 1998. *Dictionary of Louisiana Creole*. Bloomington: Indiana University Press.

Valdman, Albert, and Kevin J. Rottet, eds. 2010. *Dictionary of Louisiana French: As Spoken in Cajun, Creole, and American Indian Communities*. Jackson: University Press of Mississippi.

Wendte, Nathan A. 2020a. "A Tale of Two Triangles: Ethnolinguistic Identity among Gulf South Creoles". PhD diss., Tulane University.

———. 2020b. *"Creole" - a Louisiana Label in a Texas Context*. New Orleans: Lulu Press, Inc.

Wood, Charles Roger, and James Fraher. 2006. *Texas Zydeco*. 1st ed. Brad and Michele Moore Roots Music Series. Austin: University of Texas Press.

Discography: Clifton Chenier Lyrical Corpus (CCLC)

Note: Tracks with an asterisk (*) are not included in the CCLC for analysis purposes, but they are cited elsewhere within the chapter and included here for convenience.

C1 Clifton Chenier. 1965. "Louisiana Blues". Track 8 on *Louisiana Blues and Zydeco*. Arhoolie Records F1024, 1990, compact disc.
C2 ———. 1965. "Ay-Tete-Fee". Track 13 on *Louisiana Blues and Zydeco*. Arhoolie Records F1024, 1990, compact disc.
C3 ———. 1975. "Je Me Fu-Pas Mal". Track 9 on *Zydeco Legend!*. Maison de Soul Records, 1989, compact disc.
C4 ———. 1975. "Nonc Helaire". Track 4 on *Zydeco Legend!* Maison de Soul Records, 1989, compact disc.
C5 Clifton Chenier and His Red Hot Louisiana Band. 1978. "J'Aime Pain De Mais (I Love Corn-Bread)". Track 3 on *Live In New Orleans*. GNP Crescendo GNPD 2119, 1988, compact disc.
C6 Clifton Chenier. 1966. "Bon Ton Roulet". Track 1 on *Bon Ton Roulet! And More*. Arhoolie Records CD 345, 1990, compact disc.
C7 Clifton Chenier and His Red Hot Louisiana Band. 1978. "Jusque Parce Que Je T'Aime (Only Because I Love You)". Track 6 on *Live In New Orleans*. GNP Crescendo GNPD 2119, 1988, compact disc.
C8 Clifton Chenier. 1966. "Blues De Ma Negresse". Track 8 on *Bon Ton Roulet! And More*. Arhoolie Records CD 345, 1990, compact disc.
C9 ———. 1966. "Sweet Little Doll (Cher Catin)". Track 9 on *Bon Ton Roulet! And More*. Arhoolie Records CD 345, 1990, compact disc.
C10 Clifton Chenier and His Red Hot Louisiana Band. 1978. "Mon Vieux 'Buggy' (My Old Buggy)". Track 10 on *Live In New Orleans*. GNP Crescendo GNPD 2119, 1988, compact disc.
C11 ———. 1973. "Je Marche Le Plancher (You Know It Ain't Fair)". Track 3 on *Out West*. Arhoolie Records CD 350, 1991, compact disc.
C12 Clifton Chenier and His Red Hot Louisiana Band. 1978. "Tous Les Jours (Everyday)". Track 12 on *Live In New Orleans*. GNP Crescendo GNPD 2119, 1988, compact disc.
C13 Clifton Chenier. 1970. "Tu Le Ton Son Ton (Every Now and Then)". Track 1 on *King of the Bayous*. Arhoolie Records CD 339, 1992, compact disc.
C14 ———. 1973. "Calinda". Track 4 on *Out West*. Arhoolie Records CD 350, 1991, compact disc.
C15 ———. 1971. "Breaux Bridge Waltz". Track 16 on *Out West*. Arhoolie Records CD 350, 1991, compact disc.
C16 ———. 1975. "Sa M'Appel Fou (They Call Me Crazy)". Track 2 on *Bogalusa Boogie*. Arhoolie Records CD 347, 1990, compact disc.
C17 ———. 1971. "Ma Negresse Est Gone". Track 15 on *Out West*. Arhoolie Records CD 350, 1991, compact disc.
C18 ———. 1975. "Allons A Grand Coteau". Track 9 on *Bogalusa Boogie*. Arhoolie Records CD 347, 1990, compact disc.
C19 ———. 1981. "Ay-Ye-Yie Zydeco". Track 9 on *Live! At Grant Street*. Arhoolie Records, 2000, compact disc.
C20 ———. 1967. "Big Mamou". Track 10 on *Get It*. Demon S&C, 2012, digital release.

C21 ———. 1965. "Clifton's Two Step". Track 23 on *Louisiana Blues and Zydeco*. Arhoolie Records F1024, 1990, compact disc.

C22 ———. 1965. "Clifton's Waltz". Track 6 on *Louisiana Blues and Zydeco*. Arhoolie Records F1024, 1990, compact disc.

C23 ———. 1970. "Going La Maison". Track 5 on *King of The Bayous*. Arhoolie Records CD 339, 1992, compact disc.

C24 ———. 1969. "Gone A La Maison". Track 5 on *Sings The Blues*. Arhoolie Records CD 351, 1992, compact disc.

C25 ———. 2011. "I'm A Hog For You". Track 4 on *Live Part 2*. Demon S&C, digital release.

C26 ———. 1969. "Josephine Par Se Ma Femme (Josephine Is Not My Wife)". Track 11 on *King of The Bayous*. Arhoolie Records CD 339, 1992, compact disc.

C27 ———. 1976. "J'veux Faire L'Amour À Toi". Track 7 on *Frenchin' the Boogie*. EmArcy 982 246-9, 2004, compact disc.

C28 ———. 1975. "Je Me Reveiller Ce Matin (I Woke Up This Morning)". Track 6 on *Bogalusa Boogie*. Arhoolie Records CD 347, 1990, compact disc.

C29 ———. 1975. "Je Suis En Recolteur (I'm A Farmer)". Track 10 on *Bogalusa Boogie*. Arhoolie Records CD 347, 1990, compact disc.

C30 ———. 1966. "Jole Blonde". Track 10 on *Bon Ton Roulet! And More*. Arhoolie Records CD 345, 1990, compact disc.

C31 ———. 1966. "La Coeur De La Louisiana". Track 2 on *Voices of Americana: Clifton Chenier*. Demon S&C, 2009, digital release.

C32 ———. 1976. "La Valse De Paris". Track 9 on *Frenchin' the Boogie*. EmArcy 982 246-9, 2004, compact disc.

C33 ———. 1965. "Lafayette Waltz". Track 2 on *Louisiana Blues and Zydeco*. Arhoolie Records F1024, 1990, compact disc.

C34 ———. 1976. "Le Blues De La Vache À Lait". Track 4 on *Frenchin' the Boogie*. EmArcy 982 246-9, 2004, compact disc.

C35 ———. 1975. "Ma Mama Ma Dit (My Mama Told Me)". Track 5 on *Bogalusa Boogie*. Arhoolie Records CD 347, 1990, compact disc.

C36 ———. 1969. "Mo Veux Connaitre (Where She Slept)". Track 15 on *King Of The Bayous*. Arhoolie Records CD 339, 1992, compact disc.

C37 ———. 1976. "Moi J'ai Une P'tite Femme". Track 5 on *Frenchin' the Boogie*. EmArcy 982 246-9, 2004, compact disc.

C38 ———. 1981. "Mon Fait Mon L'ide (I Made Up My Mind)". Track 1 on *Live! At Grant Street*. Arhoolie Records, 2000, compact disc.

C39 ———. 1971. "New Ma Negress". Track 4 on *Live At St. Mark's*. Arhoolie Records CD 313, 1989, compact disc.

C40 ———. 1966. "Oh! Lucille". Track 3 on *Voices of Americana: Clifton Chenier*. Demon S&C, 2009, digital release.

C41 ———. 1969. "Paper In My Shoe". Track 8 on *Sings The Blues*. Boozoo Chavis and Eddie Shuler. Arhoolie Records CD 351, 1992, compact disc.

C42 ———. 1984. "Old Time Waltz". Track 14 on *Zydeco Legend!*. Maison de Soul Records, 1989, compact disc.

C43 ———. 1975. "Quelque Chose Sur Mon Idee (Something On My Mind)". Track 3 on *Bogalusa Boogie*. Arhoolie Records CD 347, 1990, compact disc.

C44 ———. 1977. "Road Runner". Track 6 on *Zydeco Legend!*. Maison de Soul Records, 1989, compact disc.

C45 ———. 1975. "Take Off Your Dress". Track 8 on *Bogalusa Boogie*. Arhoolie Records CD 347, 1990, compact disc.

C46 ———. 1969. "Ton Na Na (Aunt Na Na)". Track 9 on *King of the Bayous*. Arhoolie Records CD 339, 1992, compact disc.

C47 ———. 1976. "Tous Les Jours Mon Coeur Est Blue". Track 6 on *Frenchin' the Boogie*. EmArcy 982 246-9, 2004, compact disc.

C48 ———. 1966. "You Promised Me Love". Track 1 on *Get It*. Demon S&C, 2012, digital release.

C49 ———. 1966. "You Know That I Love You". Track 4 on *Voices of Americana: Clifton Chenier*. Demon S&C, 2009, digital release.

C50 ———. 1970. "Zodico Two-Step (French Two-Step)". Track 4 on *King of the Bayous*. Arhoolie Records CD 339, 1992, compact disc.

C51* ———. 1971. "J'ai Conet, C'est Pas Ma Femme". Track 5 on *Live At St. Mark's*. Arhoolie Records CD 313, 1989, compact disc.

C52* ———. 1975. "Intro and Jambalaya". Track 1 on *The King of Zydeco Live at Montreux*. Hank Williams. Arhoolie Records CD 355, 1990, compact disc.

C53* Clifton Chenier and His Red Hot Louisiana Band. 1983. "Introduction And Theme By Band". Track 1 on *Long Beach and San Francisco Blues Festival*. Arhoolie Records CD 404, 1993, compact disc.

Part 2

Translocal Perspectives

Chapter 9

Rap Kriolu Revisited

From the Transnational Diaspora to Cape Verde and Back

CHRISTINA MÄRZHÄUSER

Introduction

This chapter analyses the representation of rap music performed in Capeverdean[1] (*Kabuverdianu* or *Kriolu*), a popular music subgenre widely distributed under the labels *rap kriolu* or *cabo rap*, both in the language's homeland (i.e. on the West African Cape Verdean islands) and in the wider Cape Verdean diaspora(s) in Europe, on the African continent and in the Americas, especially in the Boston area of the United States.[2] In this chapter, Lisbon and Rotterdam are featured as important music hubs with regard to the production of rap kriolu since the 1990s. Additional examples from other diaspora settings (Boston, Paris, etc.) will be mentioned. The development of the rap scene on the Cape Verdean islands, which relied significantly on "imports" from abroad – both regarding the genre itself as well as the circulation of artists and technology – is sketched from its beginning in the 1990s up to some current developments.[3]

After the description of the local developments, interconnections between different local rap kriolu music hubs are analysed, both with regard to the production and consumption of rap music in the Cape Verdean language.

To summarize the observations on the different rap kriolu scenes and their connections, and to make the results comparable to other settings in which minority or creole languages establish their presence in the public sphere through popular music, the results are discussed within a *framework for linguistic music market analysis* designed along my research findings during the last twelve years. This framework tries to model linguistic dynamics in the music market, that is the development and growth of linguistic subgenres of musical genres into "own" markets (in both a capitalist and Bordieuan sense), which eventually broadens a language's presence in the public media scape. This development will be reconstructed in time and space for rap kriolu along the examples of the rap artists (MCs, acronym for master/mistress of ceremony; rap singers).

The analysis looks at music production and consumption networks of rap kriolu, and analyses metalinguistic discourse from song lyrics, interviews with MCs and consumers from fieldwork and audiovisual media, and written information from music press and social networks. Some quantitative data regarding rap kriolu consumption complement the qualitative data, which are backed up by scientific publications from ethnographic, sociological, linguistic and popular music studies on the (rap) music scene.

For "diaspora nations" like Cape Verde, transnational music listening and production spaces connecting the islands and the diasporas are not only a question of culture or identity – they are also a question of social prestige and financial income for rap artists.

As for the consumption of rap kriolu, local hip-hop fans of Capeverdean origin are considered the first important consumer group, but digital media consumption links different diaspora audiences, who enter into shared online discourse spaces which, in turn, make rap tracks in Capeverdean "visible" (audible, i.e. accessible through audiovisuals) to a "global", geographically dispersed/transmigratory audience with Capeverdean as the L1 or heritage language. Spreading from local, multicultural communities to wider local audiences and larger market segments, the subgenre rap kriolu has gained new audiences throughout the last ten years (2008–18).[4]

From a sociolinguistic point of view, the linguistic dynamics observed here in the international market of rap in Capeverdean are also interesting with regard to minority and non-local languages, and especially regarding Creoles. As Rosa (2018, 104) writes about Capeverdean (CV) hip-hop, this language choice is, first, a choice against the postcolonial, official dominant language(s) and, second, a source of lexical innovation in the Creole language itself, as also discussed in detail in Märzhäuser 2011a:

> CV hip hop ruptures "normative" and dominant language. It disturbs efforts to standardize through the introduction of a tremendous amount of lexical innovations [. . .] and reminds us that language is a living dynamic used to name processes that are both present and unfolding. [. . .] It reminds us of the importance between the politics of naming and the enacting of processes of social transformation.

Language in Music Production and Consumption: Analytical Framework

As a linguist, working on popular music brings along various obstacles with regard to concepts and frameworks, as it is typical for more interdisciplinary approaches. Integrating linguistic questions into popular music studies, or popular music studies insights into linguistics, remains a challenge. This new *framework for linguistic music market analysis* tries to describe the dynamics of language choice for song lyrics within the market cycles of music production and consumption for a given subgenre of popular music.

In most cases, the local adaptation of a popular music genre starts with a first phase of imitation of the input music culture in the original language, before an adaption to local language(s) takes place. The (proto)typical development of music production and consumption of a "linguistically localized" subgenre can be described along the following phases:

The first phase of linguistic adaption of a genre ("imported" in another idiom) to a local (majority or minority) language will be conceptualized as the (1) *linguistic localizing point* (or period).

The next phase is characterized by the attempts to establish the genre in the public sphere by (2) *public staging*.

Given the necessary music production infrastructure (and the means to pay for it), this is followed by (3) *recorded production* and commercial distribution and/or digital distribution via shared online media.

If the presence of the localized subgenre in public is strong enough, and its popularity grows beyond the original speaker group(s), the next phase sees a spread of the musical subgenre with regard to both production and consumption, that is there is (4) a *language crossing point* (cf. Cutler 1999; Rampton 1995, on language crossing in urban youth culture), at which non-native/non-heritage rappers choose to use the language and (5) *wider audiences* consume the music without necessarily understanding or acquiring the language.

Aspects 2 to 5 can be summarized as "entry of the subgenre in the public sphere". During phases 2 and 3, the targeted audiences are local, other diasporic and homeland linguistic ingroups. Once the audiences broaden beyond speakers of the subgenre's language in phases 4 and 5, there follows a period in which two (contradicting) language dynamics may develop, driven by marketing considerations: on the one hand, the language is perceived as a fixed, typical mark of the musical subgenre (with the language being widely used as a marketing "label"), and with artists in other geographical spaces (partly) acquiring the language or able to reproduce it language-wise.[5] In a contrary move, original artists may opt for a linguistic (re)diversification or (anglophone) internationalization in their song lyric production, in a reaction to their new audiences who do not understand the language. For this last period, it remains unclear which market effects growing popularity has regarding language in the local music scenes.

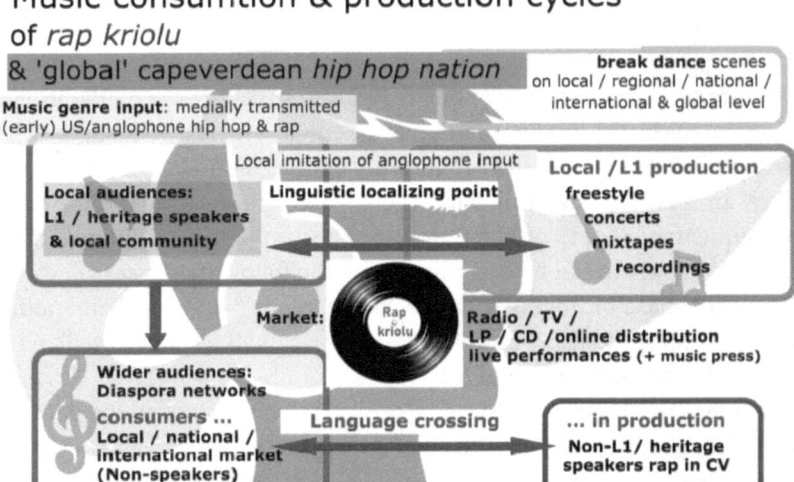

Figure 9.1 Linguistic music market analysis: consumption and production cycles.

This (sketch of a) framework is resumed in figure 9.1, which applies it to rap kriolu.

It has to be studied further whether a growing distribution of the respective linguistic music subgenre is implicitly helping the language to be "known" by more people and has the effect to increase the language's (covert) prestige. The extent to which the proposed model is useful as a descriptive framework for analysing linguistically "new" music subgenres in a more general perspective will be tested in future studies.

Rap Kriolu Histories

The popular music subgenre of rap kriolu is one of the many musical genres adopted by/for Cape Verdeans. As Hurley-Glowa (2015, 10) writes:

> Cape Verdeans have embraced multiple waves of new styles and incorporated them into the culture over the years. These include a never-ending parade of styles from the outside world including cumbia and samba in the 1960s, rock and reggae in the 1970s, and zouk and rap in the 1980s and 90s, a process made even faster today because of the internet.

This incorporation of rap from the 1980s and 1990s into Cape Verdean music (i.e. music by Cape Verdeans, whether performed in the language or not) can be observed across different geographical settings in the diaspora.

Along with rap's linguistic "localization", its musical elements have also been adapted and fused. While rap kriolu today includes musical fusion between rap and reggae/dub, trap, "softer" influences from R&B and pop, from electronic dance music styles such as Angolan-origin *kuduro* and *kizomba*, as well as fusions of rap with *batuku*, *morna* and other traditional Capeverdean styles, US American hip-hop continues to play a central role as reference culture both with respect to musical elements, and regarding ideological background and visual semiotics (e.g. in clothing and music clips). The development of different local rap scenes is frequently linked to the idea of a "global" hip-hop nation, sharing cultural practices of rap, DJing, breakdance, graffiti and lifestyle products. It is within wider, multilingual rap scenes that rap kriolu artists forged their linguistic niche in the music market. The local developments of rap kriolu in Lisbon, Rotterdam and in other diaspora contexts illustrate these dynamics. Rap music culture on the Cape Verdean islands themselves, for which the same logic of integration, adaption and fusion holds, is treated in the next section.

Lisbon

This section sketches landmarks in the development of rap kriolu in Portugal from the 1990s to the present.[6] Virtually all sources agree that the early rap scene in Lisbon was triggered by the consumption of US rap, as part of the formation of a local hip-hop culture also including beat making, DJing, breakdance and graffiti, as it is the case for many local rap scenes.[7]

> O hip hop chegou a Portugal na década de 80. Primeiro invadiu os guettos mas depressa se generalizou. [. . .] infiltrou-se nos subúrbios da cidade de Lisboa e do Porto. Zonas como Chelas, Amadora, Cacém, e Margem Sul do Tejo foram *consideradas o berço deste movimento*. (Assunção et al. 2006)
>
> Hip-hop arrived in Portugal in the decade of the 1980s. It first invaded the ghettos, but quickly generalized. It infiltrated the suburbs of Lisbon and Porto. Zones like Chelas, Amadora, Cacém, and Margem Sul (south side from Tagus river) are considered to be "cradles" of this movement. [my translation]

MC Karlon mentions that in 1994–95, they were listening to Notorious B.I.G, Wu Tang Clan, Snoop Dog and Public Enemy.[8] Local youth (especially) in suburban Lisbon identified with the settings and messages represented in US rap, but soon (in the early 1990s) they turned this musical genre into a means of expression to represent their own realities and rapped in both Portuguese and Capeverdean. The linguistic localization of rap in both languages took place within this socio-economically marginalized, multi-ethnic, first hip-hop generation, within the same, still very limited, mostly suburban hip-hop scene.⁹ Original spaces to practice (freestyle) rap in Capeverdean are the "streets" of suburban settlement areas; early home recordings took place in the MC's living rooms. As MC Jazzy G tells:

> Em 91 e 92 eu fazia Rap Kriolu, era uma coisa quase pouco explorado, mas havia bairros que já cantavam Rap em crioulo. [. . .] Comecei aqui numa altura em que a gente tinha apanha-do o Hip Hop, começou a ser os primeiros passos, mas já existia. Há pessoas que estavam fechadas em casa, mas já se fazia na altura. Eu apanhei a primeira grande onda, mais comercial, das pessoas a apresentar em crioulo. Foi assim que comecei. Eu fui dos primeiros, mas sei que houve pessoas que foram primeiros, e ninguém esta a falar deles. [. . .] O grupo de MCs que eu tinha na altura... Nós também fomos agarrar no Hip Hop Kriolu, para desenvolver-se em tal maneira que hoje em dia, digamos, que há centenas de MCs que cantam em crioulo. (Interview February 2007, cf. Märzhäuser 2011a)

> In 1991–92, I was doing rap kriolu, it was something very little explored so far, but there were suburban areas where they were already singing rap in Capeverdean. I started here in a period where people had already picked up hip-hop, there were some first steps, it already existed. There were people locked up in their homes, but they were already doing it. I caught the first big more commercial wave of people presenting rap in Capeverdean. That's how I started. I was one of the first, but I know there were people who did it first, but no one talks about them. The group of MCs I belonged to at that time . . . we clung to hip-hop kriolu to develop it in such way that today, there are hundreds of MCs rapping in Capeverdean. [my translation]

During the first years, the genre rap, as such, had to establish itself in Portugal/Portuguese, and rap kriolu stayed fairly invisible for a wider public, especially with regard to published recordings (for sure mixtapes in the form of home-recorded tracks on cassettes circulated in both languages). In the online forum Rap Tuga, a member states that "it was in 1993 when the Brazilian rapper Gabriel O Pensador released his first album that Portuguese came to be seen as the official language to sing 'lusitanian' rap".[10] For early rap kriolu in Lisbon, no external models have been mentioned apart from MC Jazzy G's reference that there were MCs rapping in CV at that time as well. Rap artists MC Jazzy G as well as MC Celso and MC Tony Dread consider themselves as early references for rap kriolu in Lisbon. Like many others, they rapped in Portuguese and CV on stage and included passages in CV in their albums as well.[11] This is also true for the early records of Boss AC and for the work of MC Chullage, both of Cape Verdean origin, two widely known Portuguese MCs, as well as for other recordings like TWA's[12] 2002 album *Miraflor*, which all included rap in CV.

The development of local kriolu and Portuguese rap in Lisbon can be interpreted as a parallel localizing phenomenon in the many suburban quarters where Capeverdean was/is the main language of daily communication in local public space, i.e. in glossotopes where CV figures as the dominant language (cf. Krefeld 2004 on the concept of glossotopes in immigration context). In his song "Doa a quem doer", Boss AC raps about the 1990s transition from a purely "underground" movement to a music culture visible in the public sphere:

> Movimento hip hop s'havia era microscópico / Até que eu e o meu "people" surgimos com "Trópico" / Domingos em Santos por trás da estação/ Centenas de putos juntos era muita confusão, mas / Ao menos tínhamos onde curtir, ouvir / ... / 94 gravar até qu'enfim/ Hernâni chamou-nos
>
> The hip-hop movement was microscopic / until me and my people came up with the 'Trópic(o)'/
>
> Sundays in Santos behind the station / hundreds of kids and a lot of confusion, but / at least we had somewhere to listen and enjoy / ... / 94 recording until finally / Hernâni called us [my translation]

The rap formation Black Company (formed in 1988)[13] had a breakthrough in 1994 with the hit song "Nadar", which together with the sampler *Rapública* (1994) produced by Hernâni (mentioned in the preceding lyrics) from Sony Records can be seen as landmarks of the rap scene in Portugal. *Rapública*, however, did not include rap in CV. According to an amateur source,[14] apart from mixtapes by DJ Kronic and DJ Sas from 1998 to 1999, Da Blazz, with musicians based in both Portugal and on Cape Verde and rapping "nearly always 50/50 kriolu-portuguese", was the first band to record an album in Capeverdean in 1999. As Rap Gravato (2017, 93) states:

> rap em criolo também ganhou espaço no movimento português nos anos 2000, ainda que não acolhido da mesma forma que o rap em português pelas editoras.
>
> Rap in kriolu gained ground in the movement in the first decade after 2000, also it wasn't picked up by the music labels in the same way as rap in Portuguese. [my translation]

It was not easy to establish hip-hop in the public sphere and on the music market, and for rap kriolu there was even less "space" in the general public. As Fradique (2003) reports, the first challenge consisted in spotting locations for hip-hop events in general and for rap concerts in particular:

> o aspecto fundamental encontra-se na capacidade de creating a space for rap performances [...],
>
> os rappers estao muitas vezes limitadas à ocupacao de infraestruturas existentes para outros fins [...], discotecas de musica Africana, bares e palcos cedidos pelas Juntas de Freguesia ou concertos organizados pelas Câmaras Municipais. (Fradique 2003, 79ff)
>
> The first fundamental aspects is the capacity to create spaces for rap performances. The rappers are often limited to occupying existing infrastructure that had a different focus: African music discos, bars and stages provided by local administration or concerts organized by city councils. [my translation]

While community-based associations and open air spaces in the suburbs were more easily accessible for organizing hip-hop events (and partly run by Cape Verdean migrants open to the new lyrical art forms in the Creole), the admission of hip-hop parties to the locations the author mentions (African discos, rock music bars, associations or spaces created by the local city administration) required sufficient recognition of the hip-hop movement as such – and of course there were financial questions as well as the issue of racism. Local authorities concerned with integration of marginalized youth, the representation of local multiculturalism and social intervention, clearly made an effort to offer cultural events attractive for local youth (as well as geographically and economically accessible to this consumer group). It is unclear to which extent "linguistic discrimination" in society played a role in the presence of rap in Capeverdean on stage, or whether it could already establish itself in official concerts at these early events in suburban spaces. In an August 2007 interview, (lusophone) MC Dama Bete states that "in Kova, Damaia, Marianas ... rappers singing in Portuguese are less respected than those rapping in kriolu" (Interview 8/2007, cf. Märzhäuser 2011a). This can be explained with the specific language ecology in these suburban "glossotopes", i.e. local communities

One of the early regular public hip-hop events in more "central" spaces in Lisbon includes those at the African disco Trópico in Santos and the music club Johnny Guitar: some events around 1994 and the series of freestyle events called Ataque Verbal[15] in Johnny Guitar broadcast live via the radio station FM Radical (Fradique 2003, 78). Fradique's reports about the Ataque Verbal-event on 6 January 1997 mention the rappers MCs Jazzy G (ex-Zona Dread, ex-Alex e os putos do Bairro), MC Jazzy G, the crew TWA and MC Italiano, artists who also performed in CV at that time. There are explicit comments on the use of Capeverdean at this event:

TWA in the house, Sam the Kid, Jazzy G sobre ao palco e inicia um longo improviso que inclui algumas partes em crioulo [. . .] se segues um duelo verbal em improviso. O crioulo é a língua principal das prestações de [MC] Italiano . . . [. . .] Italiano continua a improvisar em crioulo.

TWA in the house, Sam the Kid, Jazzy G on stage, starts a long freestyle including some parts in Capeverdean [. . .] Next, there is a freestyle verbal duelling, in which Capeverdean is the main language. MC Italiano's performance . . . [. . .] Italiano continues to improvise in Capeverdean.

While lusophone rap quickly became more popular in the second half of the 1990s thoughout Portugal, the growing local hip-hop market (beyond urban sub-urbs/ sub-culture) remained a challenge for rap kriolu, especially with regard to record labels. In 2007, MC C, band member of SAMP tells that his lyrics are not in Capeverdean because his label had been insulted as "uma editora só de pretos" (a record label for blacks only). As it was a major label, lyrics had to be in Portuguese, fearing that otherwise he wouldn't be broadcast on radio and television. However, in MC C's opinion this was not the label's politic, but a market issue:

> MC C: A nossa editora não nos prescreve nada, até porque p'ra nossa editora é muito melhor nos metemos lá a nossa cultura, mas o mercado já 'ta diferente. A questão é que eles não querem!
> Christina Märzhäuser: Mas quem?
> MC C: O sistema musical. Não querem deixar que a gente se afirme como músicos com a nossa língua, quando 'tamos num país que fala português. (Interview June 2007; cf. Märzhäuser 2011a)
> MC C: Our label doesn't prescribe us anything. It's even better for them if we put our culture there, but the market works differently. The thing is that "they" don't want it.
> Christina Märzhäuser: Who doesn't want it?
> MC C: The musical system. They don't want that we assert ourselves in our own language, while we are in a Portuguese-speaking country.

Another case of "linguistic discrimination" was reported by the two female MCs, whose producer didn't accept Capeverdean for their lyrics:

> MC Lady F: O nosso produtor - chamado produtor, ya . . . [. . .] ele disse: Não percebo crioulo, não quero em . . . (Interview August 2007; cf. Märzhäuser 2011a).
> MC Lady F: Our producer – so-called producer, ya [...] he said: I don't understand Capeverdean, I don't want (lyrics) in ...

As culture journalist M. Lança, a specialist in African art and culture in Lisbon, criticizes in 2008:

> As editoras portuguesas estão desatentas à fonte inesgotável de boa música da noite afro-lisboeta, não acreditam e não cuidam do seu 'património linguístico' - a música em língua portuguesa ou crioulo em muitos casos - como mercado de confluência de culturas.
>
> Portuguese labels are inattentive to the inexhaustible source of good quality Afro-Lisboetan music, they don't believe in it and don't care about its linguistic heritage – music in Portuguese or Capeverdean in many cases – in a market that is a confluence of cultures.

Regarding the language choice during the first decade of the twenty-first century, considerations about success on the market also played an important role, as MC A, band member of D.M. Sistas shows:

> MC A: Eu acho que no Hip Hop o crioulo não se destaca, porque há varios grupos já há anos que cantam em crioulo e não se destacam. [. . .] Porque no Hip Hop é a mensagem em português que as pessoas todas percebem. crioulo é bonito para ouvir. Podemos fazer participações ou em Kizombas ou em rap, tudo um pouco. Mas eu acho que no Hip Hop em si, onde queremos entrar, não é com o Hip Hop Kriolu que nos destacamos [. . .] Mas além de tudo acho que chegará o tempo do crioulo sobressair. (Interview 08.08.07)
>
> MC A: I think that in hip-hop, Capeverdean isn't successful, because there are many groups rapping in CV for many years now, and they aren't successful. [. . .] Because in hip-hop it's the message in Portuguese that everyone understands. Capeverdean sounds nice. We can participate (singing in CV) in Kizombas or rap, a little bit. But for hip-hop, where we want to get in, with rap kriolu we won't be successful. [. . .] But despite all this, I'm sure there will be a time for rap kriolu to gain success.

Despite these reported difficulties with local producers and labels to record rap in Capeverdean instead of Portuguese, a number of MCs and crews opted for singing in Capeverdean only – and MC A was right in anticipating rap kriolu's huge success.

The so far most successful rap kriolu artists from Portugal are the MCs of NiggaPoison, founded in 1994 by the MCs Karlon and Praga, considered pioneers in the subgenre in Portugal. They started with beatbox and freestyle raps, like many others. In 1997, they participated with raps in CV on a cassette mixtape by DJ Kronik, in 1998 were rapping in the documentary film *Outros Bairros*[16] and in three video clip recordings for the Expo 98 fair in Lisbon, and thus already had some media coverage by the end of the 1990s.

Instead of struggling against the biased language ideologies of record labels and the music market, they managed to find a different solution for their first album. Typical for many musical genres and musicians facing difficulties, to be represented by established labels, they constructed their own niche for music production and distribution when Karlon created the record label Kreduson Produson and released NiggaPoison's first EP *Podia Ser Mi* in 2001. Their second album *Resistentes*, released with the label Very Deep Records in 2006, with songs mainly in CV, was nominated for a Golden Globe Award by the television channel SIC and the journal *Caras* in 2007. In 2009, they were included in a commercial sampler *Hip Hop Fnac* with the song "Nigga". Their next album *Simplicidadi* was recorded in 2011 with *Optimus Discos*, a bigger label – again with lyrics in CV. Their albums were available in commercial record stores like FNAC.

MC Karlon is now working as a solo artist, releasing a lot of work through his company Kreduson Produson and featuring in many recordings of other rappers. As already NiggaPoison, he has fully established himself on the market as a Creole rapper (and even changed his name to Karlon Krioulo). About his 2016 album *Passaporti*, he relates that it is "a tribute to my Cape Verdean roots made with a lot of love", and in the description of his (2018) album *Griga*, he again stresses this heritage (and uses samples from traditional Cape Verdean music genres).[17]

Other MCs rapping exclusively in Capeverdean for more than a decade are MC Kromo di Guetto and MC LBC Souldjah, both with strong ties to the suburban quarter Cova da Moura (in rap lyrics and youth language often named "Kova M"), and the female MC G Fema from the neighbourhood Chelas. A female rapper from a younger generation, MC Mynda Guevara tells in an interview with Lois Varela[18] that her choice of Capeverdean for her lyrics was motivated by rap kriolu consumption of her older brother and by her Cape Verdean ancestry (a recurrent argument for language choice; see Märzhäuser 2011a).

> Lois Varela: Nasceu em Portugal, e continua pelas vistas, mas foi o Crioulo que escolheu para a s suas músicas. Sera mesmo o crioulo o dialeto do guetto que seguirá sempre, sempre vivo?
> MC Mynda Guevara MG: Sim, foi uma cena natural porque o meu irmão ouviu também bué de rap kriolu . . . rap em francês, rap tuga, rap kriolu . . . e outras línguas. Não gosto de separar, é todo a mesma cena, a mesma forma de expressar só de línguas diferentes. Mas o rap kriolu prinicpalmente porque faz parte de mim, sou caboverdiana, acho que faz todo o sentido. Apesar do sampadjudo – que é o crioulo da minha mae, canto em [. . .] badiu . . . é a forma que eu me sinto mais a vontade a me expressar.
> Lois Varela: You were born in Portugal, and continue to live here, but you chose Capeverdean for your lyrics. Does this mean that kriolu, the dialect of the ghettos will always live on?

> MC Mynda Guevara: Yes, this came very natural because my brother also used to listen to a lot of rap kriolu, but also rap in French, Portuguese rap, rap kriolu . . . and hip-hop in other languages. I don't like to make a difference, it's all the same scene, the same form of expression, only in different languages. But basically, [I chose] rap kriolu because it's part of me, I'm Capeverdean, so it really makes sense. Although the Sampadjudo dialect is the creole of my mother, I sing in Badiu [Santiago variety], that's the form I feel most at ease to express myself.

As she adds at the end of this passage, the Creole variety she raps in is "Badiu", the diatopic variety of the largest island with the capital Praia, which is also widely spoken in the Lisbon metropolitan area, and not in the "Sampadjudo" Northern variety of her mother.

Not only do speakers "cross" different varieties of Capeverdean in the diaspora, as observed, for example, in the lyrics of a freestyle session in the documentary *Nu bai – rap negro Lisboa*,[19] L1 and heritage speakers are communicating in and acquiring various secondary island-dialects in Lisbon, together with input from other Creoles such as (nearly) inter-comprehensible Kryiol from Guinea-Bissau. Kryiol-speaking MCs in Lisbon have probably been rapping in Capeverdean as well as in their own language since the 1990s. Already in 2007, MC T stresses that many lusophone listeners understood phrases like "N teni saudadi" (I miss home, loved ones) in the refrain of one of his songs, and that, due to lexical parallels, there exists considerable mutual inter-comprehension between Capeverdean and Portuguese lexis (although this doesn't necessarily hold for the creole's languages grammar). Furthermore, he states that there are already many Portuguese also speaking Capeverdean as an L2:

> porque hoje em dia há muitos, já conheço muitos Portugueses que já falam crioulo, ou lá esta, lá esta: Aqueles Portugueses do bairro. (Interview February 2007)
>
> Because today there are many, I know many Portuguese who already speak Capeverdean, that's the thing: those Portuguese from the suburban quarters.

Meanwhile, rap kriolu has further crossed borders, and there are non-Creole L1/heritage speakers performing rap in Capeverdean. The spread of rap kriolu beyond Capeverdean origins, including both PALOP and "tugas", Portuguese MCs without recent African background rapping in Capeverdean, has already been commented on by de Souza (2009, 181), who reports a conversation between two Cape Verdean MCs and an Angolan rapper in suburban Alto da Cova da Moura:

discordavam da reclamação dos rappers tuga, assim eram chamados os rappers portugueses de origem, por estes cantarem em crioulo. Para os rappers tuga esta forma de cantar, em crioulo, não tinha sentido em função de esta ser uma língua pouco praticada no país, e com isso diminuiria o alcance desta música.

The did not agree about the fact that rappers of Portuguese origin also claimed to rap in kriolu. For Portuguese rappers, it didn't make sense to sing in kriolu because it was a language not widely used in the country, thereby limiting the range of their music.

An example for MCs non-Cape Verdean descent rapping in kriolu is the 2017 track "Ca Bu Fla Ma Nau" by popular MC Piruka featuring MC Mota JR. As the Portuguese online music journal *Rimas & Batidas* (Rhymes & Beats) puts it:

> Piruka fez a sua primeira colaboração com um rapper que rima em crioulo, Mota JR, e a Internet enlouqueceu. Já soma quase sete milhões de visualizações no YouTube e bastante airplay em rádios mainstream como a Cidade. "Ca Bu Fla Ma Nau", do álbum Aclara, é o principal elo de ligação entre o grande público e o rap crioulo no momento. Crioulo ou português/É a mesma cultura.
>
> Piruka collaborated for the first time with a rapper rhyming in kriolu, Mota JR, and the internet went crazy. There are already nearly seven million clicks on YouTube and it's been broadcast many times on mainstream radio stations like Cidade. At this moment, "Ca Bu Fla Ma Nau" [Don't you say no], from the album *Aclara*, is the main link between the larger public and rap kriolu. Kriolu or Portuguese – it's the same culture.

This "merge" between both Portuguese rap subgenres and sub-scenes, namely "rap kriolu" and "rap tuga", also reflects on the consumer side. Approximately ten years ago, when I did my fieldwork-based study in Greater Lisbon, rap kriolu was still rather marginalized, and the audiences reached were most frequently Capeverdean-speaking ingroups. Today there is a wide enough audience for rap kriolu to make it attractive for non-Cape Verdean MCs to rap in Creole and be successful on the market, as highlighted in a feature in *Rimas & Batidas* about Mota JR's song "Danger":

> E quem disse que era preciso ter origens de Cabo Verde para rimar em crioulo? Ainda bem que Portugal é um país naturalmente mesclado e que celebra a sua multi-culturalidade. Mota JR adoptou o crioulo como a língua para rimar e também tem sido um caso de sucesso no meio.
>
> Who said that it was necessary to have Cape Verdean origins to rap in kriolu? Luckily, Portugal is a "naturally mixed" country celebrating its multiculturalism. Mota JR chose kriolu as the language to rhyme and he was also successful in the scene.

As for the number on "non-Cape Verdean" MCs rapping in this language, Cegonha from the Kova M recording studio, states in the online journal *Afropop*:[20]

> The next batch of artists are Afro-Portuguese rappers from around the Lisbon suburbs. All of them rap or sing in Kriolu, mostly Cape Verdean kriolu. Kriolu rap has soared in popularity recently – according to Cegonha at the Kova M Studio, there may even be more white Portuguese listening to kriolu rap than Cape Verdean-Portuguese. There are even some white Portuguese rappers who now rap in kriolu. ("Kriolu Rap From the Lisbon Suburbs", 31 July 2018)

Cape Verdean artists have been presenting at major music festivals and hip-hop events for over fifteen years by now. Participant observation from 2006 to 2011 showed that CV was included in performances by Chullage, but not by the main act Boss AC, who regularly used CV in his early career, at Festa Avante (August 2006); CV was widely used by the crew NiggaPoison in Tires (February 2007), and by various rap artists at a concert with Tony Mc Dread, J Ray, MC Jazzy and others at Musicbox Lisbon (February 2007); CV lyrics were partly used by Chullage at Festa de S. António, Lisbon (June 2007), by NiggaPoison at a concert in Oeiras, where they acted as support act before Beastie Boys (June 2007); G. Fema, Chullage, G.M. Sistas, Souljah, Halloween and other rap kriolu MCs represented in the language at Festival de Hip Hop Parque de Palmeira in Oeiras (August 2007); and even when Chullage performed in the small town Fafe in Northern Portugal (March 2008), the (non-creolophone) northern-Portuguese audience knew some of his lyrics in kriolu. The chronology of rap kriolu's presence from 2008 to 2018 could be systematically documented based on agendas of major concert locations and on festival line-ups and playlists.[21] As for recent information on rap kriolu on stage, an article on the festival Iminente in 2017 titled "Música electrónica, africana e (mais) Hip-Hop no segundo dia de Iminente",[22] mentions various Cape Verdean rappers, namely MC Vado and NiggaPoison rapping in Capeverdean, and MC Chullage, usually rapping in both languages. At this event, these rap kriolu performances alternated with rap in Portuguese and other musical style such as African(-influenced) dance music like kuduro and funaná. *Rimas & Batidas* describes the growing visibility of rap kriolu and provides the following reasons:

> O rap crioulo tem-se - de forma silenciosa - desenvolvido em quantidade e qualidade, muito por causa do crescimento de uma segunda geração de imigrantes de Cabo Verde. Nos últimos anos, a massificação das redes sociais e dos videoclipes trouxe um crescimento mais rápido a este género do hip hop nacional.

Rap kriolu has silently developed both in quantity and quality, mainly due to a second generation of immigrants from Capeverde. During the last years, the growth of social networks and video clips brought a more rapid growth to this genre of national hip-hop.

The spread of rap kriolu in Portugal can be interpreted as a musico-linguistic subgenre establishing itself in the public sphere, thereby also creating a public space of representation for a marginalized (and stigmatized) creole language. The fact that it is conceptualized as part of Portugal's "national" hip-hop shows growing acceptance of the previously rather marginalized musico-linguistic subgenre and also creates more interest in the creole language itself.

Rotterdam

A strong presence of Cape Verdean immigrants is one of the ingredients for the development of a local rap kriolu scene. Rotterdam has been a destination for many migrants from Cape Verde, and an important music hub for Cape Verdean music since the 1970s.[23] Like in many other places, rap started to "go local" here in the 1990s, and rap in Capeverdean started in this decade. The first more widely known group rapping in Capeverdean was Cabo Funk Alliance, founded in Rotterdam in 1992. Its core members were the MCs Vortex Guardian aka Angel, Jay B, Eddy Fort and Nuba, of Cape Verdean origin. One of its founders, MC Eddy Fort Moda Grog/Eddy (FMG) was born in 1950 in Mindelo on São Vicente, where he started to rap when he was 25. He landed a hit with his track "Fogo" and became popular in Cape Verde in the 1990s. His greatest success was his song "Materialista", and his first album was *CouNtDown* released as a cassette in 1994.[24] Another band member, MC Jay-B, tells about the band's early history:

> Na primeru metado das '90s trabalho stava kada vez mas poku na villa undi ki m mora. M muda di volta pa Rotterdam. M stava novamento no meio di Kabuverdianos. Ja mi era "beatcreator" dis di fim das '80s. M fika na casa di "Angel", nha irmon ki stava na movimento di Rotterdam. Nos era amigo ku "Alee" ki stava y sta na meio di movimentu di Rotterdam. Na kez dias Alee tinha gravadu um som kizomba ku artista konhesido. Y elis konxe Eddie-G (agora FMG) pa se freestyle Ingles y Kriolu. Depois de dois mix tape (fladu mesmo casette de musica) en Inglez, Holandez y Kriolu nu toma attenson die gentis, imprezas na muzika. The rest is history.

> In the first half of the 1990s, there was less and less work in the town where I lived. I moved to Rotterdam and was surrounded by Capeverdeans again. I had

already been "beat creator" since the end of the 1980s. I lived in the house of "Angel", my brother, who was already part of Rotterdam's [hip-hop?] movement. We were friends with "Alee" who was and still is part of Rotterdam's movement. In these days, Alee had recorded a Kizomba song with a well-known artist. And they knew Eddie-G (now FMG) for his freestyle in English and Capeverdean. After two mixtapes (that is, cassettes) in English, Dutch and Kriolu, people from the music industry started to notice us. The rest is history.[25]

Cabo Funk Alliance performed rap in English in the early stages of its career, but then later switched to occasional Dutch, focusing on delivering lyrics in Capeverdean.[26] The group released the albums *Cabo Alliance* (cassette) and *Hoje è quel dia* (CD, LP) in 1995, produced by Atlantic Music, and considered by some as the "most probable first ever Kriolu Hip Hop Production". However, the band's first album was mainly in English, later songs were sung in Dutch and Capeverdean, and *Hoje è quel dia* "brought a lot of fuss for breaking the 'barrier' of traditional music".[27] Cabo Funk Alliance is considered to be the pioneer of rap and hip-hop in Capeverdean beyond Rotterdam. Simultaneously, other rap and R&B groups started to develop in Rotterdam's Cape Verdean scene, and examples for early crews and MCs are Tha Real Vibe, Black Side, Djeepz, Livity and Cikay Las.

The Dutch 2018 documentary *Hoe de Kaapverdiaanse rap door Rotterdamse pioniers opkwam*[28] from the broadcaster Open Rotterdam tells the early history of rap kriolu in Rotterdam, which developed within the wider Cape Verdean immigrant community/music scene. The film description recounts the origins of rap kriolu within Rotterdam's multicultural hip-hop scene as follows:

> De grondleggers van de Kaapverdiaanse rap haalden hun inspiratie uit Amerika, waar het muziekgenre al jaren populair was. In hun eigen taal probeerden de Rotterdamse Kaapverdianen al rappend politieke kwesties onder de loep te nemen. [. . .] De Rotterdamse rapscene kreeg al snel veel complimenten, omdat hier niet alleen Kaapverdianen meededen, maar ook rappers van andere nationaliteiten. Zo versterkte iedereen elkaar.
>
> The founders of Capeverdean rap got their inspiration from America, where the music genre had been popular for years. They experimented with rapping in their own language, scrutinizing political questions. Rotterdam's rap scene gets a lot of compliments, not only for Capeverdeans, but also for rappers of other nationalities, who mutually support each other. [my translation]

As the MCs represented in the 2018 documentary confirm, rap kriolu artists in Rotterdam integrated into wider afro-diaspora (especially Afro-Caribbean) music scenes. As MC Cikay Las puts it, for the CV rap scene

"Rotterdam is the place to be". Quartel Studios is an important part of the infrastructure for local *rap kriolu* productions:

> Studio van Dhema Rush, de man die mijns inziens Kaapverdiaanse hiphop in Nederland op de kaart heeft gezet. Een veteraan in de Rotterdamse hiphopscene en in de jaren '90 zeer bekend in zowel de hiphopscene als de Kaapverdiaanse gemeenschap met de driekoppige rapgroep Tha Real Vibe.
>
> [It is the] studio of Dhema Rush, the man who, in my opinion, put Cape Verdean hip-hop on the map in the Netherlands. A veteran in Rotterdam's 1990s hip-hop scene, known in both the hip-hop scene and the Cape Verdean community with his three-person rap crew Tha Real Vibe.

This continuity of first-generation rappers turning into producers for younger generations could also be observed in other contexts. While the "old school" is still (partly) present on stage, see, for example, Gerason 90's rap track "Es ka sabi" (They don't know) from 2017,[29] it has to be further investigated whether younger generations are also actively rapping in Capeverdean and adhering to the genre as consumers. Up to now, there is little written documentation on rap kriolu in the Netherlands. However, it has been repeatedly mentioned as an important rap kriolu music hub by rappers in Lisbon.

Rap Kriolu in Other Diaspora Countries

It would require various articles to describe the different diaspora scenes of rap kriolu in more detail. Without doubt, US rappers of Cape Verdean origin played a role, especially in the US's New England region where a large community of approximately 400,000 Cape Verdeans have lived since at least the 1960s, with an estimated 35,000 in Boston's Dorchester-Roxbury neighbourhood (cf. Sieber 2005, 126). Besides Sieber (2005, 131), who highlights "Izé's remarkable fame as a French-language rapper in Paris, or hip-hop artist Dje Dje in the USA, who raps both in Kriolu and English", and some remarks in Saucier's (2011) *Native Tongues: An African Hip-Hop Reader*, one of the few scientific publications on Cape Verdean hip-hop in the United States is Rosa's (2018) paper titled "Cape Verdean Counter Cultural Hip-Hop". Rosa reports from his own experience in the 1990s:

> Jose Fernandes or DjéDjé, one of the first CapeVerdean hip-hop artists entered the scene. The circulation of the Cape Verdean language in the rap fascinated me. The merging of cultures while emphasizing *cabo-verdianidade*, especially of the variant that touched on my existence between borders, deeply resonated.

A lot of MCs of Cape Verdean descent in the United States I discovered via social media rap both in English and CV. The affirmation of Cape Verdean rappers as bilingual MCs can also be observed in other diaspora settings, as already mentioned for Rotterdam, for some MCs from Lisbon, and also for the very successful French MC Izé from Paris and his rap crew *La Mc Malcriado*. The four MCs – Stomy Bugsy, Jacky Brown, Jpax and Izé – originally from different islands of Cape Verde, all of them already experienced rappers, won the 2010 Kora Music Awards with their debut album *Nos Pobreza Ke Nos Rikéza*. Their second album, *Fidju di Kriolu* (2011), stresses the links between islands and diaspora with a special focus on Paris. The project MC Jay e Bandidos from Norway mixes CV rap with reggae in a multicultural formation (cf. Monteiro 2011). Rap lyrics including both kriolu and rap in other languages enables MCs to gain wider audiences in the respective diaspora. This is typical for multicultural rap scenes, where rap kriolu integrates into broader local hip-hop communities. On the islands, rapping only in Capeverdean is the strategy adopted by most MCs.

Rap Kriolu on the Cape Verdean Archipelago

To resume the presence of rap on the West African Cape Verdean islands in one sentence, one could simply say that it has grown exponentially during the decade from 2008 to 2018.[30] As for the genre's beginnings, more traditional local music genres and popular dance music did not easily or instantaneously make room for (cabo) rap on the islands. As Lima (2011) writes: "There are many Cape Verdean artists from other music genres who look at rap with contempt and try to marginalize it." Especially in its beginnings, the genre was often stigmatized as too "gangsta", too americanized, lyrically and musically weak. Pardue (2012, 51) states, "Kriolu rappers struggle to expand the notion of Cape Verdean music to include rap." In a text against the strong public criticism against rap, G. Silva stresses the genre's presence on the island from the 1990s to the present:[31]

> Estilo que foi popularizod ne CABO VERDE por jovens de São Vicente, na altura da "Mudança" de um estado de ditadura e partido único, para um estado alegadamente democrático. Portanto anos 90 do século XX. No te li ne século XXI e ainda no te tud te fazê ess rap.
>
> This style was made popular in Cape Verde by youth from Mindelo in the period of "Mudança", the change from a state of dictatorship and single-party state to

an allegedly democratic state, in the '90s of the twentieth century. Now, in the twenty-first century, we are still here doing rap.

Interestingly, rap has taken over some of popular music's political function as the "voice of resistance" from more traditional Cape Verdean music genres:

> cultural manifestations of the masses such as *Tabanka, Funana,* and *Batuku* were repressed by the colonial regime and the anti-colonial struggle made extensive use of "traditional" music and other popular cultural forms to mobilize people against colonial rule. The irony is that these genres continue to be contained, if not in form but in content, by neoliberal, neocolonial transnational rule. Arguably, the genre most under state surveillance and control (both formal and informal) is hip-hop. (Rosa 2018, 95)

In the work of Lima (2011, 2012, 2018), the early years of hip-hop culture on the islands and subsequent developments are described. Hip-hop as a phenomenon was imported from the United States at the end of the 1980s, starting with breakdance. As Lima (2018, 96) observes, rap was initially adopted not in the periphery, but was a phenomenon of "dominant class" youth in the two urban centers Praia (capital, on Santiago) and Mindelo (on São Vincente) who had contact with other realities, especially North America they visited in summer holidays. Breakdance was initially practised in the central squares in Praia and Mindelo. Rap only became more popular by the middle of the 1990s, triggered by the political campaigns of 1995–96 (cf. Lima 2011). But as MC Jazzy G states in an interview (2007; cf. Märzhäuser 2011a), there were already people rapping in CV in 1992. Early MCs and rap groups on the islands were Heavy H, Niggaz Badio and the female crew Chipi Girls in Praia; and IPV, Bairro Norte or PTR in Mindelo. According to Lima (2012, 279), other exterior influences triggering the development of the genre on the archipelago in the 1990s, and also the linguistic localization of rap lyrics, were the Brazilian MC Gabriel O Pensador and lusofone rap from Portugal transmitted via RTP África (and later on via internet). As his informant, MC Batchart from Hip Hop Art tells:

> Eu e o 4ARTK ouvíamos muito o hip hop lusófono. Não os old school, que na altura éramos muito novos, mas tipo o Boss AC, o Valete . . . no programa Solstício da RTP África.
>
> Me and 4ARTK listened to a lot of lusophone hip hop. Not to old school, because we were still really young at that time, but to Boss AC, Valete . . . in the program *Solstício* on RTP África.

While Valete raps in Portuguese only, Boss AC also includes some Capeverdean in his lyrics. Surely rap in Capeverdean from the diaspora in the Netherlands, Portugal and the United States soon became known on the islands as well due to migration and family visits. However, the genre seems to take more time to develop on the islands than in the diaspora. According to Lima, there was a first boom in 2000, when the genre became popular in the urban peripheries of Praia and Mindelo and spread to other places (Assomada, Tarrafal), including other islands (Santa Cruz, Porto Novo on the islands Sal and Santo Antão). The genre diversifies stylistically like pop rap (Central Side), kizomba rap (Djédjé), gangsta rap (Karaka), radical rap (GPI-Knowledge), thug rap (Caixa Baixa), gospel rap (Nax Beat) and afro-centric rap (cf. Lima 2011).

Apart from the preoccupation with the stigmatization of rap music as a "soundtrack of crime" at a moment in which it spread from the centre to the periphery[32] (expressed here as *generation thug*; cf. Pardue 2016), this passage also directs the attention to commercial aspects and questions of recording infrastructure. The question whether and where the music industry supports MCs, and at what cost music recording is accessible for rap musicians, can be considered a central issue for the genre's development. On the islands, apart from imported CV rap and very few commercialized rap kriolu recordings of local MCs (see later for early productions), ten to fifteen years ago there had been only little recorded rap music produced on the islands. Some rap tracks were even paid for by politicians during electoral campaigns – seen by many as a "corruption" of the genre's critical spirit, but driven by rappers' striving for fame and money, as Lima (2011) describes:

> Nota-se uma enorme necessidade de se alcançar a fama e ganhar dinheiro, tornando-os presas fáceis para os políticos como se viu na campanha legislativa última. No entanto, destacam-se grupos como FARP (Lém Cachorro) e Sindykatto de Guetto (Ponta D'Água) com forte envolvência em trabalhos comunitários.
>
> It can be observed that there is an enormous need to get famous and make money, and thus they are easy prey for politicians, as could be seen in the last elections. Meanwhile, there are groups which stick out like FARP (Lém Cachorro) and Sindykatto de Guetto (Ponta D'Água) who are strongly involved in community projects.

While formerly more professional rap artists mostly had to record their music abroad (if they could afford to), now there exists more professional recording facilities in Praia and Mindelo. As for thematic and ideological diversification, Lima states that (until approximately 2010?) there wasn't really a hip-hop movement, since rap had already gained a more critical, conscious touch, apart from the ongoing reproduction of a dominant discourse, and thug and gangsta rap. As Lima (2012, 278; 2018) claims, instead of historical identification figures like independence leader Amilcar Cabral, today Cape Verdean rappers serve as identification for local youth. Adopting habitus, imagery and discourse of commercial US gangsta rappers, they developed into a subterfuge for a young generation lacking professional and political perspectives.

However, rap has gained its place and diversified both with regard to musical qualities and ideological orientations of its messages, and the genre is growing at a rapid pace on the islands both with regard to production and consumption. The two urban centres of Praia and Mindelo can still be considered important local music hubs. Current names from São Vincente are the group Mad Devils[33] producing, among others, MC Reif True (EP *N Street*), MC Bieitch (EP *Sem Truque*) and MC Tiger. More widely known groups in 2018 on this island were Kiddye Bonz[34] and Wiggy Wiger.[35]

As MC Kapa Gdr, from Praia, in an interview from 26 April 2019 in the series Rap Raíz[36] states, there is more and more high-quality rap. However, he criticizes the gangsta image that some people have of rap, advocating rap as a channel for positive (but critical) message. In an 2016 interview in the article "A New Generation: The Conscious Rappers from Cape Verde",[37] MC PNC from the crew Rapaz100 Juiz tells that he started to rap in 2016: "At the beginning we just did music in the ghetto and for our friends. This year we're going to celebrate with a big party and a show." Hélio Batalha, a "conscious" hip-hop artist, states, "The hip hop movement is very young in Cape Verde. It's a big responsibility for the MCs like me to share the culture and make it a bigger movement." MC Batchart says, "The scene is new but it's growing and in a few years it's going to be big. It's hip-hop which represents the sound of this country." PNC observes about the Cape Verdean hip-hop and rap scene: "Right now it's good. There are a lot of rappers making good music. [...] hip-hop is all good right now. It's strong."

Rap's growing popularity reflects in the fact that at the 2015 CVMA (Cape Verdean Music Award, the Grammys of Cape Verdean music), a local rap album was selected as best album, "instead of Kizomba and more traditional music", as MC PNC remarks.

For certain, rap kriolu has also become more commercial in the last decade – a typical phenomenon for growing music markets. Events and festivals further increase the (island-internal and international) circulation of MCs rapping in CV. Some examples show that there is currently a broader stage for hip-hop at festivals throughout the archipelago: In July of 2016, there was a Hip Hop Summer Fest in Kebra Cabana, Praia, which featured elements such as beatboxing, parkour, cyphers, dance battles, various urban wear clothing stands, workshops on social action and stand-up comedy. (Rosa 2018, 93f). The twenty-ninth edition of the Festival de Santa Maria on Sal (13–14 September 2019), with the topic of *Uma nova consciência ambiental – uma mente consciente* (a new environmental consciousness – a conscious mind), also features a hip-hop trio of "conscious" rappers, MC Bachart, Rapaz 100 Juiz e Hélio Batalha, as announced by Irineu Almeida, the city council's director for education and culture.[38] The presence of CV rap in the public, official sphere has thus also been accomplished by MCs with a more critical attitude. The presence of rap acts from Portugal can be observed in the first post-2000 decade; a more thorough market analysis from concert agendas and festival line-ups is needed to quantify international circulation of rap artists on the islands.

Global Rap Kriolu Connections

The presence of rap kriolu in Portugal (especially Greater Lisbon), in the Netherlands (especially Rotterdam), in France (Paris), Norway, Britain (London), the United States (Boston) and on the Cape Verdean islands, attested in the data so far analysed, shows that the geographic range of this linguistic musical subgenre already extends across three continents. The transnational links between Cape Verde, Portugal, Northern Europe and the United States (and also continental Africa) exist both in consumption and production of rap kriolu. This musico-linguistic subgenre is understood, by consumers, producers and artists alike, as a link both to the distant homeland as well as to the respective local creolofone communities in diaspora. It is a complex (and definitely insider) task to understand the wider picture of connections between "homeland" and "diaspora" within the "global Cape Verdean hip-hop nation" since the 1990s. In my data from 2007 to 2008, informants from Lisbon are well aware of the transnational connections, which they also use for musical cooperation. Various informants tell about artistic cooperation with MCs from France. MC C reports about contacts to Cape Verde, Boston, Rotterdam, London and Ireland with whom he tries to collaborate, with the intention to expand the market for rap kriolu made in Lisbon to the Cape Verdean diaspora. MC Tony, in an interview from February 2007, was already very optimistic that this expansion to a wider diaspora market would be successful (cf. Märzhäuser 2011a):

> Eu acredito que, propriamente, com o Rap Português vai conseguir ultrapassar barreiras e chegar à comunidade que vive no estrangeiro [. . .] falando do Rap

Kriolu também acredito que tanto a partir de Por-tugal como a partir da Holanda como partir dos próprios Estados Unidos onde há muitos caboverdianos, ok, eles vão fazer rap em crioulo. Já conheço alguns que vão ter projecção a nível internacional, portanto, porque nós estamos a falar de línguas que têm uma expressão muito grande no mundo. [. . .] Há muitos emigrantes caboverdianos em muitos lados do mundo, e não só eles falam o Kriolu como também educam os filhos com a língua materna que é o crioulo, e os filhos acabam por agarrar o crioulo, fazer música nessa base.

I believe that Portuguese rap will cross borders and reach the community living abroad. [. . .] and speaking about rap kriolu, I believe, too, that from Portugal as well as from the Netherlands and from the US, where many Cape Verdeans live, they will rap in CV. I already know some people who will be projected on the international level, because we speak about languages which have a very wide expression in the world. [. . .] There are many Cape Verdean emigrants in many regions of the world, and not only do they speak Capeverdean, but they also educate their children in their mother tongue Kriolu, and their children cling to the creole and make music on that (linguistic) basis.

Also DJ Kronic, in an interview in 2007, sees Portugal as a point of departure of what he considers two international rap scenes (cf. Märzhäuser 2011a):

Portugal é um pouco ponto de partida de dois Raps internacionais. Para mim o rap Português é international. Porque há muitos países em que há pessoas que falam. Eu pessoalmente fui a Moçambique, em Moçambique conhecem todo o Hip Hop Português. Fiquei em casa dum gajo que era fã do Sam the Kid e tinha tudo do Sam the Kid – doze mil kilómetros daqui. Mas Angola dever ser a mesma coisa. Agora o Rap Kriolu também tem outro potencial mundial. Pode ir para todos os lados em que haja alguém a falar.

Portugal is a little bit like a starting point for two international rap scenes. For me, Portuguese rap is international. Because there are many countries where there are people who speak it. Personally, I went to Mozambik and everyone knows Portuguese hip-hop. I stayed in the house of a guy who was a fan of Sam the Kid – twelve thousand kilometres from here. And in Angola it is probably the same thing. And rap kriolu also has a worldwide potential. They can go everywhere where someone speaks it.

These international links also reflect in the music press, which often includes CV rap from different geographic spaces, for example, in features about rap kriolu releases. Deterritorialization and consumption across geographical spaces has speeded up through online platforms, as MC Kromo di Gueto relates in an interview (Campos e Simões 2011, 127).

> [Com o aparecimento do MySpace] há muita diferença porque depois de meteres o vídeo no YouTube e no MySpace também [. . .] são consultas boas mesmo. A diferença antes e depois . . ., por exemplo, porque antes eu divulgava através do CD. Se queria divulgar para a Holanda, Cabo Verde, Luxemburgo só se eu tivesse lá alguém conhecido, mandava pelo correio, que era para depois dizer: "yah, espalhem lá pelo pessoal!". Com a internet não há essa barreira, estás a perceber?, chega a qualquer lado do mundo, seja na França, seja no Japão.

> When MySpace appeared, that made a lot of difference, because thenceforth you could put your videos on YouTube and on MySpace, too [. . .] you get a good resonance. The difference from before that and after . . . for example, in the past I distributed my music on CDs. If I wanted to bring it to the Netherlands, Cape Verde, Luxemburg that was only possible if I knew somebody there, I would send them by mail, and then say: "Ya, distribute the stuff to the folks there!" With the internet, this barrier no longer exists, you know? It gets everywhere in the world, no matter whether in France or in Japan.

Connections between different music hubs exist in digital form in consumption and production, but they also arise from the constant migratory movements between islands and different diaspora communities, and from exchanges during temporary visits of diaspora family members. Pardue (2014) tells this story from participating in the suburban *bairro Kova M*,[39] which shows local interaction of MCs with different backgrounds:

> Alyson, a twenty-year-old rapper and recent immigrant from Santiago [. . .] battled rhetorically with the tales of money and labor from another rapper, Simão, who was in town from the popular Cape Verdean diasporic community of Rotterdam [. . .] The small crowd egged them on and eventually drowned out Alyson and Simao with "now, you all are here – the heart of Kriolu in Portugal. This is Kova M. Yeah!" As dozens of young men shouted *Kel li, Kova M* [. . .] others added, in English, "Black lyrics, soldiers soldiers, ghetto life."[40]

Online cooperation additionally adds to the phenomenon that rap kriolu has "no fixed geographical coordinates" and has "overcome any physical barrier", developing from local niches with audiences from "home" hip-hop communities to a transnational audience. The transnational character is also commented on in the online journal *Rimas & Batidas* by Farinha in 2017, who underlines that further deterritorialization of rap kriolu "não tem coordenadas geográficas obrigatórias e tem superado quaisquer tipo de barreiras físicas" (it doesn't have any obligatory geographic coordinates and has overcome all kinds of physical barriers) – a development resulting from ongoing migratory movements from Portugal to other locations such as London, Paris and Luxemburg (enforced by the economic crisis), and no matter where, "rap crioulo desenvolve comunidades e nichos próprios", that is it develops its own communities and niches. The article mentions MC Lass G living in London, producing songs in which he code-switches between Capeverdean and English, and lists transnational collaborations in song production, for example MC Abrov, originally from Reboleira (Lisbon), who migrated to Luxemburg and recorded a track with MC Mji, still based in Lisbon.

Since music production has become digital to a high degree, online collaborations have become common in rap music production. Sharing beats and participating in rap tracks/albums in other countries via the internet also helps international cooperation in the rap kriolu scene. MC Eddy Fort Moda Grog made a guest appearance on the 2005 album *Criol na Coraçao* by the Luxembourg-based Cape Verdean rapper Kodé, and on the album *Fidju Di Kriolu* (2011), recorded by La Mc Malcriado of France. As for sales abroad, Pardue (2014a, 64) cites MC Hezbollah:

> I know they hear my music in Dorchester [Boston neighbourhood with a large Cape Verdean community]. I sold fifty CDs there over the past couple of months. I have family out there. On the islands, in Praia I do well, especially in the Achada Santo Antonio.

As Pardue (forthcoming, 16f) summarizes, the shared discourse space of transnational rap kriolu does not only share the common language, but – in a certain segment of this music scene – also common discourse topics and positions:

> [K]riolu rappers' articulation of diaspora often detours from the conventional tropes of nostalgic recognition of past, serial emigration to several European and American points, or a longing to return to the mother archipelago. Rather, as rapper LBC demonstrates, Kriolu chronotopes can represent a wide-ranging diaspora of marginalized and displaced youth, who are critical of imperialist, corporate values.

As Rosa (2018) puts it, "The movement is emergent and proving to be powerful given that it is a subculture in communication with a wider, global hip hop nation often through digital networks and global music festivals. [. . .] there is a global sub-community that we might call the CV Hip-Hop Nation" (93, 95).

Another step is the "move" towards the African continent. MC Pericles, of Rapaz 100 Juiz, sets a new focus on collaborations with the African continent, motivated by a logic of Black Culture. "Right now we want to take our music to Africa and work with the rappers all over Africa. In Europe, we have a crew but it's just Cape Verdeans in Europe." This development can be considered of special political interest, given that rappers in various continental African languages actively and successfully intervene in their countries' political development (cf. Sow 2004, 2017, on rap in Senegal).

Discussion of Data along the Framework for Linguistic Music Market Analysis

In the following discussion, the proposed framework is used to summarize the observations about the music hubs for rap kriolu in the diaspora settings and on the Capeverdean islands.

Localizing Points in the 1990s

As shown above along the different examples in sections two and three, the "linguistic localizing point" for the musical subgenre of rap kriolu across diaspora communities and on the archipelago happened in the 1990s, parallel to the linguistic localization of rap music in many other non-anglophone hip-hop scenes. In addition to the initial stigmatization of the musical genre rap, both on Cape Verde and in the diaspora (especially through stereotypes about its crime discourse reproduced by the media), there were various language- and discrimination-related obstacles for rap in CV: for rap in the Capeverdean diaspora, firstly the language's position as a minority language hindered rappers' access to wider audiences and to the public sphere. In reaction to these difficulties, MCs either opted for rapping in the respective majority language (exclusively or alongside rap lyrics in CV), often also including English text parts (beyond single, anglophone *hip-hop speech style*[41] insertions) with the intention of targeting more international audiences and to access the broader music market. Secondly, rap kriolu tended tended to adopt gangsta-style imagery both in lyrics, outfit and videos, thereby reproducing images of marginalisation and crime, although when in fact they display the defavorable conditions of their daily life and speak up against social exclusion and racism. Linguistic re-identification with the in-group is often re-interpreted as re-ethnification, which some associate with reconnection to one's roots and the empowerment of the community, while others condemn it as self-segregation and as lack of (will for) social integration into wider society.[42] As Oliveira (2015, online) describes, "a poética do rap crioulo na cena musical contemporânea de Lisboa manifesta uma profunda cisão cultural entre o centro e a periferia onde a violência atua como norma e a vivência do gueto apresenta-se como resistência ao racismo."

Translation: The poetics of rap kriolu in Lisbon's music scene today manifests a profound cultural split between centre and periphery, where violence is the norm and daily experiences in an urban ghetto are presented as resistance against racism.

Establishment in the Public Sphere

On the Capeverdean islands, where the linguistic localization also happened in the early 1990s, there were larger difficulties at the level of production and also an initial attempt by politicians to instrumentalize rappers for their electoral campaigns. In the diaspora settings analysed more closely, rap kriolu artists managed to create their own infrastructure regarding recording and distribution, such as recording studios and record labels. First independent productions opened some doors to more commercial circuits. Rapid changes regarding rap kriolu's establishment in a broader public sphere occurred when the internet developed into a platform for music distribution. As Simões (2017, 111) illustrates along the case of Mynda Guevara, today music distribution happens mainly via online channels.

Thus, rap artists managed to establish rap kriolu not only as a suburban niche, but prepared its way to a well-established musical subgenre also represented in a wider public space for wider local audiences. While wider public recognition of individual rappers performing in Capeverdean due to their lyrico-musical skills as rappers and bilingual strategies have slowly opened local markets, the digital, transnational Cape Verdean hip-hop scene has become an attractive market for underground newcomers and established rap kriolu artists alike. Besides trends in musical taste of the youth, it is without doubt due to recent technological developments that the genre has thrived on the Cape Verdean islands as well. As online platforms quickly gain importance for music distribution, the current deterritorialization of consumer spaces allows musicians to create networks with wider audiences (and also consumer networks with numerous online forums and journals, fan blogs, etc.) for which the language serves as a central link. Connections in production and consumption between "homeland" and diaspora strengthen the transnational rap kriolu market. The overall popularity of rap as a genre reflects back onto local hip-hop culture scenes and onto different markets for rap music. How this also affects rap kriolu would be interesting to investigate.

In a music market era in which digital distribution via shared online media allows broad consumer outreach, without elevated costs, a previously marginalized music genre like rap kriolu can more easily establish itself on the market. The infrastructure for beat makers, studio recordings and video clip production has improved as well due to the accessibility of digital tools. Local recording facilities for the (sub)genre increase the quality and quantity of musical production, and through digitalization, existing local distribution channels feed into a global consumer space for music genre markets, markets which often remain selective with regard to minority languages or creole languages in postcolonial settings.

Crossing Points

One of the effects of rap kriolu's wider popularity in Portugal is the adoption of the language by rappers of non-Cape Verdean descent and by wider audiences beyond. This linguistic music market analysis of rap kriolu in Portugal shows the development of this hip-hop subgenre from a marginal "niche culture" to a more widely popular genre represented in national media and on big festivals. Consequently, rap kriolu is being listened to by non-native speaker consumers, thus bringing the creole language (which doesn't have a public discourse space or representation outside the Cape Verdean islands) to the attention of a wider public of listeners. Rap kriolu can thus be understood as a public discourse space in which this creole language is being represented for a wider audience, beyond its native and heritage speakers. It has been reported by various informants in my 2007–08 interviews that non-native consumers start to inquire about the rap lyrics' language – as the song lyrics' messages are considered especially important in the text-centred genre rap, more than this is the case with other popular genres traditionally sung in Capeverdean. Thus, rapping in Capeverdean (implicitly or explicitly) becomes a means of transmitting knowledge about the language to non-speakers (a process fairly easy, up to some point, for Portuguese-speaking audiences due to inter-comprehension possible due to the numerous lexical parallels between both languages). As MC Chullage explained in an interview with Pardue (2014b, 322):

> It's not just that I often feel more comfortable rapping in Kriolu, it's about getting everybody [non-Kriolu speakers in Portugal and rap fans around the world] to listen and go search for the meaning. It's what we all did when we first heard Public Enemy (the influential black nationalist rap group from Long Island, New York during the late 1980s and early 1990s). We didn't understand English. We looked it up. People can do that with Kriolu.

Pardue (2014a, 64) also cites MC Hezbollah, who assumes that lusofone audiences get his message rapped in Capeverdean:

Some places like Santarém and Alcobaca have invited me to headline cultural events. Not many Kriolu speakers out that was, but I think it's because poor tugas hear me and get me.

The degree of inter-comprehension between Portuguese and Capeverdean in rap lyrics, and the relation between rap kriolu input and the degree of acquisition of (passive and active competences in) Capeverdean by lusophone consumers would be worthwhile investigating. Also, it would be interesting whether these consumers try to acquire metalinguistic knowledge about the language's structures to better understand the rap kriolu lyrics they listen to.

Regarding music consumption of rap kriolu songs, quantitative figures from online streaming platforms, labels, etc. should be included in future studies to complete the analysis regarding the spread of the genre's listeners.

Outlook

As for the choice of Capeverdean for rap lyrics, most MCs emphasize their link to their Cape Verdean reference culture, both in the homeland and the local diaspora(s), and they mention this identification as an important motivation to rap in Capeverdean. As their success as rappers depends on their presence in the public sphere, for which popular music offers a (partly linguistically biased) market – both "real" and digital – it is the rappers' orientation along consumer preferences that drives their language choice as well. On the other hand, a logic of empowerment is expanded from sociopolitical topics to the use of the creole language itself: the choice of rapping in the minority language is seen as an act of resistance against linguistic hegemony, as self-affirmation for the linguistic community, as a promotion and preservation of the language itself, and as an expression of valorization of cultural and linguistic diversity. Market dynamics for sure play an important role for the success of a subgenre like rap in Capeverdean. These have been modelled here in a framework for linguistic music market analysis. To understand the development and spread of the genre in the public sphere, political and ideological aspects have to be summarized as well. Rap kriolu has been constructed – both by MCs and in the scientific literature – as a discourse space concerned with the empowerment of migrants and black communities, speaking against marginalization and racism. Across different diaspora settings, central issues in *rap kriolu* have been the socio-economic marginalization of (especially second generation) young Cape Verdean "migrants", as well as the preoccupation with the situation of this Afro-European youth and that of similar groups in other diaspora countries. Sometimes, the use of the language itself is associated with these political, sociocultural and socio-economic problems. The lyrics contain narratives about the lack of perspectives and living conditions on the Cape Verdean islands leading to strong migration, including biographical narratives about the hardship of the older generations, questioning the condition of being a "black" migrant in Europe, the sociocultural dynamics around Cape Verdean rappers in the United States, and their (partial) integration into Afro-American hip-hop communities, which require further study.

Although socio-economic problems undoubtedly have a central place in CV rap lyrics, and although it is claimed by many that the essence of being a rap performer is to assume one's responsibility about the messages of social intervention, the positions expressed in rap discourse and the range of discursive reframing of suburban socio-economic reality have to be analysed MC by MC, track by track, as they are constantly changing also due to the shifting attention of consumers and producers within the wider hip-hop music market. In light of more numerous and more widely consumed rap kriolu productions, it has to be analysed in how far rap kriolu really serves as a discourse space to speak against marginalization and racism, and to empower migrant/black communities – or whether it is used to stage "hetero-bling-bling" imageries of gangsterism and material wealth. Also, this "marginal" discourse appears to be a typical genre-topic, and as such is expected by consumers, which again turns it into a recipe for popularity and thus helps to increase sales, that is, clicks on online streaming platforms. The hip-hop inherent discursive struggle about real/underground versus commercial/sell-out rap has been documented in Portugal since 1994 for rap in Portuguese (see Fradique 2003, 120ff). The same discussion is necessary with respect to rap in Capeverdean. The line between "conscious" and "commercial" rap sometimes becomes quite thin, and consumers might not always differentiate between the depiction of a peripheral community as location of poverty and social exclusions and the use of the same scenario for a soundtrack for glorifying self-depiction in a gangsta-style rap on heroic delinquency. To some extent, rap kriolu provides a common register and a spatio-temporal setting where youth may critically reflect, share, organize and have "a possibility for the building of a transnational social movement capable of scaffolding resistance from the cultural to concrete 'bodies on the ground' political action" (Rosa 2018, 95). It is often this political message which seems to unite the rap scene across different geographical settings, sometimes interpreted as transnational discourse space for black empowerment, a logic in which rap kriolu also partly inscribes itself. As Contador (2001, 71) states, "rapping in creole"[43] produces new meanings and a lexicon for expressing "blackness" in the Portuguese context. Besides from this position defended in Contador (2001, and already in Contador and Ferreira 1997), the choice to rap in Capeverdean is not only an expression of "blackness", but also of heterogeneity, of a discourse advocating multilingual spaces and the recognition of the language itself. Rapping in Capeverdean can also be seen as an act of resistance against linguistic hegemony in the light of linguistic discrimination. As already mentioned in the literature, the conscious choice of rapping (as well or exclusively) in Capeverdean is motivated by a sense of language activism regarding the use, vitality and functional range of the language. As Rosa remarks, by choosing Capeverdean language for rap, "[y]outh who are linguistically profiled (Rosa, 2010) and oppressed are creating creative linguistic identities in and through hip hop" (2018, 103). Rosa interprets this as a move in the "post-colonial struggle for full recognition of the language" (Rosa 2018, 103). This holds for both the glottopolitical situation on the Cape Verdean islands, where Capeverdean is still awaiting full officialisation and as a minority language without official status in the diasporas (although it can be a glossotopically dominant language among creoles compared to other African migrant languages, for example, in suburban Lisbon). Up to some point, rap kriolu opens a space for CV language in the public sphere – a sphere ranging from street freestyles, broadcast home studio recordings and jams, to stage performances, and published tracks "on tape" and in online streaming and media coverage.

Notes

1. In this text, Cape Verdean(s) is used as adjective or noun for places and people. The spelling in one word (Capeverdean) refers to the language, abbreviated here as CV / cv. The language is also referred to as pt. *língua caboverdiana*/cv. *língua kauberdianu* or simply cv. *Kabuverdianu* in other texts. Speakers themselves usually refer to the language as pt. *crioulo*/cv. *Kriolu*.

2. Figures from 2014 by International Organization for Migration indicate that there are about twice as many Cape Verdeans in the diaspora than domestic residents. Of an estimated total of 700,000 Cape Verdeans abroad, 260,000 live in the United States and 100,000 live in Portugal (cf. www.iom.int/countries/cabo-verde). Figures from *Statistics Netherlands* (www.cbs.nl) indicate that 20,961 people of Cape Verdean origin (including persons with one parent from Cape Verde) live in the Netherlands. About 90 per cent of

these live in the Rotterdam metropolitan area. Precise numbers on second and subsequent generations, and on heritage speakers, are not available for Cape Verdean diasporas.

3. Scientific literature on the crioulo rap scene in Lisbon/Portugal includes Martins (1997), Cidra (2002, 2008), Domingues (2005), Raposo (2003, 2005, 2010), Souza (2009), Juan (2007), Märzhäuser (2011a, 2011b, 2011c, 2011d, 2013) and Pardue (2012, 2014a, 2014b, 2016, in press). Rap on the Cape Verdean islands is analysed in Lima (2011, 2012, 2018), Barros and Lima (2011), and Rosa (2018). For linguistic research on hip-hop culture, see Alim (2006), Alim and Pennycook (2009), Androutsopolous (2003), Stemmler and Skrandies (2007), Terkourafi (2010) or Mitchell (2001).

4. A follow-up study on rap kriolu ten years from now would be worthwhile to understand language-related music consumption dynamics.

5. This happens, for example, with well-known genres such as Salsa, where Spanish lyrics are (re)produced by non-hispanophone singers.

6. The summary of the first decade is based on the work of Fradique (2003) *Fixar o movimento – representações da música rap em Portugal*, an introductory book about the early period of the Lisbon hip-hop scene; on the ethnographic study of Martins (1997), Cidra (2002), Domingues (2005), Raposo (2003, 2005, 2010), Souza (2009), Juan (2007), Märzhäuser (2011a, 2011b, 2011c, 2011d, 2013 and respective fieldwork data) and Pardue (2012, 2014a, 2014b, 2016). In addition, materials from the music press, social media content as well as song lyrics and audiovisual sources are analysed for the first period and also to trace the spread of this subgenre of hip-hop in Portugal in the following decade (until 2018–19). Some exemplary biographies of more widely known MCs and some "newcomers" are discussed here as biographical and discourse-positional "role models" regarding language use in rap.

7. Compare, for example, the narrative of German "old school" MCs from the crew Advanced Chemistry about US rap input in the 1980s and early 1990s triggering and the subsequent linguistic localizing of rap in Heidelberg.

8. Source: From Lois Varela, "Rap Raíz #02", interview with MC Karlon, see www.youtube.com/watch?time_continue=13&v=EXC4okOtFHI, accessed 30 May 2019.

9. See Lupati (2016) on the spread oh hip-hop in Portugal's afro-decendant communities, Simões (2011) on the role of the internet for its distribution, and Simões (2017) on female rappers in Portugal

10. My translation. From http://ritmoepoesia.multiply.com (08 July 2007). *Tuga* is a clipping for Portugal used in different substandard varieties.

11. Tony Dread, *100 papas na língua* (2004).

12. TWA, abbreviation for Third World Answer or Teenagers With Attitude, is a crew from suburban Pedreira dos Hungaros, which can be considered an important location for rap kriolu origins.

13. See https://www.discogs.com/artist/1077385-Black-Company for its releases.

14. From *As nossas raízes*, https://asnossasraizesvol2.blogspot.com/search/label/--História%20HH%20Crioulo.

15. Ataque Verbal was organized by ex-Black Company DJ KGB.

16. The documentary about Pedreira do Hungaros from the series *Outros Bairros*, produced by Kiluange Liberdade, Vasco Pimentel and Inês Gonçalves, shows MC Karlon's and MC Praga's early rap kriolu practice in some segments and gives a realistic impression of the living environment. See https://www.youtube.com/watch?v=xN03tYE8Jrs, accessed 30 May 2019.

17. See www.karlonkrioulo.com, accessed 30 May 2019.

18. From Rap Raíz, "MC Mynda´Guevara, Kova M, Lisboa" [3:00], www.youtube.com/watch?time_continue=18&v=YKh4Jvz5wQM, accessed 30 May 2019.

19. Produced by Otávio Raposo in 2007. See www.youtube.com/watch?v=pOAUbcVMs4w.

20. Source: http://afropop.org/articles/playlist-kriolu-rap-from-cova-da-moura, last accessed 15 July 2022.

21. See for example the 2018 online playlist "Kriolu Rap From the Lisbon Suburbs" by Bouknight.

22. Source: Bruno Andre, "Música electrónica, africana e (mais) Hip-Hop no segundo dia de Iminente", *Desacordo*, 17 September 2017, https://jornaldesacordo.com/2017/09/17/musica-electronica-africana-e-mais-hip-hop-no-segundo-dia-de-iminente%EF%BB%BF/.

23. The label Morabeza Records (called Casa Silva until 1970), which produced recordings of more traditional genres of Cape Verdean music, among them the widely famous group "Voz de Cabo Verde" was based in Rotterdam 1965–76 X is an early example of Capeverdean musicians creating infrastructure for their music. The label then moved to Paris. Its history is described in the short film *Morabeza Records, een Kaapverdisch platenlabel uit Rotterdam*, produced in 2017 by the Stadsarchief Rotterdam, where Morabeza Records's productions are archived.

24. Source: https://upclosed.com/people/eddy-fort-moda-grog.

25. Facebook page of Cabo Funk Alliance, https://www.facebook.com/pg/Cabo.Funk.Alliance/about/?ref=page_internal.

26. www.discogs.com/artist/1635652-Cabo-Funk-Alliance?anv=Cabo+Alliance.

27. From https://sodadefestival.nl/artist/moda-grog/.

28. Translates to "how the Capeverdean rap of Rotterdam's pioneers emerged".

29. www.facebook.com/Gerason90.

30. This chapter does not analyse local rap scenes on each islands separately, nor is there, to my knowledge, a text doing so.

31. Published 18 July 2013 on https://caboverdiano.blogspot.com, originally published in *Expresso das Ilhas*.

32. And not vice versa, as is the case for many other local rap scenes, for example Lisbon.

33. Listen to https://soundcloud.com/mad-devils-of.
34. Listen to https://soundcloud.com/kiddye-bonz.
35. Listen to https://soundcloud.com/wiggy-wiger.
36. From Lois Varela (2019) "Rap Raíz", Episodio 3: Interview with MC Kapa Gdr, Praia.
37. By Team True, https://trueafrica.co/article/cape-verdean-hip-hop-artists/.
38. O País CV, "Festival de Santa Maria já tem data e quatro nomes confirmados", https://opais.cv/festival-de-santa-maria-ja-tem-data-e-quatro-nomes-confirmados/10/04/2019/.
39. In-group term for Alto da Cova da Moura.
40. Pardue (2015) interprets the "juxtaposition of Kriolu and English [. . .] [as] social practice of interest and persuasion, in this case celebrating the centrality of Kova M in reality knowledge based on experiences of blackness, masculinity, poverty, and violence".
41. See Cutler (1999) on this term.
42. See Barbosa et al. (2008) and Goís (2008) on sociological aspects of the Cape Verdean community in Lisbon, Oliveira (2015) on the complex issue of identification.
43. "Crioulo" is perceived in Contador as a contact space of languages and language variation linking different PALOP influences, including Capeverdean.

References

Alim, Samy H. 2006. *Roc the Mic Right: The Language of Hip Hop Culture*. London and New York: Routledge.
Alim, Samy H., Awad Ibrahim, and Alastair Pennycook, eds. 2009. *Global Linguistic Flows: Hip Hop Culture, Youth Identities, and the Politics of Language*. London and New York: Routledge.
Androutsopoulos, Jannis, ed. 2003. *Hip Hop: Globale Kultur lokale Praktiken*. Bielefeld: Transcript Verlag.
Assunção, C., C. Almeida, and L. Perdigão. 2006. "O hip hop 'tuga'- Das ruas de Nova Iorque para os subúrbios portugueses". www2.fcsh.unl.pt/cadeiras/plataforma/foralinha/atelier/a/www/view.asp?edicao-=06&artigo=242 (14 May 2007).
Barbosa, Carlos Elias, and Max Ruben Ramos. 2008. "Vozes e Movimentos de Afirmação: os Filhos de Cabo-verdianos em Portugal". In *Comunidade(s) cabo-verdiana(s): as múltiplas faces da imigração cabo-verdiana*, edited by Pedro Góis, 173–92. Lisboa: ACIDI.
Barros, Miguel, and Redy Wilson Lima. 2012. "Rap kriol(u): o Pan-africanismo de Cabral na Música de Intervenção Juvenil na Guiné-Bissau e em Cabo-Verde". *REALIS – Revista de Estudos AntiUtilitaristas e PosColoniais 2 (2) (Dossiê Diálogos Ibero-Africanos)*: 89–117.

Campos, R., and J.A. Simões. 2011. "Participação e Inclusão Social nas Margens: Uma Abordagem Exploratória das Práticas Culturais de Jovens Afro-descendentes. O Caso do Rap Negro". *Media & Jornalismo* 19: 117–33.
Cidra, Rui. 2002. "'Ser Real': o rap na construção de identidades na Área Metropolitana de Lisboa". *Ethnologia*, Nova Série: 189–222.
———. 2008. "Produzindo a Música de Cabo Verde na Diáspora: Redes Transnacionais, *World Music* e Múltiplas Formações Crioulas". In *Comunidade(s) Cabo-verdiana(s): As Múltiplas Faces da Imigração Cabo-verdiana*, edited by Pedro Góis, 105–26. Lisboa: ACIDI.
Contador, Antonio. 2001. *Cultura Juvenil Negra em Portugal*. Oeiras: Ed. Celta.
Contador, Antonio, and E.L. Ferreira. 1997. *Ritmo e Poesia. Os caminhos do rap*. Lisbon: Assírio and Alvim.
Cutler, Cecilia. 1999. "Yorkville Crossing: A Case Study of Hip Hop and the Language of a White Middle Class Teenager in New York City". *Journal of Sociolinguistics* 3: 428–42.
Domingues, Nuno. 2005. "Jovens Negros em Lisboa: Biografia(s) de uma Festa Hip Hop". BA thesis, University Nova de Lisboa.
Fradique, Teresa. 2003. *Fixar o Movimento. Representações da música rap em Portugal*. Lisboa: Publ. D. Quixote.
Góis, Pedro, ed. 2008. *Comunidade(s) cabo-verdiana(s): as múltiplas faces da imigração cabo-verdiana*. Lisboa: Alto Comissariado para a Imigração e Diálogo Intercultural (ACIDI).
Gravato, Fernandes. 2017. "Rap em Portugal: comunidades online, lógicas de comunicação e posicionamentos identitários na internet". Master's thesis, Universidade do Minho, Braga.
Hurley-Glowa, S. 2015. "Cape Verdeans in the Atlantic: The Formation of Kriolu Music and Dance Styles on Ship and in Port". *African Music: Journal of the International Library of African Music* 10 (1): 7–30.
Juan, Edurne de. 2007. "'Nu ta Valoriza Nos Raiz': el Rap Krioulo y la Construcción Identitaria de los Jóvenes en la Cova da Moura, Lisboa". Paper presented at First International Conference Young Urban Researchers, June 2007, Lisboa.
Krefeld, Thomas. 2004. *Einführung in die Migrationslinguistik*. Tübingen: Gunter Narr.
Lança, Marta. 2008. "A Lusofonia é Uma Bolha". *Jogos Sem Fronteiras, edições Antipáticas*, Julho 2008.
Lima, Redy Wilson. 2011. "Hip Hop: Breve História e Introdução ao Mundo do Rap Crioulo". *Buala – Palcos*, 7 July 2011.
———. 2012. "Rappers Cabo-Verdianos e Participação Política Juvenil". *Tomo* 21: 263–94.
———. 2018. "Hip Hop Praia: Rap e a Representação do Espaço Público". In *Seminário Permanente em Estudos Africanos*, edited by Ana M. Martinho Gale, 90–109. Lisboa: CHAM.
Lupati, Federica. 2016. "The African Diaspora Through Portuguese Hip Hop Music: A Case Study". *Forma Breve* 13 (Exodus: conto e recontos): 679–89.

Martins, Humberto. 1997. "Ami Cunhá Cumpadri Pitécu – Uma Etnografia da Linguagem e da Cultura Juvenil Luso-Africana em Dois Contextos Suburbanos de Lisboa". Master's thesis, Universidade de Lisboa.

Märzhäuser, Christina. 2011a. *Portugiesisch und Kabuverdianu im Kontakt: Muster des Code-switching und lexikalische Innovationen in Raptexten aus Lissabon.* Frankfurt a.M./Berlin: Peter Lang Verlag.

———. 2011b. "Capeverdean Creole in Lisbon – Young Generation's Üerspective". In *Postcolonial Linguistic Voices. Identity Choices and Representations*, edited by Eric Anchimbe and Stephen Mforteh, 299–322. Berlin and New York: Mouton de Gruyter.

———. 2011c. "Contacto de Caboverdiano e Português e Criatividade Bilingue em Letras de Rap de Lisboa". In *Actas do Encontro "Múltiplos Olhares sobre o Bilinguismo"*, edited by P. Barbosa and Cristina Flores, 145–82. Colecção Hespérides, Braga: Universidade do Minho.

———. 2011d. "Motivações na Escolha de Língua em Letras de Rap. Um Estudo com Falantes Bilingues (Português – Caboverdiano) em Lisboa". In *Linguística do português. Rumos e pontes,* edited by Mathias Arden, Christina Märzhäuser, and Benjamin Meisnitzer, 429–52. München: Meidenbauer.

———. 2013. "Sprachliche Alternanzen in Liedtexten". In *Sprache(n) und Musik. Akten der gleichnamigen Sektion auf dem XXXI.Romanistentag (Bonn, 27.09–01.10.2009),* edited by Anja Overbeck und Matthias Heinz, 91–109. München: Lincom Europa.

Mitchell, Tony, ed. 2001. *Global Noise. Rap and Hip Hop Outside the USA.* Wesleyan: University Press.

Pardue, Derek. 2012. "Cape Verdean Kriolu as an Epistemology of Contact". *Cadernos de Estudos Africanos* 24: 73–94.

———. 2014a. "Creole as Drama: Kriolu rappers extend a Cape Verdean Paradigm of Encounter". *Social Text* 119, 32 (2): 53–75.

———. 2014b. "Kriolu scenes in Lisbon: Where migration experiences and housing policy meet". *City and Society,* 26 (3): 308–30.

———. 2016. "'Cash or Body': Lessons on Space and Language from Cape Verdean Rappers and Their Beefs". *Popular Music and Society* 39 (3): 332–45.

———. Forthcoming. "Chronotope Identification in Kriolu Rap". In *Lusophone Hip Hop: "Who We Are" and "Where We Are": Identity, Urban Culture and Belonging,* edited by Rosana Martins and Massimo Canevacci, 1–21. Canon Pyon, Herefordshire (UK): Sean Kingston Publishing.

Rampton, Ben. 1995. *Crossing: Language and Ethnicity among Adolescents.* London: Longman.

Raposo, Otávio Ribeiro. 2003. "Sociabilidades Juvenis em Contexto Urbano – Um Olhar Sobre os Jovens do Bairro Alto da Cova da Moura". BA thesis, Universidade Nova de Lisboa.

———. 2005. "Sociabilidades Juvenis em Contexto Urbano. Um Olhar Sobre Alguns Jovens do Bairro do Alto da Cova da Moura". *Fórum Sociológico* 13/14: 151–70.

———. 2010. "Tu és *rapper*, representa Arrentela, és *Red Eyes Gang*: sociabilidades e estilos de vida de jovens do subúrbio de Lisboa". *Sociologia, Problemas e Práticas* 64: 127–47.

Rosa, Ricardo D. 2018. "Cape Verdean Counter Cultural Hip Hop(s) & the Mobilization of the Culture of Radical Memory: Public Pedagogy for Liberation or Continued Colonial Enslavement". *Journal of Cape Verdean Studies* 3 (1): 92–113.

Saucier, Paul Khalil. 2011. *Native Tongues: An African Hip-Hop Reader*. Trenton: Africa World Press.

Sieber, Timothy. 2005. "Popular Music and Cultural Identity in the Cape Verdean Post-Colonial Diaspora". *Etnográfica* IX (1): 123–48.

Simões, José Alberto. 2010. *Entre a Rua e a Internet: Um Estudo Sobre o Hip Hop Português*. Lisboa: Imprensa de Ciências Sociais.

Simões, Soraia. 2017. "Fixar o (in)visível: papéis e repertórios de luta dos primeiros grupos de rap femininos a gravar em Portugal (1989–1998)". *Cadernos de Arte e Antropologia* 7 (1/2018): 97–114.

Souza, Angela Maria de. 2009. "A Caminhada é Longa . . . e o Chão tá Liso: O Movimento Hip Hop em Florianópolis e Lisboa". PhD thesis, Universidade Federal de Santa Catarina, Brasil.

Sow, Ndiémé. 2004. "Mots Contre Maux: Le Rap Sénégalais, Entre Art du Langage et Activisme Social". *Anadiss* 25: 76–83.

———. "Encyclopédie de ker gi: Entre Récréation et Re-création d'une Identité Linguistique". *Revue du GRADIS – Questioner les cultures urbaines* 2: 1–16.

Stemmler, Susanne, and Timo Skrandies, eds. 2007. *Hip Hop und Rap in Romanischen Sprachwelten – Stationen einer Globalen Musikkultur*. Frankfurt: Peter Lang.

Terkourafi, Marina, ed. 2010. *The Languages of Global Hip Hop*. London and New York: Continuum.

Online Sources (Blogs, Websites, Social Media, Online Music Press)

Blog AfroPop Worldwide, https://afropop.org, Article:
Bouknight, Sebastian (31 July 2018) "Playlist: Kriolu Rap From the Lisbon Suburbs".

Blog Caboverdiano, http://caboverdiano.blogspot.com, Gilson F. R. Silva aka G.Silva (18 July 2013) "HipHop Criol ta vivo e no te que oi vivo na melon", published in Expresso das Ilhas, posted 18 July 2013.

Online Journal *Buala*, www.buala.org, Articles:
António Guterres, Joaquim Arena, LBC, periferia (18 March 2011). "A África das periferias de Lisboa: a produção artística na periferia".
Lima, Redy Wilson (07 July 2011). "Hip hop: breve história e introdução ao mundo do rap crioulo".

Monteiro, Eurídice (10 August 2011) "Hip Hop da Diáspora: Malcriado, Chullage e Bandidos".
Lima, Redy Wilson (06 November 2012). "Rap dos anos 90 em Cabo Verde, o fenómeno Tchipie".
Oliveira, Susan de (24 August 2015). "Indígenas, imigrantes, pobres: o afropolitanismo no rap crioulo" – Parts 1 & 2.

Online Journal *Rimas e Batidas*. www.facebook.com/rimasebatidas, Articles:
Monteiro, Eurídice (10 August 2011) "Hip Hop da Diáspora: Malcriado, Chullage e Bandidos".
Farinha, Ricardo (28 January 2017) "20 músicas de rap crioulo para o arranque do ano".

Webpage "Cabo Forum – Cabo Hip Hop" (from France), https://web.archive.org/web/20080404025037/http://membres.lycos.fr/ cabosite95/newpage2.html.
Webpage "Cabo Funk Alliance", www.facebook.com/pg/Cabo.Funk.Alliance/about/?ref=page_internal.
Webpage "Gang do Moinho", www.facebook.com/GangdoMoinho.HipHopTuga.
Webpage "H2Tuga", https://www.facebook.com/h2tugapt/.
Webpage "Hip Hop Tuga", https://www.facebook.com/hiphoptugasite.
Webpage "Hip Hop Tuga", https://www.facebook.com/hiphoptugaa/.
Webpage "HipHopWeb", https://www.facebook.com/HipHopWeb/.

Audiovisuals: Films and Songs

Documentary "Nu bai – rap negro Lisboa". 2006. Produced by Raposo, Otávio. https://www.youtube.com/watch?v=pOAUbcVMs4w.
Documentary "23 minutos sobre Rap Underground". Produced by GRC/Migalhas. www.youtube.com/watch?v=xAQth9jSplA&feature=youtu.be.
Interview by Varela, Lois. 29 March 2019. "Rap raíz" #02 Karlon, Rap Raiz Tv. https://www.youtube.com/watch?time_continue=13&v=EXC4okOtFHI.
Documentary "Music of Resistance". 2009. Broadcasted on Al Jazeera. www.musicofresistance.com/chullage.html.
Song by Apollo G and Garry – "Tempo antigo". Produced by DJ Michel, MIXTAPE "Sucess after Struggle (S.A.S)", V. https://www.youtube.com/watch?v=CdwpnmYQ9X8 &list=PLK9etAEsNSHy_CxuRioSiVQeFHAy7VHsb [30.05.2019: 12.194.537 Clicks].

Chapter 10

Authentic Crossing?

Jamaican Creole in African Dancehall

ANIKA GERFER

Introduction

Media products such as music recordings have for some decades been one of the most important means through which people all around the globe come into contact with different varieties of English. Although media products have already been studied extensively in cultural studies and linguistic anthropology, sociolinguistic research has neglected them for a long time. The omnipresence, complexity and social relevance of language performances offer unprecedented opportunities for the analysis of prevailing language ideologies, the performance of social styles and identities for various (symbolic) purposes, as well as transnational and transcultural flows of standard and non-standard linguistic resources in the process of globalization (Coupland 2007; Pennycook 2007). Performed language is different from everyday language in that it is scripted and rehearsed, and thus stylized, that is, self-aware and sometimes hyperbolic, with particular forms often associated with specific genres (Bell and Gibson 2011, 557–58). Language is a highly pertinent tool in the creation and display of an artist's identity. The performance of an artist's staged identity often diverges from their "real", off-stage identity. In language performances, being authentic has been found to result from "context-dependent discursive practices" (Akande 2012a, 241), that is, "specific [. . .] patterns of discursive representation [which] can achieve the quality of experience that we define as authentic" (Coupland 2003, 417–18).

Authenticity in traditional variationist sociolinguistics has often been equated with vernacular language, that is a person's in-group, "natural" speech style. In the Labovian sense, authenticity correlates with geographically and socially demarcated linguistic communities. This view of authenticity is strongly related to the concept of "place".

Blommaert (2010, 1), however, advocates that in consequence of globalization processes these "classic distinctions and biases" should be reconsidered. Instead of focusing on "static variation, on local distribution of varieties" sociolinguistics needs to "rethink itself as a sociolinguistics of *mobile resources*" (Blommaert 2010, 1; emphasis mine). In this light, discursive practices through which speakers construct and perform authenticity in non-territorialized locations, such as in stylized, mediated language (Bucholtz 2003, 403; Lacoste, Leimgruber and Breyer 2014, 9), become worthwhile in sociolinguistic research. Globalization processes have led to the worldwide dissemination of languages and cultures. In the course of these developments, vernaculars have spread across the world in unprecedented speed and forms, such as within the global "mediascape" (Appadurai 1996). They have consequently become globally available and prestigious linguistic resources which are reappropriated in different contexts. As a consequence, they become detached from their previous associations of social class and stigma (Coupland 2011; Mair 2013).

As indicated earlier, performed language contrasts with the kind of "authentic speech" which has been of key interest in traditional sociolinguistics. Performed language, as scripted, rehearsed, intentionally styled and "initiative" (Bell 1984), has therefore often been characterized as "a form of strategic deauthentication" (Coupland 2001, 345). However, the connection between performed language and authenticity is multifaceted and deserves careful attention in sociolinguistic research. Authentic "belonging" cannot exclusively be controlled by a speaker but is sometimes negotiated by others, as is the case with singers, whose performances are scrutinized by the audience (Coupland 2014, 29–30). Authenticity is a complex and context-dependent concept which can play a crucial role in an artist's success, and which can be achieved or discredited through language (Coupland 2003; Sebba and Dray 2012). Inauthentic or stereotypical uses of linguistic forms may be perceived as fake and be condemned by the audience (Lopez and Hinrichs 2017, 3; Terkourafi 2010). A commonly applied strategy of achieving authenticity in language performances is via the co-occurrence of global and local (linguistic) elements, also labelled "glocalization" (Robertson 1995). For instance, hip-hop artists all over the world fuse foreign (especially African American English) and local linguistic resources in order to both maintain a local identity and "keep it real", but at the same time be loyal to hip-hop's American origins (O'Hanlon 2006). Lee (1982, 105) further identifies a link between language use and financial success when he points out that

[t]he popular singer [...] can only exist provided that he or she attracts a *paying* [emphasis mine] audience. The singer must therefore be in a constant state of dialogue with the audience and must "communicate" to them, a situation which is only possible when the "language" used is understood by both sides.

Thus, the combination of global and local linguistic resources does not only add to a performer's authenticity with regard to genre appropriateness, but it also enables them to reach a wider audience and hence be financially successful.

The present study investigates the linguistic behaviour of African dancehall performers, some of which have been harshly criticized by their fellow artists for using "fake [Jamaican] patois" (Sarpeah 2017) and for copying Jamaicans instead of performing in their local languages. I examine how African dancehall singers "cross" (Rampton 1995) into Jamaican Creole (JC) in their songs by analysing songs by Shatta Wale (Ghana), Patoranking (Nigeria) and Redsan (Kenya) and comparing them to contemporary successful Jamaican dancehall artists. More specifically, I aim to find out (1) which JC phonetic, morphosyntactic and lexical features are used most frequently; (2) whether and to what extent the African artists incorporate features of other languages; and (3) which notions of authenticity apply to the African dancehall performances.

A mixed-methods approach combining quantitative and qualitative research methods gives insight into the dynamic relationship of the coexistence of various linguistic resources and the construction of authenticity in a globally available and increasingly prestigious music genre. An auditory analysis is carried out to investigate the performers' use of JC phonetic features. In order to find out whether the artists' use of JC is systematic and consistent, a quantitative phonetic and morphosyntactic analysis is conducted. Besides this quantitative approach, the performers' use of Jamaican lexemes and the incorporation of additional local languages is analysed qualitatively.

Crossing and Authenticity in Music Performances

Performers such as singers often diverge from their "natural" speaking voice and model their language towards an outgroup with whom they wish to identify – a sociopsychological process labelled "referee design" (Bell 1984). For instance, some pop and rock artists have been found to adopt an Americanized singing style for multiple reasons, including genre appropriateness, that is "Americanness" as indexical of mainstream pop music and commercial considerations (Gibson and Bell 2012; O'Hanlon 2006; Simpson 1999; Trudgill 1983). A parallel concept to Bell's (1984) referee design is Rampton's "crossing" (1995), which focuses on the appropriation of a language or variety by speakers "who aren't accepted members of the group" (270). Crossing, in contrast to referee design, "involves a sense of movement across quite sharply felt social or ethnic boundaries" (Rampton 2009, 287). Over the past few decades, crossing has been extensively studied in various performance and non-performance contexts (see for example Bucholtz 1997; Cutler 2003; Hewitt 1986; Rampton 1995; Sebba and Dray 2012). Language crossers usually do not have full competence in the target language or variety, and therefore tend to choose only some socially significant variants of a truncated repertoire (Blommaert 2010, 103) to display their affiliation (Bucholtz 1997, 73).

Due to colonization processes, multilingualism and language contact have been the norm in postcolonial settings for several centuries. Therefore, the dissemination of languages across national borders, which in these settings are usually inventions or fictions, has always been a rather natural and expected process. However, communication and the global spread of languages have been facilitated and taken on new forms through new media and the Internet. As part of the global mediascape, languages have thus been spreading all across the globe, resulting in the movement, borrowing, blending and reappropriation of languages and cultures in terms of transcultural flows (Pennycook 2007, 6). Nowadays, performers have unprecedented access to a wide range of varieties and languages which they incorporate into their performances. For example, non-US American hip-hop artists mix local languages with features of African American English to "keep it real" on a local scale and, at the same time, express their affiliation to the American origins of the music genre (see Akande, 2012a, for Nigerian hip-hop; Lee, 2011, for Korean hip-hop; and O'Hanlon, 2006, for Australian hip-hop). Nigerian hip-hoppers additionally adopt features of JC to make their performances more accessible to an international audience (Akande 2012a). In her pop reggae song *Work* (2016), Rihanna uses features of Caribbean English Creole, and possibly African American English, to display her "co-existing identities" (Jansen and Westphal 2017), while Trinidadian ragga soca artists have been found to mix Trinidadian Creole English and JC phonology to index and "give credence to a specific Trinidadian experience, one of political, social and economic disenfranchisement and marginalization" (Leung 2009, 526). Blommaert (2005) demonstrates how South African radio DJ Pakaay crosses into JC; "Dread Talk" (Pollard 2000), which is a subvariety of JC spoken by members of the Rastafari movement; African American

English; and Township English in his hip-hop/reggae show. In his ethnographic study on German reggae subculture, Westphal (2018) shows that the performers mostly use stereotypical features which enable them to perform a subcultural identity. In these performances, language crossers are not fully proficient or fluent in their target varieties; instead, they deploy individual features of a truncated repertoire to mark "packages of identity features" (Blommaert 2005, 231). In contrast to this, Gerfer (2018) shows that some non-Jamaican reggae artists adopt a wide range of JC phonetic, morphosyntactic and lexical features both in singing and in speaking.

Music performances show stylized, affected and sometimes exaggerated language through which artists can create and display new identities. Instead of treating authenticity as a fixed and static concept, which in traditional sociolinguistic terms has been interpreted as vernacular language use in views of "place", that is origin and ownership, performance sociolinguistics needs to consider the creation of authenticity through linguistic (and extra-linguistic) practices in the moment of performing (Sebba and Dray 2012, 271). Authenticity is a decisive factor in an artist's success: Language representations which are perceived as stereotypical or inauthentic may be disparaged, leading to a decrease in sales figures. This suggests that authenticity is a complex notion and therefore does not lend itself to a sole, fixed definition but is context-dependent and dynamic. Authenticity can be achieved through particular ways of speaking and forms of discursive representation (Coupland 2003, 417–18). In the performance of pop and rock music, for example, adopting an Americanized accent can be perceived as either authentically pop/rock or as inauthentic, depending on the "cultural schema" of the audience (Bell and Gibson 2011, 565; Gibson 2010). Likewise, indie rock artists index authenticity by rejecting the "fake" Americanized accent of mainstream pop and engage in an "initiative act of identity" (Beal 2009, 238; Gibson and Bell 2012, 160) by singing in their vernacular voices. The core hip-hop value of authenticity, or "keepin' it real" (Mitchell 2003, 45), is an important and multifaceted issue which is accomplished by different artists in different ways. Australian hip-hoppers, for instance, maintain a local authenticity and identify with their target audience, that is, young Australians, by rapping predominantly in Australian English, including broad phonetic features. This emphasizes a distinction between Australian and US American hip-hop (O'Hanlon 2006, 194). Rapping in one's vernacular instead of adopting foreign voices can thus be expressive of one's personal identity, which is perceived as authentic and "real" in a Labovian sense of the concept. Authenticity can also be accomplished through glocalization, that is, through the fusion of foreign and local resources, which has been examined in Nigerian or Japanese hip-hop (see Akande 2012a and Pennycook 2003, respectively). Lee (2010) argues that non-US American rappers who copy American gangsta hip-hoppers would be perceived as inauthentic because they would not "keep it real"; but not including some global hip-hop features is not interpreted as "real" either. This is in line with Mitchell (2001, 298), who describes authenticity in hip-hop as a dynamic process which involves linguistic, social and political components, resulting in complex way of "indigenization and syncretism". A parallel concept through which authenticity can be created is "translocalization", a process in which "locality [is] transported into locality" (Blommaert 2010, 79). Instead of suggesting that these localities become "more 'global' or 'deterritorialized'", translocalization sees these localities "as local as before", with new meanings being imported into such local systems, "where they are changed and interpreted on the basis of such systems" (Blommaert 2010, 79).

Authenticity in the context of dancehall music is still an under-researched field. Some studies, however, have suggested that the use of JC is strongly associated with the performance of reggae and dancehall music and is even expected by audience members with very limited knowledge of JC (Gerfer fc.). Westphal (2018), who examines performers' language use at a German outdoor reggae event, finds that many of the interviewed audience members of the "outside audience" do not know any or only very little JC. However, this "partial language gap" (Westphal 2018, 109) between the German reggae performers and large parts of the audience does not have a negative effect on the audience's perception of the local artists' use of JC as natural and authentic, since they feel it reflects a "peaceful hippiesque atmosphere" (Westphal 2018, 109). In her study on Réunionese dancehall, Bremner (2015) argues that artists cross into English and JC to transfer their covert yet global prestige onto Réunionese Kréol. Similar to Westphal (2018), she shows that the inclusion of potentially unfamiliar JC lexical items apparently is not detrimental to the audience's identification with the music, which shows that intelligibility is not essential for achieving authenticity (Bremner 2015, 120). In the context of such heteroglossic (Bakhtin 1981) music performances, authenticity proves to be a highly complex conception which depends on multiple factors, such as music genre, setting (that is, an artist's origin and linguistic background) and audience expectations. By mixing local languages with global elements, such as the prestigious supercentral non-standard varieties African American English and JC (Mair 2013, 263–65), artists create and perform authenticity in individual and dynamic ways.

The Global Spread of Jamaican Creole and Dancehall

JC is an English-based Creole spoken as the first language by most Jamaicans. Despite its long-term prevalence across all sectors of Jamaican society, JC is not standardized or fully recognized but coexists with the country's sole official language, (Standard) Jamaican English, which is usually acquired at school. Due to colonial language ideologies, JC has been associated with a low social status and lack of education. After Jamaica's independence in 1962, the colonial distribution of linguistic power has been disrupted as part of decolonization processes. As a growing sense of national identity started to emerge, JC evolved into a linguistic symbol of a Jamaican national identity (Schneider 2007, 234–36). Although the status of JC has improved since the country's independence, it has remained in an inferior position to Jamaican English in local contexts (Westphal 2015, 195). On a global scale, however, JC has gained covert prestige and has developed into a language which has supercentral status (Mair 2013, 264). Several factors have supported this change in prestige, including shifts in power relations and identity politics, travel and migration, as well as Jamaican popular music (Devonish 2007; Hinrichs 2011; Mair 2013). Through outmigration of West Indians to metropoles such as Toronto and London, JC has crossed national borders and has become part of the sociolinguistic structure of these cities (Hinrichs 2014; Kerswill 2014). Additionally, JC has developed into an expressive of ethnic identity for the wider black community (Sebba 1993) and been appropriated by white British adolescents for numerous reasons (Hewitt 1986; Rampton 1995; Sebba and Dray 2012). The most important driving force behind the global spread of JC, however, is the worldwide success of Jamaican popular music (Cooper 2004).

The development of ska, rocksteady and reggae in Jamaica during the 1960s was heavily affected by American rhythm and blues. This influence had a huge impact on language use in early reggae music, leading artists to sing in English and adopting typical American English forms (Farquharson 2017, 10). By the 1970s, JC started being incorporated into reggae music alongside an increased insertion of Dread Talk (Pollard 2000) due to the impact of Rastafari on roots reggae songs. This political-religious countercultural movement has gathered supporters all over the globe and has played a major role in the global spread of JC and Dread Talk (Mair 2013, 14; Winer 1990, 36). The emergence of Jamaican dancehall is usually dated to the late 1970s, although its occurrence among the working classes had already started a couple decades earlier (Stolzoff 2000, xii). Early forms of the music genre reflected a "ghetto glorification of sex, guns, and the drug trade" (Thomas 2004, 81), which sharply contrasted with the emphasis on social critique and a belief in black redemption focused on in previous reggae music. Current dancehall music has been referred to derisively as "slackness" music (Cooper 2004, 73–79) which is "vulgarly degrading to Jamaica's moral fiber" (Thomas 2004, 81) by many (upper-class) observers. Additionally, on the one hand, dancehall has been viewed as politically conservative by some Jamaicans because unlike roots reggae music, dancehall disavowed from the revolutionary politics of the 1970s and instead reflected "personal melodramas" (Thomas 2004, 81). On the other hand, Cooper (1989, 12) sees dancehall as a form of "verbal marronage" through which singers criticize the conservatism of Jamaican social relations, such as the defamation of homosexuality, which is entrenched in local values formed by a fundamentalist reading of the Bible (Manuel, Bilby and Largey 1995, 178). The variability of Jamaican dancehall has led Stolzoff (2000, 1) to characterize dancehall as "a field of active cultural production" and "a means by which black lower-class youth articulate and project a distinct identity in local, national, and global contexts".

Dancehall has been dominated by JC since its beginnings. Dancehall artists, by refusing to sing in English and providing working-class Jamaicans with an amplified voice and a means through which they could express their own experiences, adopted an anti-colonial stance and have substantially added to the legitimacy of JC (Farquharson 2017, 11). The worldwide dissemination of JC has been accelerated by the growing international popularity of reggae music brought forth by Bob Marley and other Jamaican roots reggae artists as well as the globalization of the sound system in dancehall culture. Sound systems are mobile clubs which originated in Kingston's inner city in the 1950s. The sound system tradition and dancehall space have travelled through outmigration from Jamaica to diverse locations all over the world. While dancehall events were still an underground phenomenon during the 1990s, once they started gaining in popularity, artists travelled to Jamaica to acquire JC (Cooper 2012, 78–86). Dancehall and JC have since been adapted to new locations and fostered their own local expressions. For instance, Hewitt (1986) and Sebba and Dray (2012) demonstrate that JC is the prestige language at sound system and MCing events in Great Britain. Bremner (2015) argues that Réunionese dancehall artists adopt JC features to transfer its prestige onto Réunionese Kréol, and Westphal (2018), analysing language use at a German outdoor reggae event, shows that JC, Dread Talk, Standard English and German coexist in the reggae performances, which can thus be described as "both global and local", as the performers do not only orient themselves towards a "global absent referee (that is, Jamaica, Rastafari, reggae)" but also "model their performances according to the needs of a local [German] audience" (110).

The adoption and appropriation of JC in language performances beyond sound system events has been examined in numerous music genres, such as Trinidadian ragga soca (Leung 2009), Nigerian hip-hop (Akande 2012a), pop reggae (Jansen and Westphal 2017) and global reggae (Gerfer 2018; fc.). Similarly, the use of JC has been examined in a South African hip-hop/reggae show in which the radio DJ Pakaay style-shifts between (Standard) English, JC, Dread Talk, African American Vernacular English, and Township English (Blommaert 2005, 224–32). Lopez and Hinrichs (2017) analysed the use of JC and Dread Talk by a European American character in the 2013 Volkswagen Super Bowl commercial. In most of the cases described earlier, JC is not deployed as a fully acquired language, but performers insert some salient features of a truncated repertoire as an index of authenticity and internationality (Akande 2012a; Bremner 2015; Westphal 2018), a working-class identity (Leung 2009), coexisting identities (Jansen and Westphal 2017) and belonging to the global reggae community (Gerfer 2018). JC, as a (formerly) stigmatized and discriminated but at the same time covertly prestigious language, is taken up in music, which has always provided a rather liberal space, giving access to a variety of languages, styles and voices (Farquharson 2017, 8). Artists from different linguistic backgrounds who sing in their local languages, such as Réunionese Kréol (Bremner 2015), Trinidadian Creole English (Leung 2009) and Nigerian Pidgin (NP) (Akande 2012a), include features of JC to transmit its prestige to their local languages and create globally authentic performances.

Dancehall has a long history in West African countries like Ghana and Nigeria, but it stayed underground for some time due to a lack of acknowledgement as part of African culture, and the prevalence of hip-hop and the more established reggae culture. Since the early 2000s, however, dancehall artists have been able to promote events and release music without mainstream support via the Internet. Dancehall is now becoming more fashionable, with performers gaining popularity across the continent and beyond. Their language in performing has recently been an issue of public debate: While dancehall artists Shatta Wale and Stonebwoy from Ghana fight over who performs the "better" version of JC, critics have excoriated their use of English and JC instead of singing in their local languages.

The two West African countries of Ghana and Nigeria as well as the East African country of Kenya are multilingual countries in which English is the official language and mainly used in formal contexts. In Ghana, more than fifty languages are spoken. In the South, the Akan dialect Twi is a lingua franca, while Hausa, introduced to northern Ghana from Nigeria, is a lingua franca in the North and in linguistically diverse quarters in the Southern cities (Huber 2013, 394). Ghanaian Pidgin (GP) is a predominantly oral, informal and Southern-urban language which is not officially recognized or standardized (Huber 2013, 394). Similarly, Nigeria is a highly multi-ethnic and multilingual country, where more than five hundred indigenous languages are spoken next to the country's official language English and NP (Eberhard, Simons and Fennig 2019). NP is used daily by more than 75 million of the 150 million inhabitants of Nigeria and throughout the Nigerian diaspora. It is therefore the most widely spoken Creole language in the world (Faraclas 2013, 417). The major native languages in Nigeria in terms of population are Hausa, Yoruba and Igbo. Kenya's official languages are English and Swahili. In total, more than sixty languages are spoken in Kenya (Eberhard, Simons and Fennig 2019). Most languages which are spoken locally belong to either to the Niger-Congo language family or the Nilo-Saharan, which are spoken by the country's Bantu and Nilotic populations, respectively. While Kenya's various ethnic groups typically speak their mother tongues within their own communities, the two official languages, English and Swahili, are used as lingua francas throughout the country.

Data and Methods

The present study draws on both quantitative and qualitative methods to investigate the linguistic behaviour of African dancehall artists and compare it to Jamaican performers. The songs were chosen according to "popularity", that is the most frequently streamed songs on Spotify and YouTube. A quantitative analysis of seven phonetic and seven morphosyntactic features serves to investigate whether African dancehall artists systematically cross into JC. Table 10.1, based on Devonish and Harry (2008) for phonetic and Patrick (2008) for morphosyntactic features, displays the features analysed in the dancehall songs, their JC realizations and examples. The use of Jamaican lexemes and local languages is considered in the qualitative part of the linguistic analysis. Additionally, I analysed further JC phonetic and morphosyntactic features (namely the insertion of a bilabial glide after bilabial plosives, syllable amalgamation across word boundaries, copula forms, multiple negation and the negative marker *na* as well as the use of modal auxiliaries) qualitatively due to low token counts.

Table 10.1 JC Phonological and Morphosyntactic Features

Phonological Feature	JC Variant	Example
LOT/CLOTH	[a]	*top* [tap]
THOUGHT	[aː]	*talk* [taːk]
GOAT	[uo] ~ [ua]	*phone* [fuon]
FACE	[ie] ~ [iɛ] ~ [ia]	*wake* [wiak]
MOUTH	[oʊ] / [ɔŋ]	*now* [noʊ] / *down* [dɔŋ]
Palatal and labial-velar consonants	Insertion of semi-vowel sequences [w] after /p, b/ and [j] after /k, g/	*boy* [bwaɪ] / *girl* [gjal]
Vowel assimilation across syllable boundary	Syllable amalgamation	*go on* [gwaːn], *do it* [dwiːt]

Morphosyntactic Feature	JC Variant	Example
Number marking	Post-nominal affix *-dem*[a]	*the youth-dem*
Copula	Copula *a*	*she a wise*
Progressive aspect	a. Progressive *a* + verb b. ∅ + verb + *in'/ing*	a. *them always a smile* b. *them always smiling*
Negation	1. Negative concord 2. Negative marker *na*	1. *me never hear no man* 2. *you na know the end*
Modal auxiliary	*haffi*	*them haffi come*
Prepositions	e.g. *inna, fi, pon*	*him inna di club* *the girl deh pon the floor*
Infinitive marker	*fi*	*me want fi go home*

[a] It needs to be noted that plural marking via postposed elements also exists in NP English (see for example Faraclas 2013, 428). Therefore, Patoranking's use of this feature is further analysed qualitatively.

A total of 988 phonetic and 286 morphosyntactic tokens were analysed in the lyrics of eighteen songs for the African artists. The Jamaican comparison group produced a total of 851 phonetic and 307 morphosyntactic tokens in the lyrics of fifteen songs (see table 10.2).

The Jamaican comparison group consists of the contemporary successful performers Damian Marley, Gaza Slim, Mavado, Sean Paul and Vybz Kartel, while the African dancehall songs come from Patoranking (Nigeria),

Table 10.2 Number of Tokens Analysed per Artist

Feature	N Jamaicans	N Patoranking	N Shatta Wale	N Redsan
THOUGHT	46	22	34	29
LOT/CLOTH	182	51	55	49
MOUTH	92	25	43	27
Palatal consonants	118	18	25	61
GOAT	233	110	113	85
FACE	180	90	71	80
Total phonetic tokens	**851**	**316**	**341**	**331**
Number marking	38	10	11	17
Progressive aspect	84	39	30	30
Prepositions	136	28	32	47
Infinitive marker	49	11	15	16
Total grammatical tokens	**307**	**88**	**88**	**110**

Shatta Wale (Ghana) and Redsan (Kenya). Patrick Nnaemeka Okorie, aka Patoranking, is a Nigerian reggae-dancehall singer and songwriter. He started as a dancer in the streets and was primarily exposed to Bob Marley as a child. He has won several major African awards and has produced his music under VP Records, an independent label based in New York. In addition to Nigerian English and NP, he speaks Yoruba and Igbo. Charles Nii Armah Mensah Jr. is known as Shatta Wale. He is the most awarded dancehall artist in Africa and the second most awarded musician in Ghana. Shatta Wale was introduced to dancehall as a young man when cousins from London started bringing new releases from Jamaica with them. He has collaborated with Jamaican performers Mavado, Popcaan and Jah Vinci. He speaks English as well as GP, Ewe, Ga and Twi. Redsan, born as Swabri Mohammed in Nairobi, Kenya, is one of the most well-renowned ragga and dancehall artists in East Africa. He has won several East African music awards and has toured Europe and the United States several times. He speaks (Kenyan) English and Swahili.

Results

Figure 10.1 shows the percentage of JC realizations of six phonetic features in the Jamaican and African dancehall performances.

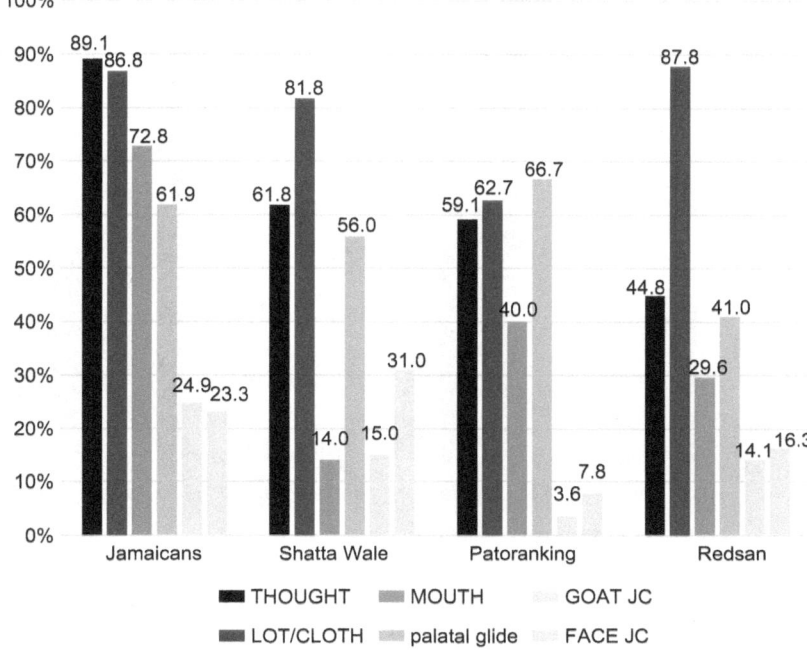

Figure 10.1 Comparison of JC phonetic variants between Jamaican and African dancehall artists.

Although all variants occur in every artist's performance, the Jamaican artists use higher rates of the JC variants of THOUGHT (41/46, 89.1 per cent), MOUTH (67/92, 72.8 per cent) and GOAT (58/233, 24.9 per cent) than the African dancehall performers. The JC variant of LOT/CLOTH is used very frequently by all artists, with Redsan (43/49, 87.8 per cent) even exceeding the Jamaican artists (158/182, 86.8 per cent). The insertion of a palatal glide occurs often similarly often in all artists' songs. The JC GOAT diphthong is used most often by the Jamaicans (58/233, 24.9 per cent), followed by Shatta Wale (17/113, 15.0 per cent) and Redsan (12/85, 14.1 per cent), while Patoranking uses it only in 3.6 per cent (4/110) of the cases. The JC variant of FACE is used more frequently in the African dancehall performances; Shatta Wale (22/71, 31.0 per cent) even uses it more often than the Jamaicans (23.3 per cent).

Figure 10.2 compares the percentages of JC variants of four grammatical features in the Jamaican and African dancehall songs. Again, all features occur in all artists' songs, with number marking being used more often by Shatta Wale and Redsan than by the Jamaicans. For Patoranking's use

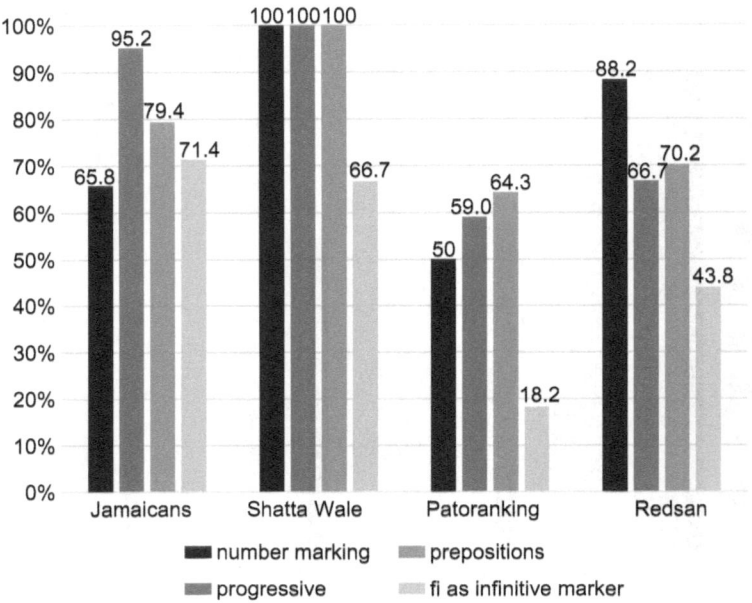

Figure 10.2 Comparison of JC grammatical variants between Jamaican and African dancehall artists.

of this feature, the situation is more complex: since plural marking via postposed elements does not only exist in JC but also in NP (see Faraclas 2013, 428), a qualitative analysis of Patoranking's use of this feature is inevitable to ascertain which linguistic resource he draws upon in the respective cases. As Patrick (2008, 435) notes, JC accepts the co-occurrence of the post-nominal affix -*dem* and plural -*s*. Patoranking uses this feature in three out of ten instances:

(1) the haters-dem want we to fall off
 the haters PL want 1-PL-OBJ-PRO INF. MARKER fall off
 the enviers want us to fall off (Patoranking, "Another Level")

(2) the haters-dem a loving [...] we
 the haters PL PROG loving 1-PL-OBJ-PRO
 the enviers love us (Patoranking, "Another Level")

(3) me haters-dem miss
 1-SG-POSS-PRO haters PL miss
 my enviers miss (Patoranking, "Writing on the Wall")

The co-occurrence of the postnominal affix -*dem* and -*s* exists in JC but neither in NP nor in GP; therefore, at least for these three cases it can be concluded that Patoranking draws on JC. Examples 4 and 5, however, display more problematic cases:

(4) some   boy [bwaɪ]-dem   say   money money   over   everything
    some   boy PL   say   RED   over   everything
    some boys say money over everything (Patoranking, "G.O.E.")

(5) some   boy [bwaɪ]-dem   say   a   me   the one   a   loot
    some   boy PL   say   COP   1-SG-SUBJ-PRO   the one   NON-COMPL   loot
    some boys say I'm the one to rob (Patoranking, "G.O.E.")

In examples 4 and 5, Patoranking uses the postnominal affix -*dem* for plural marking, which exists both in NP and JC. Therefore, this information alone does not suffice to determine whether he draws on NP or JC. However, Patoranking realizes *boy* as [bwaɪ] in both instances, which is typical of JC and does not occur in NP. It can thus be argued that the co-occurrence of this salient JC phonetic feature with plural marking in the same phrase indicates that Patoranking draws on JC.

(6) some   friend-dem   good   while   some   friend-dem   kala
    some   friend-PL   good   while   some   friend PL   kala
    some friends are good while some friends are dangerous (Patoranking, "Friends")

(7) some   friend-dem   good   while   some   friend-dem   bad
    some   friend-PL   good   while   some   friend PL   bad
    some friends are good while some friends are bad (Patoranking, "Friends")

(8) me   friend-dem   come   around
    1-SG-POSS-PRO   friend PL   come   around
    my friends come around (Patoranking, "Friends")

Examples 6 to 8 contain instances of plural marking via postposed -*dem* as well. In contrast to examples 4 and 5, here, it is impossible to determine whether Patoranking draws on JC or NP. The only feature hinting at NP can be found in example 6, in which he uses the slang word *kala*, which probably originated in Port Harcourt or Warri (both in South-South Nigeria) and means "gun" or "bullet" (F. Oyebola, personal communication, 24 April 2020).

The JC progressive aspect occurs in 100 per cent (30/30) of Shatta Wale's performances, followed by the Jamaican comparison group (80/84, 95.2 per cent). Redsan (20/30, 66.7 per cent) and Patoranking (23/39, 59.0 per cent) still use the JC variant in more than half of the cases. The use of Jamaican prepositions differs considerably among the artists: While Shatta Wale uses it in 100 per cent (32/32), Redsan (33/47, 70.2 per cent) and

Patoranking (18/28, 64.3 per cent) use lower rates than the Jamaicans (108/136, 79.4 per cent). The infinitive marker *fi* is the only feature that is used more often by the Jamaicans (35/49, 71.4 per cent) than by all African artists.

Additionally, the insertion of a bilabial glide is used by all three African dancehall artists and occurs in the word *boy*, for instance, "Some *boy* [bwaɪ] them say money money over everything" (Patoranking, "G.O.E.") and "Them want fi use some *boy* [bwaɪ] fi fight me now" (Shatta Wale, "Scam Dem"). Redsan inserts a bilabial glide in the word *balling*: "Work it out as I'm watching and *balling* [bwaːlɪn]" ("Badder than Most"). Besides, the use of syllable amalgamation across morpheme boundaries is used by Patoranking and Shatta Wale:

(9) so we *go on* [gwaːn] live we na go sorrow
so we're going to live, we're not going to sorrow (Patoranking, "Another Level")

(10) me hear enough argument a *go on* [gwaːn]
I hear that a lot of debate is going on (Shatta Wale, "Reality")

Table 10.3 lists further grammatical features in the artists' songs. It shows that the JC copula *a*, multiple negation and the preverbal negator *na* are used by all artists in several songs. Shatta Wale and Redsan further deploy the JC modal verb *haffi* (have to) and the second-person plural pronoun *unu*, which is used both as a subject pronoun (for example, *unu make me smile*) and as a possessive pronoun (*big up unu crew*).

Additionally, Shatta Wale uses distinct features of GP (see Huber 2008) in his song "Life Changer", that is, the copula *bì* (11) as well as the habitual marker *dè* (12) (Huber 2008, 397), for instance:

(11) I no bì magician
1-SG-S-PRO NEG COP magician
I'm not a magician (Shatta Wale, "Life Changer")

(12) I dè believe in myself
1-SG-S-PRO HAB believe in myself
I believe/have been believing in myself (Shatta Wale, "Life Changer")

In addition to the aforementioned features of JC and GP, the artists use additional grammatical features, such as copula absence, the absence of subject–verb concord, *no* as a preverbal negator, the complementizer *seh* and the relativizer *weh*. Since these features do not only exist in JC but can be found in NP and GP as well, it is impossible to determine which linguistic resources the performers draw on respectively. Therefore, they can only be

Table 10.3 Additional JC Grammatical Features in Songs by Patoranking, Shatta Wale and Redsan

Morphosyntactic Feature	Patoranking	Shatta Wale	Redsan
Copula *a*	This *a* no cheating zone ("Cheating Zone") Them *a* friend killer ("Friends") Girl *a* you me picture ("Killing Me")	Dancehall *a* me thing ("Dancehall King") Man *a* still holy ("Kill Them") This *a* reality ("Reality") Man *a* scammer ("Scam Dem")	You *a* wise girl ("Ma Babie") Them *a* high ("Shoulder Back") You *a* the hottest girl ("Touch Me There")
Preverbal negator *na*	We *na* borrow ("Another Level") Me *na* go anywhere ("G.O.E.") Girl you *na* go injure ("Killing Me") Me *na* know ("Writing on the Wall")	We *na* worry (Dancehall King) Me *na* want them come near me ("Kill Them") We *na* fear them face ("Reality") Jah know me *na* faking ("Scam Dem")	We *na* take off ("Badder than Most")
Multiple negation	This *ain't no* cheating zone ("Cheating Zone") Me *na* need *no* mixture ("Killing Me")	Me *no* take *no* nonsense ("My Ting") Tell them *not* to watch *no* nitweetity ("Reality") Me *na* take *no* fooliness ("Scam Dem")	Take *no* game from *no* one ("Ma Babie")
Modal *haffi*	—	You *haffi* listen when me talk ("Reality") Them seh me *haffi* go pon a training ("Scam Dem")	Dancehall *haffi* shine ("Live it Up") You *haffi* walk ("Ma Babie") Shoulder back everybody *haffi* do ("Shoulder Back") You alone *haffi* excite me ("Touch Me There")
Pronoun *unu*	—	*Unu* all funny ("Scam Dem")	*Unu* fine ("Badder than Most") Big up *unu* crew ("Shoulder Back") *Unu* make me smile ("Touch Me There")

referred to as non-standard grammatical features in more general terms. By using these non-standard forms, African dancehall artists reach a wide West African audience, who are familiar with many of these non-standard features. This is due to the fact that NP and GP serve as lingua francas in these multilingual settings in which many local languages are not mutually intelligible (Huber 2013).

Table 10.4 provides an overview of various Rastafarian lexemes as well as dancehall party vocabulary and their respective meanings used by the African dancehall artists. It can be seen that the artists mix lexemes originally associated with the Rastafari belief system with vocabulary typically occurring in a dancehall setting.

In addition to these typical Rastafarian and dancehall party lexemes, Patoranking's songs display some Yoruba lexical items, such as *Eledumare* and *Oluwa* (both meaning "god"; Patoranking, "G.O.E."), *fisi* (add to it), *Ofada* (a Nigerian dish) and *okada* (motorcycle taxi). Patoranking and Shatta Wale further associate their performances with their home countries by referring to place names, such as Port Harcourt in Nigeria (Patoranking, "G.O.E.") as well as Nima and Korle Gonno, which are cities in the Accra region (Shatta Wale, "Dancehall King"); important dates, such as Independence Day in Nigeria (the first of October; Patoranking, "Writing on the Wall"); and groups of people, such as the Akoko, a large Yoruba cultural subgroup (Patoranking, "Friends"). Shatta Wale localizes his performance even further by including names of prominent Ghanaians, for example, Jerry John Rawlings (former head of state and president of Ghana), Yvonne Nelson (Ghanaian actress, model, film producer), Sammy Forson (Ghanaian-Zambian media personality) and Azumah Nelson (Ghanaian former professional boxer).

Notions of Authenticity in Multilingual African Dancehall Performances

The results have demonstrated that the three African dancehall artists heavily cross into JC on a phonetic, morphosyntactic and lexical level. In contrast to previous studies on the use of JC in performances (see for instance Akande 2012a; Blommaert 2005; Sebba and Dray 2012; Westphal 2018), the African performers do not only use phonetic and morphosyntactic features of a truncated repertoire but include assorted features on different levels of linguistic variation. Some of these features, such as the insertion of a palatal glide, the JC variant of LOT/CLOTH, number marking and the use of typical Jamaican prepositions, are used at least as often as by the

Table 10.4 Rastafarian and Dancehall Party Lexemes in the Artists' Songs

Rastafarian Lexemes	Meaning	Artists and Songs
Jah	god (Pollard 2000, 79)	Patoranking, "Another Level" and "G.O.E." Shatta Wale, "Kill Them Wif Prayers", "Reality" and "Scam Dem"
Babylon	oppressive system (Pollard 2000)	Patoranking, "Friends"
Selassie	Ethiopian emperor, worshiped by Rastafarians as the reincarnated Messiah	Patoranking, "G.O.E." Shatta Wale, "Kill Them Wif Prayers"
irie	alright; good (Pollard 2000, 47)	Patoranking, "Another Level"
overstand	understand (Pollard 2000, 102)	Shatta Wale, "Reality"
chalice	marijuana pipe (Allsopp 2009, 146)	Patoranking, "G.O.E."
ganja	marijuana (Cassidy and Le 2002, 194)	Patoranking, "Friends" Shatta Wale, "Dancehall King"
Dancehall Party Vocabulary	Meaning	Artists and Songs
wine (originally Trinidadian English Creole)	to dance erotically (Allsopp 2009, 606)	Patoranking, "Another Level" Redsan, "Badder than Most", "Livet It Up" and "Touch Me There"
selector	person playing music (Stolzoff 2000, 54–56)	Redsan, "Shoulder Back"
big up (originally hip-hop)	expression of support (Richardson 2006, 29)	Shatta Wale, "Dancehall King", "Everybody Like My Ting" Redsan, "Shoulder Back"

Jamaican performers. The use of Jamaican lexemes is restricted to genre-specific items which refer to religion and the Rastafari movement (Dread Talk; Pollard 2000) and vocabulary belonging to a dancehall/party register.

In addition to the prevalent use of English and JC in their dancehall songs, Patoranking, Shatta Wale and Redsan incorporate (some of) their native languages to authenticate their performances on a local level, orientate their performances towards different referees and display "coexisting identities" (Jansen and Westphal 2017): First, the use of JC is associated with dancehall music, which originated in Jamaica, that is, it is genre-related. JC therefore does not only serve to refer to a Jamaican outgroup referee but, additionally, to address a global audience that is familiar with the use of Jamaican features in this music genre, expects it and deems it authentic. Second, the artists incorporate features of NP and GP, which serve as lingua francas in Nigeria and Ghana, respectively. In some cases, they overlap with JC due to similar substrate influences. By including these lingua francas, the artists can reach a supraregional audience. And third, the audience on a micro level is addressed through regional African languages like Yoruba and Swahili. The three African performers further localize their performances by referring to local place names, important dates in their country's history and nationally prominent people.

As professional musicians, African dancehall artists indigenize the dancehall genre and create new identities by putting multilingual performances on display. Authenticity is an important concept in linguistic performances because the audience's appraisal and their perception of a performance as "real" and authentic, or inauthentic, can have a tremendous impact on the artists' commercial success: "We value authenticity and we tend to be critical of pseudo-authenticity" (Coupland 2003, 417). As discussed earlier, the creation of authenticity in music performances which involve language crossing depends on various interdependent factors, such as the music genre, the audience and their "cultural schema" (Bell and Gibson 2011, 565), and an artist's background. As regards the music genre, the African dancehall performers' use of JC authenticates their performances: They neither "overshoot" (Bell and Gibson 2011, 568), that is, use higher rates of JC variants than the Jamaican comparison group throughout, nor do they ignore JC's association with Jamaican popular music. Dancehall artists who copy Jamaican dancehall artists are perceived as inauthentic and fake because they do not stay true to the classic assumption within variationist sociolinguistics that authenticity is related to the notion of "place" (Lacoste, Leimgruber and Breyer 2014; Sarpeah 2017). However, not including any features of JC would probably not be interpreted as authentic either due to factors such as genre appropriateness or audience expectation. What an audience expects to see and hear is inextricably linked to what they associate with a particular music genre; however, different audiences may characterize the linguistic behaviour of the three African dancehall performers as either authentic or inauthentic, depending on their own linguistic background and their language ideologies. For instance, individuals who prefer to keep it "linguistically pure" (Akande 2012b) and view authenticity vis-à-vis the geographical context in which languages developed would interpret the use of global linguistic resources alongside local ones, resulting in multilingual performances, as a threat to the status of local languages. Similarly, authentic language use in the context of performances may still be interpreted in terms of origin and ownership, as demonstrates the utterance by entertainment critic Akwasi Ernest who says that "Ghanaian dancehall artistes will be beaten to death in Jamaica if they speak Patois" (Asante 2016).

The African dancehall performers under study are aware that crossing into JC can authenticate their performances concerning the music genre and make it accessible to a global audience. For instance, Patoranking explains that by crossing into JC, the artists pay tribute to the Jamaican language: "It is not our language. We love how [Jamaicans] sound not because we are trying to be like them. It's just for the love of how they sound and that is why we do it" (Okumu 2016). This statement shows that Patoranking actively uses JC in his songs because of his love for the language. Another reason for using JC is expressed by Shatta Wale, who has been attacked publicly for singing in JC. He states in an interview that Ghanaian dancehall artists use JC as well as local languages to "make [their music] unique" and reach their community (Junia 2016). If artists were to sing in their local languages only, they would probably reach a rather small audience. Regional African languages may even benefit from co-occurring with globally available and prestigious varieties: People all over the world come into contact with Pidgin Englishes and other African languages *because* they are mixed with English and JC – languages which the audience already understands and expects in the performance of dancehall music. In turn, local languages may gain in prestige and receive more international attention.

The present study has shown that African dancehall artists glocalize the dancehall music genre by adjusting it to their individual needs. They authenticate their performances on various levels by using globally available features of English and JC as well as Pidgin Englishes (NP and GP English) and local languages, such as Yoruba and Swahili. This practice constructs heteroglossic (Bakhtin 1981) performances which are intelligible to audiences from different linguistic backgrounds and authentic in terms of originality and creativity. Comparable to non-US American hip-hop (Akande 2012a; Pennycook 2007), Réunionese dancehall (Bremner 2015) and Trinidadian ragga soca artists (Leung 2009), the three African singers cross into JC, a language which has acquired prestige in the context of dancehall music and has been detached from its associations with stigma and inferiority. JC is available to artists all over the world, who use it for different kinds of identity work, for instance to transfer its prestige onto their indigenous languages and authenticate their performances globally, supraregionally and locally.

Discography

Damian Marley. 2005. "Welcome To Jamrock". Track 1 on *Welcome to Jamrock*. Universal Records, MP3 file.
———. 2012. "Make It Bun Dem". Track 1 on *Make It Bun Dem*. Big Beat Records, MP3 file.
———. 2017. "Here We Go". Track 2 on *Stony Hill*. Republic Records, MP3 file.
Gaza Slim. 2012. "Always". Track 2 on *Girl Boss – The Realest Girl*. Adidjahiem Records, MP3 file.
———. 2012. "Everything Fi Hold Him". Track 3 on *Girl Boss – The Realest Girl*. Adidjahiem Records, MP3 file.
———. 2012. "Independent Ladies". Track 4 on *Girl Boss – The Realest Girl*. Adidjahiem Records, MP3 file.
Mavado. 2005. "Never Believe You". Track 1 on *Never Believe You*. DASECA Productions, MP3 file.
———. 2015. "My League". Track 1 on *My League*. We The Best Music Group, MP3 file.
———. 2018. "Caribbean Girls". Track 20 on *Reggae Mix Tape Vol.2* (mixed by DJ Wayne). Tad's Record Inc, MP3 file.
Patoranking. 2014. "Friends". Track 1 on *Friends*. Foston Musik, MP3 file.
———. 2016. "Another Level". Track 1 on *Another Level*. Foston Musik, MP3 file.
———. 2016. "Cheating Zone". Track 3 on *God Over Everything*. Universal Music, MP3 file.
———. 2016. "G.O.E". Track 2 on *God Over Everything*. Universal Music, MP3 file.
———. 2016. "Killing Me". Track 5 on *God Over Everything*. Universal Music, MP3 file.
———. 2016. "Writing On The Wall". Track 7 on *God Over Everything*. Universal Music, MP3 file.
Redsan. 2012. "Ma Babie". Track 14 on *Best of Kenyan Local Classics*. Dope Ent, MP3 file.
Redsan. 2018. "Badda Than Most". Track 2 on *The Baddest*. RCA Records Label, MP3 file.
Redsan. 2018. "Shoulder Back". Track 3 on *The Baddest*. RCA Records Label, MP3 file.
Redsan and Nyla. 2018. "Touch Me There". Track 15 on *The Baddest*. RCA Records Label, MP3 file.

Redsan and Shinde. 2009. "Unbreakable". MP3 file.
Redsan and Victoria Kimani. 2017. "Live It Up". Track 1 on *Live It Up*. Epic Nation, MP3 file.
Rihanna. 2016. "Work". Track 4 on *Anti*. Westbury Road Entertainment, MP3 file.
Sean Paul. 2002. "Get Busy". Track 5 on *Dutty Rock*. Atlantic Records, MP3 file.
———. 2002. "Like Glue". Track 4 on *Dutty Rock*. Atlantic Records, MP3 file.
———. 2005. "Temperature". Track 11 on *The Trinity*. Atlantic Records, MP3 file.
Shatta Wale. 2014. "Everybody Like My Ting". Track 33 on *Answers (The Hybrid)*. SM4LYF Records, MP3 file.
Shatta Wale. 2015. "Scam Dem". Track 10 on *Magical Year Mixtape*. SM4LYF Records, MP3 file.
———. 2016. "Kill Dem Wif Prayers". Track 18 on *After the Storm*. Shatta Movement Music Production, MP3 file.
———. 2016. "Reality". Track 10 on *After the Storm*. Shatta Movement Music Production, MP3 file.
———. 2017. "Dancehall King". Track 3 on *Answers (The Hybrid)*. SM4LYF Records, MP3 file.
———. 2017. "Life Changer". Track 1 on *Life Changer*. Shatta Movement Empire, MP3 file.
Vybz Kartel. 2011. "Summer Time". Track 8 on *The Gaza Don*. Adidjahiem Records, MP3 file.
———. 2011. "Yuh Love". Track 6 on *Kingston Story*. Mixpak Records, MP3 file.
———. 2016. "Fever". Track 7 on *King of The Dancehall*. Adidjahiem Records, MP3 file.

References

Akande, Akinmade T. 2012a. "The Appropriation of African American Vernacular English and Jamaican Patois by Nigerian Hip Hop Artists". *ZAA* 60 (3): 237–54.
———. 2012b. *Globalization and English in Africa: Evidence from Nigerian Hip-Hop*. New York: Nova Science.
Allsopp, Richard, ed. 2009. *Dictionary of Caribbean English Usage*. Kingston: University of the West Indies Press.
Appadurai, Arjun. 1996. *Modernity at Large: Cultural Dimensions of Globalisation*. Minneapolis: University of Minnesota Press.
Asante, Nana Afrane. 2016. "Ghanaian Dancehall Artistes Bashed over 'Fake' Patois". Accessed 3 March 2019. https://3news.com/ghanaian-dancehall-artistes-bashed-over-fake-patois/.
Bakhtin, Michail Michailowitsch. 1981. *The Dialogic Imagination: Four Essays*. Translated by Caryl Emerson and Michael Holmquist, edited by Michael Holmquist. Austin: University of Texas Press.
Beal, Joan C. 2009. "'You're not from New York City, You're from Rotherham': Dialect and Identity in British Indie Music". *Journal of English Linguistics* 37 (3): 223–40.

Bell, Allan. 1984. "Language Style as Audience Design". *Language in Society* 13 (2): 145–204.
Bell, Allan, and Andy Gibson. 2011. "Staging Language: An Introduction to the Sociolinguistics of Performance". *Journal of Sociolinguistics* 15 (5): 555–72.
Blommaert, Jan. 2005. *Discourse: A Critical Introduction*. Cambridge: Cambridge University Press.
———. 2010. *The Sociolinguistics of Globalization*. Cambridge: Cambridge University Press.
Bremner, Natalia. 2015. "Keepin' it Real? Engaging with Language Politics in Réunion through the Juxtaposition of English and Réunionese Kréol in Dancehall Music". *Journal of Romance Studies* 15 (1): 111–30.
Bucholtz, Mary. 1997. "Borrowed Blackness: African American Vernacular English and European American Youth Identities". PhD diss., University of California.
———. 2003. "Sociolinguistic Nostalgia and the Authentication of Identity". *Journal of Sociolinguistics* 7 (3): 398–416.
Cassidy, Frederic Gomes, and Robert Le Page, eds. 2002. *Dictionary of Jamaican English*. Cambridge: Cambridge University Press.
Cooper, Carolyn. 1989. "Slackness Hiding from Culture: Erotic Play in the Dancehall". *Jamaican Journal* 22 (4): 12–31.
———. 2004. *Sound Clash: Jamaican Dancehall Culture at Large*. New York: Palgrave Macmillan.
———. 2012. *Global Reggae*. Kingston: Canoe Press.
Coupland, Nikolas. 2001. "Stylisation, Authenticity and TV News Review". *Discourse Studies* 3 (4): 413–42.
———. 2003. "Sociolinguistic Authenticities". *Journal of Sociolinguistics* 7 (3): 417–31.
———. 2007. *Style: Language Variation and Identity*. Cambridge: Cambridge University Press.
———. 2011. "Voice, Place and Genre in Popular Song Performance". *Journal of Sociolinguistics* 15 (5): 573–602.
———. 2014. "Language, Society and Authenticity: Themes and Perspectives". In *Indexing Authenticity*, edited by Véronique Lacoste, Jakob Leimgruber, and Thiemo Breyer, 14–42. Berlin: De Gruyter.
Cutler, Cecelia. 2003. "Yorkville Crossing: White Teens, Hip Hop and African American English". In *The Language, Ethnicity and Race Reader*, edited by Roxy Harris, 314–27. London: Routledge.
Devonish, Hubert. 2007. *Language and Liberation: Creole Language Politics in the Caribbean*. 2nd ed. Kingston: Arawak Publications.
Devonish, Hubert, and Otelemate G. Harry. 2008. "Jamaican Creole and Jamaican English: Phonology". In *Varieties of English 2: The Americas and the Caribbean*, edited by Edgar W. Schneider, 256–89. Berlin: De Gruyter.
Eberhard, David M., Gary F. Simons, and Charles D. Fennig, eds. 2019. *Ethnologue: Languages of the World*. Twenty-second ed. Dallas: SIL International. http://www.ethnologue.com.

Faraclas, Nicholas. 2013. "Nigerian Pidgin English". In *The Mouton World Atlas of Variation in English*, edited by Bernd Kortmann and Kerstin Lunkenheimer, 417–32. Berlin: De Gruyter.

Farquharson, Joseph T. 2017. "Linguistic Ideologies and the Historical Development of Language Use Patterns in Jamaican Music". *Language & Communication* 52 (1): 7–18.

Gerfer, Anika. 2018. "Global Reggae and the Appropriation of Jamaican Creole". *World Englishes* 37 (4): 668–83.

Gerfer, Anika. Forthcoming. "Jamaican Creole in Global Reggae and Dancehall Performances: Language Use, Perceptions, Attitudes". Unpublished manuscript.

Gibson, Andy. 2010. "Production and Perception of Vowels in New Zealand Popular Music". MPhil thesis, Auckland University of Technology.

Gibson, Andy, and Allan Bell. 2012. "Popular Music Singing as Referee Design". In *Style-shifting in Public: New Perspectives on Stylistic Variation*, edited by Juan Manuel Hernández Campoy and Juan Antonio Cutillas-Espinosa, 139–65. Amsterdam: Benjamins.

Hewitt, Roger. 1986. *White Talk Black Talk*. Cambridge: Cambridge University Press.

Hinrichs, Lars. 2011. "The Sociolinguistics of Diaspora: Language in the Jamaican Canadian Community". *Texas Linguistics Forum* 54: 1–22.

———. 2014. "Diasporic Mixing of World Englishes: The Case of Jamaican Creole in Toronto". In *The Variability of Current World Englishes*, edited by Eugene Green and Charles F. Meyer, 169–94. Berlin: De Gruyter.

Huber, Magnus. 2008. "Ghanaian Pidgin English: Morphology and Syntax". In *Varieties of English 4: Africa, South and Southeast Asia*, edited by Rajend Mesthrie, 381–94. Berlin: De Gruyter.

———. 2013. "Ghanaian Pidgin English". In *The Mouton World Atlas of Variation in English*, edited by Bernd Kortmann and Kerstin Lunkenheimer, 394–409. Berlin: De Gruyter.

Jansen, Lisa, and Michael Westphal. 2017. "Rihanna Works Her Multivocal Pop Persona: A Morpho-syntactic and Accent Analysis of Rihanna's Singing Style". *English Today* 33 (2): 46–55.

Junia, Pep. 2016. "Shatta Wale Speaks to MTV Base UK". *ENewsGh*. Accessed 3 March 2019. https://enewsgh.com/2016/09/shatta-wale-speaks-mtv-base-uk.

Kerswill, Paul. 2014. "The Objectification of 'Jafaican': The Discoursal Embedding of Multicultural London English in the British Media". In *The Media and Sociolinguistic Change*, edited by Jannis Androutsopoulos, 428–55. Berlin: De Gruyter.

Lacoste, Véronique, Jakob Leimgruber, and Thiemo Breyer, eds. 2014. *Indexing Authenticity*. Berlin: De Gruyter.

Lee, Ed. 1982. "The Foremost Medium: The Voice". In *Pop Rock and Ethnic Music in School*, edited by Graham Vulliamy and Ed Lee, 102–26. Cambridge: Cambridge University Press.

Lee, Jamie Shinhee. 2010. "Glocalizing *Keepin' it Real*: South Korean Hip-Hop Playas". In *The Languages of Global Hip Hop*, edited by Marina Terkourafi, 139–62. London: Continuum.

———. "2011. Globalization of African American Vernacular English in Popular Culture". *English World-Wide* 32 (1): 1–23.

Leung, Glenda Alicia. 2009. "Negotiation of Trinidadian Identity in Ragga Soca Music". *World Englishes* 28 (4): 509–31.

Lopez, Qiuana, and Lars Hinrichs. 2017. "'C'mon, Get Happy': The Commodification of Linguistic Stereotypes in a Volkswagen Super Bowl Commercial". *Journal of English Linguistics* 45 (2): 130–56.

Mair, Christian. 2013. "The World System of Englishes: Accounting for the Transnational Importance of Mobile and Mediated Vernaculars". *English World-Wide* 34 (3): 253–78.

Manuel, Peter, Kenneth M. Bilby, and Michael D. Largey. 1995. *Caribbean Currents: Caribbean Music from Rumba to Reggae*. London: Latin American Bureau.

Mitchell, Tony, ed. 2001. *Global Noise: Rap and Hip Hop outside the USA*. Middletown: Wesleyan University Press.

———. 2003. "Doin' Damage in my Native Language: The Use of 'Resistance Vernaculars' in Hip Hop in France, Italy, and Aotearoa/New Zealand". In *Global Pop, Local Language*, edited by Harris M. Berger and Michael Thomas Carrol, 3–17. Jackson: University Press of Mississippi.

O'Hanlon, Renae. 2006. "Australian Hip Hop: A Sociolinguistic Investigation". *Australian Journal of Linguistics* 26 (2): 193–209.

Okumu, Phiona. 2016. "Dancehall's New Star Patoranking Talks Ghana, Changing Labels and Jamaica's Influence". *True Africa*. Accessed 4 March 2019. https://trueafrica.co/article/dancehalls-new-star-patoranking-talks-ghana-changing-labels-jamaicas-influence/.

Patrick, Peter L. 2008. "Jamaican Creole: Morphology and Syntax". In *Varieties of English 2: The Americas and the Caribbean*, edited by Edgar W. Schneider, 609–44. Berlin: De Gruyter.

Pennycook, Alastair. 2003. "Global Englishes, Rip Slyme, and Performativity". *Journal of Sociolinguistics* 7 (4): 513–33.

———. 2007. *Global Englishes and Transcultural Flows*. London: Routledge.

Pollard, Velma. 2000. *Dread Talk: The Language of Rastafari*. Kingston: Canoe Press.

Rampton, Ben. 1995. *Crossing: Language and Ethnicity among Adolescents*. London: Longman.

———. 2009. "Crossing, Ethnicity and Code-switching". In *The New Sociolinguistics Reader*, edited by Nikolas Coupland and Adam Jaworski, 287–98. London: Palgrave Macmillan.

Richardson, Elaine. 2006. *Hiphop Literacies*. London: Routledge.

Robertson, Robert. 1995. "Glocalization: Time–Space and Homogeneity-Heterogeneity". In *Global Modernities*, edited by Mike Featherstone, Scott Lash and Robert Robertson, 25–44. London: Sage.

Sarpeah, Adu. 2017. "The Fake Patois Used By Shatta Wale, Stonebwoy, Others Can't Be Labeled As Dancehall". *Ghbase.com*. Accessed 10 March 2019. https://www.ghbase.com/fake-patois-used-shatta-wale-stonebwoy-others-cant-labeled-dancehall-root-eye/.

Schneider, Edgar W. 2007. *Postcolonial English*. Cambridge: Cambridge University Press.

Sebba, Mark. 1993. *London Jamaican: Language Systems in Interaction*. London: Longman.

Sebba, Mark, and Susan Dray. 2012. "Making it Real: 'Jamaican,' 'Jafaican' and Authenticity in the Language of British Youth". *ZAA* 60 (3): 255–73.

Simpson, Paul. 1999. "Language, Culture and Identity: With (Another) Look at Accents in Pop and Rock Singing". *Multilingua* 18 (4): 343–67.

Stanley Niaah, Sonjah. 2004. "Kingston's Dancehall: A Story of Space and Celebration". *Space and Culture* 7 (1): 102–18.

Stolzoff, Norman C. 2000. *Wake the Town and Tell the People: Dancehall Culture in Jamaica*. Durham: Duke University Press.

Terkourafi, Marina, ed. 2010. *The Languages of Global Hip Hop*. London: Continuum.

Thomas, Deborah A. 2004. *Modern Blackness: Nationalism, Globalization, and the Politics of Culture in Jamaica*. Durham: Duke University Press.

Trudgill, Peter. 1983. *On Dialect: Social and Geographical Perspectives*. Oxford: Blackwell.

Westphal, Michael. 2015. "Linguistic Decolonization in Jamaican Radio". *ZAA* 63: 179–197.

———. 2018. "Pop Culture and the Globalization of Non-standard Varieties of English: Jamaican Creole in German Reggae Subculture". In *The Language of Pop Culture*, edited by Valentin Werner, 97–115. New York: Routledge.

Winer, Lise. 1990. "Intelligibility of Reggae Lyrics in North America: Dread ina Babylon". *English World-Wide* 11 (1): 33–58.

Chapter 11

Jamaican in Transatlantic Contact Spaces

Linguistic Practices in African Reggae, Dancehall and Other Popular Musics

ANDREA HOLLINGTON

Introduction

The high profile of Jamaican music has led to a worldwide phenomenon of Jamaican language practices being adopted in local music. Especially on the African continent, which is historically and ideologically linked to its African diaspora in the Americas, the Jamaican language enjoys great popularity in local music scenes, for instance, in Ethiopia (Hollington 2016) and Zimbabwe (Hollington 2018). Instead of zooming into a particular music scene, this chapter seeks to take a step back and look at the broader picture of the role of Jamaican in transatlantic language contact in music. With music examples from various anglophone African countries, including Kenya, Uganda, Zimbabwe, Ghana and Nigeria, this chapter will discuss trends in creative and conscious language contact in reggae, dancehall and African popular music (often also referred to as "Afrobeats"[1]) music. The analysis will include not only the incorporation of Jamaican linguistic practices (e.g. through borrowing or translanguaging), but also take into account historically shared experiences and ideologies that inform linguistic discourses and practices relevant in popular music. The discussion will also include common African Caribbean cultural-linguistic practices. The objective is to shed light on the complexities of language contact, shared histories and cultural connections in the transatlantic contact space, with a special focus on the role of Jamaican in music practices.

Transatlantic connections and cultural links between Africa and the Caribbean (or the Americas in a broader perspective) have been the focus of many academic studies (see for instance Gilroy 1993; Mahler 2018). Music and language as sociocultural practices have received much scholarly attention, resulting in diverse contributions to the understanding of contact, flows and influences in transatlantic spaces (see for instance Bilby 2004,

Farquharson 2012; Hollington 2016, 2018; Jaji 2014; Manuel and Fiol 2007; Mufwene 1993; Parkvall 2000; Stanley Niaah 2008). This chapter will tie in with previous studies on language in music practices by looking at transatlantic connections between Jamaica and various African music examples, in particular from anglophone countries. One aim is to illustrate the dispersion of Jamaican language practices in various art forms in Africa and discuss the reasons and motivations for this in the context of the high profile of Jamaican music in Africa and beyond. The objective of this chapter is therefore to present an overview of Jamaican in African popular music practices, but also to shed light on shared phenomena in Jamaican and African language practices in popular music beyond the dominant linguistic paradigm of unidirectional transfer, by looking at the Atlantic as a dynamic contact zone (cf. Gilroy's concept of the Black Atlantic, 1993).

In this regard, it is important to acknowledge another issue of transatlantic contact, namely that of shared phenomena which might not be traced to the unidirectional migration of a particular linguistic feature, but can rather be attributed to shared histories, language practices and cultural conceptualizations in the transatlantic contact space. Here, we will look at culturally influenced metaphors in the field of emotion.

The many different domains and cultural contexts, as well as diachronic and synchronic layers of language contact, testify to the complexities of the transatlantic contact zone. On the one hand, these complexities have been created by numerous breaks and disruptions throughout the histories of the Atlantic World (slave trade, trafficking, migration, slavery and other forms of unfree labour, conquests, colonialism, neocolonialism, etc.). On the other hand, people in many African societies share (these and other) historical and contemporary experiences with people in Jamaica (e.g. colonialism, oppression, life in the ghetto), which create common ground for shared as well as migrated and adopted linguistic practices: There are examples of parallel developments and contact-induced practices in language and music which are partly due to shared histories and experiences and also to the dynamics of multilateral contact in the Atlantic World.

Important keywords in these dynamics are *consciousness* and *agency*, which are aspects that have often been overlooked or dismissed in the study of language practices in the transatlantic contact zone, particularly so-called Creole languages (see Faraclas forthcoming; Hollington 2015). Music constitutes a space in which the exchange and combination of ideas and practices from different cultural, geographical or linguistic backgrounds can be studied, especially with regard to the conscious ways in which artists and musicians use linguistic and musical repertoires. For Jamaican music, scholars have produced a number of works that discuss the ways in which African music practices have influenced the developments of Jamaican music styles (see for instance Bilby 2004, 2016; Reckord 1998; Lewin 2000). While it is undeniable that African languages and music had a great impact on the making of Jamaican linguistic and musical practices through the involuntarily migrations of enslaved Africans to the island,[2] it is important to stress that Jamaican music culture has influenced practices on the African continent as well, especially in popular music. While the global popularity of reggae has affected African music scenes and developments since the 1970s, dancehall music is having a great impact in recent years. In a world characterized by phenomena of globalization, cross-cultural and transatlantic exchanges and collaborations are facilitated and so is the flow of information and communication through the internet. While the use of the Jamaican language in African popular music might seem to be a very small and specialized niche of language contact, the quantity of examples of translanguaging involving Jamaican in popular music in various (anglophone) African countries reveals the impact of these practices. The music is very popular, as is evident when looking at views and likes on platforms such as YouTube and Spotify, as well as when witnessing the great success of concerts and tours of the artists involved, and the airplay on radio and television. Research on African youth languages has shown that popular music also influences the ways in which youth and adolescents communicate (see, for instance, Nassenstein and Hollington 2016; Hollington and Nassenstein 2017).

This chapter will – in an attempt to present an overview of various phenomena of Jamaican–African language contact in music – look at a range of popular music examples from anglophone African countries, including Nigeria, Ghana, Ethiopia, Kenya, Uganda and Zimbabwe. In particular, I will examine language use in the lyrics of songs from African and Jamaican artists and illustrate how these artists engage in translanguaging (Garcia and Wei 2014) and other creative linguistic practices.[3] The following section will introduce and analyse the lyrics of song examples from different African countries with special regard to the use of Jamaican. A special form of Jamaican–African language contact in music is presented in collaborative tunes, songs sung together by African and Jamaican artists. This special form is increasing in popularity and will be addressed in the subsequent section. Then we will look at common linguistic practices, in particular metaphors, which are based on shared cultural and historical experiences. This involves the use of emotion metaphors in popular music on both sides of the Atlantic. The final section will summarize the findings and draw conclusions on the diversity of linguistic practices in this overview perspective on Jamaican–African language contact in music.

African Music Practices

Reggae and dancehall have been popular in many African societies (especially, but not exclusively, in anglophone countries), and musicians in various African countries have adopted Jamaican musical and linguistic styles. From internationally renowned reggae stars such as Alpha Blondy, Lucky Dube and Tiken Jah Fakoly, to globally popular dancehall artists such as Shatta Wale or Winky D, numerous artists have adopted elements of Jamaican music and language, as well as other cultural practices (e.g. clothing and hairstyle, food or herbs) in their music and (public) lifestyle. Apart from the Jamaican-originated music genres reggae and dancehall, this chapter will also look at diverse types of African popular music (often referred to as "Afrobeats" or "Afropop", see footnote 1) which emerged in the last decade often as pan-African and highly influential music styles with strongholds in Nigeria and Ghana, among other places, including the diaspora. By discussing music examples from reggae, dancehall and African popular music, I will focus on language practices in the song lyrics. I want to stress that while reggae and dancehall constitute distinct music genres, distinctions between the three music styles in African practices are not always easy, since there are overlaps and mutual influences. Reggae artists may cross over into dancehall and vice versa. The relationship between reggae and dancehall and the ways they merge have been discussed by several scholars, often viewing the emergence of these popular music genres as a continuum. Stanley Niaah (2010, 4), for instance, writes:

> Dancehall is largely understood as an incarnation of reggae from the 1980s to the present, or as part of the continuum of Jamaican popular music since the rhythm and blues of the late 1950s, music that has largely been consumed in dance halls. However, the difference in the dancehall era is the degree to which live dancehall styles influence what appears on vinyl, developing performing styles, a new generation of singers, bands with fresh playing styles, reliance on digital rhythms, explicit lyrics, new dance moves and sound clashes.

With regard to language practices in these music genres, Farquharson (2017) shows that – unlike mento music before, and dancehall and reggae music later – in the 1960s, rocksteady and early reggae were primarily sung in English (and not Jamaican), which the author attributes to the heavy influence of American rhythm and blues music on the development of these music genres. From the 1970s onwards, more Jamaican language practices entered the music and performances and became characteristic of dancehall – and not only in Jamaica. Through the international popularity of Jamaican music, the Jamaican language has come to be used by artists, sound systems and musicians all over the world.

African popular music publicly labelled as "Afrobeats" (see note 1 for a short discussion of the problematics of this term) emerged in Africa as well as in the diaspora and can be regarded as a versatile and heterogeneous style: "It [Afrobeats] simply means the new sound of Africa, which takes in diverse influences that take inspiration from its African roots and is combined with the sounds of rap, reggae/dancehall, and even R&B" (Khan 2017).[4] Given the complexity of these music genres and their interrelation, a detailed definition or differentiation between the genres will not be a part of this chapter.

In the remainder of this section, we will look at the lyrics of songs from various African countries and discuss the ways in which the respective artists include elements of the Jamaican language in their often multilingual music performances. This will include music from Kenya, Uganda, Zimbabwe, Ghana and Nigeria, and will thus attempt to provide a preliminary overview of Jamaican language practices in anglophone Africa. I have written elsewhere about this form of language contact in Ethiopia (Hollington 2016), and a fresh look at Ethiopia and its special ties to Jamaica is presented by Tomei (chapter 12, this volume). Moreover, Gerfer (chapter 10, this volume) also discusses Jamaican language practices in African dancehall.

It should be emphasized that looking at the lyrics in their written form, as presented here in this chapter, constitutes an act of isolating and "fixing" extracted forms of lyrics from often dynamic and fluid linguistic and musical practices.[5] The readers are thus encouraged to watch the YouTube videos themselves to get a more holistic view of the songs. Moreover, I want to point out that the various music scenes and the language practices therein are much more than the songs in their final recorded form. Communicative practices in the studio, on the stage, on social media, in rehearsal rooms and so on, involving producers, managers, sound engineers, musicians, backing vocalists, stage hands, and of course the fans and listeners need to receive much more attention in studies of the linguistics of popular music.

Song Example 1 – Kenya: Wyre, "Kingston Girl" (Excerpt)

Chorus	translation (only Kiswahili parts)
Kingston gyal won't you come take a walk with me	
Kingston gyal won't you come take a walk with me	
nikupeleke hadi Kenya come back home	Let me take you to Kenya
nikupeleke hadi Kenya come back home	Let me take you to Kenya
Verse 2	
me waan fi take you to a town called Nairobi	
take you round pon a *matatu* de whole day	minibus
take you to me family so dat you know me	
make we eat dat *nyama choma* de whole day	roasted meat
baby come ina me yaad	
let me show you how me waan treat you from de start	
memba dat [remember that]	
so let me take you to a country	
dat me call me yaad	
dung ina East Africa[6]	

In this song, which the Kenyan artist released with the renowned Jamaican record label Chimney Records, Wyre uses the Jamaican language alongside English and Kiswahili. While the Kiswahili elements are marked in italics in the lyrics of song example 1, the non-marked parts present a mix of Kenyan English and Jamaican. Wyre's translanguaging practices in this regard reflect his conscious choices from multilingual linguistic resources, which fulfil several functions: (1) The singer creates aesthetically appealing lyrics with a transnational flow by combining different linguistic resources and creating multilingual rhymes. (2) The marking of identity in this regard is a multilayered phenomenon which links the artist to the global reggae scene, as well as to Jamaica and Kenya. Various scholars have discussed the use of Jamaican by non-Jamaican reggae and dancehall artists as a marker of authenticity (see the discussion in Gerfer, chapter 10, this volume; as well as, for instance, Hollington 2018; Westphal 2018). Moreover, the artist's use of Kiswahili marks his Kenyan identity and places the song in a local context. On another level, the translanguaging practices in the lyrics highlight the multilingual dimension of the song, which also expresses multilevel identity constructions in both local and global spheres. Interestingly, the song also addresses the theme of repatriation (the returning of descendants of enslaved Africans to the African continent), which is quite popular in reggae songs through the influence of Rastafari. Here, the singer uses the African language, Kiswahili, to express the act of bringing his beloved to Kenya, accompanied by the repeated phrase "come back home".

The fact that many African reggae and dancehall artists employ translanguaging in their songs (as will become evident later in this chapter) testifies to the creative use of multilingualism that has been described for many African societies (see for instance Lüpke and Storch 2013; Harnischfeger, Leger and Storch 2014; Lüpke 2010). Growing up in essentially multilingual societies endows artists, and people in general, with sociolinguistic skills that enable smooth bricolaging with the diverse linguistic resources at their disposal.

The use of Jamaican linguistic practices, as stated earlier, marks authenticity and belonging to the global reggae/dancehall scene, but it also illustrates transatlantic language contact. The artist makes use of Jamaican language practices with regard to phonetic features, for example, the insertion of a palatal glide/semivowel after velar stops as in *gyal* (girl), the dissolving of consonant clusters through deletion accompanied by vowel lengthening as in *waan* (want), and the replacement of dental fricatives [θ/ð] with alveolar stops [t/d] as in *de* (the) and *dat* (that). On the morphosyntactic level, Wyre uses the object pronoun *me* in subject position (*me waan*, "I want") and as a possessive pronoun (*me family*, 'my family'; *me yaad*, 'my yard/home'), and he makes use of the infinitive marker *fi* and the locative prepositions *pon* and *ina*. He also uses the emblematic and common Jamaican forms *dung* 'down' and *memba* 'remember'. Moreover, the artist uses terms with distinct semantics in Jamaican like *yaad*, which means 'home', and refers to his homeland Kenya.

Song Example 2 – Uganda: Sheebah Karungi, "Nkwatako" (Excerpt)

Verse 1   translation (Luganda parts)
Come right now back ina mi yaad,
Settle the issue
baby *tetulwana*,   baby let us not fight

now let me talk to you,	
sit down.	
bambi tetuyomba.	please let us not quarrel
Gwe nyini bintu byenyina tondeka my so,	you are the owner of the things I have, don't leave me
be straight to I and I *tugende mu maaso,*	let us go forward
why yuh coup pon mi like dat?	
Nnga atalina na mugaso soh	As if I don't have any value
when mi open mi eyes	
what do you see in me eyes	
baby I'm so lazy	
I'm so lazy	
cause everyday you changing	
you better stop your ways	
Baby I'm so crazy I'm so crazy	
Chorus	
Nkwatako,	please touch me
kano kozze nyambako	now that you have accepted (me) – please help me
Kuluno nze nfiirako	this time please take care of me (lit. die for me)
kabibe bizibu nyumizako	whether it's about troubles,
please tell me about them	
Nkwatako,	please touch me
baby *nsuuttako,*	baby calm me down
Togenda nkuumako	don't go – wait for me
Leero tonvako	don't leave me today[7]

In her song "Nkwatako" (Touch Me), Queen Sheebah Karungi combines Luganda, the major Bantu language of Uganda, with English and Jamaican linguistic resources. While the chorus is basically in Luganda, the verses illustrate her creative translanguaging technique (see verse 1 in the excerpt – Luganda in italics, English and Jamaican unmarked). While we can observe the use of the same – globally prominent – linguistic elements as markers of authenticity, namely, the use of the first-person pronoun *mi* in subject position and as possessive pronoun (*when mi open mi eyes*), the locative *ina* and the term *yaad* (yard, usually with the meaning 'home'), the artist also incorporates Rasta Talk (also known as Dread Talk, Iyaric; see Birhan 1981; Pollard 1994; Schrenk 2015) into her song, as shown in the following, a line in which she combines English, Rasta Talk and Luganda.

(1)	be	straight	to	I	and	I	tu-gend-e	mu	maaso
be	straight	to	1SG	and	1SG	1PL-go-SUBJ	LOC	CL6.eye

be straight to me, let's go forward

The expression *I and I* (also spelled I-an-I) is usually employed by Rastafari to replace personal pronouns such as I, me, you and we, and expresses oneness, a concept of feeling community, as well as a connection to Rastafari views. McFarlane (1998, 107) states that *I and I* "is a means by which Rastas communicate their basic philosophy or concept of themselves, their community, and the world" and that "the I-an-I locution creates a linguistic device that provides a new sense of self-liberation for a people of the African diaspora".

The expression *I and I* is frequently used in reggae songs, which are often influenced by Rastafari due to the high number of Rastafari reggae artists. Since *reggae* music enjoys great popularity in Uganda, as well as in many other African countries, it is no surprise that expressions from Rasta Talk are understood and adapted by fans and local artists. By using Jamaican and Rasta Talk elements in her lyrics, Sheebah Karungi, like the other artists discussed here, links her music to global reggae and dancehall, expresses identity, creates a transnational linguistic style, and appeals to both local and global audiences.

Song Example 3 – Zimbabwe: Spiderman, "She Love Me" (Excerpt)

Verse 1
mi use Microsoft phone
fi a chat you know
she haffi tell mi seh
Spider you mi babyboy
we haffi buss up every ting
[...]
she haffi tell mi seh you bad to di bone
mi buss up di song, get ina di studio
mi buss up on di song
and di gyal dem waan fi come[8]

Spiderman is one of the youngest Zimdancehall artists in Zimbabwe. At the age of twelve he had already performed with renowned Jamaican dancehall artists Capleton, Agent Sasco, Mavado and Mr Vegas, the latter being the one who gave him his stage name Spiderman (Machakaire 2013). In his song "She Love Me", Spiderman not only incorporates Jamaican elements in his song, but attempts to sing more or less entirely in Jamaican. While I have only represented a short excerpt of the lyrics here, the entire song features Jamaican, or his adaption of the Jamaican language. The artist also has numerous songs which he sings in chiShona, his mother tongue and the major language of Zimdancehall, the Zimbabwean version of dancehall music, while inserting elements, phrases and snippets of Jamaican. This is a common translanguaging practice in Zimdancehall and beyond. Elsewhere (Hollington 2018), I have written about Zimdancehall music and multilingual language practices therein. The song chosen for this chapter highlights the role of Jamaican in Zimdancehall in another way. Apart from the creative translanguaging practices that bring African languages and Jamaican together (processes that are often also influenced by English, the dominant colonial language), some artists make more extensive use of Jamaican. For European (and American) artists, Jamaican language use has been discussed with regard to artists such as Gentleman (Germany) and Alborosie (Italy) (see Gerfer 2018). In the example presented here, a young Zimbabwean artist uses Jamaican language practices in his music (see also his song "I Need Some Time", which likewise features large amounts of Jamaican language rather than isolated elements). While Spiderman makes more extensive use of Jamaican than the other artists introduced earlier, the linguistic features of Jamaican that he uses are quite similar, which seems to support the assumption that there are stereotypical (in terms of their frequency in Jamaican language forms used by non-Jamaicans) linguistic elements of Jamaican that are commonly used to mark identity and authenticity (see Westphal 2018). This includes the aforementioned use of the pronoun *mi*, the infinitive marker *fi*, the progressive marker *a*, the complementizer *seh* and the auxiliary *haffi*, as well as phonetic features such as the replacement of dental fricatives [θ/ð] with alveolar stops [t/d] as in *di* ('the'). Moreover, this artist makes extensive use of the term *buss up* [bos op], which has become an en vogue expression in global/African dancehall music in the last years for something or someone great, hot or smashing. The term can therefore be regarded as one of the many emblematic features that mark Jamaican(ness) and thus authenticity, as well as belonging to the global reggae scene. However, in Jamaica, the expression belongs to the more obsolete forms of slang and is not so commonly used anymore.[9]

Song Example 4 – Ghana: Shatta Wale, "Dancehall King" (Excerpt)

Ina di whole Ghana,
Di gyal dem a link up Bandana,
Shatta Wale
Some call mi di godfada
Ina NBT wi a ride Hammer
Nima a mi yaad ah
Korle Gonnor godfada
Big up every youth aahh
Every ghetto youth aahhhh
Every ghetto gyal weh know seh mi a number one
Dancehall king
Ina di whole Ghana
Di gyal dem a link
Ina di whole Ghana
Shatta movement ting
Ina di whole Ghana
Money makers ting
Ina di whole Ghana[10]

When looking at songs from West Africa, in particular Ghana and Nigeria, the issue of language contact becomes more complicated, as the local creolized varieties based on English (Ghanaian Pidgin English and Nigerian Pidgin English, aka Naijá) share a number of features with Jamaican, so it is not always unequivocally clear from which variety a certain element in the song lyrics was taken. While phonetic features such as the replacement of interdental fricatives [θ/ð] with alveolar stops [t/d] are similar in Jamaican and Ghanaian Pidgin (e.g. *di*, 'the'; *dem*, 'them'), other features, such as the aforementioned *gyal* (girl), are more typical markers of Jamaican: I have not come across any attestations of an insertion of a palatal glide after velar stops in Ghanaian Pidgin English, despite the prominence of palatalization in Akan (see Boadi 1988). In fact, it seems that the palatalization rule of Akan is not applied to English loanwords, which might be an indicator against its development in Ghanaian Pidgin English (see the discussion in Adomako 2013).

The locative *ina*, the use of the first-person pronoun *mi* in subject position and as a possessive pronoun (its use in subject position is attested in Ghanaian Pidgin English; see Huber 2013), and the use of the third-person pronoun as plural marker (e.g. *di gyal dem*, 'the girls') might be less marked in this contact scenario (although Ghanaian Pidgin English uses other means to mark nominal plurals; see Huber 2013). The issue is complex because the scenario is characterized by creolized varieties based on English that have similar historic linguistic influences, as many of the enslaved Africans who were active in the formation of Jamaican were speakers of West African languages. So, specific features found in the lyrics of today's popular music might be found in varieties on both sides of the Atlantic, as in the following cases: the lyrics presented earlier feature the relative marker *weh* and the complementizer *seh*, two grammatical phenomena which are commonly used in Jamaican and which are also used in Ghanaian Pidgin English (Huber 2013).

Interestingly, the artist uses the Jamaican progressive marker *a* instead of the typical Ghanaian Pidgin English *dè* in the following example 2,[11] and the Jamaican copula *a* instead of Ghanaian *bi* in example 3.

(2) Di   gyal   dem   a   link up   Bandana[12]
    DET   girl   PL   PROG   link up   Bandana
    The girls are linking up Bandana

(3) Every   ghetto   gyal   weh   know   seh   mi   a   number   one
    every   ghetto   girl   REL   know   COMPL   ISG   COP   number   one
    Every ghetto girl that knows I am (the) number one

This, however, is an observation that only relates to the excerpt of lyrics presented here. In other instances, the grammatical markers of Ghanaian Pidgin English also feature in the lyrics of Ghanaian popular music (see Gerfer, chapter 10, this volume).

Later in the song, Shatta Wale makes use of the lexeme *pumpum*, which, although of suggested African origin in terms of etymology (see Farquharson 2012), is quite a popular Jamaican word with explicit semantics ('vagina'[13]) and is part of the core vocabulary of global dancehall discourse with respect to "slackness", that is, straightforward sexual lyrics:

(4) say   pumpum   mi   love   gyal   dem   a   mi   flavor
    say   vagina   ISG   love   girl   PL   COP   ISG   flavor
    Say I love vaginas, girls are my taste

The song example from Ghana shows the complexity and multilayeredness of transatlantic language contact: the lyrics feature a Jamaican lexeme which is a supposed African retention (*pumpum*) and which goes back to the historic language contact created through the transatlantic slave trade. Then there are linguistic features that are similar in the contact varieties on both sides of the Atlantic (Jamaican and Ghanaian Pidgin English), such as the relative marker *weh* and the complementizer *seh*, which might be due to the similarities of the (historic) language contact situations. Finally, the artist uses Jamaican linguistic elements which are perceived as typical markers of Jamaicanness and common features in the global reggae/dancehall repertoire. In that regard, the multilayeredness of the linguistic features also reflects the heteroglossic practices of the artist.

African–Jamaican Collaborations

While the previous section has illustrated how popular and widespread the use of Jamaican is in various African popular music scenes, this section is dedicated to a special form of language contact in music, namely, the collaboration of Jamaican and African artists and the production of songs that they sing together. While this form of African–Jamaican collaborative work in music has a long tradition (see, for instance, the album *From the Heart of the Congo*, produced by the well-known Lee Scratch Perry, featuring the Congolese musicians Seke Molenga and Kalo Kawongolo in 1991; or the song "Yela" by Senegalese Baaba Maal, featuring the Jamaican-descended British-based reggae artist Macka B, produced by Island Records in 1992), the number of collaborative songs has increased in this period of "global reggae", with the international popularity of dancehall music and the recent global popularity of African popular music. For instance, the British-based Jamaica-descended reggae artist Maxi Priest released the song "This Woman", together with the popular Nigerian Yemi Alade; Zimbabwe's most famous Zimdancehall artist Winky D released "My Woman", featuring the Jamaican "King of the Dancehall" Beenie Man; and the well-known Nigerian artist Mr Eazi featured the celebrated Jamaican Chronixx in his song "She Loves Me". The song "Nakupenda pia", by the aforementioned Kenyan artist Wyre alongside the Jamaican Alaine, in which both artists playfully make use of each other's language, has received much attention. A similar form of linguistic creativity featuring language contact can be observed in "Kamata", a song by the Kenyan artist Zikki, featuring Jamaican Tarrus Riley. While there are many other examples, this section will look a bit more closely at two songs, namely "Key to the City" by Tiwa Savage and Busy Signal, and "Fire Daughter" by Treesha, featuring Queen Ifrica.

Song Example 5 – Nigeria and Jamaica: Tiwa Savage featuring Busy Signal, "Key to the City" (Excerpt)

Chorus (Tiwa Savage)
who got de key to de city
who got de fine face pretty pretty
I got de man dem witty witty
oh oh oh oh oh oh
who got de key to de city
who got de fine face pretty pretty
I gat de man dem witty witty
oh oh oh oh oh eh
Hook (Tiwa Savage)
De way I wine my body boneless
All your friends dey must to confess
Imma give it to you, so no stress
Get your body right there's no rest
De way I wine my body boneless
All your friends dey must to confess
Imma give it to you, so no stress
Get your body right there's no rest
Verse 1 (Busy Signal)
(Riddim)
Bus'! Aye!
Gyal, wine up your body fi mi baby na, na, na
Oh na-na-na
You bubble it and get de keys to de city like la, la, la
Oh na-na-na
So mi seh, "whe you waan?", gyal and mi seh, "whe you waan?"
You bubble it and bruk it down, like you a break de law
De way you wine, you're representing Mama Africa
Caribbean, and den we link up ina Canada
Busy remix with Tiwa from Nigeria
We have de keys to the city, we no commoner
And if you love it, buss a blank, and go so, "Tra-la-la!"[14]

In this collaboration, the Nigerian artist Tiwa Savage, who usually sings in Nigerian Pidgin English and Yoruba, flavoured with various English elements, contributes a heteroglossic voice to the song. For instance, the song excerpt features not only Naija (or Nigerian Pidgin English), but also language forms that are typical of American English, and African American Vernacular English in particular, such as *imma* and the extensive use of *got*. It is not only her choice of lexemes and grammatical forms but also her pronunciation and phonetic choices that contribute to the polyphonous and transnational flair of the song, as the singer combines Nigerian and American phonetic features and prosody. The Jamaican dancehall artist Busy Signal adds Jamaican language practices to the song and adds another level to this linguistically multidimensional song. In his Jamaican section, Busy Signal uses some of the elements that were discussed earlier as being used by the various African artists, such as the use of the first-person pronoun *mi* in subject position and as possessive (here in combination with the possessive *fi*, 'for'), the palatal glide in *gyal*, the reduction of consonant clusters (*waan* for 'want'), and the replacement of dental fricatives with alveolar stops (*de* for 'the'), which is also typical for Naija, as can be seen in Tiwa Savage's parts. Moreover, the artist makes use of several typical Jamaican expressions that relate to dance styles or moves, such as *whine/ whine up your body, bubble* and *bruk it down*, which, although typical Jamaican dancehall markers, the artist also relates to Africa, as well in the line *de way you whine, you're representing Mama Africa*. This is followed by an emphasis of the Nigerian–Jamaican or rather African–Caribbean connection made in this song as he mentions the places in the next lines. The first verse closes with a call on the listeners to show their appreciation: *and if you love it buss a blank and go so "tra-la-la"*. The expression *buss a blank*, another emblematic idiom frequently used in Jamaican music, refers to the paying of respect/ showing of appraisal by imitating a gunshot (with the hand pointing the "gun finger" and the mouth making the gun sound).

Apart from the "main lyrics", a significant contribution to the linguistic encounter between the two artists is achieved by the backings and shouts that each artist contributes to the other one's part. For example, Busy Signal adds short expressions such as *turf, busy, brrrb, gyal* and *no stress* to Tiwa Savage's chorus and the recurring hook. While this is a common practice in collaborative dancehall songs, it also highlights the dialogic style of the song and adds to its multilingual and heteroglossic dimension. As is the case with the earlier Ghanaian song example, the language varieties in contact here share a number of features that distinguish them from (Standard) English: for instance, as the excerpt shows, the use of the third-person plural pronoun *dem* as a plural marker and, as mentioned, the replacement of [ð] by [d]. In fact, perceived and shared linguistic commonalities may add to the bond between Africa and its diaspora in Jamaica that music artists and others emphasize, which is built on shared or similar experiences with imperial oppression, colonialism, life in the ghetto, and a positive evaluation of African identity and black consciousness, among other themes. In a recent interview, Mr Eazi, another Nigerian artist who collaborated with the Jamaican artist Chronixx, emphasizes the shared roots of Jamaican and African music cultures:

> The roots of almost all popular music genres are in Africa, at least the basis, the rhythm. And there has always been a connection between Africa and the West Indies. When I grew up, the biggest songs in the clubs were Dancehall. Searching for inspiration we looked at the Caribbean. The ancestors of the people there, who create Dancehall, came from Africa after all. So it is only natural that the music styles influence each other.[15] (Milz 2019, 39)

Song Example 6 – Kenya, Germany, Jamaica: Treesha Featuring Queen Ifrica, "Fyah Daughter" (Excerpt)

Verse 1 (Treesha)
mi seh not because mi pretty
don't you think it can get ugly
I a kill dem softly
still da one ya a go hard
when mi step out
mi no waan no hypocrites around mi
mother of di earth
I bring balance and set de laws
protecting di children and di elders from creation
when necessary stepping on the frontline of the war
balance to mi king
togedda building up di nation
I too wear di rifle dem plenty ammunition
Am a lioness
be ever bless
ready fi go conquer anything weh come fi tes'
am a lioness
goddess ina flesh
di universal woman represent
Chorus (Treesha)
I a real fyah dawta yeah
I an I a hol' di order yeah
a real fyah dawta yeah

lioness a hol' di order
I a real fyah dawta yeah
lioness a hol' di order yeah
a real fyah dawta
I no long to slaughter
I a hol' di order[16]

In this song, the Kenyan singer Treesha, who is based in Germany, collaborates with Jamaican artist Queen Ifrica. Like Busy Signal in the song above, the Jamaican artist Queen Ifrica contributes a verse featuring Jamaican to the song and also represents a strong Rastafari influence, both through her persona and her lyrics, in which she refers to Empress Menen, the wife of Emperor Haile Selassie, who is often called upon by Rastafari to emphasize the balance (King Alpha and Queen Omega) and equality of man and woman.

Treesha, in this song as well as in her other releases, makes extensive use of Jamaican language elements and blends in well with Queen Ifrica's part. Her linguistic competence in Jamaican shows a deeper level of immersion as she uses most of the linguistic features of Jamaican already discussed in this chapter, including phonetic and morphosyntax features. Apart from those Jamaican elements, the artist also makes use of language forms that are typical of Rasta Talk (Schrenk 2015; Pollard 1994) and that are commonly used by Rastafari artists in their music.[17] Language forms like *I an I* (discussed in the previous section with regard to the Ugandan music example) are strong markers of Rastafari philosophy and concepts of communality, an aspect which underlines the message of the song which speaks about female empowerment and solidarity. Female perspectives and voices are also invoked by the use of feminine versions such as *lioness* and *dawta* ('daughter'). The use of these terms and the message of the song as a whole also reflect the (semantic) context of the entire riddim production, as the riddim is called Lioness Order and the compilation features only female artists. Moreover, and unlike in the other song examples, Treesha uses the pronoun *I* rather than *mi*, a choice which might be influenced by the significance of *I* [ai] in the Rastafari concept of word, sound and power. Metaphors and images like *fyah dawta* ('fire daughter') and *lioness* highlight the connection to Rastafari and the expression of a global Rastafari identity even more: the (biblical) fire is an important and oft-used image, a metaphorical means of fighting against oppression, to "burn" down Babylon, and also to express power and strength, as in the expression *more fyah*. The image of the lion (and the lioness) is a common theme in Rastafari creations from song lyrics to T-shirt prints, and Rastafari are often referred to as "lion", the latter representing strength and royalty.[18] Moreover, this song and Treesha's languages use also confirm that Rasta Talk is more commonly used in reggae than in dancehall.

Shared Cultural Conceptualizations in Music

In this section, I want to shed light on a phenomenon related to the language contact scenario under discussion, namely, cultural conceptualizations in language. These can result in shared practices in popular music on both sides of the Atlantic. It has already been mentioned that many of the historical contact phenomena are due to the involuntary migration of enslaved Africans to the Americas. Various scholars have described how lexemes and grammatical features, as well as semantic structures of Jamaican, historically derive from African languages (see, for instance, Alleyne 1988; Bilby 1983; DeCamp 1967; Farquharson 2012; Hall-Alleyne 1984, 1990, 1996; Kouwenberg 2008, 2009; Kouwenberg and LaCharité 2004; Hollington 2015, 2017; Mittelsdorf 1978; Warner-Lewis 1996, 2003). The term "cultural conceptualization" refers to culturally influenced cognitive processes that our mind undertakes in order to structure and make sense of our experiences in the world (Kövecses 2006). As shared cultural knowledge, conceptualizations spread across a group of people and result in strong manifestations in languages (Sharifian 2011). This includes phenomena such as metaphors, metonymies, categories, schemas and cultural models.

One area in which cultural conceptualizations, and metaphors in particular, can be studied, is that of emotion as embodied experience. In many languages, parts of the (human) body feature prominently in linguistic expressions of emotions; however, their underlying conceptualizations may differ. In a previous study (Hollington 2017), I have discussed how certain Jamaican metaphorical expressions such as *red yai* (< English "red" + "eye", referring to envy and jealousy) and *bad main* (< English "bad" + "mind", referring to envy, malevolence or begrudging) are based on (West) African cultural conceptualizations with corresponding expressions in West African languages.[19] Languages of the Akan and Gbe cluster, plus other languages spoken in present-day Ghana and Ivory Coast and beyond, illustrate that the concepts of *red eye* and *bad mind* are rooted in local cultural scripts of the respective emotions (see Hollington 2017). While the existence of expressions based on these conceptualizations in Jamaica goes back to the language contact brought about by the transatlantic trade in enslaved

Africans, the use of these metaphors on both sides of the Atlantic in popular music testifies to the significance of these cultural concepts in the Atlantic space. The expression *bad mind* is frequently used in Jamaican and West African popular music, in particular in dancehall. For instance, Femi Kuti, son of the legendary Nigerian artist Fela Kuti, uses the expression in his song "Oyimbo" (see line seven in song example 7).

Song Example 7 – Nigeria: Femi Kuti, "Oyimbo"

I beg leave me
My life I dey think
No disturb me
With nonsense gist
The fine things of life
These people don't see
Their bad mind
No gree make them get better dream
So with their crooked legs
Them waka go redeem
But salvation comes from within
Seek and ye shall find
Definitively with music
Whose rich
harmonies and melodies
Will truly bring peace
All in the name of peace
We fight and kill to find justice
For me na only music
From the voice of the soul we speak
Wetin concern me with English my brothers
Na them kuku bring them selfish my sisters
They bank Africa money like the Swiss
Oyimbo don kill Africa finish[20]

Moreover, the aforementioned Ghanaian artist Shatta Wale has a song called "Dutty Badmind". While the word *dutty* [dʌtɪ] seems to be a Jamaican loan, the word *badmind*, as argued earlier, has a history in both regions and is a commonly used expression in the dancehall and beyond. Interestingly, the word *dutty* testifies to the multilayered contact history as well. While it is easily regarded as an English loan (< "dirty"), when used as an adjective, the term can also mean "soil, ground", as in the following proverb popularly known through Bob Marley's song "Dem Belly Full":

(5) *De rain a fall but de doti tuff*
It is raining but the ground is (still) tough (hard)

With this meaning, the Jamaican term is considered to be of African origin, and in particular from Akan. Farquharson explains:

> dóti, dórti '(a) earth, soil; the ground; (b) excrement, dung' (2) Àkán (Akyem) dɔ̀té 'soil, earth, clay, mud' [. . .]. (3) It appears that *dirt(y)* was copied into quite a few African languages either from English directly, or via a contact variety. However, most of these mean dirt, rubbish or filthy which sets them off from Jamaican *dóti* which means 'ground, earth'. [. . .]
>
> The DJE [Dictionary of Jamaican English] derives the word from the Àkán etymon accepted here but claims influence from English dirt, dirty. In the case of Àkán we are either dealing with a case of accidental resemblance with the English adjective [. . .] or an English loan into Àkán. Evidence against the second option comes from prosody since we know that bisyllabic English words are regularly borrowed into Àkán with a High-Low tone melody [. . .]. The Low-High tone pattern of the Àkán word makes an English derivation less plausible. (4) Àkán (GOC). (Farquharson 2012, 260)

In Jamaica, the term *badmind* is used abundantly in dancehall music. The following list illustrates a few examples of songs where the expression features in the song title (adapted from Hollington 2017):[21]

Artist	Song
Vybz Kartel	"Too badmind"
Mavado	"Badmind a go kill dem slowly"
I-Octane ft. Bounty Killer	"Badmind dem a pree"
Beenie Man	"Badmind people"
Elephant man	"Bun bad mind"
Alkaline	"Dutty badmind"
Popcaan	"Badmind a kill dem"
Aidonia ft. Jah Vinci	"Badmind cyah stop we"
Chan Dizzy	"Hello badmind"

The frequent and emblematic use of the expression *badmind* in dancehall music may have led to an increase in its use in West African music. The examples seem to show that the parallel history of the term and its underlying conceptualization (which led to mutual intelligibility of the figurative and embodied semantics of the expression) have enabled and multiplied its use as a trending expression in the lyrics of dancehall and other forms of popular music on both sides of the Atlantic. In this regard, shared (linguistic/semantic) histories and life experiences can increase contemporary transnational entanglements and linguistic flows.

Conclusion

This chapter has presented an overview of transatlantic linguistic entanglements and contact in African popular music. Special attention has been paid to the role of the Jamaican language in this contact space and the ways in which African artists in different regions adopt and adapt Jamaican language practices. The discussion has also included the shared histories and historical language contact that have connected Africa and Jamaica for centuries. The historical background and contemporary practices testify to the dynamicity of the Atlantic contact zone. Moreover, the abundance of Jamaican language practices in music all over (anglophone) Africa exemplifies the importance of music as a space of language contact. In this regard, globalization and digital communication have facilitated language contact in music through easy ways of sharing new productions and releases and collaborating across the Atlantic. Since the transatlantic contact space in music comprises much more than the song lyrics looked at in this chapter, further research perspectives include investigating language contact in a broader picture: How do artists express themselves and interact with fans on stage and in their social media profiles? Which language practices are used in the studio, especially in collaborative situations?[22] How do artists and fans learn Jamaican?[23] What are the perceptions of Jamaican language use in African popular music?[24] Thus, popular music as a space of transatlantic language contact still requires more research to arrive at a broader and more nuanced picture of language contact in various communicative situations.

Acknowledgements

I am grateful to the Global South Studies Center, University of Cologne, for supporting my research. I would like to thank Dennis Akena and Innocent Mwaka for their help with transcription and translation of the Luganda parts of the Ugandan song example. Moreover, I am indebted to Mary Chambers for proofreading and copyediting the manuscript. I also thank the two reviewers for commenting on the draft of this chapter.

Abbreviations

CL	class (noun class)
COMPL	complementizer
COP	copula
DET	determiner
LOC	locative
PL	plural
PROG	progressive
REL	relative
SG	singular
SUBJ	subjunctive

Notes

1. While the name "Afrobeats" has become quite popular, there are also critical voices regarding its use. In an article on okayafrica, for example, Korede Akinsede (2019) writes: "To name something is to claim ownership. And with the Western music industry's long tradition of appropriation, ownership of Africa's latest export is something Africans on the continent cannot risk losing. Currently, 'Afrobeats' is used as a catch-all term for all popular music emerging from the African continent." And later the author suggests: "The ever-present 'afro-' prefix still follows the tradition of portraying Africa in monolithic terms. A much simpler and respectful solution, is to refer to what is currently known as 'Afrobeats' as pop music from a specific country (i.e. Ghanaian Pop Music) and to other established musical styles by their local names – 'highlife,' 'fuji,' 'gqom,' 'bongo flava' and so forth, equipping new listeners with the right vocabulary to experience the varying cultures." To mark the problematic nature of the term, it is used in quotation marks in this chapter.

2. To be more precise, not only has the involuntarily migration of enslaved Africans played a role in this scenario, but also other forms of migration, in particular Africans coming to Jamaica as indentured laborers in the aftermath of the abolition of slavery in the nineteenth century (see Schuler 1980).

3. The analysis will rely on versions of the songs posted on YouTube. Links will be provided in further footnotes.

4. https://www.huffpost.com/entry/an-conversation-with-the-queen-of-afrobeats-tiwa-savage_b_59c3ff70e4b0ffc2dedb5bdb (accessed April 2019).

5. Furthermore, it needs to be pointed out that the spelling in this chapter is rather inconsistent as it follows local conventions (such as spellings used by artists and fans on social media and other platforms) rather than phonemic representation.

6. See and listen to the full song at https://www.youtube.com/watch?v=mVyztZXPFCQ (accessed April 2019).

7. See and listen to the full song at https://www.youtube.com/watch?v=FBl2bEerZlw (accessed April 2019).

8. See and listen to the full song at https://www.youtube.com/watch?v=4P05_pQ5-5c (accessed April 2019).

9. It might be interesting to further investigate if dancehall artists across Africa more commonly use Jamaican speech forms that are already outdated or not so popular anymore in Jamaica.

10. See and listen to the full song at https://www.youtube.com/watch?v=CYiCIyhqo1o (accessed April 2019).

11. A similarity here might be that both progressive markers, the Jamaican *a* and the Ghanaian *dè*, are derived from locative copulas. It should be noted that habitual reading of the copula in example 2 might be possible as well.

12. "Bandana" is the former stage name of Shatta Wale.

13. Farquharson (2012) discusses the possible adaption of this term and shows that the meaning "vagina" has developed as a euphemism and was not part of the lexical semantics of the suggested Akan etymon.

14. Listen to the song and watch the video at https://www.youtube.com/watch?v=LfnTZLage8g (accessed May 2021).

15. My translation from the original German publication of the interview.

16. Listen to the song at https://www.youtube.com/watch?v=5QIyeEP6Cto (accessed May 2021).

17. It might be relevant that the entire production, the riddim collection Lioness Order produced by Oneness Records, is themed in a conscious and Rastafari-influenced manner, focusing on the figure of the lioness, who stands for a strong and conscious women. Conscious, in this context, refers to positive, good-minded, natural practices or persons, or simply refers to consciousness of living arrangements.

18. On the one hand, the lion is regarded as the king of the animals; on the other hand, pictures of His Majesty Haile Selassie, the Ethiopian emperor central in Rastafari beliefs and philosophy, with his lions that he kept, are well known among Rastafari.

19. While I am only considering the two expressions *bad main* and *red yai* here, I want to emphasize that there are numerous other shared cultural conceptualizations in Jamaican and West African languages (see Hollington 2015).

20. Listen to the song at https://www.youtube.com/watch?v=NraW1OOGRB8 (accessed May 2021).

21. This list is by no means complete and only lists examples where the term *badmind* features in the song title.

22. For instance, Chill Spot Records, a Zimdancehall recording label and studio in Harare, Zimbabwe, has recorded several Jamaican artists, such as Turbulence, I-Octane and Romain Virgo, who had come to Zimbabwe to perform at concerts.

23. As some young artists and fans have told me in Zimbabwe, music and the internet (forums, Facebook groups, etc.) play an important role in this regard.

24. As Gerfer (chapter 10, this volume) points out, the perceptions are not always positive, as in the case of Shatta Wale (Ghana).

References

Adomako, Kwasi. 2013. "Underapplication in Akan Loanword Adaptation". *International Journal of Linguistics* 5 (5): 174–96.

Akinsete, Korede. 2019. "Call Us by Our Name: Stop Using 'Afrobeats'". Okayafrica, 4. February 2019. Accessed May 2020. Online available here: https://www.okayafrica.com/afrobeats-genre-name-stop-op-ed/.

Alleyne, Mervyn C. 1988. *Roots of Jamaican Culture*. London: Pluto Press.

Bilby, Kenneth. 2004. "Performing African Nations in Jamaica". *Contours* 2 (2): 184–92.

———. 2016. *Words of Our Mouth, Meditation of Our Heart: Pioneering Musicians of Ska, Rocksteady, Reggae and Dancehall*. Middletown: Wesleyan University Press.

Bilby, Kenneth M. 1983. "How the 'Older Heads' Talk: A Jamaican Maroon Spirit Possession Language and Its Relationship to the Creoles of Suriname and Sierra Leone". *Nieuwe West-Indische Gids* 57 (1–2): 37–88.

Birhan, Iyawta Farika. 1981. *Iyaric: A Brief Journey into Rastafari Word Sound*. San Jose: Queen Omega News Communications Unlimited Company.

Boadi, Lawrence A. 1988. "Problems of Palatalisation in Akan". *Journal of West African Languages* XVIII (1): 3–16.

DeCamp, David. 1967. "African Day-Names in Jamaica". *Language* 43 (1): 139–49.

Faraclas, Nicholas. Forthcoming. "Politics and Identities". In *The Routledge Handbook of Creole Languages*, edited by Umberto Ansaldo and Miriam Meyerhoff. London and New York: Routledge.

Farquharson, Joseph T. 2012. *The African Lexis in Jamaican: Its Linguistic and Sociohistorical Significance*. PhD thesis, University of the West Indies, Mona, Jamaica. Accessed March 2019. Available at: http://works.bepress.com/joseph_farquharson/1/

———. 2017. "Linguistic Ideologies and the Historical Development of Language Use Patterns in Jamaican Music". *Language & Communication* 52: 7–18.

García, Ofelia & Li Wei. 2014. Translanguaging: Language, Bilingualism and Education. Hampshire/New York: Palgrave Macmillan.

Gerfer, Anika. 2018. "Global Reggae and the Appropriation of Jamaican Creole". *World Englishes* 37 (4): 668–83.

Gilroy, Paul. 1993. *The Black Atlantic: Modernity and Double Consciousness*. Cambridge, MA: Harvard University Press.

Hall-Alleyne, Beverly. 1984. "The Evolution of African Languages in Jamaica". *ACIJ Research Review* 1: 21–46.

———. 1990. "The Social Context of African Language Continuities in Jamaica". *International Journal of the Sociology of Language* 85: 31–40.

———. 1996. "An Ethnolinguistic Approach to Jamaican Botany". In *African Continuities in the Linguistic Heritage of Jamaica* [ACIJ Research Review 3], edited by Maureen Warner-Lewis, 1–40. Kingston: African-Caribbean Institute of Jamaica.

Harnischfeger, Johannes, Rudolf Leger, and Anne Storch, eds. 2014. *Fading Delimitations. Multilingual Settlements in a Convergence Area*. Köln: Köppe.

Hollington, Andrea. 2015. *Traveling Conceptualizations: A Cognitive and Anthropological Linguistic Study of Jamaican*. Amsterdam: Benjamins.

———. 2016. "Movement of Jah People: Language Ideologies and Music in a Transnational Contact Scenario". *Critical Multilingualism Studies* 4 (2): 133–53.

———. 2017. "Emotions in Jamaican: African Conceptualizations, Emblematicity and Multimodality in Discourse and Public Spaces". In *Consensus and Dissent. Negotiating Emotion in the Public Space*, edited by Anne Storch, 81–104. Amsterdam: Benjamins.

———. 2018. "Transatlantic Translanguaging in Zimdancehall: Reassessing Linguistic Creativity in Youth Language Practices". *The Mouth* 3 (special issue: Critical Youth Languages Studies – Rethinking Concepts): 105–23.

Hollington, Andrea, and Nico Nassenstein. 2017. "From the Hood to Public Discourse: The Social Spread of African Youth Languages". *Anthropological Linguistics* 59 (4): 390–413.

Jaji, Tsitsi Ella. 2014. *Africa in Stereo: Modernism, Music, and Pan-African Solidarity*. Oxford: Oxford University Press.

Khan, Ahmad. 2017. "A Conversation with the Queen of Afrobeats: Tiwa Savage". Huffpost Sept 21, 2017. Online available at: https://www.huffpost.com/entry/an-conversation-with-the-queen-of-afrobeats-tiwa-savage_b_59c3ff70e4b0ffc2dedb5bdb.

Kouwenberg, Silvia. 2008. "The Problem of Multiple Substrates: The Case of Jamaican Creole". In *Roots of Creole Structures: Weighing the Contribution of Substrates and Superstrates*, edited by Susanne Michaelis, 1–27. Amsterdam: John Benjamins.

———. 2009. "Africans in Early English Jamaica (1655–1700): The Akan-dominance Myth". In *Freedom: Retrospective and Prospective*, edited by Swithin R. Wilmot, 32–44. Kingston: Ian Randle.

Kouwenberg, Silvia, and LaCharité, Darlene. 2004. "Echoes of Africa: Reduplication in Caribbean Creole and Niger-Congo Languages". *Journal of Pidgin and Creole Languages* 19 (2): 285–331.

Kövecses, Zoltán. 2006. *Language, Mind and Culture*. Oxford: Oxford University Press.

Lewin, Olive. 2000. *Rock It Come Over: The Folk Music of Jamaica*. Kingston: University of the West Indies Press.

Lüpke, Friederike. 2010. "Multilingualism and Language Contact in West Africa: Towards a Holistic Perspective". *Journal of Language Contact*, THEMA 3 (1): 1–12.

Lüpke, Friederike, and Anne Storch. 2013. *Repertoires and Choices in African Languages*. Berlin: Mouton De Gruyter.

Machakaire, Tarisai. 2013. "Zim's Youngest Dancehall Artiste". *Daily News*, issue 13. January 2013. Accessed April 2019. Available at: https://www.dailynews.co.zw/articles/2013/01/13/zim-s-youngest-dancehall-artiste.

Magnus Huber. 2013. "Ghanaian Pidgin English". In *The Survey of Pidgin and Creole Languages* (Volume 1: English-based and Dutch-based Languages), edited by Susanne Michaelis, Philippe Maurer, Martin Haspelmath, and Magnus Huber. Oxford: Oxford University Press. Accessed April 2019. Available online in the Atlas of Pidgin and Creole Language Structures Online: https://apics-online.info/surveys/16#.

Mahler, Anne Garland. 2018. *From the Tricontinental to the Global South. Race, Radicalism, and Transnational Solidarity*. Durham and London: Duke University Press.

Manuel, Peter, and Orlando Fiol. 2007. "Mode, Melody, and Harmony in Traditional Afro-Cuban Music: From Africa to Cuba". *Black Music Research Journal* 27 (1): 45–80.

Milz, Georg. 2019. "Strictly Business. Interview with Mr Eazi". *Riddim Magazine* 2/2019: 58–61.

Mittelsdorf, Sibylle. 1978. *African Retentions in Jamaican Creole: A Reassessment*. PhD diss., Northwestern University, Illinois.

Mufwene, Salikoko, ed. 1993. *Africanisms in Afro-American Language Varieties*. Athens: University of Georgia Press.

Nassenstein, Nico, and Andrea Hollington. 2016. "Global Repertoires and Urban Fluidity: Youth Languages in Africa". *International Journal of the Sociology of Language* 242: 171–93.

Parkvall, Mikael. 2000. *Out of Africa: African Influences in Atlantic Creoles*. London: Battlebridge.

Pollard, Velma. 1994. *Dread Talk: The Language of Rastafari*. Kingston: Canoe Press.

Reckord, Verena. 1998. "From Burru Drums to Reggae Ridims: The Evolution of Rasta Music". In *Chanting Down Babylon: The Rastafari Reader*, edited by Nathaniel Samuel Murell, William David Spencer, and Adrian Anthony McFarlane, 231–52. Philadelphia: Temple University Press.

Schrenk, Havenol M. 2015. "The Positive-Negative Phenomenon and Phono-Semantic Matching in Rasta Talk". In *Youth Language Practices in Africa and Beyond*, edited by Nico Nassenstein and Andrea Hollington, 271–91. Berlin: Mouton de Gruyter.

Schuler, Monica. 1980. *Alas, Alas Kongo: A Social History of Indentured African Immigration Into Jamaica, 1841–1865*. Baltimore: John Hopkins University Press.

Sharifian, Farzad. 2011. *Cultural Conceptualisations and Language: Theoretical Framework and Applications*. Amsterdam: Benjamins.

Stanley Niaah, Sonjah. 2008. "A Common Space: Dancehall, Kwaito and the Mapping of New World Music and Performance". *The World of Music* 50 (2): 35–50.

Warner-Lewis, Maureen, ed. 1996. *African Continuities in the Linguistic Heritage of Jamaica* [ACIJ Research Review 3]. Kingston: African-Caribbean Institute of Jamaica.

———. 2003. *Central Africa in the Caribbean: Transcending Time, Transforming Culture*. Kingston: University of the West Indies Press.

Westphal, Michael. 2018. "Pop Culture and the Globalization of Non-standard Varieties of English: Jamaican Creole in German Reggae Subculture". In *The Language of Pop Culture*, edited by Valentin Werner, 97–115. New York: Routledge.

Chapter 12

Jamaric Reggae

Jamaican Speech Forms in Contemporary Ethiopian Reggae Music

RENATO TOMEI

Introduction

In Ethiopia, the presence of an international Rastafari community using Jamaican as its vehicular language has influenced part of the local population both linguistically and in a more broadly cultural sense. This influence is particularly visible in the musical output of Ethiopian youth, not only in Shashamane, where the Rastafari community lives,[1] but throughout the country, as also described in the author's previous research on the linguistic acquisition and choice of Jamaican speech forms (JSF) in Shashamane (Tomei 2015) and the rest of Ethiopia (Tomei 2017). This chapter represents a further development of these studies as it investigates the presence of JSF on the Ethiopian reggae scene through the analysis of song lyrics and live performances of popular contemporary Ethiopian artists, supported by several interviews and personal conversations as well as audio and video recordings.

To allow the disciplinary contextualization of the phenomenon under scrutiny, the present investigation begins addressing some of the most relevant findings and conclusions of Tomei 2015:

a. The contact between JSF and the national language led to the development of a new youth speech form called Jamaric (Tomei 2015, 194).

Jamaric is to be seen as the result of a creative process including the formation of new words featuring both Amharic and JSF.

Other studies conducted into youth linguistic practices have highlighted the influence of JSF and their evolution into global registers (Rampton 2006; Blommaert 2005). As argued by Canagarajah (2013, 26, 180–84), the translingual proficiency of speakers has to be addressed with a practice-based approach, focusing on performative competence and the linguistic strategies employed to achieve communicative success in the "contact zone". The observation of the linguistic phenomena occurring in these contact zones has also favoured the development of more recent approaches focusing on translingual practices, or translanguaging (García and Wei 2014; Canagarajah 2013).

b. In the case of Ethiopian youth, the process of acquisition and the choice of JSF can be defined as a conscious acquisition in terms of language and is also related to identity; linguistic choice results from the exercise of a personal, individual and free choice, and it is a reflection of a recognized group identity (Tomei 2015, 193).

The present research considers the fundamental connections between language and identity formation and expression, particularly focusing on Afro-Caribbean ties, taking its cue from the works of Le Page and Tabouret-Keller (1985), Riley (2007), Mühleisen (2002), Allsopp (1996, 2006, 2010), Alleyne (1989), Rickford (1987), Devonish (1986, 2003), Makoni (2003), Mufwene (2010) and Winford (1985) in what specifically concerns the field of black linguistics.

Furthermore, considering the social and cultural context of Addis Ababa, where issues of mobility, context and access to resources are primary, this study also draws from theoretical perspectives provided by recent studies into urban sociolinguistics (Blommaert 2010; Smakman and Heinrich 2015, 2018).

More specifically, the scenario under scrutiny can be classified as a significant case in the emerging field of studies into African Urban Youth Languages, which investigates and describes the linguistic creativity of the new generation of speakers in metropolitan areas of Africa, highlighting the role of the speaker's agency and consciousness in the definition of linguistic choice (Kießlingand Maarten 2004; Nassenstein and Hollington 2015; Ebongue and Hurst 2017).

c. The fields of music and artistic performance offer the highest degree of individual creativity and variational stylistic choice in expressing oneself through JSF. The use of JSF, associated with the specific musical genre (reggae), stimulates a sense of group identity and belongingness among the youth (Tomei 2015, 194).

In the process of writing the lyrics of a song, the construction of rhyme and the choice of words are determined not only by poetics and aesthetics, but also by factors related to identity and the need to express it. The inextricable connections between youth-speak and the language of music have been examined at great length, in particular in the context of the global spread of hip-hop, reggae and dancehall as genres providing youth with a universal tool to express critical thoughts and as a means of resistance to the system (Alim 2006; Alim, Ibrahim and Pennycook 2009; Mitchell 2001; Berger and Carroll 2003; Cooper 2004; Hope 2006; Stanley Niaah 2010).

This contribution focuses on the presence of Jamaican and Jamaric speech forms in the contemporary music context of Ethiopia, with particular regard to the reggae scene. While it is beyond the present scope to provide a description of Ethiopian music at large – as it reflects the national diversities in terms of ethnic, religious and social belonging – it is important to stress how, in Ethiopia, music is an integral part of the culture and plays a fundamental role in tradition and its practices (religious ceremonies, celebrations, community practices, rituals and so forth). Its history, development and relevance have been the subject of several research projects and publications, from the first accounts of sacred chants and rituals by European explorers and missionaries (Alvares 1520; Prutky 1751; Lobo 1623; Isenberg and Kraft 1843; Burton 1856) to the descriptions of new styles and registers in more recent times (Kebede 1971, 1980, 1992; Levine, 1965, 2000; Sàrosi, 1967; Powne 1968).

Furthermore, addressing the issue of music in Ethiopia implies considering in the first instance the history of the Tewahedo Orthodox Church. Notable in that history is Yared, an Ethiopian saint, who, centuries before the definition of scales in traditional Western music, developed a musical notation system which is still in use in contemporary Ethiopian music today. Yared introduced music and sacred chants into the rituals and ceremonies of the church, and the system of formal religious education has integrated many of these liturgical chants into monastic practices, thus preserving a precious and unique part of the orthodox tradition (Kebede 1992).

In parallel with the development of religious music, the specificity of the Ethiopian pentatonic modal system has provided a strong impetus to the development of a long-standing musical tradition which has produced a vast repertoire of popular music. Taking their cue from the tradition inaugurated as far back as 1924 during the regency of Haile Selassie I by the Arba Lijoch (forty children) Brass Band, the first band/orchestra in Ethiopia, many music ensembles have developed, accompanying famous singers (Kasuka 2013, 23–24). In particular, the years between 1950 and 1970 were extremely prolific in terms of music production, distribution and performance.

More recently, the introduction of genres of music popular in Western countries has contributed to the development of new musical output, blending local traditions and the use of traditional instruments with different music patterns and clichés. Some of these have been studied and described by several authors. Ethio-jazz and its most influential exponent, Mulatu Atsatke, is a case in point (Shinn and Ofcansky 2013; Falceto 2001).

By contrast, only sparse attention has been devoted to the contemporary scene, which, along with traditional and popular repertoires, features the emergence of new genres and styles, such as Ethio-rock, Ethiopian hip-hop and Ethiopian reggae. These represent an extremely fertile seam for research, in particular for what concerns linguistic hybridization and creativity, as the lyrics of the songs – mainly written in Amharic, the official language of Ethiopia – actually draw from different linguistic and cultural sources (that is, translanguaging).

The present study is based on research conducted by the author in Ethiopia between 2017 and 2019, into the presence of JSF within the reggae community of Addis Ababa and Shashamane. It also refers to a previous research (2008–13), resulting in the 2015 publication. With reference to the generation of data, the complexity of the scenario described compels the adoption of a combination of data collection methods and techniques, and integrated textual typologies: interviews (semi- and unstructured), focus groups, conversational situations (dialogues, monologues, storytelling), video and audio recordings of conversations and performances (live shows, DJ sets, backstage conversations), lyrics of songs as well as conversations on Skype and WhatsApp. Furthermore, the author has followed the moderate participant observation approach.[2]

The JSF featured in the provided examples have been transcribed using the Cassidy–JLU Writing System, developed by Di Jamiekan Langwij Yuunit (the Jamaican Language Unit) of the University of the West Indies on the basis of the model proposed by Frederic Cassidy in 1961 (JLU 2009).

Reggae in Ethiopia: A Bicentric System

The reasons for the high popularity of reggae music in Ethiopia are not restricted to the appeal of its captivating sonorities and deep basslines. The presence of numerous Rastafari individuals – temporary visitors or members of the Rastafari community that went to Ethiopia to settle in Shashamane or other areas of the country – clearly represents an additional element explaining the widespread diffusion of reggae, this being one of the most influential vehicles of transmission of Rastafari tenets and principles at an international level. As reported by Reckord (1998, 243), Mortimer Planno, one of the leaders of the Rastafari movement in its early stages, defined reggae music as a "positive, non-violent force that will gain power for Rastafari in Jamaica and abroad, and freedom and supremacy for the black man". Indeed, the "black dimension" issue plays a fundamental role in the spread of this music genre among a new generation of Ethiopians.

In November 2018, UNESCO inscribed the "Reggae music of Jamaica" on the Representative List of the Intangible Cultural Heritage of Humanity. The official website reports:

> While in its embryonic state Reggae music was the voice of the marginalized, the music is now played and embraced by a wide cross-section of society, including various genders, ethnic and religious groups. Its contribution to international discourse on issues of injustice, resistance, love and humanity underscores the dynamics of the element as being at once cerebral, socio-political, sensual and spiritual. The basic social functions of the music – as a vehicle for social commentary, a cathartic practice, and a means of praising God – have not changed, and the music continues to act as a voice for all.

However, the most important factor to be considered is the strong connection between Jamaica and Ethiopia, particularly in the Rastafari worldview, which identifies this African country as Zion, the Promised Land, to which the faithful hope to return; the New Jerusalem where the throne of King David is still represented by Haile Selassie I (Owens 1976; Campbell 1987; Bonacci 2015). Although reggae, as a genre, falls into the category of secular music, it incorporates concepts of spirituality and mysticism deeply connected to the Ethiopian tradition, as visible in the lyrics of Rastafari artists, from Bob Marley and Dennis Brown to Chronixx and Jesse Royal, recent stars of the international scene.

While the present article focuses on Jamaican words and fixed expressions featured in the lyrics of Ethiopian reggae songs, there are many Jamaican reggae songs featuring Amharic words, for example, the famous "Igziabeher (Let Jah Be Praised)" by Peter Tosh; "Ababajanoy" by Don Carlos; or "Sattaamasagana", "Tenayistillin" and "Y mas gan" by the Abyssinians. This reflects the fact that, as the language of Emperor Haile Selassie I, Amharic is considered by Rastafari members to be a sacred language, and one that should be learnt by all African descendants in preparation for returning to Ethiopia. As reported by the *Jamaica Observer*, the Language Training Centre in St Andrew offers courses in Amharic, from beginners to advanced levels, taught by Ethiopian Dr Tesfaye Mulu.

The majority of the students are members of the Rastafari community (Johnson 2013).

The presence of reggae music in Ethiopia is better defined by segmenting two binary spatial opposites, the "centre" and the "periphery", and looking at the factors that support the distinction. This scenario presents several analogies with the Jamaican dichotomy of "town" and "country". Here, the Jamaican capital city of Kingston (town) is also the musical capital in terms of production, distribution and performance of, and exposure to, the latest hits and trends, while in the rest of the island (country) it is easier to find live performances of roots reggae artists and bands, often marketed as tourist attractions for those who want to experience a stereotypical tropical Jamaica, far from the bustling atmosphere of Kingston.

By contrast, Ethiopia features a bicentric system, where, besides the capital Addis Ababa – representing the centre of the reggae business, as Kingston does in Jamaica – there is another centre, Shashamane, where the most authentic reggae sound and messages come from. The two centres have similarities as well as significant differences. The differences, being particularly relevant to the present discussion, are summarized in table 12.1. The table illustrates what is clearly an unbalanced situation, highlighting the absence of an organized music business in Shashamane. There is a substantial number of talented young reggae artists, both from the repatriated community and the local population, who, in order to pursue their musical careers, are eventually forced to move to Addis Ababa.[3]

Yet, Shashamane represents the heart of reggae music in Ethiopia. As noted earlier, the presence of a Rastafari community, comprising mostly Jamaican members, confers on this place a very particular status, and it represents a unique opportunity for Ethiopian reggae lovers and artists to come into contact not only with Jamaican native speakers, but also with reggae artists who have either settled in Ethiopia or who are just visiting.[4]

There is a sort of prestige associated with Shashamane such that reggae artists and singers feel they need to establish a connection with the local context. The main artists of the national scene always include at least one clip shot of the Jamaica Sefer in their videos, featuring the typical Rastafari settlement (with the colours of the Ethiopian flag and the Lion of Judah painted on walls, gates, buildings, cars) and members of the Rastafari community. Famous examples are "Bob Marley" (2008) by Teddy Afro featuring Haile Roots, "Asio Bellema" (2012) by Jah Lude featuring Tadele Roba, and "Feeling Irie" (2016) by Ras Jany and Don Deltafa.

Table 12.1 The Music Context: Differences between Addis Ababa and Shashamane

	Addis Ababa	Shashamane (Jamaica Sefer)
Social context and life patterns	Largest city of Ethiopia[a]	Small area surrounding the town[b]
	Job opportunities and facilities	Scarce job opportunities and facilities
	Cold climate – life mainly indoors (workplace, house, malls and shopping centres, lounges and bars)	Warm climate – life mainly outdoors (streets, community meeting places, yards[c])
Music scene	Prevalence of live shows	Prevalence of sound system
	Prevalence of musicians and singers	Prevalence of selectors and DJs[d]
	Mainly roots reggae	Mainly dancehall
Venues and events	Numerous venues hosting live reggae events[e]	Only one venue hosting live reggae events
	Numerous venues hosting sound system events (music clubs, hotels, bars, lounges)	Less than five venues hosting sound system events (bars, lounges)
Production	Numerous professional recording studios and rehearsal venues	Less than five home recording studios and no rehearsal facilities
	Reggae labels offices and studios	No officially registered reggae labels
	Network of music professionals (producers, musicians, beat makers, studio engineers, video makers, graphic designers, promoters)	No organized music business

Promotion	Numerous artist management and booking agencies	No artist management or booking agency
	Numerous radio and TV stations with weekly reggae programmes	No radio or TV stations

[a] According to the latest population census, conducted by the Ethiopian national statistics authority in 2007, Addis Ababa had a population of 3,384,569. However, the United Nations World Population Prospects reports that the metro area population of Addis Ababa in 2020 is 4,794,000. https://population.un.org/wpp. Accessed 23 July 2020.

[b] Jamaica Sefer (or Melka Oda) is the name given by the local population (*sefer* in Amharic means area) to the area surrounding the town of Shashamane (total population: approximately 130,000) where most of the members of the Rastafari community live.

[c] The term *yard* has to be interpreted as the house, and more specifically the whole area surrounding it. The yards, in Jamaica as well as in Shashamane, represent an environment open to social interactive practices, including music (Cassidy and Le Page 2002 [1967]).

[d] Regarding the terminology, there is a distinction among job titles. (a) Selector: in Jamaica, the one who "selects" the songs to be played during a show or party. See also Reynolds 2006. This person is referred to as a DJ (disc jockey) in most of the rest of the world. (b) DJ: originally (late 1960s) delivering improvised lyrics on instrumental tracks to the audience (Cooper 2004, 297). This style subsequently developed into a specific subgenre, the DJ style. Currently, many of the most popular Jamaican artists are DJs (for example Shabba Ranks, Beenieman, Bounty Killer, Sizzla, Capleton, Damian Marley). See also Hope (2006, 33) and Katz (2012). (c) Singer: in its traditional interpretation, the artist performing songs providing melodies and harmonies (examples are Bob Marley, Dennis Brown, Garnett Silk, Luciano, Jah Cure). (d) Artist: often used as an umbrella term to identify reggae selectors, DJs, singers and musicians.

[e] When the author visited Ethiopia for the first time, in 2004, there was a very popular club called Medora where it was possible to eat traditional Jamaican food while listening to reggae music. At that time, Medora, as well as Illusion, Ambassador, Safari (later Harlem Jazz) and other clubs in the capital, also organized reggae sessions and concerts with the participation of very large audiences. Currently, in addition to the multitude of bars, restaurants and lounges keeping weekly reggae nights, the main venues for live shows and events are Villa Verde and the African Jazz Village of the Ghion Hotel, where Bob Marley performed during his visit to Ethiopia in 1978.

The Artists, Their Language(s) and Lyrics

As noted, reggae music is very popular in Ethiopia. This chapter does not aim to offer an exhaustive panorama of the contemporary scene which features countless artists and performers. Currently, the most popular Ethiopian singers are Johnny Ragga (born Yohannes Bekele, one of the first artists to perform Jamaican-inspired reggae in the country), Haile Roots, Jah Lude, Sami Dan, Ras Biruk, Ras Jani and Daggy Shash, representing the new generation of Ethiopian reggae. Yet, the celebrity in this field is Teddy Afro, born Tewodros Kassahun, who began his career in 2001 with his first album, *Abugida*. In addition to these singers, there are many reggae selectors and DJs working in clubs, bars, and on radio and television, mainly in Addis Ababa.

The Rastafari community makes a significant contribution to the local reggae scene. King Kong, Sydney Salmon, Teddy Dan and Ras Kawintaseb are the most popular singers from this community. Since returning to Ethiopia – between the end of 1990 and early 2000 – they have made a significant contribution to the development of the music scene. Younger artists, such as Jahziel Naphtali, Static Levy, and Intellect also known as Benjamin Beats, are also attracting large audiences and providing hit songs for the new generation.

In terms of linguistic issues, Ethiopian reggae presents a complex scenario. While Ethiopian artists already have a multilingual background (Ethiopian languages such as Amharic, Afaan Oromo and Tigrinya), which is detectable in the lyrics of the songs, the international singers and performers add another element to the linguistic mosaic being examined, as the majority of them have Jamaican origins (King Kong, Sydney Salmon, Teddy Dan, Jahziel Naphtali and Static Levi). Ras Kawintaseb and Benjamin Beats were born in Trinidad and Tobago, and England, respectively. Notwithstanding the different origins and linguistic backgrounds, JSF are used by all these artists in their songs and live shows, and by selectors and DJs during their performances.

Clearly, the multilingualism of the Ethiopian singers represents an added value with regard to their professional skills, as they can confidently access different language domains and use different codes. Moreover, their JSF competence allows them to use an additional gamut of sounds, rhymes and poetics, and to strengthen the connection with Jamaican reggae.

The present study specifically focuses on the linguistic behaviour of Ethiopian singers and DJs, their creativity and translingual practices, analysing the lyrics of popular songs released in the last fifteen years and highlighting the presence of JSF.

Furthermore, in addition to the lyrics of the songs, the excerpts provided are part of the linguistic corpus of non-transcribed materials (interviews, audio and video recordings of linguistic practices, conversations and interactions) gathered by the author during field research.

Acquisition of Linguistic Features

Concerning the acquisition of linguistic features, the data gathered during this research expand the existing corpus of JSF used by young people in Ethiopia provided by the previous publications on the subject (Tomei 2015, 2017; Hollington 2016).

For a more accurate description of the markers denoting the influence of JSF on Ethiopian youth involved in the local music scene, the features detected have been organized into different categories and highlighted in the lyrics of the songs. The selection of macro areas has been made with reference to the related literature (Cassidy and Le Page 2002 [1967]; Cassidy 2007 [1961]; Patrick 2003; Bailey 1966; Pollard 2000).

- Morphosyntactic features
- Phonological features
- Interjections and fixed expressions
- Features of Rastafari/reggae-specific usage

The examples feature the original lyrics of the song, an interlinear gloss and a free translation.

Morphosyntactic Features

Nouns: use of *dem* added to the noun in order to show plurality (Cassidy 2007)

Example 1 – Song: "Ancheee (Ehy You)" by Daggy Shash

Daggy Shash	*kom*	*fi*	*di*	*gyal-**dem***
Daggy Shash	come	for	the	girl-PL

Daggy Shash comes (sings) for the girls

Pronouns and deictics: personal pronoun (example 2) and proximal deictic (example 3) (Patrick 2003)

Example 2 – Song: "Kulfun Sechign/Give Me the Key" by Jonny Ragga

Ier	*ou*	*mi*	*a go*	*krai!*
Hear	how	I	FUT	cry!

Hear how I will sing!

Example 3 – Radio programme: "Whatever is Clever" (EBC National Radio) hosted by DJ Ezee

Reggae and more Reggae, yes people!   Wi lov da ting ya, yu nuo?
Reggae and more Reggae, yes people! We love the thing DEM, you know?
Reggae and more Reggae, yes people! We love this thing, you know?

Verbs: the case of *a* as pre-verbal marker (example 4), no overt past-tenses marker (example 5), absence of *s* for the third-person singular (example 6), the case of *a* and *a go* for the continuous and future-tense (example 7), modals (example 8)

Example 4 – Song: "Hello Africa" by DJ Dulas featuring Dagy Lion

*Ai-man **a** kom   fram Africa, Ai-man **a** kom   fram   Ethiopia*
I-man VB come from Africa, I-man VB come   from   Ethiopia
"I come from Africa, I come from Ethiopia"

Example 5 – Song: "One Way Ticket" by Jonny Ragga

*Lang taim yu **tel** mi se   yu   liivin Babylon*
Long time you tell me CONJ you leaving Babylon
You have been saying you are leaving Babylon for a long time

*Shashamane! Som a dem de aredi an dem **mek** di wok don*
Shashamane! Some of them ADV already and they make the work done
Shashamane! Some of them are already there and they have done their work

Example 6 – Song: "One Way Ticket" by Jonny Ragga

*Step outta Babilon, Shasha   **open**   ar   and*
Step out of Babylon, Shashamane open her hands
Leave Babylon, Shashamane opens her hand

Example 7 – Song: "Kulfun Sechign/Give Me the Key" by Jonny Ragga

*Ier   ou   mi   **a go**   krai!*
Hear how I   FUT   cry!
"Hear how I will sing!"

Example 8 – Song: "One Way Ticket" by Jonny Ragga

*Big   disizhan **hafi**   mek   fi   get   out   a   Babylon*
Big   decision MOD make to   get   out   of   Babylon
It takes a big decision to get out of Babylon

Negation: *Neva* (example 9) indicates perfect, and *No* (example 10) is associated with non-perfect actions/events.

Example 9 – Song: "Hule Hule" by Ras Jany featuring Jerusalem
*Do   it   laik   yu   **neva**   do   it   bifuor*
Do   it   like   you   NEG   do   it   before
Do it like you have never done before

Example 10 – Live performance by Daggy Shash (Addis Ababa, September 2017)
*Silekta   skwiiz   da   ridim!   Mi   **no**   av   taim   fi   wies,   ziin?*
Selector   squeeze   the   rhythm!   I   NEG   have   time   to   waste,   seen?
Selector start the track! I do not have time to waste, do you understand?

Phonological Features

Phonological changes of the complex vowels /ia/ and /ua/ (examples 11 and 12),[5] phonological variation v > b (example 13), stops instead of fricatives (example 14), the deletion of consonants (example 15).

Example 11 – Song: "Hello Africa" by DJ Dulas featuring Dagy Lion
Wiek   *op   di   die   an   **wiek** op   di   nait*
Wake   up   the   day   and   wake up   the   night
Wake up in the day and wake up in the night

Example 12 – Song: "Mi Phone a Ring" by Ras Jany
*A   uu   dat   mek a   **fuon**   kaal fi   mi   ina mi   styudiyo taim?*
Is   who that   make a   phone call   for me   in   my   studio   time?
Who is calling me during studio time?

Example 13 – Song: "Mi Phone a Ring" by Ras Jany
*Dem   no   av   a   fiks   taim   fi   kaal? Ras   Jany   **bex**!*
They   NEG   have   a   fixed   time   for   call? Ras   Jany   vexed!
Don't they have a fixed time to call? Ras Jany is upset!

Example 14 – Radio programme: "Whatever is Clever" (EBC National Radio) hosted by DJ Ezee
*Wi   lov   da   **ting**   ya,   yu   nuo?*
We   love   the   thing   ADV,   you   know?
We love this thing, you know?

Example 15 – Song: "Mi Phone a Ring" by Ras Jany
Wa?   *Mi   fuon   iz   ringin*
What?   My   phone   is   ringing

Furthermore, the following excerpt, from an interview the author conducted with DJ Dulas, shows that the acquisition of Jamaican phonology can also entail interference with Amharic words, as in the case of the pronunciation of the name Haile Selassie I:

> Renato Tomei: How do you pronounce the name of the emperor of Ethiopia?
> DJ Dulas: *AiliaiSelassiai*![6]
> Renato Tomei: Is this the Amharic pronunciation?
> DJ Dulas: No, in Amharic it's *Sellasi*. People who read and know say *Sellasi*, but who listen to reggae music or is among Rastas say *Selassiai*. I say *Selassiai* because, as a youth, I was inspired by music, and it's all about *Aitiopia* and *Selassiai*. And then, don't forget, I am a Shasha youth, so I have always been at the celebrations for His Majesty birthday or coronation, since I was a kid.
> It is pure energy when the MC[7] says "Greetings people, welcome to the coronation of *Ailiai*", and the crowd answers "*Selassiai*". And then again, "*Jah*" (the MC), "*Rastafarai!*" (the crowd). So, for me, there is no problem to change. (Addis Ababa, October 2018)

Interjections and Fixed Expressions

There is consensus that the umbrella term *interjections* covers a wide range of terms, "from the smallest particle and phoneme to extended sentences, inclusive of exclamations and vocative structures. It also extends to exclamations like cursing, blessings, and greetings" (Masiola 2018, 1). They have been given a recognized status within the continuum progression ranging from emotional "sounds" to significant verbal utterances and sentences (Wierzbicka 1992). Consequently, definitions vary as they may also fit into diverse slots (Wilkins 1992).

There are aspects of interjections analysed along the trend of speech act theories, recognizing that there is a "language of interjections" (Poggi 2009) and that there are also psychological, behavioural and acquisitional factors (Stange 2009). A more recent focus is the aspect of interjections and non-verbal communication with gesturality, combining the "seeing and showing" in a continuum (Wharton 2003). This is an important item, especially when analysing video recordings and in describing the interactional sequence.

With regard to interjections, the following occurrences have been detected: affirmative (example 16) and negative (example 17).

> Example 16 – Song: "Hule Hule" by Ras Jany and Jerusalem
> Aleee!   **Bum!   Bum**   ina   di   daansaal   ruum!
> EXLAM   IDEO   IDEO   in   the   dancehall   room!
> Alè! Boom! Energy in the party!

As also explained by DJ Dulas, one of the most popular disc jockeys in the capital, during an interview with the author in 2018:

> *Boom* is the most used one. Most people just say *boom* because they love the sound, and they know it means something good. When the people want to big me up, or big up the show, they tell me "Yo, DJ Dulas, *Boom!*" There is nothing to know about it: from they say *boom*, they know it's big, you know? (Addis Ababa, October 2018)

Example 17 – Song: "Pick It Up" by Jonny Ragga
[voicemail: "Leave your name and number after the tone and I will get back to you"]
[kiss-teeth]
Cho!

Kiss-teeth is the metalinguistic representation of a specific gesture widely used in Jamaica and in the Caribbean. *Cho!* is one of the interjections generally associated with the kiss-teeth gesture and related to it in function and use (Patrick and Figueroa 2002).

Other Jamaican interjections detected are *chuu* (< English "true"), *ye man* (< English "yeah man"), *aarait* (< English "alright") – affirmative, and *ihn ihn/ehn ehn* (no) – negative.

Other categories identified by analysing the data are: rhetorical questions (example 18), swear words,[8] and other fixed expressions (example 19):

Example 18 – Song: "Hello Africa" by DJ Dulas featuring Dagy Lion
I am Dagy Lion Station, this is a music studio collaboration!

Wa	**di**	**man**	**se,**	**DJ**	**Dulas?**
What	the	man	say,	DJ	Dulas?

What do you say, DJ Dulas?

During an interview, DJ Dulas, addressing the issue of the use of Jamaican expressions within the reggae community of Addis Ababa, stated:

> We can find all these things in Jamaican songs, you know? Especially in Addis, it's the music. People don't know what it means, they just use the words. *Wa da man se* sounds good, it carries a *vibe*. So, we use it all the time. (Addis Ababa, October 2018)

Other rhetorical questions detected are *wa a gwaahn?* (< English "what is going on?"), *yu no siit/ziit?* (< English "don't you see it?"), *yu no?* (< English "you know?"), *ziin?* (< English "do you see it?") and *yu no ier?* (< English "don't you hear?"). These are used to reinforce statements and arguments in conversation, as "backchannel signals" to reinforce assertions, solicit agreement and stimulate attention, as an enhanced phatic function.

A further category is represented by those words used in case of strong surprise or of the exceptionality of an event. Even though considered markedly vulgar words or "improper" in terms of register, they are ethnically marked as Jamaicanism. Under this category, the following have been detected: *raasklaat, bomboklaat* and *blodklaat*. However, the use of curse words seems to be a very limited phenomenon, especially if compared with the majority of international contexts in which reggae music has fostered the assimilation of JSF. There is no trace of the aforementioned words in the lyrics of the vast repertoire of Jamaric songs. The only occurrences recorded pertain to DJ talk and personal interactions during dancehall parties and live shows.

This is also confirmed by DJ Dulas:

> In general, in Ethiopia the youth keep their mouth clean. It's not like outside. Here we know the meaning and we keep our mouth clean, you know. Also, Rastas don't like bad words. Neither do Ethiopians. (Addis Ababa, October 2018)

He makes a further distinction between Shashamane and Addis Ababa for what concerns the context and the appropriateness related to the use of swear words:

> In Addis there is no time to use them. And no place. I mean, for youth like me, born in Shasha, it's different. We use the words because we know them, but at the same time we know when and where not to use them. In Addis, many don't know exactly the meaning, so they may use them out of context. (Addis Ababa, October 2018)

Example 19 – Conversation with DJ Ezee (November 2019)
Yu don nuo mi breda! Mi plie Reggae sins mi wuz a yuut
You don't know my brother! I play Reggae since I was a youth
You know already my brother! I play Reggae since I was a child

Other detected Jamaican fixed expressions are *a so mi se* (< English "is so I say") and *a so mi a diil wid* (< English "that's my style").

Features of Rastafari/Reggae Specific Usage

With reference to the Rastafari use of language, it is the case of all those words falling under the three categories proposed by Pollard (2000):

1. Known words with a new meaning (semantic shift).

   Example 20 – Song: "Bob Marley" by Teddy Afro featuring Haile Roots
   Unite yourself, black people rise! Unite yourself, be wise, be wise!
   Unite yourself, **Babylon, Babylon, Babylon** *fall.*

"Babylon" represents here the sociopolitical and economic institutions that oppress the masses and their corruption (Reynolds 2006, 5). This word is used extensively in the lyrics of reggae songs: see for example Bob Marley's "Babylon System", "Chant Down Babylon", "Exodus", and "Africa Unite".

2. Words undergoing conceptual substitutions, or words "that bear the weight of their phonological implications with some explanations" (Pollard 2000, 46).

   Example 21 – Song: "Feeling Irie" by Ras Jany and Don Deltafa
   Dis iz a speshal **livikieshan**
   This a special **dedication**

As many words in Dread Talk, the word *liv-ikieshan* is the product of a lexical permutation in affixation, where the first three letters *ded* (dead) are replaced by *liv* (live). Being a dedication associated to a positive concept, the word should not include sounds/words recalling negative concepts. Other examples are *op-pressor, ci-garette* and *week-end*, respectively becoming *down-pressor* (not up), *blind-garette* (not see) and *strong-end* (not weak).

3. The *ai* words (first-person conceptualization).

   Example 22 – Song: "Melkam Yamarech" by Haile Roots
   African uman,   riil uman,   **Ai an ai** *uman,   riil   uman*
   African woman, real woman, I   and I   woman, real woman
   African woman, real woman, my woman, real woman

Ai (I) represents the main feature of DT as it linguistically defines the individual redemption obtained by Rasta through their faith and emphasizes the centrality of the human being as in connection with the rest of the Creation. In particular, the form *ai an ai* (also *I & I*) represents the unity between man and God (I), which comes over I. As reported by Pollard (2000), the Jesuit father Joseph Owens published in 1976 a brief description of the Rastafari movement and theology where, in recording the choice of avoiding the use of the object pronoun /me/ in subject position by some members of the community, he argues that it is perceived as "expressive of subservience, as representative of the self-degradation that was expected of the slaves by their masters" (Owens 1976 quoted in Pollard 2000).

Also those words undergoing conceptual substitution (category 2), where *ai* generates the lexical permutation in affixation, have been considered part of this category, as in the case of *aiwa* (also *iwah, howa, iowa*), which translates as "hour, present time" (Reynolds 2006, 64).

> Example 23– Song: "Lambadina" by Teddy Afro
> *Ina mi main, ina mi aiz, Mi si di rait ina dis aiwa*
> In   my mind, in my eyes, I see the right in this hour
> In my mind, in my eyes, I see the truth in this time

In addition to the categories identified by Pollard, the present analysis also considers other significant elements, such as forms of greeting (example 24), forms of address (example 25) and words used within the musical context of Jamaican reggae and dancehall and internationally known and spread during recent decades (example 26) (Le Page and Tabouret-Keller 1985; Chevannes 1994; Alleyne 1989; Pollard 2000; Reynolds 2006; Cooper 2004; Hope 2006).

> Example 24 – Song: "Affi Go" by Ras Biruk
> **Greetings in the mighty name of His Imperial Majesty**
> **Emperor Haile Selassie the First, Jah Rastafari**

This is one of the most famous greeting formulas uttered by Rastafari members, especially before starting a meeting or any official gathering, sometimes with some variations. Its international popularity is due to its use by Bob Marley in the introduction to one of his most famous songs, "Rastaman Vibration" (1976).

Other forms of greetings detected are *blesed lov* (< English "blessed love"), *muor lov* (< English "more love"), *bles op* (< English "bless up") and *airi* (< "nice, hearty"; Reynolds 2006).

> Example 25 – Facebook message (Messenger) sent by Ras Biruk (March 2019)
> *Yes mi **Bredren**, everything bless!*
> Yes my brother, everything blessed!

Bredren, also *bredrin* (< English "brother") – and *sistren* for females – denotes brotherhood or religious communion (Reynolds 2006, 18), and it is used by the members of the Rastafari community to address their fellows.

Other forms of address detected are *jred, nati, king* and *faiyah* (< English "fire").

Example 26 – Song: "Feeling Irie" by Ras Jany and Don Deltafa
Pul it op, pul it op, pul it op!
Start it over! (the song)

Many other reggae-related words/expressions have been detected. The most frequently used are *big op, mash op da plies* (< English "smash the place"), *masiv* and *nof rispek* (< English "enough respect").

It is worth mentioning that the contemporary Ethiopian reggae scene is characterized by an increasing use of JSF, employed to mark authenticity and a connection to the original Jamaican reggae. This is particularly noticeable, for example, in the case of the stage names singers choose for themselves. According to Hollington (2018, 115):

> While choosing a stage name is certainly an act of identity (as the name stands for the self), it can also reflect various sign-relations on the indexical, iconic and symbolic level.

Indeed, the names of contemporary artists are extremely significant at indexical, iconic and symbolic levels, as they feature words largely used by Rasta: *Haile Roots, Jah Lude, Sami Dan, Ras Biruk and Ras Jani, Daggy Shash.*

Conversely, Teddy Afro's use of JSF is confined to a few distinctive words and expressions. This could be explained by the fact that, having started his career a decade before the contemporary artists, he has been less exposed to the linguistic influence of the Jamaican community and, consequently, he has a limited competence of JSF – what Blommaert (2010, 103) defines as a "truncated repertoire".

Translanguaging

One of the most prominent features observed in the context under scrutiny is the creativity of the singers and artists, who freely select, from their full linguistic repertoire, words and expressions to make meaning and assert their identity. As defined by García and Wei (2014, 25), "a translanguaging space acts as a Thirdspace which does not merely encompass a mixture or hybridity of first and second languages, instead it invigorates languaging".

The international mobility of Ethiopian reggae artists and the deep relationship between the Ethiopian homeland and its many diasporic communities around the world (mainly the United States, Canada and Europe) together create an audience that is highly heterogeneous in its cultural and linguistic features. Consequently, the artists develop a genuine creativity, based on the capability of drawing from different social and linguistic sources. Indeed, there are many songs highlighting the power of language which, particularly in the context of music, can inspire the most creative ways to achieve its main aim, that is, to deliver the message. Examples are the song "Fayamo" by Jah Lude (2013), which addresses the universality of language lauding the heterogeneity of Ethiopian languages and cultures, and the song "Chiggae" by Haile Roots (2011), who plays with language and music, associating the "chikchika" (in the Ethiopian music tradition, the tell-tale triplet rhythm) with "reggae", further confirming the high degree of musical/linguistic hybridization.

As stated by DJ Dulas, JSF offer great opportunities in this regard:

> Everywhere in the world people know that Jamaican language is music language. It's easy to put things in Patwa because you can do it as you want. It's not straight, you can bend it, and you can twist it, and it still sounds the same. (Addis Ababa, October 2018)

In Zimbabwe, extensive translanguaging is common in many reggae and dancehall songs, in youth language practices and also in everyday communication between multilinguals (Hollington 2018). In the same way, Ethiopia presents an evolving scene in which the youth share a multilingual repertoire drawing mainly from Amharic, JSF and English. Jamaric represents the result of this creativity, as well as a useful tool in music. The singer Sydney Salmon confirms this:

> The youth here are learning the Jamaican language, and they are mixing it with the local language. What they are creating is really beautiful.
>
> We call it *Jamaric*! (Shashamane, February 2013)

In this regard, the lyrics of the songs and the DJ talk practices analysed represent a case in point.

In the vast repertoire of Ethiopian reggae, there are songs written entirely in Amharic or entirely in Jamaican (and English), and others in which the artist creatively combines Amharic and JSF (Jamaric). Many of these songs are directly inspired by Jamaican sources, in terms of lyrics, content and music. "Bezu Were", a popular song by Ras Biruk, is a clear example in that regard. The melody of the chorus, as well as the instrumental, echo a very famous Jamaican song, "Tenement Yard" by Jacob Miller. Furthermore, the lyrics, mainly written in Amharic, translate the Jamaican words and play on the similarities and the assonance between words in the two languages (both *susu* and *shushu* are respectively the Jamaican and Ethiopian equivalent of "to whisper behind the back" or "to gossip").

> Example 27 – Song: "Bezu Were" by Ras Biruk
> ብዙ ወሬ፣ወሬ፣ወሬ   ብዙ ሱሱሱሱሱ
> Bezu were were were,   bezu ***Sususususu***
> Too many rumours, too many rumours
> ብዙ ወሬ፣ወሬ፣ወሬ፣ወይኔ   ብዙ ሀሜት፣ ሀሜት፣ ሀሜት   ብዙ ሹሹሹሹሹ
> Bezu were were were, weine! Bezu amet amet amet,   bezu Shushushushushu
> Too many rumours – Oh no! Too much malice, too many rumours
> There are numerous examples of this phenomenon, and its diachrony observation highlights rapid development of new words and expressions.

More interestingly, the increasing level of linguistic competence in JSF among Ethiopian youth is producing effects that go far beyond the concepts of language mixing and switching. As reported by DJ Dulas:

> Jamaican has a positive effect on Amharic language. Yes man, for real! We can style it out, *geba*? (< English "do you understand?") *Yu siit/ziit*?
> Some Jamaican words are similar to Ethiopian words, but they have different meanings. We say "***Wha a gwaansetat***", but what we really mean is "Wagahunsetat". You see, we just style it out. (Addis Ababa, October 2018)

Wagahunsetat, which literally translates as "give her the price", is a common expression used in various contexts: it may refer to a buying-and-selling situation (give her the right price); it may also refer to punishment (give her a lesson); in youth jargon, it has a sexual connotation. Ethiopian youth exposed to JSF often substitute the Amharic *Wagahun* with *Wha a gwaan*, without changing the meaning of the expression, demonstrating how the linguistic practices of these youths are characterized by a high degree of interchangeability between JSF and Amharic words and expressions as part of the same repertoire.

Another recurrent expression used by Ethiopian youth and featuring JSF is *Beka Jah*. It is used in conversational contexts in which an interlocutor wants to end a dispute in a peaceful way. This expression is always associated with a specific gesture, the fist bump, largely used in Jamaica. *Beka* is an Amharic verbal form which translates as "to suffice" or "to be enough"; it is also used as a volitive interjection meaning "stop it". Both the word *Jah* and the fist bump have been introduced into Ethiopia by Jamaicans and, more specifically, by Rasta, who use the former to refer to God and the latter as a symbol of peace and respect.

Moreover, besides linguistic innovations, the cultural permeability characterizing the music scene under scrutiny also challenge social paradigms, as demonstrated by the recent proliferation of songs addressing issues which in the past have been peripheral to music production in Ethiopia, such as politics, poverty and injustice.9

In this sense, Teddy Afro represents the most significant example, as the content of some of his songs, inspired by social justice issues (for example the banned yet very popular "Yasteseryal"), have led to a conflictual relationship with the government, eventually culminating with his arrest in 2007. More recently, the singer Sami Dan, with his 2016 album *Keras Gar Negeger*, crosses the thematic boundaries of contemporary Ethiopian music clichés, exposing the public to critical and controversial topics regarding the national socio-economic conditions, such as discrimination, unfair legislation and underdevelopment. "Dimts Alba Sew", for example, presents significant similarities with numerous Jamaican reggae songs, in particular as it condemns the indifference and disregard of the people for the suffering of their fellow men:

> Example 28 – Song: "Dimts Alba Sew" by Sami Dan
> ዝምታዬ መልሶዉ እኔዉ ላይ ይጮዉሀል ይጠይቀኛል
> Zimitaye meleso yenewo lai yechewale yeteyekegnale
> My silence comes back to me, it shouts and questions me
> የተራበዉን አይቼ ሳልፎዉ የተጨነቀዉን ሳልሰማዉ
> Yeterabeun ayiche salfow, yetechenekeun salsemaw
> I've seen the hungry and walk past, I haven't listened to the worried man
> ለቸገረዉ ምንም ሳላካፋለዉ ለራሴ ብቻ ነዉ ለካ እምኖረዉ
> Lechegerew menem salakafilow lerase bicha now leca minoraw
> I haven't shared with the needy, Oh Gosh, I am so selfish!

It is not a direct translation of the words of Jamaican songs, rather of the concepts, which are recontextualized and adapted to the Ethiopian sociocultural scene.

In this regard, DJ Dulas observes:

> We are starting using not only Jamaican words, but also **ideas**, **concepts**. For example, Sizzla sang "Step aside" long time ago, and now we are singing it in Amharic. Something that never happened before. It's not about love for girls, you know? Ethiopians always sing and listen to love songs, that's nothing new. What's new is to talk openly about how we suffer, how we must fight every day to make it. And this is a Jamaican thing. (Addis Ababa, October 2018)

The sociopolitical conditions that have triggered the development of Jamaican reggae, providing a voice for the voiceless, reverberate in the lyrics of the songs of Sami Dan and many other singers, opening new horizons for Ethiopian reggae music.

In the words of David Katz:

> Reggae sprang from desperation, fashioned by those with little at hand as an expression of their predicament. Its rallying cry against injustice and its growing influence ensure that the music will remain a continual source of inspiration. (Katz 2012, 11)

Conclusions

In line with recent studies on youth linguistic practices, the present research shows how, in Ethiopia, a new generation of speakers is using linguistic creativity "in order to construct and express their identity" (Nassenstein and Hollington 2015, 14–15).

The influence of Jamaican linguistic and cultural practices is particularly evident in the context of Ethiopian reggae music, where composers and performers frequently use a wide variety of JSF. The adoption of these features, occurring in music and interactions, has been described through the analysis of the lyrics of Ethiopian singers and artists, and other sources of data (live performances, personal conversations, text messages).

While Amharic and English feature most prominently, JSF seem to be employed as essential elements to emphasize and highlight authenticity and connection to the original Jamaican reggae. Moreover, if compared with the pioneers of Ethiopian reggae, the new generation of artists shows an increasing use of JSF and a conscious approach to Jamaican extralinguistic features.

The multilingualism of Ethiopian singers, as observed, allows them not only to display a wider range of sounds, rhymes and poetics, but also to access different language domains using different codes. Moreover, the translanguaging approach, in particular as it manifests itself in the context of music, has allowed the observation of further developments in terms of linguistic acquisition and choice of JSF by Ethiopian youth, such as the creation of new Jamaric words.

In 1976, at the inaugural meeting of the Society for Caribbean Linguistics, Richard Allsopp presented a paper titled "Case for Afrogenesis", providing the basis for further research into Creoles, emphasizing the role of African languages in the development of these languages and providing an alternative approach within the debate surrounding the origin of Creole languages (monogenesis versus polygenesis). Since then, numerous scholars have followed in his footsteps, investigating and describing the linguistic connections between African languages and Caribbean Creoles (Rickford 1987; Alleyne 1989; Devonish 1986). Moving from their output and accomplishments, the present contribution aims at expanding the context of analysis: the large presence of Jamaican words, expressions and formulas in Ethiopian reggae music suggests the existence of a circular flow, a transatlantic linguistic journey, going from Africa to the Caribbean and then back to Africa again, which thus produces new and authentic ways of development and expression. Inspired by the culture and linguistic practices of their ancestors, the decision of the members of that community to return to Africa and settle in Ethiopia could consequently implicate a linguistic move from Afro-*genesis* to Afro-*revelation*.

Notes

1. The Rastafari community of Shashamane was established after the donation of 500 acres of land by the Emperor Haile Selassie in 1948. The "land grant" was originally assigned to the members of the black diaspora scattered around the world and of those who had supported the liberation of the country during the Italo-Ethiopian war. The first pioneers arrived mainly from the Caribbean (Montserrat, Jamaica, Barbados). The community is now composed of members repatriated from all over the world, who have recently received Ethiopian identity cards and been legally registered in the country. For a more accurate account of the repatriation movement, see Bonacci (2015).

2. According to DeWalt and DeWalt (2011, 2), participant observation is seen as a way to collect data in "naturalistic settings by ethnographers who observe and/or take part in the common and uncommon activities of the people being studied". Furthermore, moderate participation occurs when the ethnographer seeks to "maintain a balance between being an insider and an outsider, between participation and observation" (Spradley 1980, 60).

3. For a more detailed description of the music scene of Shashamane, see the docufilm *Youths of Shasha – The Movie*, produced by the author for the association Youths of the World, which describes the existence of natural musical talent within the young multi-ethnic community and, at the same time, the absence of any kind of support for their artistic skills. The movie is accessible at https://www.youtube.com/watch?v=UV-gBrY-R30.

4. Many Jamaican reggae artists have been to Shashamane (Bob Marley, Dennis Brown, Bob Andy, Freddie McGregor, the Marley family, Morgan Heritage, Luciano, Mickey General, Fred Locks, Sizzla, Protoje, Chronixx, Jesse Royal and a few others) and some of them, for example King Kong, Teddy Dan and Sydney Salmon, have decided to settle there. The name of this

locality is well known among the international audience as it is mentioned in the lyrics of many songs, and there is also a famous sound system called Shashamane International, based in New York and owned by two Americans with Kenyan origins who have never been to Ethiopia. Notwithstanding its international fame, Shashamane does not offer basic music facilities (professional recording studios, radio stations), as highlighted by table 12.1. As stated by Brother Flippin, one of the Jamaican pioneers who returned to Ethiopia in 1975, most of those artists singing about Shashamane have never been there, nor have they contributed to the development of the local music scene (interview featured in the documentary *Youths of Shasha – The Movie*).

5. For a description of the phonetic changes of the phoneme /a/ when sharing the syllable nucleus with the vowels /i/ and /u/, and producing the phonetic realizations [iɛ] and [uo], see Devonish and Otelemate (2004, 454).

6. In Amharic, the name of the Emperor is ቀዳማዊኃይለሥላሴ (Qadamawi Haile Sellasie), where Qadamawi translates as "the First". In English literature, the name has different spellings: Haile Selassie/Sellassie/Sellasie 1st/I. In particular, the use of the Roman numeral "I" has fostered the pronunciation *ai* (also written Selassie-I). The same pronunciation is extended to the name of the emperor before coronation, Ras Tafari, which becomes Ras Tafar*ai* (also written Rastafar-I). See also Pollard (2000).

7. MC, master of ceremonies, is a term also used in hip-hop culture and identifies the person entertaining the audience and using the microphone. See also Alim, Ibrahim and Pennycook (2009).

8. Concerning the use of Jamaican swearwords, see Farquharson, Forrester and Hollington (2020).

9. In Ethiopia, the most popular and best-selling songs are love songs. There is also a long tradition of war songs. Apart from few yet significant examples (see Beyene 2019), social protest and political opposition have not featured significantly in the music of the past century. See also Sàrosi (1967) and Powne (1968).

References

Alim, Sami. 2006. *Roc the Mic Right: The Language of Hip Hop Culture*. London: Routledge.

Alim, Sami, Awad Ibrahim, and Alistair Pennycook, eds. 2009. *Global Linguistic Flows: Hip Hop Cultures, Youth Identities and the Politics of Language*. London: Routledge.

Alleyne, Marvin. 1989. *The Roots of Jamaican Culture*. London: Pluto.

Allsopp, Richard, ed. 1996. *Dictionary of Caribbean English Usage*. Kingston: University of the West Indies Press.

———. 2006. *The Case for Afrogenesis and Afrogenesis of Caribbean Creole Proverbs*. Society for Caribbean Linguistics. Kingston: University of the West Indies Press.

———. 2010. *New Register of Caribbean English Usage: Centre for Caribbean Lexicography*. Kingston: University of the West Indies Press.

Arrowsmith-Brown, James Henry, ed. 1991 [1751]. *Prutky's Travels to Ethiopia and Other Countries [Hakluyt Society Second Series No. 174]*. London: The Hakluyt Society.

Bailey, Beryl Loftman. 1966. *Jamaican Creole Syntax: A Transformational Approach*. Cambridge: Cambridge University Press.

Beckingham, Charles Fraser, and George Wynn Brereton Huntingford, eds. 2010 [1958]. *The Prester John of the Indies: A True Relation of the Lands of Prester John Being the Narrative of the Portuguese Embassy to Ethiopia in 1520 written by Father Francisco Alvares*. Vol. 1. Translation of Lord Stanley of Alderley [1881]. The Hakluyt Society, Series II: CXIV. London: Ashgate.

Berger, Harris M., and Michael Thomas Carroll. 2003. *Global Pop Local Language*. Jackson: University Press of Mississippi.

Beyene, Zenebe. 2019. "From an Emperor to the Derg and Beyond: Examining the Intersection of Music and Politics in Ethiopia". In *Music and Messaging in the African Political Arena*, edited by Uche Onyebadi, 1–21. Hershey: IGI Global.

Blommaert, Jan. 2005. "In and Out of Class, Codes and Control. Globalization, Discourse and Mobility". In *Dislocations/Relocations: Narratives of Displacement*, edited by Anna De Fina and Mike Baynham, 128–43. Manchester: St Jerome Publishers.

———. 2010. *The Sociolinguistics of Globalization*. Cambridge: Cambridge University Press.

Bonacci, Giulia. 2015. *Exodus! Heirs and Pioneers, Rastafari return to Ethiopia*. Kingston: University of the West Indies Press.

Burton, Richard. 1856. *First Footsteps in East Africa*. London: Tylston and Edwards.

Campbell, Horace. 1987. *Rasta and Resistance: From Marcus Garvey to Walter Rodney*. Trenton: Africa World Press.

Canagarajah, Suresh. 2013. *Translingual Practice: Global Englishes and Cosmopolitan Relations*. London and New York: Routledge.

Cassidy, Frederic G. 2007 [1961]. *Jamaica Talk: Three Hundred Years of the English Language in Jamaica*. Kingston: Universities of the West Indies Press.

Cassidy, Frederic G., and Robert Le Page. 2002 [1967]. *Dictionary of Jamaican English*. Kingston: University of the West Indies Press.

Chevannes, Barry. 1994. *Rastafari: Roots and Ideology*. Syracuse: Syracuse University Press.

Cooper, Carolyn. 2004. *Sound Clash: Jamaican Dancehall Culture at Large*. London: Palgrave.

Da Costa, Manuel Gonçalves, ed. 1984. *The Itinerário of Jerónimo Lobo*. London: Hakluyt Society.

Devonish, Hubert. 1986. *Language and Liberation: Creole Language Policies in the Caribbean*. London: Karia.

———. 2003. "Language Advocacy and 'Conquest' Diglossia in the Anglophone Caribbean". In *The Politics of English as a World Language*, edited by Christian Mair, 157–78. Amsterdam and New York: Rodopi.

Devonish, Hubert, and Harry G. Otelemate, eds. 2004. "Jamaican Creole and Jamaican English: Phonology". In *A Handbook of Varieties of English: A Multimedia Reference Tool. Volume 1: Phonology. Volume 2: Morphology and Syntax*, edited by Bernd Kortmann and Edgar Werner Schneider, 450–80. Berlin: Mouton de Gruyter.

DeWalt, Kathleen Musante, and Billie R. DeWalt. 2011. *Participant Observation: A Guide for Fieldworkers*. Plymouth: Alta Mira Press.

Ebongue, Augustin Emmanuel, and Ellen Hurst 2017. *Sociolinguistics in African Contexts: Perspectives and Challenges*. Berlin: Springer.

Falceto, Francis. 2001. *Abyssinie Swing: A Pictorial History of Modern Ethiopian Music*. Addis Ababa: Shama Books.

Farquharson, Joseph T., Clive Forrester, and Andrea Hollington. 2020. "The Linguistics of Jamaican Swearing: Forms, Background and Adaptations". In *Swearing and Cursing: Contexts and Practices in a Critical Linguistic Perspective*, edited by Nico Nassenstein and Anne Storch, 147–64. Berlin, Boston: De Gruyter.

García, Ofelia, and Li Wei. 2014. *Translanguaging: Language, Bilingualism and Education*. Basingstoke: Palgrave Macmillan.

Hollington, Andrea. 2016. "Reflections on Ethiopia n Youths and Yarada K'wank'wa: Language Practices and Ideologies". *Sociolinguistic Studies* 10: 1–2.

———. 2018. "Transatlantic Translanguaging in Zimdancehall: Reassessing Linguistic Creativity in Youth Language Practices". *The Mouth* 3 (special issue: Critical Youth Languages Studies – Rethinking Concepts): 105–23.

Hope, Donna. 2006. *Inna di Dancehall: Popular Culture and the Politics of Identity in Jamaica*. Kingston: University of the West Indies Press.

Isenberg, Charles William, Johann Ludwig Krapf, and James MacQueen. 2011 [1843]. "Chapter III". *Journals of the Rev. Messrs Isenberg and Krapf, Missionaries of the Church Missionary Society: Detailing their Proceedings in the Kingdom of Shoa, and Journeys in Other Parts of Abyssinia, in the Years 1839, 1840, 1841, and 1842* (Cambridge Library Collection – Religion): 160–86. Cambridge: Cambridge University Press.

(The) Jamaican Language Unit/Di Jamiekan Langwij Yuunit. 2009. *Ou Fi Rait Jamiekan – Writing Jamaican the Jamaican Way*. Kingston: Arawak Publications.

Johnson, Richard. 2013. "Develop a Love for Amharic". *Jamaica Observer*, April 28, 2013.

Kasuka, Bridgette. 2013. *Prominent African Leaders Since Independence*. Cape Town: New Africa Press.

Katz, David. 2012. *Solid Foundation: An Oral History of Reggae*. London: Jawbone Press.

Kebede, Ashenafi. 1971. "The Music of Ethiopia: Its Development and Cultural Setting". PhD diss., Wesleyan University.

———. 1980. "The Sacred Chant of Ethiopian Monotheistic Churches: Music in Black Jewish and Christian Communities". *The Black Perspective in Music* 8 (1): 21–34.

———. 1992. *Roots of Black Music*. Englewood: Prentice-Hall.

Kießling, Roland, and Mous Maarten. 2004. "Urban Youth Languages in Africa". *Anthropological Linguistics* 46 (3): 303–41.
Le Page, Robert B., and Andrée Tabouret-Keller. 1985. *Acts of Identity: Creole-based Approaches to Language and Ethnicity*. Cambridge: Cambridge University Press.
Levine, Donald N. 1965. *Wax and Gold: Tradition and Innovation in Ethiopian Culture*. Chicago: Chicago University Press.
———. 2000 [1974]. *Greater Ethiopia: The Evolution of a Multiethnic Society*. Chicago: Chicago University Press.
Makoni, Sinfree, Geneva Smitherman, Arnetha F. Ball, and Arthur K. Spears, eds. 2003. *Black Linguistics: Language, Society, and Politics in Africa and the Americas*. London: Routledge.
Masiola, Rosanna. 2018. *Interjections, Translation, and Translanguaging: Cross-Cultural and Multimodal Perspectives*. Lanham: Lexington Books.
Mitchell, Tony, ed. 2001. *Global Noise: Rap and Hip-Hop Outside the USA*. Middletown: Wesleyan University Press.
Mufwene, Salikoko. 2010. "The ET Column: Globalization and the Spread of English: What Does It Mean to be Anglophone?" *English Today* 26: 57–59.
Mühleisen, Susanne. 2002. *Creole Discourse: Exploring Prestige Formation and Change Across Caribbean*. Amsterdam: John Benjamins.
Nassenstein, Nico, and Andrea Hollington, eds. 2015. *Youth Language Practices in Africa and Beyond*. Berlin: Mouton de Gruyter.
Owens, Joseph. 1976. *Dread: The Rastafarians of Jamaica*. Kingston: Sangster.
Patrick, Peter. 2003. "Creole, Community, Identity". In *The Politics of English as a World Language*, edited by Christian Mair, 249–77. Amsterdam and New York: Rodopi.
Patrick, Peter, and Esther Figueroa 2002. "Kiss-teeth". *American Speech* 77 (4): 383–97.
Poggi, Isabella. 2009. "The Language of Interjections". In *Multimodal Signals: Cognitive and Algorithmic Issues*, edited by Anna Esposito et al., 170–86. Berlin: Springer.
Pollard, Velma. 2000. *Dread Talk: The Language of Rastafari*. Montreal and Kingston: McGill-Queen's University Press and Canoe Press UWI.
Powne, Michael. 1968. *Ethiopian Music, an Introduction: A Survey of Ecclesiastical and Secular Ethiopian Music and Instruments*. London and New York: Oxford University Press.
Rampton, Ben. 2006. *Language in Late Modernity. Interaction in an Urban School*. Cambridge: Cambridge University Press.
Reckord, Verena. 1998. "From Burru to Reggae Riddims: The Evolution of Rasta Music". In *Chanting Down Babylon*, edited by Nathaniel Samuel Murrel, William David Spencer, and Adrian Anthony McFarlane, 231–52. Philadelphia: Temple University Press.
Reynolds, Dennis Jabari. 2006. *Jabari Authentic Jamaican Dictionary of the Jamic Language*. Waterbury: Around the Way Books.
Rickford, John R. 1987. *Dimensions of a Creole Continuum*. Stanford: Stanford University Press.

Riley, Philip. 2007. *Language Culture and Identity*. London: Continuum Academic.
Sàrosi, Bálint. 1967. "The Music of Ethiopian Peoples". *Studia Musicologica* 9: 9–20.
Shinn, David H., and Thomas P. Ofcansky, eds. 2013. *Historical Dictionary of Ethiopia*. Lanham: Scarecrow Press.
Smakman, Dick, and Patrick Heinrich. 2015. *Globalising Sociolinguistics: Challenging and Expanding Theory*. London: Routledge.
———. 2018. *Urban Sociolinguistics: The City as a Linguistic Process and Experience*. London: Routledge.
Spradley, James P. 1980. *Participant Observation*. Orlando: Harcourt College Publishers.
Stange, Ulrike. 2009. *The Acquisition of Interjections in Early Childhood*. Hamburg: Diplomica.
Stanley Niaah, Sonjah. 2010. *Dancehall: From Slave Ship to Ghetto*. Ottawa: University of Ottawa Press.
Tomei, Renato. 2015. *Jamaican Speech Forms in Ethiopia: The Emergence of a New Linguistic Scenario in Shashamane*. Newcastle: Cambridge Scholars Publishing.
———. 2017. "Contact Languages Counteracting Language Planning Policies: A New Lingua Franca in the Oromia Region (Ethiopia)". *Cultus* 10: 108–23.
Wharton, Tim. 2003. "Interjections, Language, and the 'Showing/Saying' Continuum". *Pragmatics and Cognition* 11 (1): 39–91.
Wierzbicka, Anna. 1992. "The Semantics of Interjection". *Journal of Pragmatics* 18: 159–92.
Wilkins, David. 1992. "Interjections as Deictics". *Journal of Pragmatics* 18: 119–58.
Winford, Donald. 1985. "The Concept of Diglossia in Caribbean Creole Situations". *Language in Society* 14 (3): 345–56.

Sitography

Daggy Shasha. "Ancheee!!!". https://www.youtube.com/watch?v=NjPe9hMeCHI.
DJ Dulas featuring Dagy Lion. "Hello Africa". https://www.youtube.com/watch?v=GsynprIrFuE.
Haile Roots. "MelkamYamarech". https://www.youtube.com/watch?v=8LmiVSGMtHA.
Jacob Miller. "Tenement Yard". https://www.youtube.com/watch?v=g5sOdcK2hp4.
Jah Lude featuring Tadele Roba. "Asio Bellema". https://www.youtube.com/watch?v=uitISGfz-ys.
Jonny Ragga. "Kulfun Sechig". https://www.youtube.com/watch?v=nE6uUFRu_VU.
Jonny Ragga. "One Way Ticket". https://www.youtube.com/watch?v=MmFDGyQxsi4&index=2&list=PLizDlWrwP3YQpWbI87gsejvxzDUJySmXC.
Ras Biruk featuring Lenny Kurlou. "AffiGo!". https://www.youtube.com/watch?v=26pRngNmovI.
Ras Charmer. "Such a Long Way". https://www.youtube.com/watch?v=oCIjKZOKRRQ.

Ras Jany. "Mi Phone a Ring". https://www.youtube.com/watch?v=8HJhsqY_uuc.
Ras Jany and Don Deltafa. "Feeling Irie". https://www.youtube.com/watch?v=CZByyoIOJpk.
Ras Jany featuring Jerusalem. "Hule Hule". https://www.youtube.com/watch?v=MkxjaffrPKI.
Sami Dan. "Dimts Alba Sew". https://www.youtube.com/watch?v=Mq_T5buEAGM.
Sizzla Kalonji. "Step Aside". https://www.youtube.com/watch?v=2zNslfvPiHk.
Teddy Afro. "Lambadina". https://www.youtube.com/watch?v=wxV-n9iSkEs.
Teddy Afro featuring Haile Roots. "Bob Marley". https://www.youtube.com/watch?v=2FT1rHQYP0s.
UNESCO website. https://ich.unesco.org/en/RL/reggae-music-of-jamaica-01398.
Youths of Shasha – The Movie. https://www.youtube.com/watch?v=UV-gBrY-R30.

Chapter 13

Caribbean Identity in Pop Music

Rihanna's and Nicki Minaj's Multivocal Pop Personas

LISA JANSEN AND MICHAEL WESTPHAL

Introduction

Music as an intrinsic part of pop culture condenses linguistic and cultural complexities. Pop culture in general, and music in particular, serves as a major driving force for the global spread of English varieties (Pennycook 2007). These include both internationally prestigious varieties that carry overt prestige, such as American English (AmE), and language varieties that have long been marginalized and stigmatized – for example, African American English (AAE) or Caribbean English Creoles (CECs). In singing, all varieties occur as somewhat abstracted forms, that is as singing styles. An American or Americanized singing style, for instance, combines typical standard (e.g. rhoticity and /t/-flapping) as well as non-standard (PRICE monophthongization and the negator *ain't*) features predominantly associated with the United States (e.g. Simpson 1999). Music has played a crucial role in elevating these varieties to imitation-worthy linguistic resources and continues to strengthen their position in pop culture and as supercentral varieties in the World System of Englishes (Mair 2013). This study focuses on Rihanna and Nicki Minaj and their role in promoting the global spread of CECs. Both artists are known, heard and seen across the globe displaying their (Afro-)Caribbean heritage through their pop personas.

Adopting a qualitative, multimodal approach, we investigate how these two internationally successful artists explicitly draw attention to their Caribbeanness. A linguistic analysis of their performances sheds light on their use of CECs, complemented by a visual analysis of the accompanying music videos which exemplify the display of Caribbean tropes. Apart from the production side, the audience's perception of and attitudes towards Rihanna's and Minaj's performances are considered, using the video platform YouTube, which invites for comments and metalinguistic discussions.

In this chapter, we first discuss the multimodality and multivocality of pop performances and then briefly present background information on Rihanna and Minaj. The following sections illustrate the methods and results of our multimodal analysis. In the conclusion, we discuss the results on the use and perception of CECs in Rihanna's and Minaj's performances at the intersection of the sociolinguistics of globalization and performance.

Music as a Multimodal Product

Artists like Rihanna and Minaj are international pop personas. A persona is a publicly projected role which can consist of interacting real as well as artificial identities or alter egos. These can have different voices which display coexisting identities (Jansen and Westphal 2017, 5; Trudgill 1983, 158–60). Most performances where an artist displays their persona are not authentic in a traditional sociolinguistic sense but stylized linguistically, since language use, from writing lyrics to singing, is planned and rehearsed, and visually, by staging performers and songs in music videos (Bell and Gibson 2011). Additionally, further types of representation on (social) media platforms, from interviews to Tweets to fashion labels and perfumes, are produced to project the artists and their work.

As globally successful pop performers, Rihanna and Minaj travel the globe and explicitly put different language varieties on display wherever they go. The spread of singers' linguistic styles and resources is facilitated by being part of the vast and ever-growing mediascape (Appadurai 1996), where their work is not only produced and reproduced but the audience has the opportunity to participate and interact. This highlights another important aspect of music's inherent multimodality: the audience. The role of the audience as the counterpart of the performer has long been neglected in linguistic research, although it plays a vital role in performances (Bell and Gibson 2011, 563; Jansen 2018). The audience carefully scrutinizes and evaluates how performers act on and off stage. It expects to be entertained by skilful performances. Ultimately, the audience plays a decisive role in assessing whether a performance and, in turn, the performer is successful. The audience's evaluation in the form of newspaper articles, blog entries, YouTube comments or any other possible medium of participation can give insight into attitudes towards language performances and identity constructions.

Music as Space for Negotiating Identity

In sociolinguistic research of music, various motivations for choosing a particular singing style[1] have been investigated and discussed. Trudgill's seminal text (1983) explores why many British singers of the 1950s and 1960s preferred an Americanized singing style. American music genres have dominated the field since they first emerged in the US South, turning their singing style into a linguistic role model. This type of active referee design (Bell 1992) has over decades turned into a well-established trend and a quasi-natural way of singing. Sounding American is not necessarily an active choice but has developed into a default emulation of a conventionalized singing style associated with originally American music genres such as pop and rock (Beal 2009). Hence, using an Americanized singing style nowadays is rather associated with mainstream music than with America itself.

Out of this American sounding status quo (re-)emerged the trend of "going local". Punk as well as indie pop and rock bands choose to stand out from this well-established Americanized singing style and actively stylize the local by mediating their vernaculars (Beal 2009; Trudgill 1983). Not only does the "going local" trend contribute to a display of various accents, dialects or varieties, but it also leads to localness and localization becoming part of the respective genres' philosophies. Indie bands authenticate themselves by stylizing the local. Hip-hop provides the very similar credo of "keepin' it real" (O'Hanlon 2006, 201–02), which calls on rappers to stay true to their roots, be authentic. This idea is so inextricably linked to hip-hop that localized varieties are an integral part of this genre around the globe (Pennycook 2007). In the United States, where hip-hop has originated as an African American subculture, AAE is the dominant vernacular of hip-hop (Richardson 2006, 1–21). AAE has also become an integral part of rap performances by non-African American artists around the world (see Akande, 2012, for Nigerian examples; Eberhardt and Freeman, 2015, for Australian examples). While some of these artists cross entirely into AAE in their performances (Eberhardt and Freeman 2015), others combine AAE with other English varieties and languages to a "linguistic bricolage" (Eckert 2008, 456; see also Akande 2012; Pennycook 2007). Thus, AAE is used to perform a hip-hop identity in subcultures. At the same time, AAE, as a stigmatized variety in the United States, has become a commodity in rap performances, which is also adopted by non-African American mainstream artists (Eberhardt and Freeman 2015).

The discourse of Jamaican Creole (JC) in music is similar to that of AAE. JC is the first language of the majority of Jamaicans but is not fully standardized or fully officially recognized on the island. While JC is codified, for example, in terms of spelling (e.g. Cassidy and Le Page 2002), this codified form is only applied in specific cases but not by the wider population (Deuber and Hinrichs 2007). In Jamaica, it coexists with the country's sole official language, English, which in practice means Standard Jamaican English. JC has a long history of linguistic discrimination as "broken English" similar to other CECs. In the course of the twentieth century, the status of JC and other CECs has improved markedly, as they are now often valued as symbols of national identity (Devonish and Harry 2008, 256–57; Patrick 2008, 609–10). The local and global popularity of Jamaican popular music has saliently contributed to the increased value of JC (Mair 2013, 264). Current dancehall music is dominated by JC whether performed by Jamaican artists (Farquharson 2017, 11) or non-Jamaicans (Gerfer 2018). While some non-Jamaican artists almost exclusively use JC in their songs (Gerfer 2018), other performers mix it with other varieties of English (Akande 2012) or languages (Chapter 10; Westphal 2018). JC has not only become a global resource for the performance of a subcultural reggae persona, but it is also used in other genres: Leung (2009, 527) shows how Trinidadian artists combine JC with Trinidadian English Creole in ragga soca music "to give voice to a distinctive Afro-Trinidadian identity".

Most studies have focused exclusively on (recorded) performances of lyrics, whereas the perspective of the audience and other modalities of pop performances, such as music videos, interviews or social media posts, have been largely neglected (see, however, Jansen 2022). There is a wide body of research on hip-hop and AAE, and a growing discourse on JC in reggae and dancehall, but other music genres and CECs are still under-researched. This study presents a multimodal analysis of Rihanna's and Minaj's multivocal pop personas. We investigate how these two mainstream artists combine different linguistic resources (with a focus on CECs) as well as visual modalities in their performances. Additionally, we analyse how the audience reacts to their multivocality. In detail, we aim to answer the following research questions:

- Which linguistic resources do Rihanna and Minaj use in their performances? Are there patterns?
- Which other modalities are used to construct their pop personas?
- How does the audience perceive the performances?

Data and Method

Rihanna and Minaj are both globally successful pop artists who live in the United States and have Caribbean roots. Rihanna was born (1988) and raised in Barbados, but relocated to the United States in 2005 when signing her first major label contract. Minaj was born in Trinidad (1982), the larger island of the twin-island state of Trinidad and Tobago, but grew up in Queens, New York City. Furthermore, they combine different musical styles (R 'n' B, hip-hop, reggae, pop) and the performance codes associated with said genres (AAE, JC, AmE). Their linguistic repertoires potentially also include the vernaculars of their home islands, Bajan and Trinidadian English Creole. These diverse varieties are part of their multivocal pop personas, which reflect their African American and Caribbean American identities.

We explore how Rihanna and Minaj perform their Caribbeanness from a production and perception point of view. The YouTube videos of Rihanna's single "Work" (A) and Minaj's feature in Jamaican singer Mavado's "Give It All to Me" (B) serve as the primary data. "Work" has received heightened media attention due to Rihanna's use of CEC (Jansen and Westphal 2017) and "Give It All to Me" is a typical example of a collaboration of Minaj with a Caribbean artist. In addition, we analysed a social media performance of Minaj speaking JC, which is part of a behind-the-scenes video (C). This performance went viral and fans reposted the excerpt of Minaj speaking JC on YouTube (D, E). For Rihanna, we included an interview in which she states she had to change her accent for her career (F). Table 13.1 shows an overview of the YouTube videos.

For the two music videos and Minaj's social media performance, we analysed the diverse linguistic resources in the performances of both artists with regard to morphosyntax, lexis and accent. In order to demonstrate the complex linguistic variation, we identified individual linguistic features that are typical of CECs (Allsopp 2003; Hackert 2012; Roberts 2007), in particular JC (Cassidy and Le Page 2002; Devonish and Harry 2008; Patrick 2008) and Bajan (Blake 2008), AAE (Green 2002) and AmE (Kretzschmar 2008; Simpson 1999). In our visual analysis, we focused on the use of Caribbean semiotic resources in the music videos.

In addition, we examined the perception of the audience towards Rihanna's and Minaj's multivocal performances by conducting a qualitative content analysis (Kuckartz 2012) of YouTube comments on all videos. First, we preselected 100 comments from each video that addressed the artists' language or identity. If the 100th comment was at the beginning of

Table 13.1 Overview of Data

	Title of Video	Date of Publication	YouTube Channel	Views[a]	Comments[a]	Selected Comments
A	"Rihanna - Work (Explicit) ft. Drake" https://www.youtube.com/watch?v=HL1UzIK-flA&ab_channel=RihannaVEVO	22 February 2016	Rihanna	1,033,027,998	385,474	103
B	"Mavado – Give It All To Me ft. Nicki Minaj" https://www.youtube.com/watch?v=9sbuoFy32Kc	4 November 2013	Mavado Gully Official	49,852,327	4,815	88
C	"Nicki Minaj Anaconda Video: Behind The Scenes Vlog" https://www.youtube.com/watch?v=4riuBBmcpLs	7 August 2014	Nicki Minaj	14,544,038	2,567	109
D	"Nicki minaj drunk talk comments" https://www.youtube.com/watch?v=ZNgwiugN9oo	8 August 2014	Valan Turkish	208,647	191	38
E	"nickiminajjamaican accent//2015" https://www.youtube.com/watch?v=6_CJJMDSIHg	8 August 2015	macckeLLy	85,704	100	22
F	"Rihanna on her accent" https://www.youtube.com/watch?v=5dnrohN4PoA	12 April 2014	The Celeb Factory	3,270,679	1,458	116

[a] On 27 February 2019.

a discussion or mid-discussion, the following comments belonging to that discussion were included as well. Ultimately, the data collection includes 219 comments on Rihanna and 257 on Minaj. We then developed a coding scheme deductively: the comments were closely read and grouped into similar and distinctive statements. Subsequently, codes were allocated to these groups. This process was repeated until the need for new codes was saturated. The developed codes were refined to establish meaningful and comprehensible categories. The codes were summarized in a codebook, which also includes anchor examples and coding instructions to ensure methodological transparency.

Audiovisual Analysis

Rihanna's single "Work", which features Canadian rapper Drake, is a multilayered composition on several levels. Musically, it mixes dancehall, pop music, contemporary R 'n' B and hip-hop. On a content level, Rihanna addresses the work she has to put into her career, romantic relationships and fulfilling sexual desires. While Drake's part is monostylistic in "informal English", Rihanna combines CECs, most notably JC and Bajan, with AmE and possibly AAE.

On a morphosyntactic level, the lyrics (see the appendix) contain various CEC features: modal auxiliary *hafi* and quotative *se* (line 2: *he se me hafi work*); the absence of 3 SG {-s} (line 3: *he see*); future marker *a go* (line 5: *when you a go learn*); the personal pronouns *me* and *him* in subject position (line 6: *me na care if him hurt*); copula absence and negator *na* (line 10: *you na righteous*). The majority of these features is used in most CECs, all of them are pervasive in JC: for example, copula absence is very frequent in all CECs, whereas negator *na* is prevalent in JC but is absent in Bajan (Hackert 2012, 716). However, Rihanna also uses Standard English (StE) grammar: she employs StE pronouns *I, me, my, you* and *your*, negation with do-support, SV concord and StE copula forms.

Rihanna's accent variation in "Work" shows a similar linguistic repertoire. Her accent is marked by features typical of Caribbean Englishes and Creoles: for example, the realization of FACE as a monophthong (line 12: *adoration*; line 13: *patience*; line 14: *decoration*; line 15: *foundation*); word-final consonant cluster absence (line 9: *dealt, nicest*; line 11: *text*; line 19: *act*); and TH-stopping (line 15: *with, the*). Rihanna's accent is also marked by word-initial H-absence (lines 6, 7, 8: *him*; line 6: *hurt*), a salient feature of JC. On an accent level, Bajan is crucial to Rihanna's linguistic repertoire. Particularly in the chorus, Rihanna's pronunciation is marked by a high degree of nasalization and an under-articulation of consonants, creating a typical Bajan sound pattern (Roberts 2007, 96–97). Two further Bajan accent features are Rihanna's almost consistent rhotic pronunciation and her realizations of *act* and *it* (line 8) with a word-final glottal stop. Yet, Rihanna's performance also includes AmE pronunciation patterns: she realizes TH as an interdental fricative in *that* (lines 16–18) and *this*; retains consonant clusters in *believed* (line 12) and *don't* (lines 22, 23); realizes FACE with an upgliding diphthong [eɪ] in *baby* (line 22), *babe* (line 30) and *say* (line 30); and realizes the BATH tokens in *chance* (line 24) and *past* (line 26) as [æ].

The analysis shows that the most salient variation in Rihanna's performance is between CECs, mostly JC and Bajan, and AmE. AAE is another potential influence, as Rihanna uses several morphosyntactic and accent features shared by AAE and CECs but no AAE-exclusive characteristics. However, this variation is not random but correlates with the mode of discourse. The CEC accent and morphosyntactic features occur most consistently in the chorus (lines 1–6) and the first verse (lines 7–11). In these parts of the song, Rihanna rather speaks, which seems to bring out her Caribbean voice. In contrast, her singing style in the last two verses (lines 12–30) is mainly produced with an AmE accent. Although Rihanna combines different CECs, AmE and potentially AAE, she does not blend them completely. Her multivocal persona is constructed by the coexistence and only partial overlap of diverse linguistic features.

Similar to the strong presence of CEC in the lyrics, the video produced for "Work" also highlights a wide range of visual images prototypical of the Caribbean. The video portrays a dancehall event, set in a Caribbean restaurant in Toronto, called The Real Jerk. The venue is decorated with the pan-African colours black, red, green and yellow, which trigger associations with the Caribbean, reggae and Rastafari. Rihanna displays a dancehall queen persona, wears a Bajan flag as an accessory and performs typical dancehall moves such as a specific type of wining (being in a crouched position with her hands on her knees).[2] The audience drinks Jamaican (Red Stripe) and Trinidadian (Carib) beer, consumes marijuana and eats jerk chicken – a Jamaican specialty.

In her interview (video F, "Rihanna on her accent"), Rihanna reports on the linguistic pressure of having to adapt her accent for the sake of interviews and business conversation to make sure that she is clearly understood. The ability to switch from her Caribbean language use towards AmE norms is crucial for her music and acting career. She does not mention that she had to accommodate her accent towards AmE, but this norm seems to be implied. For Rihanna it is clear that her Bajan accent is unintelligible for people outside the Caribbean and that switching to AmE is an essential skill.

Nicki Minaj's music performance "Give It All to Me" is a collaboration with the Jamaican dancehall artist Mavado (see the appendix for lyrics). In this song, she has a rap (lines 1–12) and a singing part (lines 13–21). The song mixes dancehall with hip-hop and pop elements. The lyrics express feelings of (hetero)sexual attraction and desire, but Minaj's rap part is a typical self-referential battle rap, including self-praise and dissing other rappers. Whereas Mavado's language use is entirely in JC, Minaj's linguistic repertoire is similarly multivocal to Rihanna's: she uses an abundance of CEC features which are all typical of JC (but not Trinidadian English Creole) and mixes them with AmE and AAE. On a morphosyntactic level, Jamaican features include conjunction *se* (line 2: *tell dem se*), pronoun *dem* and *me* in subject position as well as past marker *did* plus aspectual *a* (line 4: *everything me did a start dem borrow*), copula absence (line 2: *we straight*; line 3: *the flow tight*; line 8: *these bitches my sons*) and the preposition *ina* (line 21: *pretty gang ina the place*). For individual tokens Minaj employs a Caribbean pronunciation: she pronounces TH as a stop in *everything* (line 4), *the* (lines 3, 21) and *them* (lines 1–3). The realization of FACE in *straight* with a downgliding diphthong as [ˈʃtrɪeːt] (line 2) is typical of JC. She also uses several lexical items prototypical of Jamaica, dancehall and Rastafari with a Jamaican pronunciation. *Bad gyal* (line 9), realized as [bad gjal] with a lowered TRAP and a palatal glide, is Minaj's dancehall catchphrase and *tell dem (se)* (lines 1–3) is a typical dancehall catchphrase. *Lick* (line 1: *lick a shot*) is prevalent in JC (Cassidy and Le Page 2002, 273). The term *burn fire*, realized as [bon faɪja], is a Rastafarian "fire bon metaphor" (Cooper 2004, 179–206). Thus, Minaj expresses her Caribbeanness mainly through JC and a reggae and dancehall register, while Trinidadian English Creole is not part of her linguistic repertoire.

While these JC features are highly salient, the baseline of Minaj's rap part is a typical hip-hop register (e.g. Richardson 2006), characterized by AAE as well as lexical items and tropes specific to hip-hop. She uses several AAE features: copula absence and TH-stopping (shard with CECs) and PRICE monophthongs (line 8: *I tied my* [aː taːd maː]). She also uses several lexical items specific to hip-hop, such as *flow*, *tight* and *bitches* (Richardson 2006, 18, 33–34). Minaj employs the prototypical hip-hop tropes of bling-bling (i.e. the celebration of materialism), referring to her expensive car (line 6: *coupe black and blue*), and toughness, invoking the image of a gun (line 1: *lick a shot*) and dissing other rappers (line 8: *these bitches my sons*).

AmE is also part of Minaj's performance. All TRAP (except *bad*) and BATH vowels are realized as [æ] (line 6: *black*; line 10: *Instagram*; line 15: *man*; line 12: *ask*; line 14: *dance*) and her accent is categorically rhotic, in contrast to Trinidadian English and Trinidadian English Creole, which are both non-rhotic; all FACE (except *straight*) and GOAT tokens are realized as upgliding diphthongs [eɪ] and [oʊ] (lines 18–19: *baby, own*). Except for the CEC and AAE morphosyntactic features listed, Minaj's grammar is dominantly StE. For example, she uses the StE pronouns *I, me, my, you* and *your*.

Similar to Rihanna's performance in "Work", Minaj's multivocal performance combines different varieties but does not blend them completely as the distribution patterns with the mode of discourse. The rap part (lines 1–12) can be characterized as a hip-hop register into which Minaj inserts several prototypical JC features. The singing part of her performance (lines 13–21) is in StE grammar with an AmE pronunciation.

The video to "Give It All to Me" depicts a beach party. The participants drink cocktails and perform dancehall-style dance moves. They also wave flags from different Caribbean countries, such as Grenada, Barbados, Bahamas, Jamaica, Trinidad and Tobago, and Haiti. Minaj is shown holding a Trinbagonian flag, which she waves towards the camera in her last verse of the rap part (line 12: *Caribbean girls run it, ask Riri*, i.e. Rihanna). In this way, Minaj highlights her Caribbeanness visually and reinforces it by aligning herself with Rihanna.

The embedding of JC and Caribbean images into her performance is typical of several songs of Minaj, especially collaborations with Caribbean artists. She also uses JC in social media. In the performance selected, Minaj supposedly imitates a "rant video" of a female Jamaican who insults her ex-boyfriend and his lover.[3] Minaj's "mock-rant" performance is highly repetitive and a concatenation of individual but not necessarily connected utterances with a high density of prototypical Jamaican lexical, grammatical and accent features. Central to this performance is the word *bloodcloth*, realized as [blɔdklaːt] (lines 4, 5, 7), a Jamaican cuss word referring to a sanitary towel (Allsopp 2003, 107) which is used as a discourse marker expressing speaker stance. She also repeatedly uses the Caribbean expression *vex* (very angry; lines: 2–3; Allsopp 2003, 582). On a morphosyntactic level, she employs JC pronouns 1 SG *me* in subject position (lines 2, 3) and in possessive case (lines 3–4) and 2 PL *unu* (line 4). She also uses the negator *na* in *why me na vex* (line 2). Her accent is marked by downgliding FACE (line 3: *baby* [bɪebɪ]) and GOAT (lines 6–9: *know* [nʊo]) diphthongs, the realization of STRUT as [o] (line 3: *but*) and TH-stopping (line 4: *father*; line 10: *that*). In the video, it is clearly transparent that Minaj steps into a performance mode

(Bell and Gibson 2011, 557) when imitating JC and switches back to her baseline at the end of the scene. She intentionally uses JC in an exaggerated way as a symbolic resource to achieve a comic effect, and the audience (e.g. her entourage in the video) also receives it as comedic.

Qualitative Content Analysis of YouTube Comments

The content analysis shows that the comment section of YouTube videos is a fruitful space not only for metalinguistic discussions, ranging from discourse on language labels to perceptions and attitudes to ideologies, but also for forming and strengthening group identity. According to the two main preselection criteria, language and identity are the main topics discussed in this section.

Overall, the language performances of both artists are vital points for discussion and introduce many different descriptive labels. These were initially broadly sorted by their most defining descriptions, that is for most cases their regional allocation. For instance, descriptions like "Jamaican Patwa", "jamaica dialect" and "Jamaican accent" were subsumed under the code **Jamaican**. This process led to identifying seven major language codes (listed from most to least frequent): **Jamaican** (JAM), **Bajan** (BAJ), **English** (ENG), **Patois/Creole** (Patois),[4] **Caribbean** (CARIBBEAN), **Trinidadian** (TRI), **broken English** (brENG). Apart from describing the artists' language performances, matters of intelligibility turned out to be a heatedly debated topic within this discourse. To illustrate this debate, four codes were created: **unintelligibility** included cases in which subjects state that they do not understand the language used in the form of a request for a translation. The code **translations** covers all types of serious translations or explanations provided to make the performed language intelligible for others. **Mock transcriptions** subsumed all kinds of ridiculing and nonsensical lyrics imitating the sounds perceived, not the actual language. **Insults** were coded accordingly when the artist and her language behaviour were verbally attacked.

The perception of the singers' identities was not as diverse as the language descriptions. When a subject stated that the singer is Trinidadian, from Trinidad (and Tobago) or was born on Trinidad, the code **she is Trinidadian** (Trini) was allocated. The same coding rules apply for **she is Bajan** (Bajan), **she is Caribbean** (Caribbean), **she is from Jamaica/Queens/NYC** (Queens) and **she is American** (American). Since Rihanna and Minaj mix and blend various linguistic resources in their performances, the topic of inauthenticity occurred within the data. Whenever a comment accused one of the artists of being fake (e.g. stating that Minaj as a Trinidadian should not use JC) the code **inauthenticity** was allocated. Comments expressing positive attitudes or solidarity with the performers and their language were labelled **positive**.

Figure 13.1 shows that Minaj's performance is predominantly characterized as Jamaican followed by Patois. Only some name it Trinidadian, but it is hardly called Caribbean. English does not occur at all. In contrast, Rihanna's language is mainly classified as Bajan with the label English in second place. Only few subjects call it Caribbean or Jamaican. Overall, these labels show that although one language is clearly dominant for the respective artist, there are a range of other language influences perceived by the subjects. The term "broken English" occurs in a few comments but is interestingly not used pejoratively and by Caribbean subjects themselves. In general, the results confirm the Caribbeanness of the singers' performances, but nonetheless a multitude of labels is provided and heated debates over the most appropriate language descriptions take place. It is not just the general language label that is discussed but also its further specification, that is descriptive terms such as accent, dialect or language, as the following excerpt on Rihanna's language performance in "Work" exemplifies. This discourse, however, seems to be essentially an inner-Caribbean one:

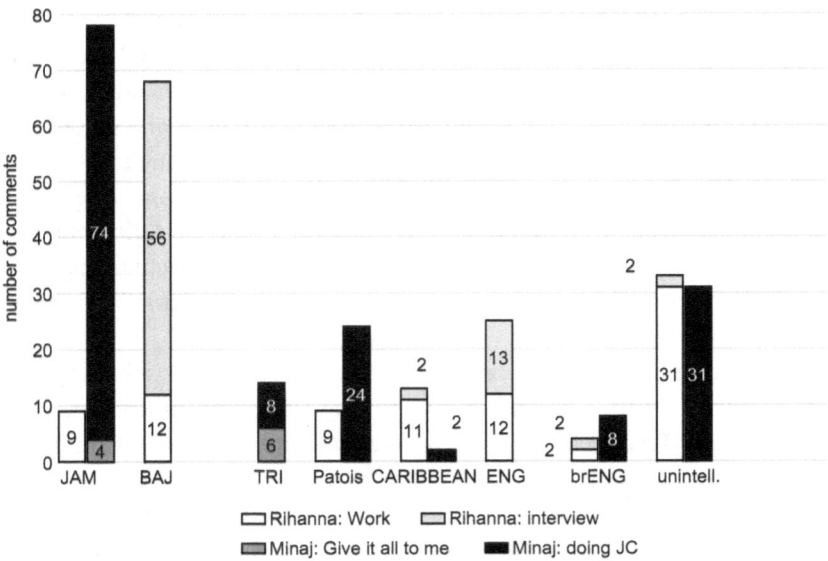

Figure 13.1 Language labels and unintelligibility.

- "Rihanna is from Barbados she is speaking <u>patwa</u> for those who think she is <u>not speaking English</u>"
- "She's speaking <u>caribbean dialect</u>."
- "she's speaking a <u>Caribbean language</u>."
- "It's a language but it's also the <u>Caribbean accent</u> that makes it hard to understand."
- "she is speaking <u>bajain</u>"
- "Rihanna used <u>Barbadian English</u> in some of the verses"
- "she speaking <u>creole</u>"

Figure 13.1 illustrates that the more the subjects speculate about the variety used (i.e. more different language labels are used), the higher the degree of unintelligibility. Rihanna's performance in "Work" and Minaj's imitation of JC reach high ratings of unintelligibility as opposed to their other videos analysed. This observation goes hand in hand with the denser and less prototypical use of CEC features. The discussions on matters of intelligibility demonstrate a rift between an in-group, subjects directly or indirectly identifying as Caribbean, and a non-Caribbean out-group. The latter mostly reveals itself by admitting difficulties in understanding the performances. Such comments range from questions, "What language is she speaking in?", to mock translations, "All I heard was wer wer wer wer wer wer wer wer der der der der der der mer mer mer mer mer", or even insults, "she's a bitch that doesn't even know how to properly talk". The latter two are exclusively found in comments concerning Rihanna's performance in "Work". It is striking that although one video of each performer is widely considered unintelligible, the respective reactions and counter-reactions unfolding are quite different. In case of Rihanna's "Work", eleven mock transcriptions and nine insults are posted. One subject even provides a mock translation for the entire song pointing out that "Drake's part [is] in English", making a transcription obsolete, and then continuing with "(Rihanna again) Gimmy adder worg worg worg worg worg worg". This example shows a clear juxtaposition of Drake's intelligible English and Rihanna's unintelligible mixture of CECs, which clearly serves as a source of amusement and ridicule. The in-group often reacts in a defensive, them-versus-us fashion. It defines the out-group and dissociates itself from them: "ignorant people who love visiting the islands but have a problem with the native tongue". Concerning Minaj's imitation of JC in her mock-rant, however, most comments on unintelligibility are rather neutral and much less offensive. Most subjects simply ask about information on the language used and others provide this information, offering not mocking but serious transcriptions or translations of her imitation of JC:

- "Can someone translate?"
- "she basically said that he and drake were gonna make the people lose their minds, then she proceeds to ask wht yall knew about swiffer and pinesol (cleaning objects). then she says they dont now about these things that can be purchased at the dollar store"

Figure 13.2 highlights that while the subjects seem to know that Rihanna is from Barbados, the identity labels used to describe Minaj are more mixed. Although she is a US American citizen, she is overwhelmingly identified as Trinidadian and only few consider her American. Some specifically mention her growing up in Jamaica, Queens, New York City. Negative evaluations of Minaj's JC performance are mainly based on the perception of Minaj's identity and her performance as fake. Among the comments that overall describe her as inauthentic, there are negative statements from Jamaicans who dislike her use of "their language": "I'm tired of this chick keep talking Jamaican Patwa. Rep your own country, leave Jamaica Alone". And there are subjects who note that she does not represent Trinidad but Jamaica instead: "Nicki Minaj being repping JA way more THAN her Trinidadian culture. . .". She is also criticized for

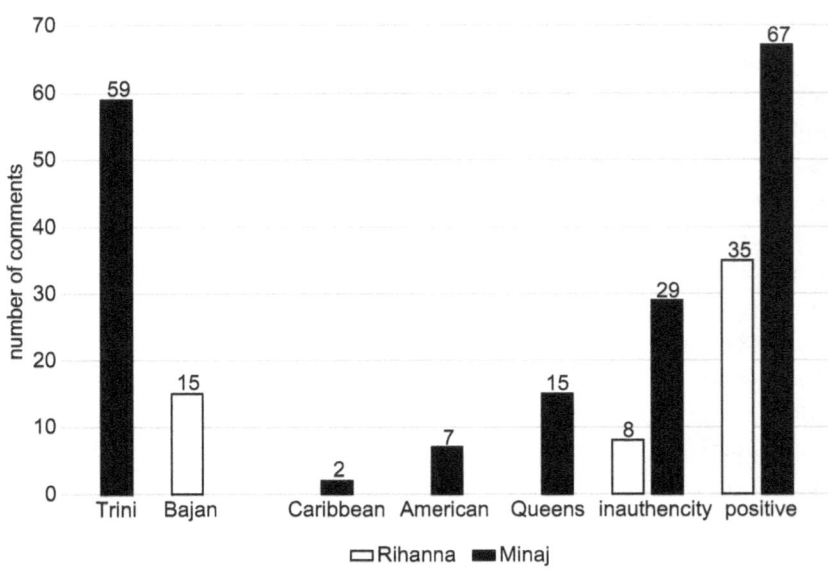

Figure 13.2 Rihanna and Minaj: identity labels, inauthenticity, positive comments.

faking JC: "She sounds like a bad freshwater yankee.⁵ That didn't sound Jamaican. Neither did it sound Trini". When others come to her defence they often mention her upbringing in Jamaica, Queens, New York City, as a valid reason why she could be fluent in JC. So although being accused of appropriating JC on the one hand, she is praised for her performance and for representing the Caribbean and Trinidad on the other: "tehe..I love when she talks in our Jamaican Accent..lol.." or "MY girl Nicki representing Trinidad & Tobago in style". As Minaj refers to Rihanna (Riri) in her music performance, we additionally counted fifty-eight reposts (not included in figure 13.2) of her utterance "Caribbean girls run it, ask Riri" in the comment section, with which, against all critique, she validates herself as a Caribbean artist.

In the case of Rihanna, inauthenticity appears to be a minor issue and it only comes up in comments to her interview. Here, subjects either mention that she has lost her Bajan accent for an American one or that she is imitating it. What is more striking are thirty-two comments by fellow Caribbeans and speakers of other stigmatized varieties expressing solidarity and sharing similar experiences of having to accommodate to standard English to be understood and accepted: "I have a Hispanic accent and when i apply for a job or i have a job interview i am nervous because of my accent – [...] its seen as unprofessional. If you aren't Hispanic dont talk like you know what we go through". Although Rihanna does not score as many positive evaluations as Minaj, which is probably explained by less debate on identity and authenticity taking place in general, one of the main characteristics mentioned is that her accent is *sexy*.

Performing Caribbean Identity in Pop Music

Both Rihanna and Minaj use a range of different varieties to express their multivocal pop personas. They combine CECs with AmE and AAE to perform both a Caribbean and African American identity. In "Work", Rihanna highlights her home vernacular Bajan and combines it with JC and AmE. Minaj's musical performance mainly uses AAE and a hip-hop register in combination with AmE and individual JC features. The performance of Minaj's Caribbeanness relies strongly on JC and associations with other Caribbean artists. Trinidadian English Creole is never part of her pop persona. While Minaj's social media performance is a close imitation of a Jamaican and dancehall referee (Bell 1992; Gerfer 2018), the two mainstream pop performances combine CEC features with other language varieties into a "linguistic bricolage" (Eckert 2008, 456) –

similar to findings in previous research on the globalization of JC and AAE in music (Akande 2012; Leung 2009; Pennycook 2007; Westphal 2018).

However, there is no complete blend of these resources and their distribution is not random but correlates with the mode of discourse. CECs and AAE are predominantly used in rapped and spoken parts, while AmE is largely reserved for singing. This structured bricolage displays the complexity of Rihanna's and Minaj's multivocal pop personas being both Caribbean and African American: there is no identity conflict (Trudgill 1983) but fluid coexistence.

Both artists use an abundance of cultural references in their videos to construct their Caribbeanness. They draw on and reinforce stereotypes. The Caribbean is connected to promiscuous dancing, the consumption of marijuana and alcohol, and a carefree party vibe. Especially in "Work", Caribbean culture and language are exoticized and commodified as sexy. Minaj's performances reinforce different stereotypes of JC. The fully functional Creole language is reduced to a symbolic resource for cussing and comic relief in the mock-rant and serves mere emblematic function (Blommaert 2010, 29) in "Give It All to Me".

The perceptions of the multivocal performances are multifaceted. Among an out-group audience there is a discourse of unintelligibility ranging from interest, to ridicule and linguistic discrimination, and is met with harsh resistance from an in-group. The results on intelligibility corroborate further reactions on the internet concerning Rihanna's "Work", which include ridiculing memes and posts devaluing CEC as gibberish (Jansen and Westphal 2017). However, CEC is also valued as exotic and sexy in the comments. An in-group discourse on inauthenticity is mainly notable for Minaj: comments accuse her of cultural appropriation (Eberhardt and Freeman 2015) of JC and denial of her Trinidadian heritage. Still, the appreciation for promoting the Caribbean is more dominant. Rihanna's Caribbeanness is never questioned, and her statements about the pressure of linguistic accommodation are met with solidarity. While Rihanna's and Minaj's performances are almost unequivocally perceived as Caribbean, there is much variation when it comes to describing their language use. The diverse labels and the debates surrounding them give insight into language ideological debates in the Caribbean dealing with the status of CECs: the ideologically loaded labels range from language, to dialect, accent and broken English. This debate also shows that there are vastly diverging ideas about what Creole and Patois actually are on a folk-linguistic level (Sebba and Dray 2012, 263).

The results demonstrate that language production and perception relate closely to each other. Performances with a high density of CEC features on several linguistic levels ("Work" and Minaj's mock-rant) trigger more uncertainty about the exact labels, more comments on intelligibility, more negative reactions and thus more heated discussions. In contrast, Minaj's insertion of a few prototypical JC items into her rap combined with a Trinidadian flag and her affiliation to Rihanna is largely celebrated.

In sum, the analysis shows that CECs are a central aspect of Rihanna's and Minaj's pop personas, who put these historically marginalized languages on display for a global audience. However, in this mainstream pop mediascape (Appadurai 1996), Creoles undergo noticeable changes. JC has come to represent CECs and Caribbeanness in general but is often presented in a stereotypical and truncated (Blommaert 2010, 102–36) manner. Furthermore, the use of Creoles beyond stereotypical features is met with stigmatization by non-Caribbean audiences. In pop culture, CECs are only a commodity if artists are able to code-switch to the predominant AmE norms. This conclusion corroborates Blommaert's (2010, 41–62) descriptions of the new linguistic inequalities caused by globalization.

In conclusion, we wish to make a case for researching music as a multimodal phenomenon in linguistics. Pop music does not only provide a space for the production and spread of CECs and other language varieties but also for the negotiation of language ideologies and performed identities. YouTube videos and comments provide rich data for the analysis of the dynamic process of language production and perception.

Notes

1. "Singing style" does not only refer to various linguistic resources that can be incorporated but also to the "mode of discourse" (Simpson 1999, 351), that is the manner, in which a song is delivered. Simply put, whether an artist raps, does melodic storytelling, or sings – to name but a few modes of discourse.

2. Wining – "dance erotically by swinging the hips vigorously while thrusting the buttocks back and forth" (Allsopp 2003, 606).

3. Jamaican Matie, "TERRIANN VS WIFEY MELISSA......OVA KEVIN", YouTube Video, 7:27, 3 December 2013, https://www.youtube.com/watch?v=YuhL84n7zIQ

4. The language codes are based on the subjects' metalinguistic descriptions of the performances. **Jamaican** (JAM) (Patois) differs from **Patois/Creole** in that the codings for the latter do not provide a precise

description of the performance as Jamaican (Patwa or Creole) but instead claim that, for example: "It's patois, Caribbean dialect derived from English".

5. Fresh-water Yankee – "a native West Indian person who picks up a North American accent after a short visit to the US or Canada" (Allsopp 2003, 244).

Audiovisual Sources

Hank Huled. "Nicki Minaj Drunk Talk". YouTube video, 0:32. 8 August 2014. https://www.youtube.com/watch?v=ZNgwjugN9oo.

Jamaican Matie. "TERRIANN VS WIFEY MELISSA......OVA KEVIN". YouTube video, 7:27. 3 December 2013. https://www.youtube.com/watch?v=YuhL84n7zIQ.

Mavado Gully Official. "Mavado – Give It All To Me ft. Nicki Minaj". YouTube video, 3:52. 4 November 2013. https://www.youtube.com/watch?v=9sbu0Fy32Kc.

Nicki Minaj. "Nicki Minaj Anaconda Video: Behind The Scenes Vlog". YouTube video, 2:48. 7 August 2014. https://www.youtube.com/watch?v=4iiuBBmcpLs.

Rihanna. "Rihanna – Work (Explicit) ft. Drake". YouTube video, 7:34. 22 February 2016. https://www.youtube.com/watch?v=HL1UzIK-flA&ab_channel=RihannaVEVO.

Skelly gvz. "Nicki Minaj Jamaican Accent// 2015". YouTube video, 0:15. 9 August 2014. https://www.youtube.com/watch?v=6_CJJMDSIHg.

TheCelebFactory. "Rihanna on Her Accent". YouTube video, 0:50. 12 April 2012. https://www.youtube.com/watch?v=5dnrohN4P0A.

References

Akande, Akinmade. 2012. "The Appropriation of African American Vernacular English and Jamaican Patois by Nigerian Hip Hop Artists". *ZAA* 60 (3): 237–54.

Allsopp, Richard. 2003. *Dictionary of Caribbean English Usage*. Kingston: UWI Press.

Appadurai, Arjun. 1996. *Modernity at Large: Cultural Dimensions of Globalisation*. Minneapolis: University of Minnesota Press.

Beal, Joan. 2009. "You're Not from New York City, You're from Rotherham: Dialect and Identity in British Indie Music". *Journal of English Linguistics* 37 (3): 223–40.

Bell, Allan. 1992. "Hit and Miss: Referee Design in the Dialects of New Zealand Television Advertisements". *Language and Communication* 12 (3/4): 327–40.

Bell, Allan, and Andy Gibson. 2011. "Staging Language: An Introduction to the Sociolinguistics of Performance". *Journal of Sociolinguistics* 15 (5): 555–72.

Blake, Renée. 2008. "Bajan: Phonology". In *Varieties of English 2: The Americas and the Caribbean*, edited by Edgar Schneider, 312–19. Berlin: de Gruyter.

Blommaert, Jan. 2010. *The Sociolinguistics of Globalization*. Cambridge: Cambridge University Press.

Cassidy, Frederic, and Robert B. Le Page. 2002. *Dictionary of Jamaican English*. 2nd ed. Kingston: UWI Press.

Cooper, Carolyn. 2004. *Sound Clash: Jamaican Dancehall Culture at Large*. New York: Palgrave Macmillan.

Deuber, Dagmar, and Lars Hinrichs. 2007. "Dynamics of Orthographic Standardization in Jamaican Creole and Nigerian Pidgin". *World Englishes* 26 (1): 22–47.

Devonish, Hubert, and Otelemate Harry. 2008. "Jamaican Creole and Jamaican English: Phonology". In *Varieties of English 2: The Americas and the Caribbean*, edited by Edgar Schneider, 256–89. Berlin: de Gruyter.

Eberhardt, Maeva, and Kara Freeman. 2015. "First Things First, I'm the Realest: Linguistic Appropriation, White Privilege, and the Hip-Hop Persona of Iggy Azalea". *Journal of Sociolinguistics* 19 (3): 303–27.

Eckert, Penelope. 2008. "Variation and the Indexical Field". *Journal of Sociolinguistics* 12 (4): 453–76.

Farquharson, Joseph. 2017. "Linguistic ideologies and the Historical Development of Language Use Patterns in Jamaican Music". *Language & Communication* 52: 7–18.

Gerfer, Anika. 2018. "Global Reggae and the Appropriation of Jamaican Creole". *World Englishes* 37 (4): 668–83.

Green, Lisa. 2002. *African American English: A Linguistic Introduction*. Cambridge: Cambridge University Press.

Hackert, Stephanie. 2012. "Regional Profile: The Caribbean". In *The Mouton World Atlas of Variation in English*, edited by Bernd Kortmann and Kerstin Lunkenheimer, 704–33. Berlin: de Gruyter.

Jansen, Lisa. 2018. "Britpop is a Thing, Damn It: On British Attitudes towards American English and an Americanized Singing Style". In *The Language of Pop Culture*, edited by Valentin Werner, 116–35. London: Routledge.

Jansen, Lisa. 2022. *English Rock and Pop Performances: A Sociolinguistic Investigation of British and American Language Perceptions and Attitudes*. Amsterdam: John Benjamins.

Jansen, Lisa, and Michael Westphal. 2017. "Rihanna Works her Multivocal Pop Persona: A Morpho-Syntactic and Accent Analysis of Rihanna's Singing Style". *English Today* 33 (1): 46–55.

Kretzschmar, William. 2008. "Standard American English Pronunciation". In *Varieties of English 2: The Americas and the Caribbean*, edited by Edgar Schneider, 37–51. Berlin: de Gruyter.

Kuckartz, Udo. 2012. *Qualitative Inhaltsanalyse. Methoden, Praxis, Computerunterstützung*. Basel: Beltz Juventa.

Leung, Glenda. 2009. "Negotiation of Trinidadian Identity in Ragga Soca Music". *World Englishes* 28 (4): 509–31.

Mair, Christian. 2013. "The World System of Englishes: Accounting for the Transnational Importance of Mobile and Mediated Vernaculars". *English World-Wide* 34 (3): 253–78.

O'Hanlon, Renae. 2006. "Australian Hip-Hop: A Sociolinguistic Investigation". *Australian Journal of Linguistics* 26 (2): 193–209.
Patrick, Peter. 2008. "Jamaican Creole: Morphology and Syntax". In *Varieties of English 2: The Americas and the Caribbean*, edited by Edgar Schneider, 609–44. Berlin: de Gruyter.
Pennycook, Alastair. 2007. *Global Englishes and Transcultural Flows*. London: Routledge.
Richardson, Elaine. 2006. *Hiphop Literacies*. London: Routledge.
Roberts, Peter. 2007. *West Indians and their Language*. Cambridge: Cambridge University Press.
Sebba, Mark, and Susan Dray. 2012. "Making It Real: 'Jamaican', 'Jafaican' and Authenticity in the Language of British Youth". *ZAA* 60 (3): 255–73.
Simpson, Paul. 1999. "Language, Culture and Identity: With (another) Look at Accents in Pop and Rock Singing". *Multilingua* 18 (4): 343–67.
Trudgill, Peter. 1983. "Acts of Conflicting Identity: The Sociolinguistics of British Pop-Song Performance". In *On Dialect: Social and Geographical Perspectives*, edited by Peter Trudgill, 141–60. Oxford: Blackwell.
Westphal, Michael. 2018. "Pop Culture and the Globalization of Non-Standard Varieties of English: Jamaican Creole in German Reggae Subculture". In *The Language of Pop Culture*, edited by Valentin Werner, 95–115. London: Routledge.

Appendix

Rihanna's Lyrics in "Work"

1. work work work work work work
   wɜ̃k wɜ̃ wɜ̃ wɜ̃ wɜ̃ wɜ̃k
2. he se me hafi work work work work work work
   ɔ se mɪ afɪ wɜ̃k wɜ̃ wɜ̃ wɜ̃ wɜ̃ wɜ̃k
3. he see me do me dirt dirt dirt dirt dirt dirt
   ɔ̃ sɪ mɪ dʊ mɪ dɜ̃ dɜ̃ dɜ̃ dɜ̃ dɜ̃ dɜ̃
4. so me put in work work work work work work
   sɔ̃ mɪ pɔ? ɔn wɜ̃ wɜ̃ wɜ̃ wɜ̃ wɜ̃ wɜ̃
5. when you a go learn learn learn learn learn learn
   wɛ̃n jʊ ã gɔ̃ lɜ̃n lɜ̃n lɜ̃n lɜ̃ lɜ̃ lɜ̃
6. me na care if him hurt hurt hurt hurt hurting
   mɪ nã kɛɹ ɪf ɪm ɜ̃t ɜ̃t ɜ̃ ɜ̃ ɜ̃tɪn
7. dry me a desert him no time to have you lurking
   dɹaɪ mi a dɪsɜ̃ːt ɪm na taɪm tə hæv jɔ̃ lɜ̃ːkɪn
8. him a go act like him na like it
   ɪm ã gɔ̃ æʔ laːɪʔ ɪm na lãːɪk ɪʔ

9	you know I dealt with you the nicest	
	jə no aɪ del wɪd jə də naːɪsɪs	
10	nobody touch me you na righteous	
	nəbadi tʌtʃ mi jə na raɪtʃəs	
11	no bother text me in a crisis	
	na badə teks mɪ ɪn ə kɹaɪsəs	
12	I believed all of your dreams adoration	
	aɪ bəliːvd ɑl əv jəʳ dɹiːmz adəɹeːʃan	
13	you took my heart and my keys and my patience	
	jə tʊk maːɪ hɑːɹt ən maːɪ kiːz ən maːɪ peːʃans	
14	you took my heart on my sleeve for decoration	
	jə tʊk maːɪ hɑːɹt ɑːn maːɪ sliːv fə dekəɹeːʃan	
15	you mistaken my love I brought for you for foundation	
	jə mɪˈstekən maɪləv aɪ bɹɔː fə ju fə faʊnˈdeːʃan	
16	all that I wanted from you was to give me	
	al ðæ aɪ wanəd fɹəm ju wəz tu ɡɪv miː	
17	something that I never had something that you never seen	
	sʌmθɪn ðæt aɪ neva hæd sʌmθɪn ðæt juː neva siːn	
18	something that you never been mh	
	sʌmθɪn ðæt juː neva biːn m̃ː	
19	but I wake up and act like nothing's wrong	
	bət aɪ weɪk ʌp ən æʔ laːɪ nʌɾnz ɹaŋ	
20	just get ready fi	
	dʒəs ɡeʔ redi fɪ	
21	before the tables turn turn turn turn turn turn	
	bɪˈfɔː də teɪblz tə̃n tə̃n tə̃ tə̃ tə̃ tə̃n	
22	beg you something please baby don't you leave	
	beɡ juː sʌmθɪn pliːz beɪbi doʊnt juː liːv	
23	don't leave me stuck here in the streets uhu	
	doʊnt liːv miː stək hɪəɹ ɪn ðə stɹiːts əhə	
24	If I get another chance to	
	ɪf aɪ get əˈnʌðɹ tʃæns tuː	
25	I will never no never neglect you	
	aɪ wɪl nevə no nevə nəˈɡlekt you	
26	I mean who am I to hold your past against you	
	aɪ miːn huː əm aɪ tə hoʊld jəʳ pæs əɡenst juː	

27	I just hope that it gets to you
	aɪ dʒəst hoʊp ðæt ɪt gets tə juː
28	I hope that you see this through
	aɪ hoʊp ðæt juː siː ðɪs θruː
29	I hope that you see this true
	aɪ hoʊp ðæt juː siː ðɪs truː
30	what can I say please recognize I'm trying babe
	wat kæn aɪ seɪ pliːz rekəgnaːz aɪm traːɪɪn beɪb

Nicki Minaj's Lyrics in "Give It All to Me"

1	hey yo Mavado tell dem lick a shot hollow
	eˈ jo moˈvadə tɛl ɛm lɪk ə ʃat halə
2	tell dem se we straight arrow
	tɛl ɛm se ˈwi ˈʃɹɪeːt ˈaɹə
3	tell dem the flow tight narrow
	tɛl ɛm də ˈfloː taɪ ˈnaɹə
4	everything me did a start dem borrow
	ˈɛvɹɪˌtɪŋ mə dɪda staˈt dɛm baɹə
5	cruised up link my dudes up
	kɹuːzd ʌp lɪŋk ma duːdz ʌp
6	the coupe black and blue yup it's bruised up
	ðə kuːp blæk ən blʊ jʌp ɪz bɹuːzd ʌp
7	I'm like who's up girls is used up
	aˈm laˈk huːz ʌp gɝlz ɪz juːzd ʌp
8	these bitches my sons I tied my tubes up
	ðiˈː ˈbɪtʃəz maː sʌnz aː taːd maː tuːbz ʌp
9	tell dem again bad gyal toast is oozed up
	tɛl ɛm əˈgɛn bad gjal toʊst ɪz uːzd ʌp
10	I hit up Instagram post some nudes up
	aɪ hɪt ʌp ɪnstəgɹæːm poʊst sʌm nuːdz ʌp
11	uh burn fire rev it pop a wheelie
	ʌ bɔn faɪja ɹɛv ɪt pap a wiːlɪ
12	Caribbean girls run it ask Riri
	kɛˈɹɪbiːən gɝlz ɹʌn ɪt æsk ɹɪɹɪ
13	I'll handle you
	aːl hændl juː

14	let me dance for you	
	lɛmɪ dæns fə juː	
15	I might be thinking about leaving my man for you	
	aː maɪt bi θɪŋkɪn baʊt livɪn maː mæːn fə juː	
16	I'll handle you	
	aːl hændl juː	
17	let me dance for you	
	lɛmɪ dæns fə juː	
19	I might be thinking about leaving my mans for you yeah yeah	
	aː maɪt bi θɪŋkɪn baʊt livɪn maː mæːns fə juː jə jə	
18	make me your own baby	
	meɪk mɪ jɚ oʊn beɪbə	
19	make me your own baby	
	meɪk mɪ jɚ oʊn beɪbeɪ	
20	I'm here I'm here I'm here	
	aːm hɚ aːm hɚ aːm hɜːɹ	
21	pretty gang ina the place	
	pɹɪtɪ gæŋ ɪna də pleɪs	

Nicki Minaj's Social Media Performance

1	gal a want to se	
	gal a wɔn də se	
2	why me na vex	
	waɪ mɪ na vɛks	
3	but me baby father a vex yo	
	bot mə bɪebɪ faːda a vɛks jaː	
4	me daughter a vex unu bloodclaat	
	me daːtaː a vɛks ʌnə blədklaːt	
5	[…] me and Drake a go mad dem bloodclaat whereabout	
	mɪ an dɹɪek a go ma dem blədklaːt weəbəʊt	
6	what you know 'bout Swiffer	
	we jʊ nʊo əbəʊt swɪfɐ	
7	you know 'bout bloodclaat Pine-Sol	
	jʊ nʊo əbəʊt blədklaːt paɪn saːl	
8	you know 'bout Pine-Sol	
	jʊ nʊo əbəʊt paɪn saːl	

9	and you know 'bout Swiffer I a get that a dollar store
	an jʊ nʊo əbəʊt swɪfɐ aɪ a get dat a dala stɔːɹ
10	se you know 'bout that
	se jʊ nʊo əbəʊt dat
11	[...] are y'all crazy I'm already drunk
	ɑ jɔl kɹeɪzi aːm ɔlɹɛdi dɹʌŋk

Contributors

Marie-Eve Bouchard is an Assistant Professor in the Department of French, Hispanic and Italian Studies at the University of British Columbia.

Nickesha T. Dawkins is a Linguistics Lecturer in the Department of Language Linguistics and Literature (LLL) at The University of the West Indies, Cave Hill campus.

Hubert Devonish is Professor Emeritus of The University of the West Indies. His research has focused on phonology, language planning, and Creole languages in education

R. Sandra Evans is a Lecturer at The University of the West Indies, St. Augustine, Trinidad.

Joseph T. Farquharson is Senior Lecturer in Linguistics at The University of the West Indies, Mona, and Coordinator of the Jamaican Language Unit.

Ronald T. Francis is an assistant lecturer at The University of the West Indies, St. Augustine, Trinidad.

Anika Gerfer is a doctoral candidate and research assistant at the English department of the University of Muenster, Germany.

Andrea Hollington is a postdoc researcher at the University of Mainz, Germany.

Lisa Jansen and Michael Westphal are both post-doctoral researchers at the University of Münster, Germany.

Byron M. Jones is a Lecturer in Linguistics in the Department of Modern Languages and Linguistics at The University of the West Indies, St. Augustine, Trinidad.

Renato Tomei is Associate Professor of English Language and Translation at the University for Foreigners of Perugia, Italy,

Christina Märzhäuser teaches linguistics of Portuguese, Spanish and French and worked at the departments of Romance Languages of the Universioties of Munich, Erlangen, Mannheim, Kassel Praia (Cape Verde), Braga (Portugal), Vienna and as visiting researcher at UC Berkeley. Her research focus is on language contact and multilingualism, heritage languages, language and music, and syntax-semantics interface. She is affiliated with LMU Munich, Universidade do Minho, Braga and FLUC Coimbra.

Nathan Wendte is an associate professor of linguistics in the Department of Anthropology at the University of Virginia in Charlottesville, Virginia USA

Guyanne Wilson is a Senior Lecturer in English Linguistics at the Technical University of Dortmund

Index

aesthetic, 4, 263, 285
anglophone, 2, 80, 181, 195, 218, 258–262, 278
Angolar, 8, 64, 66, 67, 69, 72, 75, 77, 79
appropriation, 34, 234, 239, 279
authenticity, 1, 2, 4, 5, 7–10, 49, 58, 65, 69–71, 74–76, 81, 142, 143, 231–233, 235, 236, 239, 248, 250, 251, 264, 265, 267, 301, 305, 323, 324, 326–328

calypso, 3, 4, 20, 25, 28, 29, 34, 35, 40, 50, 53, 55, 58, 139, 142
Canada/Canadian, 6, 58, 108, 151, 271, 302, 319, 330
Cape Verde/Cape Verdean, 6, 9, 66, 67, 81, 82, 193, 194, 196–225
Caribbean, 2, 10, 11, 17–19, 27–29, 37, 40, 41, 44, 51–53, 55–59, 138–144, 146, 147, 151, 154, 155, 164, 208, 234, 258, 271–273, 285, 297, 305, 306, 313, 317, 319–330
change, 4, 5, 8, 9, 20, 22, 38, 58, 59, 100, 106, 108, 138, 146, 151, 163, 170, 171, 203, 210, 219, 236, 237, 246, 288, 295, 296, 307, 317, 329
chutney, 22, 28–31, 34, 138, 142
code-switching, 4, 80, 81, 138, 142
colonial, 2, 3, 10, 18, 37, 38, 66, 71–73, 77, 81, 162, 211, 237, 238, 259, 267, 273

dancehall, 1, 3, 6–10, 37, 40, 41, 43, 44, 53, 58, 94, 97, 100, 103–106, 108–112, 115, 116, 118–127, 131–135, 138, 139, 142, 150, 154, 233, 236–244, 246–252, 258, 260–264, 266–270, 272, 273, 275–278, 286, 290, 296, 298, 300, 302, 316, 319–322, 327
Dennery Segment, 8, 37, 39–46, 53–57, 59, 60
diaspora, 5, 6, 9, 11, 37, 41, 58, 67–69, 139, 193, 194, 196, 197, 204, 208–210, 212, 214, 216–219, 221–224, 240, 258, 261, 262, 266, 272, 306
discursive, 8, 42, 181, 222, 231, 232, 235

emblematic, 9, 164, 264, 267, 272, 277, 328
English, 5, 6, 8, 10, 11, 17, 19, 20, 34, 37–39, 42, 44–49, 55–60, 80, 84, 89, 90, 93, 94, 97–101, 103, 108, 132, 138, 140–143, 147, 154, 160, 162, 164, 167, 168, 173, 182, 208–210, 216–218, 220, 226, 231, 232, 234–242, 249, 251, 262, 263, 265, 267–272, 275–277, 297, 298, 300–303, 305, 307, 313, 315–317, 319, 321–325, 327, 328, 330
Ethiopia/Ethiopian, 6, 10, 249, 258, 260, 262, 280, 284–294, 296, 298, 301–307
ethnic/ethnicity, 7, 18–19, 23–24, 28, 30, 34, 70, 75, 155, 157, 160–163, 165–166, 169, 182, 198, 234, 237, 240, 286, 288, 298, 306
ethnography, 1, 11

Forro, 8, 64, 66–67, 69, 71–72, 75–79, 82–83

French, 9, 37–38, 44, 51, 56–59, 138, 142, 159, 162–168, 171, 173, 175, 180–163, 204, 209–210

Ghana/Ghanaian, 6–7, 9–10, 233, 239–240, 242, 248, 250–251, 258, 260–262, 268–270, 272, 275–276, 279–281
Guyana, 7, 19, 22, 23–24, 34

habitus, 8, 42–43, 45, 49–50, 52–53, 58–59, 213
Haiti/Haitian, 4, 6, 161, 166, 322
heritage language, 5–6, 73, 194
heteroglossic, 7, 236, 251, 270–272

identity, 1–5, 7–11, 15, 18, 23–24, 39, 44–45, 50–51, 58, 64–65, 67, 69–71, 74–75, 77–82, 89, 101, 103–104, 107–108, 132–135, 138–139, 142, 144, 149, 152, 153–155, 160–163, 166–167, 169, 180, 182, 194, 231–232, 235, 237–239, 252, 263–264, 266–267, 273–274, 285, 301, 305–306, 313–317, 323, 326–328

Jamaica/Jamaican, 2–3, 5–11, 18–19, 37, 40, 43, 49, 53, 89–97, 99–101, 103–106, 108, 112, 126, 131, 134, 142–144, 150–152, 231, 233, 235, 237–246, 248–251, 258–279, 284, 286–292, 296–398, 300–307, 316–318, 320–324, 326–327, 329–330

Kenya/Kenyan, 9–10, 233, 239–240, 242, 256, 260, 262–264, 270, 273–274, 307
Kwéyòl, 8, 37–39, 42, 45–50, 55–61, 63

language attitudes, 1, 8, 89, 100, 180
language contact, 1, 4, 11, 49, 234, 258–262, 264, 268–270, 275, 278

language ideologies, 1, 4–5, 8, 64–71, 81–82, 138, 202, 231, 237, 251, 329
language use, 3–5, 7–9, 37–39, 44–45, 65, 70, 89–90, 93–96, 97, 99–101, 138–139, 141–146, 151, 153, 155, 160, 180–181, 224, 232–233, 235–238, 251, 260, 267, 278, 281, 314, 320–321, 323, 325, 328
linguistic capital, 43–44, 50, 54, 57, 72
linguistic market, 8–9, 42–44, 72
Louisiana, 2, 9, 159–168, 171, 173, 175–177, 180–189
Lung'ie, 64, 67
lyrics, 3–5, 8, 10–11, 19–22, 25–26, 28, 30–31, 39, 41–45, 48–60, 68, 79, 84, 90–94, 103, 106, 111–114, 127, 130–133, 139, 146–147, 151, 160, 167–170, 179, 182, 194–195, 199, 201, 203–204, 206, 208, 210–211, 216, 218, 220–224, 241, 260–264, 266–269, 272, 274, 278, 284–285, 287–288, 291–293, 298–299, 302, 305, 307, 314, 316, 319–321, 323

metalinguistic, 4, 71, 170, 194, 221, 297, 314, 323, 329
migration, 4–6, 11, 52, 212, 222–223, 237, 259–260, 275, 279
morphosyntactic, 4–5, 164, 167–168, 172, 233, 235, 240–241, 247, 248, 264, 293, 319–322
multilingualism, 1, 4–5, 12–13, 86–87, 155, 234, 264, 292, 305
multivocal, 8, 10, 13, 156, 255, 313–314, 316–317, 320–322, 327–328

nationality, 2, 7, 239
Nigeria/Nigerian, 6–7, 9–10, 33, 143, 233–234, 236, 239–242, 245, 248, 250, 253, 256, 260–262, 268, 270–273, 276, 315

performance, 2, 8–10, 17, 19–22, 28, 31, 33–35, 42–43, 62, 70, 72, 81, 105–107, 138–139, 142–147, 149–156, 159, 161, 165, 180, 182, 200–201, 206, 223, 231–236, 238–239, 242–243, 245, 248, 250–252, 262, 264–267, 289, 292, 295, 305, 313–317, 320–329
phonetic, 3, 5, 8, 103, 106, 108, 110–111, 116, 118, 121, 130–134, 146–147, 149, 152, 169, 133, 235, 240–243, 245, 248, 264, 267, 268, 272, 274, 307
pidgin, 6, 62, 86, 143, 251, 268
pitch, 8, 109, 111, 115–119, 121–123, 131–134, 137
popular music, 1, 3, 5–7, 8, 13, 19–20, 25, 35, 69, 80, 84, 89–91, 93–96, 100–101, 136, 141, 156, 193–196, 211, 221, 228–229, 237, 250, 255, 258–262, 269–270, 273, 275–276, 278–279, 286, 316
postcolonial, 2, 17–19, 31, 35, 52, 63, 73, 156, 194, 220, 228, 234, 257
practice theory, 8
pragmatic, 5, 12–13, 61, 171, 311

quantitative, 5, 89–90, 108, 114, 194, 221, 233, 240

rap kriolu, 6, 9, 193–194, 196–210, 212, 213–225
reggae, 1, 5–6, 10, 12, 62, 92, 94, 97, 100, 102, 109, 136, 139, 142–144, 153–154, 156–157, 161, 196–197, 210, 234–239, 242, 252, 254–258, 260–264, 266–267, 270, 275, 281, 283–306, 309–310, 312, 316–317, 320–321
repertoire, 143, 159–161, 167, 182, 184, 234–235, 239, 248, 259, 270, 282–283, 286, 287, 298, 301–303, 317, 319, 321

revitalization, 9, 60, 73, 83, 85, 87, 159, 160, 166–167, 182–183
rhyme, 3–4, 45, 68, 110, 205, 263, 285, 292, 305
riddim, 13, 40–41, 44–46, 50, 55–58, 99, 271, 274, 280, 283, 310

São Tomé and Príncipe/Santomean, 2, 8, 64–88
singing, 4, 21–22, 24–28, 32–33, 64–65, 72, 74, 77–82, 94, 97, 100, 138, 141–146, 150, 151–154, 159, 198, 200, 202, 233, 235, 239, 251, 304, 307, 313–315, 320–322, 328–329
soca, 9, 20, 22, 26, 28–31, 34–35, 37, 40–41, 50, 54–57, 59–62, 94, 97, 138–139, 141–147, 149, 151, 153, 155, 157–158, 234, 238, 252, 256, 316
sociolinguistics, 3–5, 12–13, 86–88, 103, 135–137, 156–157, 160, 183–184, 227, 231–232, 235, 250, 254–256, 285, 308–309, 311, 314
speech act, 3, 8, 20–22, 26, 28, 30–35, 43, 296
St Lucia/St Lucian, 8, 37–39, 41–42, 44–47, 49–63, 151
syntactic, 4–5, 13, 38, 46, 48, 56, 156, 164, 167, 168, 177, 178, 182

transatlantic, 10, 258–360, 264, 269, 275, 278, 306
translocal, 7, 9, 10, 167, 236
transnational, 194, 211, 214, 216–217, 219, 222, 231, 256, 263, 266, 272, 278, 282–283
Trinidad and Tobago /Trinbagonian, 2, 3, 7, 19–20, 22–24, 29–32, 34–37, 41, 55, 147, 151–153, 157, 295, 317, 322

Uganda/Ugandan, 10, 258, 260, 262, 264–266, 274, 278

variation, 1, 5, 40, 47, 85, 87, 103, 106–108, 110, 116–121, 124, 126, 130–136, 140, 146, 150, 153, 155, 156, 160, 173, 184, 226, 231–232, 248, 250, 254, 255, 285, 295, 300, 317, 319
vowels, 3, 8–9, 46–47, 103–104, 108–111, 114, 116–121, 123–127, 130–134, 136, 140, 141, 145, 148, 152–153, 164, 255, 295, 307, 319–320, 328

Zimbabwe/Zimbabwean, 10, 258, 260, 262, 266–267, 270, 280, 302
zydeco, 9, 159–161, 164–165, 167, 181–183, 186

www.ingramcontent.com/pod-product-compliance
Lightning Source LLC
Chambersburg PA
CBHW031544300426
44111CB00006BA/164